Jaina Scriptures and Philo

Interest in Indian religion and comparative philosophy has increased in recent years, but despite this the study of Jaina philosophy is still in its infancy. This book looks at the role of philosophy in Jaina tradition, and its significance within the general developments in Indian philosophy.

Bringing together chapters by philologists, historians and philosophers, the book focuses on karman theory, the theory of conditional predication, epistemology and the debates of Jaina philosophers with representatives of competing traditions, such as Ājīvika, Buddhist and Hindu. It analyses the relationship between religion and philosophy in Jaina scriptures, both Digambara and Śvetāmbara, and will be of interest to scholars and students of South Asian Religion, Philosophy and Philology.

Peter Flügel is Chair of the Centre of Jaina Studies at the School of Oriental and African Studies, University of London, UK. He is the series editor for the Routledge Advances in Jaina Studies series.

Olle Qvarnström is Professor of History of Religions at Lund University, Sweden.

Routledge advances in Jaina studies
Series Editor: Peter Flügel

School of Oriental and African Studies
Jain Studies have become an accepted part of the Study of Religion. This series provides a medium for regular scholarly exchange across disciplinary boundaries. It will include edited collection and monographs on Jainism.

1 **Studies in Jaina History and Culture**
Disputes and dialogues
Edited by Peter Flügel

2 **History, Scripture and Controversy in a Medieval Jain Sect**
Paul Dundas

3 **The History of Vegetarianism and Cow-Veneration in India**
Ludwig Alsdorf
Edited by W. Bollée

4 **Jaina Scriptures and Philosophy**
Edited by Peter Flügel and Olle Qvarnström

Jaina Scriptures and Philosophy

Edited by Peter Flügel and Olle Qvarnström

Routledge
Taylor & Francis Group
LONDON AND NEW YORK

First published 2015
by Routledge

2 Park Square, Milton Park, Abingdon, Oxfordshire OX14 4RN
711 Third Avenue, New York, NY 10017

Routledge is an imprint of the Taylor & Francis Group, an informa business

First issued in paperback 2018

British Library Cataloguing in Publication Data
A catalogue record for this book is available from the British Library

Library of Congress Cataloging-in-Publication Data
Jaina scriptures and philosophy / edited by Peter Flügel, Olle Qvarnström.
pages cm. – (Routledge advances in Jaina studies)
1. Jainism–Sacred books. 2. Jaina philosophy. I. Flügel, Peter.
II. Qvarnström, Olle.
BL1310.4.J36 2015
294.4'82–dc23 2014048786

ISBN: 978-1-138-83989-2 (hbk)
ISBN: 978-1-138-31963-9 (pbk)

Typeset in Times New Roman
by Wearset Ltd, Boldon, Tyne and Wear

MIX
Paper from responsible sources
FSC www.fsc.org FSC™ C013985

Printed in the United Kingdom
by Henry Ling Limited

Contents

Figures

Tables

Contributors

Nalini Balbir is Professor of Indology at the University of Paris-3 Sorbonne-Nouvelle. Her main fields of research are Pāli and Jain studies (www.iran-inde.cnrs.fr/IMG/pdf/publNBalbir.pdf), both scriptures and practices. Among her recent publications on various facets of Jainism are an introductory essay to the English translation of E. Leumann's *Übersicht über die Āvaśyaka-Literatur* by G. Baumann (L.D. Institute of Indology, 2010), a translation of Ācārya Nemicandra's *Dravyasaṃgraha* (Hindi Granth Karyalay, 2010) and *Paṭadarśana (Tīrthaṃkara praṇīta dharmadeśanā antargata Śatruṃjaya māhātmya) (The Glory of Shatrunjya as Depicted in a 19th Century Jain Scroll)* (Jain Vishva Bharati University, 2010; with Dr K.K. Sheth). She is the co-author with K.V. Sheth, K.K. Sheth and C.B. Tripathi of the *Catalogue of the Jain Manuscripts of the British Library* (British Library, Institute of Indology, 3 vols, 2006). She is also engaged in the Jainpedia website project which provides descriptions of digitized images of Jain manuscripts in the UK, together with an encyclopedia of Jainism online (www.jainology.org/jainpedia/).

Piotr Balcerowicz (www.orient.uw.edu.pl/balcerowicz) is Professor of Sanskrit and Indian Studies at the University of Warsaw. Until 2011 he served as Professor of International Relations at the University of Social Sciences and Humanities, Warsaw. He specializes in philosophical traditions of Asia and the West as well as in intercultural relations and the contemporary history of Asia, especially South Asia, Central Asia and the Middle East. His publications include: *Jaina Epistemology in Historical and Comparative Perspective* (Stuttgart, 2001; reprinted: Delhi, 2008), *Afghanistan: History – People – Politics* (Warsaw, 2001), *Jainism – An Ancient Indian Religion: History, Ritual, Literature* (Warsaw, 2003), *History of Classical Indian Philosophy. Part One: Beginnings, Analytical Trends and Philosophy of Nature* (Warsaw, 2003), *Jainism and the Definition of Religion* (Mumbai, 2009), *Early Asceticism in India: Ājīvikism and Jainism* (Routledge, 2015). He has also edited a number of volumes, including: *Logic and Belief in Indian Philosophy* (Delhi, 2010), *Art, Myths and Visual Culture of South Asia* (Delhi, 2011), *World View and Theory in Indian Philosophy* (Delhi, 2012), *Encyclopedia of Indian*

Philosophies, Vol. 14: *Jaina Philosophy*, Part II (Delhi, 2013), *Encyclopedia of Indian Philosophies*, Vol. 17: *Jaina Philosophy*, Part III (Delhi, 2015).

Johannes Bronkhorst is Professor of Sanskrit and Indian Studies at the University of Lausanne. He has written numerous articles and books about the history of Indian thought, including the circumstances in which these forms of thought could develop. His recent books are: *Greater Magadha: Studies in the Culture of Early India* (Leiden, 2007), *Buddhist Teaching in India* (Boston, 2009), *Absorption: Two Studies of Human Nature* (www.bronkhorst-absorption.info; 2009), *Buddhism in the Shadow of Brahmanism* (Leiden, 2011), *Language and Reality: On an Episode in Indian Thought* (Leiden, 2011).

Anne Clavel is an associate member of the Centre of Jaina Studies, SOAS, and specializes in Jain Philosophy. After her PhD Dissertation on Akalaṅka's theory of knowledge, she wrote several papers dealing with Jain Epistemology and Logic, for instance: "Śvetāmbaras and Digambaras: a Differentiated Periodization?" in *Periodization and Historiography of Indian Philosophy*, ed. E. Franco (Vienna, 2013); "Is the *Syādvāda* True Only From a Certain Point of View?" in *Jaina Studies: Proceedings of the DOT 2010 Panel in Marburg, Germany*, ed. J. Soni (New Delhi, 2012); "La perception peut-elle échapper au concept? La contribution jaina au débat indien", *Antiquorum Philosophia* 5 (2011). She taught Sanskrit and Indian Culture at the Universities of Lyon and Aix-en-Provence in France.

Anna Aurelia Esposito is Assistant Professor at the University of Würzburg, Germany. She has conducted research on South Indian drama manuscripts and published critical editions of the dramas *Cārudatta* and *Dūtavākya* of the so-called "Trivandrum Plays". She is currently working on the transmission of religious and moral contents in Jain narrative literature, with a special focus on Saṅghadāsa's *Vasudevahiṇḍī*. Her recent publications are: "The Prakrit of the Vasudevahiṇḍī – an Addendum to Pischel's Grammar", *Zeitschrift für Indologie und Südasienstudien* 28, 2011; "How to Combine the Bṛhatkathā with Jain World History – Reflections on Saṅghadāsa's Vasudevahiṇḍī", *Jaina Studies: Proceedings of the DOT 2010 Panel in Marburg, Germany*, ed. Jayandra Soni (New Delhi, 2012); and "Didactic Dialogues: Communication of Doctrine and Strategies of Narrative in Jain Literature", *Dialogue in Early South Asian Religions: Hindu, Buddhist, and Jain Traditions*, ed. Brian Black and Laurie Patton (Farnham, 2014).

Peter Flügel, D. Phil Johannes Gutenberg-Universität Mainz, Reader at the Department of the Study of Religions at the London School of Oriental and African Studies (SOAS), Founding Chair of the Centre of Jaina Studies at SOAS, has published widely on Jaina history and culture. See: www.soas.ac.uk/jainastudies. He is editor of the Routledge Advances in Jaina Studies series, the *International Journal of Jaina Studies*, *Jaina Studies – Newsletter of the Centre of Jaina Studies* and hosts the Annual Jaina Studies Workshop at SOAS. For the Routledge series he has also edited *Disputes and Dialogues: Studies in Jaina History and Culture* (London 2006) and *Jaina Law and Society* (London, 2015).

Shin Fujinaga is Professor of Philosophy at Miyakonojo National College of Technology, Miyakonojo, Japan. He received a BA in Ethics from Kumamoto University and an MA in Indian Philosophy from Hiroshima University, Japan. Between 1981 and 1983 he studied Jaina logic under the guidance of Muni Jambuvijaya, Pandit D. Malvania and Professor Nagin Shah, and in 2000 gained a PhD in Indian Philosophy from Hiroshima University. His main publication is *Jaina kyo no Issaichisya Ron (A Study of Sarvajña in Jainism)* (Kyoto, 2001). At present he is working on Jaina *vinaya.*

Prem Suman Jain has served as professor and dean at M.L. Shukhadia University, Udaipur (India) and as director in the National Institute of Prakrit Studies and Research, Bahubali Prakrit Vidyapith, Shravanabelagola. He has edited rare Prakrit and Apabhramsa manuscripts and published more than 60 books and 170 research papers in the field of Jainological and Prakrit Studies. Dr Jain has been the recipient of many State and National Awards along with the President of India Samman for Pali-Prakrit 2006, at Rashtrapati Bhavan New Delhi. The notable Acharya Tulsi Prakrit Award was bestowed on him in 2014 for his contributions in the field of Prakrit Studies. At present he is working on ancient Prakrit texts like the *Bhagavatī Ārādhanā* and the *Kuvalayamālākahā.* Some of the books written and edited by him are: *Kuvalayamālākahā kā Sāṃskṛtika Adhyayana (Cultural Study of the Kuvalayamālākahā)* (Vaiśālī, 1975), *Prākṛit Svayam Śikṣaka* (Jaipur, 1976, 2004 5th edn), *Significance of Prakrit Narrative Literature* (Mysore, 1989), *Jaina Saṃskṛti aur Paryāvarana Saṃrakṣana (Jaina Culture and the Protection of the Environment)* (Udaipur, 2000), *Śaurasenī Prākṛt Bhāṣā evaṃ Vyākaraṇa (Śaurasenī Prakrit Language and Grammar)* (Delhi, 2001), (Edited) *Sukumālasāmicariu of Vibudha Śrīdhara* (Jaipur, 2004), *Jaina Dharma kī Sāṃskṛtik Virāsat (Cultural Heritage of Jaina Religion)* (Delhi, 2005), *Tīrthaṅkara Mahāvīra and His Religion of Compassion* (Shravanabelgola, 2008), *Prakrit Primer* (New Delhi, 2010), *Prakrit Ratnakāra* (Shravanabelgola, 2012), etc.

Olle Qvarnström is Professor of History of Religions at Lund University, Sweden. He has conducted research on Brahmanism, Buddhism and Jainism, especially philosophical and theological traditions, their doctrinal system and praxis, mutual influence and conflict. In the field of Jaina systematic philosophy, he has studied philosophers such as Siddhasena Divākara, Haribhadrasūri and Hemacandra. His current research on Jainism involves Jain art and the relationship between Jainism and Islam during the Delhi Sultanate.

Jayandra Soni retired in May 2012 from the Department of Indology and Tibetology, Philipps-Universität Marburg, Germany, where he taught Indian languages (Sanskrit, Hindi, Gujarati) from October 1991. Born and brought up in South Africa where he did his BA, he studied further in India (Banaras Hindu University PhD in 1978) and Canada (McMaster University PhD in 1987). He presently lives in Austria and teaches part-time courses on Indian philosophies and religions at the University of Innsbruck. He is continuing his research into Indian philosophy, including special studies in Jaina philosophy on which he has also written several articles. His books include *Philosophical Anthropology in Śaiva Siddhānta* (Delhi, 1989). He edited *Jaina Studies: Proceedings of the DOT 2010 Panel in Marburg, Germany* (New Delhi, 2012). Together with Michael Pahlke and Christoph Cueppers he edited *Buddhist and Jaina Studies: Proceedings of the Conference in Lumbini, February 2013* (Lumbini, 2015). His publications can be seen here: www.staff.uni-marburg.de/~soni/.

Herman Tieken taught Sanskrit and later also Tamil at the University of Leiden. His main fields of interest are Kāvya literature in Sanskrit, Prākrit, Apabhraṃśa as well as Tamil, Jaina canonical texts and the Sanskrit epics. A recent publication, together with Peter Khoroche, is *Poems on Life and Love in Ancient India: Hāla's Sattasaī* (Albany, 2009); another is *Between Colombo and Cape Town. Letters in Tamil, Dutch and Sinhala, Sent from Ceylon to Nicolaas Ondaatje, Exile at the Cape of Good Hope (1728–1737)* (Delhi, 2014).

Kenji Watanabe is a part-time lecturer of Pāli at Taisho University, Sugamo-Tokyo, Japan. He received a BA with *A Study in the Kirātārjunīya of Bhāravi* in 1974 and an MA with *A Study of the Uttarajjhāyā* in 1976 from Taisho University. He studied Middle Indo-Aryan languages and Jaina Studies at Ghent University in Belgium under the guidance of Prof. Dr Jozef Deleu in 1969–71 and 1974. One of his many articles is "Avoiding all Sinful Acts by both Buddha and Mahāvīra" in the *Bulletin d'Études Indiennes*, No. 11 (Paris, 1993). He edited *Jain Studies in Honour of Jozef Deleu* (Tokyo, 1993) and published the monograph *Jainism* (in Japanese) (Tokyo, 2005).

Introduction

Philological and linguistic research on the Jaina Āgamas, the principal focus of the once dominant "Jainology and Prakrit Studies" approach, has become a rarity nowadays, while the study of systematic Jaina philosophy, based on sources in Sanskrit, Middle- and New Indo-Aryan languages, is given more attention. Even in departments of philosophy, where until recently the study of Indic philosophy for comparative purposes has largely been neglected, a plethora of new publications are emerging. The study of systematic Jaina philosophy – both in its own right, as part of the history of ideas in India, and in relation to the Jaina canon and its early commentaries – is, however, still in its infancy.

This book constitutes a small contribution to the effort to rectify this incomplete and lopsided understanding of the Jaina tradition. It includes original, previously unpublished contributions of leading scholars in the field of Jaina studies, addressing questions concerning the relationship between religion and philosophy in Prakrit and Sanskrit Jaina texts, Digambara and Śvetāmbara. One of the main aims of the book is thus to link research on canonical and non-canonical sources, however preliminary. In an attempt to understand Jaina philosophy and its significance for developments in Indian philosophy generally, some of the articles focus especially on Jaina theories of karma, conditional predication (*syādvāda*) and epistemology, as well as on debates of Jaina philosophers with representatives of Ājīvika, Buddhist and Brāhmaṇical philosophy.

The book brings together specialists from different disciplines, in particular philologists, historians and philosophers. In recent years, interdisciplinary research has proved extremely fruitful in the otherwise highly specialized domain of Jaina Studies and has re-energized a once stagnant field.

The articles collected in this volume are divided into three thematically distinct sections, "Scriptures", "Karma Theory and Ethics" and "Philosophy". They were all delivered at the 11th Jaina Studies Workshop on "Jaina Scriptures and Jaina Philosophy" held at SOAS on 12 March 2009. The workshop was organized by Peter Flügel (SOAS), Olle Qvarnström (Lund University) and Nicholas Barnard (Victoria and Albert Museum). It was sponsored by the Centre of Jaina Studies at SOAS, The Swedish Research Council/Lund University and the V&A Jain Art Fund.[1] Four papers presented at the conference are, for various reasons, not included in this volume: Frank van den Bossche's "Haribhadra Sūri on

Yogācāra", Bansidhar Bhatt's "Is Pārśva the Twenty-Third Jina a Legendary Figure? A Critical Survey of Early Jaina Sources", Paul Dundas's "Textual Authority in Ritual Procedure: The Śvetāmbara Jain Controversy Concerning *Īryāpathikīpratikramaṇa*" and Peter Flügel's "Reflections on the Origins of the Jaina Doctrine of Karman". Bossche abstained from publishing his paper, Bhatt decided to let his keynote lecture serve as a foundation for his forthcoming book on Pārśva (which is scheduled to appear in this series), Dundas's paper has already been published in the *Journal of Indian Philosophy* 39 (2011) 327–350, and Flügel's had already partly been published as "Prologue" in *Mathematical Sciences in the Karma Antiquity. Vol. 1: Gommaṭasāra (Jīvakāṇḍa)* by Laxmi Candra Jain in collaboration with Prabha Jain (Jabalpur: Gulab Rani Karma Science Museum & Shri Brahmi Sundari Prasthashram Samiti), 2008: 1–15.

This book has been dedicated to Professor Dr Willem B. Bollée, formerly Professor of Indology at the University of Heidelberg, a doyen of Jaina Studies for more than sixty years.[2] A complete bibliography of his publications has been included at the end of this book.

Notes

1 See the abstracts in *Jaina Studies – Newsletter of the Centre of Jaina Studies* 4 (2009) 5–10: www.soas.ac.uk/jainastudies/newsletter/file50273.pdf, and the conference report by Kristi Wiley, "Jaina Scriptures and Philosophy: SOAS Jaina Studies Workshop 2009", *Jaina Studies – Newsletter of the Centre of Jaina Studies* 5 (2010) 10–12: www.soas.ac.uk/jainastudies/newsletter/file57740.pdf.

2 Professors Willem B. and Annegret Bollée were present at the SOAS conference, when it was announced to whom the conference volume would be dedicated.

Part I
Scriptures

1 On the composition of the *Uttarajjhāyā*

Herman Tieken

Introduction

The *Uttarajjhāyā* consists of 36 chapters, each of which forms a small, complete treatise in itself. What is striking about this text is the great variety in the form and contents of the individual chapters, ranging from mere lists of elements from the doctrine and practice of the Jaina faith and chant-like poetry to edifying stories. As a compilation the *Uttarajjhāyā* contains material from different ages derived from different sources.[1] According to Charpentier the text has grown out of a slim collection of lectures on general religious topics and legends. The increase was attributed by him to attempts to adapt the text to a more scientific approach.[2] In connection with the later additions Charpentier refers in particular to the last nine chapters, which, however, he believed were not added in one go as they do not form an uninterrupted series. Though he does not deny the possibility that in the arrangement of the chapters of the *Uttarajjhāyā* one may find "traces of a certain plan", this must according to him have been the result of an unconscious process.[3]

In what follows I intend to reconsider Charpentier's findings and show that the arrangement of the chapters in the *Uttarajjhāyā* does follow a plan, the material having been divided into four broad sections each of which deals with a particular step on the path to final liberation. The order of the chapters within these sections, however, is an entirely different matter, as is, for instance, the principle behind the alternation between stories and doctrine. From the cases discussed no clear picture emerges which can be applied generally. It is difficult on this, "micro", level to take away the impression of the *Uttarajjhāyā* as an random, unsystematic collection of different types of materials (lists, stories) from different sources. By way of conclusion I would like to venture a suggestion as to what might have been the function of a highly varied type of text like the *Uttarajjhāyā*.

The division of the *Uttarajjhāyā* into four sections

To start with I will go through the text with big strides, trying to lay bare its division into the four sections, each describing a different step of the path leading to final liberation. After that the contents of some of the individual sections will be discussed in more detail.

The first two chapters are skipped here. As will be argued below, they form a kind of preface to the text as a whole. In Chapter 3, then, which is titled *Cāuramgijja*, four "limbs" (*aṃgāṇi*) are enumerated: birth as a human being (*māṇusatta*), the acquisition of knowledge (*suī*), living in accordance with the principles thus acquired (*saddhā*) and perseverance in self-control (*saṃjamammi vīriya*) (3.1/97). In the stanzas 2–10 each of these items is further specified: *māṇusatta* in 2–7, *suī* in 8, *saddhā* in 9 and *saṃjamammi vīriya* in 10. It is stressed that these conditions are very difficult to reach; the magic word is *dullaha* (e.g. 3.1/97: *cattāri paramaṃgāṇi dullahāṇiha jaṃtuṇo*, 3.8/104: *suī dhammassa dullahā*). The tone is the following: given the effects of *karma* it is very rare to be born as a human being, while for a human being it is, in turn, not easy to acquire the right type of knowledge, and even if one succeeds in this it remains extremely hard to live according to these principles; at the end of it all, while living an ascetic life, an extreme form of great endurance is required. But the reward is high: "He who has been born as a human being, who having listened to the *dhamma*, lives according to this *dhamma*, and who as an ascetic is highly energetic, such a man prevents the inflow of *kamma* and shakes of the 'dust' "[4] and "he will reach the highest *nirvāṇa*".[5]

The function of this chapter appears to be a kind of table of contents of the text, the remainder of which is devoted to the four topics listed in this very same order: *māṇusatta* in chapters 4–9, *suī* in 10–11, *saddhā* in 11–28 and *samjama* (under the name of *tava*) in 28–36.

Chapters 3 and following elaborate upon *māṇusatta*, or human existence. The (human) body is needed to be able to annihilate old *kamma*, which is accomplished by ascetic practices (6.13/174). Human existence is explicitly called the starting capital (*māṇusattaṃ bhave mūlaṃ*, 7.16/194). Unfortunately, life is not perfect (*asaṃkhaya*) and therefore one should be careful in what one does and not wait until old age, when it will be too late to do anything about it (4.1/117). Thus, the "fool" (*bāla*) who lives carelessly will at the time of his death tremble with fear, i.e. the fear of being born again; he dies the death against one's will (*akāmamaraṇa*) (5.16/145). People who possess the right type of knowledge and live virtuous lives, on the other hand, will have no reason to be afraid at the time of their death; they die what is called the death according to one's will (*sakāmamaraṇa*) (5.29/158 and 32/161 respectively). This theme of the opposition between the fool living carelessly (*pramatta, bāla*) and the careful wise man (*apramatta, paṃḍia*) returns prominently in Chapters 6, 7 and 8.

Chapter 9 contains the story of the life of King Nami. To this story I will return below. What I want to point out here is that it opens with an explicit reference to Nami's birth as a human being: *caiūṇa devalogāo uvavaṇṇo māṇusammi loyammi*, "After [Nami] had descended from the world of the gods and had been born in the world of men".

In Chapter 10 all the four conditions or requirements for reaching final liberation are addressed once more, each stanza ending with a refrain in which Mahāvīra warns his pupil Gautama not to spoil the opportunity and be careful (*samayaṃ goyama mā pamāyae*). First *māṇusatta* is dealt with (see 10.4/294: *dullabhe khalu māṇuse bhave*), then *suī* (16/306: *laddhūṇa vi māṇusattaṇaṃ āyariyattaṃ puṇarāvi dullahaṃ*, 18/308: *uttamadhammasuī hu dullahā*) and *saddhā* (19/309 *laddhūṇa vi uttamaṃ suiṃ saddahaṇā puṇarāvi dullahā*), and finally the life of a solitary wandering ascetic (29/319 *ceccāṇa dhaṇaṃ ca bhāriyaṃ pavvaio hi se aṇagāriyaṃ*, 30/320 *mā taṃ bitiyaṃ gavesae*, see also the word *saṃjae* in 36/326). From the chapter itself it does not become clear if the text serves as a conclusion to the preceding section or as an introduction to the next one by going through all the four points once more. However, a comparison with Chapter 28, for which see below, suggests that 10 serves rather as an introduction to the next topic of *suī*, or the acquisition of knowledge, by placing it in its context. The *suī* section is short, consisting only of this introduction and Chapter 11, titled *bahussuyapujja*, or "Praise of the very learned". Chapter 11 first provides lists of various characteristics of good and bad pupils. Half way through, a learned man is praised through a series of comparisons ("He is like a well-broken horse, like a bull with pointed horns, etc.) and the section ends appropriately with the statement that "one who is searching for the highest truth should devote himself to study" (*suyam ahiṭṭhijjā uttamaṭṭhagavesae*, 11.32/359).

Unlike the beginnings of the sections on *suī* and *saṃjama*/*tava* (the latter begins with 28, for which, see below), the opening of the section on *saddhā* is not marked in any way. It is not immediately clear where after 11 the section begins. Below I will try to show that the topic of *saddhā* begins with Chapter 12 and is concluded by 27.

With the thirtieth chapter, titled *tavamagga*, we have arrived at the fourth subject of our list, *saṃjamammi vīriya*. Most probably, however, the section already begins with Chapter 28. The latter chapter, titled *mokkhamaggagatī*, introduces a set of four conditions or requirements for liberation, which, while the terms differ, largely overlaps with the earlier one found in Chapter 3. The twenty-eighth chapter mentions, and at the same time defines, *nāṇa*, *daṃsaṇa*, *caritta* and *tava*, which, if we take *daṃsaṇa* and *caritta* together (for which, see below), agree with *suī*, *saddhā*[6] and *saṃjamammi vīriya* respectively. In presenting once more the complete list of items (except the first one) dealt with in the *Uttarajjhāyā*, this chapter resembles Chapter 10 found between the section on *māṇusatta* and *suī*. However, by its use of the terms *nāṇa* and *daṃsaṇa* instead of *suī* and *saddhā* 28 seems to go with the section that follows rather than with the one that precedes. Though the omission of something corresponding to *māṇusatta* is problematic, Chapter 28 seems to serve to place the following topic of *tava* in the context of the text as a whole. See in this connection 28.35/1099:

nāṇeṇa jāṇaī bhāve daṃsaṇeṇa ya saddahe
caritteṇa na giṇhāi taveṇa parisujjhaī.

By knowledge one knows existence(s), by right view one lives [according to this knowledge], by good conduct one remains free from *kamma* and by austerities one is purified [from old *kamma*].[7]

As already indicated, Charpentier believes that the contents of the final section of the *Uttarajjhāyā* lack homogeneity. This is a point to which I will return below. What should be noted here is that all the chapters do deal, directly or indirectly, with *tava*.

It will have become clear that the *Uttarajjhāyā* is not a random collection. Instead, it systematically describes in four sections the four different hurdles to be taken on the path to final liberation. In this connection the following points need closer attention. In the first place the exact boundary between the sections on *suī* and *saddhā* will have to be determined. A problem is that this part of the text consists mainly of stories, the contents of which are often difficult to narrow down to one specific theme. In this connection I will also discuss the position of the Nami story in the *māṇusatta* section. Second, we have to have a closer look at the contents of the final section of the text, which, as said, is claimed to lack coherence. And, third, I will turn to the first two chapters of the text which I have provisionally labelled a preface. An attempt will be made to explain how this works.

The demarcation of the sections on *suī* and *saddhā*

The exact demarcation of the sections on *suī* and *saddhā* is no easy task, in the first place because *saddhā* is a highly inclusive term and in the second place because the text in this part contains mostly stories, the contents of which are, as indicated, often difficult to narrow down to one specific theme. *Saddhā* is synonymous with *sammatta*, "right faith", and *daṃsaṇa*, which is in fact an abbreviation of *sammattadaṃsaṇa*. It is opposed to *micchatta* (*daṃsaṇa*), "wrong faith". Among other things it seems to denote a positive attitude towards the principles of the Jaina faith and a strong determination in carrying out these principles. In this connection I want to quote 28.15/1079:

> *tahiyāṇaṃ tu bhāvāṇaṃ sabbhāve uvaesaṇaṃ*
> *bhāveṇa saddahaṃtassa sammattaṃ taṃ viyāhiyaṃ,*
>
> The [right] attitude [*sabbhāve*] a person assumes who believes with his whole heart what he has been taught about these things [the nine so-called *tattvārtha*s mentioned in the preceding stanza], is called right faith.

In the next stanzas *sammatta* is equated with *ruī*, or love for or devotion to the doctrine, which includes, for instance, love which comes by nature (*nisaggaruī*) and love which comes forth only on command (*āṇāruī*), after a complete course of study (*vitthāra*) or only after a brief exposition (*saṃkheva*) (see 28.16/1080ff.). *saddhā* clearly also includes the eagerness to learn, or being an inquisitive pupil. Other elements involved in *sammatta* (= *saddhā*) are enumerated in stanza 28.31/1095. These are, in Jacobi's translation,

> that one has no doubts [about the truth of the tenets] [*nissaṃkiya*]; that one has no preference [for heterodox tenets] [*nikkaṃkhiya*]; that one does not

> doubt its saving qualities [*nivvitigiṃchā*]; that one is not shaken in the right belief [because heretical sects are more prosperous] [*amūḍhadiṭṭhī*]; that one praises the pious [*uvavūha*]; that one encourages [weak brethren] [*thirīkaraṇa*]; that one supports or loves the confessors of the Law [*vacchalla*]; and that one endeavours to exalt the law [*pabhāvaṇa*].[8]

As indicated, *sammatta* is opposed to *micchatta*, or "entertaining false or wrong views". See in this connection also 28.28/1092, in which *sammattasaddahaṇā* is equated with *vāvanna-kudaṃsaṇa-vajjaṇā*, "the avoiding of corrupted and wrong views".

Saddhā appears to be clearly distinguished from *suī* or *nāṇa*, which denote (the acquisition of) the knowledge of the constituent elements of the world and the process of liberation. As said, *saddhā* refers instead to the fervour, singlemindedness and persistence with which a person pursues these principles (and not those of other faiths, which would be *micchatta*). At the same time there is an overlap with *caritta*, "right conduct", third in the list of four (*nāṇa*, *daṃsaṇa*, *caritta* and *tava*) mentioned in Chapter 28. See in this connection stanza 28.29/1093: "Right conduct [*caritta*] is not possible without right faith [*sammatta*]. Right conduct is to be included in the category of right faith. Right faith and right conduct operate simultaneously, but right faith precedes".[9] This complex *caritta*/*saddhā* is in turn clearly distinguished from the following category of *saṃjama*, or *tava*. The purpose of *caritta*/*saddhā*, which includes, for instance, the five *samiti*s and the three *gutti*s, is to prevent the influx of new *kamma*, while the specific function of *saṃjama*/*tava* is to destroy old *kamma*.[10]

In discussing the chapters between 11 and 28 I will first consider the non-story chapters, that is 15–17, 24 and 26–27. Chapter 11, which deals with *suī*, is followed by three chapters with stories. Then follow three chapters, 15–17, which deal with the life of a monk. Chapter 15 describes the true *bhikkhu*, who, for instance, is content with a simple bed and lodging (15.4/498), does not despise tasteless food (13/507) and lives alone (16/510). It is clear that with this chapter we are no longer in the realm of *suī* but in that of *saddhā*, which, it should be remembered, to a large extent overlaps with *caritta*, or conduct. The same applies to Chapter 16, which deals mainly with rules concerning celibacy (e.g. 16.13/523: the monk should avoid the company of women), and Chapter 17, which describes the bad monk, who after having attained the rare (*dullaha*) benefit of insight flaunts all principles and starts to live as he likes (18.1/530).

Chapter 24, hedged in between two story chapters, appears to deal with topics typically belonging to *saddhā*, namely the five *samiti*s and the three *gutti*s. This is followed by another story, after which Chapter 26 follows, dealing with correct behaviour. After a list, which includes things like asking a superior's permission and showing respect to him, rules follow concerning the division of the day and night into four parts each and the duties a monk has to perform during these periods. All these seem to be typically *saddhā* topics.

Chapter 27 seems to make in an almost playful way a transition to the next section on austerities. It deals with bad pupils, "who break down through a want of steadfastness" (*bhajjaṃtī dhiidubbalā*, 27.8/1055) or "act in opposition to the words of his teacher" (*āyariyāṇaṃ taṃ vayaṇaṃ paḍikūlei*, 11/1058). The teacher should abandon them and use his time by practicing austerities instead (*caittāṇaṃ daḍhaṃ pagiṇhaī tavaṃ*, 16/1063), which is precisely the topic of the next section beginning with Chapter 28.

With regard to the stories in the section comprised by Chapters 11–28 it has already been noted that it is difficult to connect a particular story exclusively with one specific topic. Any decision on this point carries with it a certain element of arbitrariness if special attention is paid to certain parts of the story only while other elements are neglected. In what follows, nevertheless an attempt is made to find out where amidst these stories the topic switches from *suī* to *saddhā*. In going through the stories in the *Uttarajjhāyā* I will begin at the end of a long, uninterrupted series of such stories, namely with Chapter 23, working my way backwards to Chapter 18. This series of stories is found in between chapters, which, as I have tried to show, are concerned with matters related to *saddhā*. One might therefore expect that the stories of Chapters 18–23 deal one way or an other with that very same matter.

Chapter 23 contains the dialogue between Kesī and Goyama. This dialogue seems to present a relatively easy case, in that it has only one aim, namely to establish the superiority of the Jaina faith at the cost of the teachings of Pārśva. As such the story deals, directly or indirectly, with several of the elements of *saddhā* mentioned in 28.31/1095 referred to above, like *nissaṃkiya*, "having no doubts [about the truth of the tenets]", *nikkaṃkhiya*, "having no preference [for heterodox tenets]", *nivvitigiṃcā*, "not doubting the saving qualities of the Jaina faith" and *amūḍhadiṭṭhī*, "not being in the right belief [because heretical sects are more prosperous]". Furthermore the story may be taken to exemplify the *sammatta-micchatta* opposition mentioned above, with Pārśva representing the *micchatta* standpoint.

One of the themes, if not the main theme, of the Rahanemi story in Chapter 22 is that of a monk neglecting his vows and returning to his former life of vice. Fortunately the hero, Rahanemi, is just in time stopped from doing so. For the remainder of his life he sticks faithfully to his vows (*sāmaṇṇaṃ niccalaṃ phāsejāvajjīvaṃ daḍhavvao*, 22.47/834). This aspect of the story clearly belongs to the realm of *saddhā*. Going further backwards, the story of Samuddapāla in Chapter 21 is basically an excuse to enumerate the five vows (21.12/775), some characteristics of good conduct (probably 13/776) and the hardships a monk has to endure in the course of his ascetic career (14–22/777–785).[11] I do not think that there can be any objection to connecting this chapter with *saddhā*.

Chapter 20 consists of a dialogue between King Seṇiya and an ascetic on the topic of *aṇāhatta*, "being without a protector". The king is asked how he can claim to protect his subjects when he is not even able to take good care of himself and secure his own liberation from rebirth. In the course of his exposition the ascetic gives a sermon, titled Mahāniyaṃṭhijja Mahāsuya (20.38–53/741–756), which forms a tract onto itself.[12] In the sermon the ascetic describes people who after having adopted the *niyaṃṭhadhamma* lose their purpose and grow lax (*niyaṃṭhadhammaṃ labhiyāṇa vī jahā sīyaṃti ege bahukāyarā narā*, 20.38/741), as a result of which they need protection. As such this tract, which gave the chapter its name and clearly forms its centre-piece, deals with one of the main aspects of *saddhā*. A similar theme is found in Chapter 19, which deals with the parents of Miyāputta who try to talk their son out of his decision to leave home and become a wandering monk. They fail, however, to break Miyāputta's determination, a theme central to *saddhā*.

Chapter 18 deals with the conversion of Saṃjaya, the king of Kaṃpilla, in the presence of the monk Gaddabhāli. After his conversion he is approached by a king who like himself has given up his kingdom in order to become a monk, but seems bothered by uncertainty about such questions as to whether there is a soul or not and about the role of *viṇaya* and *nāṇa* (or literally *aṇṇāṇa*) in the process of liberation. In stanzas 18.24–32/574–582 Saṃjaya puts forwards Mahāvīra's standpoints on these issues. Next he tells the king that a wise man accepts the existence of the soul and avoids the belief in its non-existence, urging him to accept this faith and to live accordingly, however hard this may be.[13] After that, ostensibly to reassure the king of the correctness of his decision to give up kingship and become a monk, Saṃjaya supplies a list of former kings who have done precisely that.

Going by this summary it is tempting to include this story, like those which follow, into the category of *saddhā*. In that case Chapters 18–23 seem to form an uninterrupted series of stories exemplifying aspects of *saddhā*. As indicated, this was more or less expected. In this respect the situation of the story chapters 12–14 is different. These three chapters are found in between the chapters on *suī* (11) and *saddhā* (15). The question is where the latter topic begins.

Again I will proceed by going backwards. The story of the king of Usuyāra, his *purohita* priest, their wives and their sons deals basically with these persons' determination to leave home and adopt the life of a wandering ascetic, and their relatives' attempts to prevent them from doing so. It begins with the priest's sons decision to leave home and their father's unsuccessful attempt to dissuade them. The sons are, as they say themselves, "full of right faith" (*sammattasaṃjuyā*, 14.26/467), and "Faith will enable [them] to discipline [their] passions" (*saddhā khamaṃ ṇe viṇaittu rāgaṃ*, 14.28/469). The situation repeats itself when the priest wants to leave home as well and his wife tries to dissuade him, and once more, with the king, his sons and his wife. This story seems to go with *saddhā*. It is to be noted, however, that while the stories in the series 18–23 mainly deal with a monk's conduct and his determination after he has left home, or, in the negative sense, his return to his former life of vice, this story deals with the aspirant monk's attempt to leave home itself. In fact, the very same theme is found in Chapter 13, which contains the story of Citta's failure to convince King Baṃbhadatta that he should give up his kingdom and the pleasures that go with worldly life, and to become a monk.

The first story of this group of three is of an entirely different order. It depicts a confrontation between a Jaina monk, on the one hand, and priests officiating at a sacrifice, on the other. The Jaina monk, called Hariesa, originally belonged to the very low caste of the *sovāga*s (Skt *śvapāka*s). When, while begging, he arrives at a sacrificial arena, he is met by a bunch of brahmins, who tell him to be off as the food at the sacrifice had been especially meant for them. In the meantime a Yakṣa who has taken pity on the monk replies on his behalf that he is actually the only true recipient of the food and that they are just brahmins in name. At that moment young men (*kumāra*; it is not clear if they are "princes", that is, the royal patron's sons, or the sons of the main priest) appear, rushing forward and beating up the monk. At the same moment the royal patron's daughter appears on the scene. She tries to stop the boys, for in the monk she has recognized the great saint to whom her father had wished to give her in marriage but who had refused her. Upon this, Yakṣas appear, who beat the boys to death. The main priest now recognizes the monk's superiority, asks for forgiveness and offers him food. At that moment perfumed rain falls down from the sky and we hear the gods praising the brahmin's gift to the monk (12.36/395: *ahodāṇaṃ ca ghuṭṭhaṃ*) and declaring that of the status acquired by birth and the ascetic life the latter has proved to be the stronger (12.37/396: *sakkhaṃ khu dīsai tavoviseso na dīsaī jāiviseso koī*).

The story is concluded by a dialogue in which brahmins (plural!) ask the monk on what his claim that he is the only worthy recipient of the sacrificial food is based, as the food normally goes to brahmins. The dialogue proceeds in the following fashion: the brahmins ask the ascetic where his fire is, his fireplace, his sacrificial ladle and his dried cowdung, and the ascetic replies that penance is his fire, life (soul) his fireplace, *joya* (*yoga*) his ladle and *kamma* his fuel (12.43–44/402–403).

The story seems to elaborate on two themes: the one concerns the belief that the status one has acquired at birth forms no real hurdle in becoming a good ascetic, and the second concerns the Jaina monk's superiority in particular in relation to the brahmin. Thus we see how the lowly *sovāga* Hariesa has become a truer brahmin than those who are brahmins by birth. By the first theme Hariesa's story seems to establish a link with the section on human birth dealt with in Chapters 3–9, ignoring as it were the section on knowledge that comes in between in Chapters 10–11. The second theme may well have served as a fitting introduction to the section on *saddhā*, or a Jaina monk's faithfulness to the ascetic path. In this connection it is telling that the final story in the *saddhā* section in Chapter 25 once more deals with the very same question of who is the true brahmin, the Vedic brahmin or the Jaina ascetic monk. In Chapter 25 the Jaina monk Jayaghosa arrives at the end of a period of fasting at the sacrifice of Vijayaghosa, who chases him away with the argument that he gives food only to learned Vedic brahmins. Jayaghosa retorts that the latter do not know what is essential and starts an exposition on what makes a true brahmin (e.g. "he who does not utter lies out of anger, for a joke, out of greed or out of fear, him we call a real brahman", *taṃ vayaṃ būma māhaṇaṃ*; 25.23/975). He manages to convince Vijayaghosa, who next begs him to accept food from him. At this point the two stories, the one about Hariesa and the other about Jayaghosa, each go their own ways. As we have seen, Hariesa accepts the food and ends his fast

(12.35/394: *bāḍhaṃ ti paḍicchai bhattapāṇaṃ*). This is followed by the passage referred to above, in which the life of the Jaina monk is compared to that of the Vedic brahmin. Jayaghosa in Chapter 25, by contrast, does not accept the food, saying that he does not need it and that he had rather that Vijayaghosa leave home so that he need no longer roam around on the vast sea of *saṃsāra*.[14] This refusal of the food offered appears to be part of the larger undertaking of annihilating former *kamma* and to reach liberation. For we next read how Vijayaghosa "goes into houselessness" (25.42/994), and how both he and Jayaghosa and Vijayaghosa destroy their former *kamma* and reach the highest perfection.[15] This ending seems to make for a smooth transition to the next section which deals with the annihilation of former *kamma* through extreme asceticism. In the same way the final part of Chapter 12 might be taken as a kind of advertisement of the section that follows on the way of life of the ascetic monk.

If the above analysis is correct, it would mean that the section on *saddhā* indeed begins with Chapter 12. It thus begins with a story, which is echoed by the very last story in the section. This last story, however, does not form the end of the section; two more chapters follow, one on, among other things, the duties of the monk during the different parts of the day and night (Chapter 26) and the other, Chapter 27, on pupils who ignore their teachers' advice. By saying that a teacher, rather than wasting his time on these pupils, had better devote his time to austerities, this chapter, after Chapter 25 with its story on Jayaghosa and Vijayaghosa, makes for a second transition to the next section on austerities, which begins with Chapter 28.

It is also possible to recognize some kind of logic in the order of the stories in the *saddhā* section. Thus, while the first batch of stories, 13–14 and 18–19, seems to depict men who want to become monks, the sequence 20–23 deals with men after they have become monks. It should be added, though, that the distinction is not as clear-cut as that. Thus, as we saw, 18 first relates how King Saṃjaya became an ascetic monk and next how he supported another king in his decision of having become a monk. In this way Chapter 18 goes with 13–14 as well as with 20–23.

Ten out of the sixteen chapters of the *saddhā* contain stories. These stories seem to form a tract in itself, with their own introduction and ending, and, allowing for some overlap of themes, showing at least a trace of a logical order. Admittedly, the latter finding relates only to the broad division of the stories into two categories; the principles involved in the order of the individual stories clearly need a further and much more detailed study. This also applies to the distribution of the chapters with non-story material found in between the story chapters. It is interesting to note that while the story chapters are concluded with Chapter 25 the other chapters have, as indicated above, their own conclusion, namely in 27. In this way both the story chapters as well as the non-story chapters seem to compete with each other for the main role in the *saddhā* section.

The story about how King Nami became a monk

All this leaves us with one more story, namely the one about Nami in Chapter 9. If Chapter 10 does function indeed as an introduction to the section of *suī* (Chapter 11), this story would form a kind of climax to the *māṇusatta* section. The story tells how King Nami successfully resists Indra's attempts to prevent him from carrying out his decision to give up the power and the pleasures that go with the life of a king, and become a monk. As such the story would have fitted excellently in the section on *saddhā*. What then might have determined its position in the *māṇusatta* section instead? In this connection I want to draw attention to the opening line of the story (9.1/229), already briefly mentioned above: *caiūṇa devalogāo uvavaṇṇo māṇusammi loyammi*, "having descended from the world of the gods, he was born in the world of men". This particular information does not come out of the blue. In the preceding chapters only human beings are said to be able to reach final liberation, as this requires the destruction of the human body as a means to annihilate one's old *kamma*: "One should sustain this [human] body for the annihilation of one's old *kamma*" (*puvvakammakhayaṭṭhāe imaṃ dehaṃ samuddhare*, 6.13/174). In Chapters 7 and 8 several "destinations" are mentioned, namely beside that of men, those of gods (*devagaī*), creatures from hell, animals (*naragatirikkhattaṇa*, 7.16/194)[16] and demons (*uvavajjaṃti āsure kāe*, 8.14/222).[17] It is difficult after all this to treat the opening line of the Nami story as just a coincidence: after various byways discussed in the preceding chapters it brings us right back to the central topic of the section, namely human existence. The story itself by the word *paṃḍiya* in the very last line returns to one of the themes of the first few chapters of the section, namely that the opportunities of this life should not be squandered foolishly but used "wisely" (9.62/290).

The coherence of the fourth section

As already indicated, Charpentier was bothered by the apparent lack of order and coherence among the last nine chapters of the *Uttarajjhāyā*.

It is unfortunately not entirely clear what he expected on this point. In this respect I have argued that the situation has changed anyhow, for the last nine chapters coincide with our final section on *saṃjamammi vīriya* or *tava*. The question now should be if these chapters relate to that topic and if so, how. At this point it is to be remembered that the purpose of *tava* (or *saṃjama*) is to destroy old *kamma* (*khavettā puvvakammāiṃ saṃjameṇa taveṇa ya*, 28.36/1100).[18] It should therefore not come as a surprise that the section beside chapters on *tava* also contains chapters on *kamma*. The text indeed vacillates between these two topics, though, in a way that is not easy to predict. Thus in the twenty-ninth chapter 73 stages are distinguished in the process leading to the destruction of *kamma* and final liberation. They go from *saṃvega*, or the "longing for liberation", through various aspect of right conduct and ascetic practices to *akammayā*, or "the state of complete freedom from *kamma*". Next

Chapter 30 makes a clear distinction between the prevention of inflow of new *kamma*, for which rules of conduct like the five *samiti*s and the three *gutti*s suffice (30.3/1179), and the destruction of old *kamma*, which requires more drastic measures. Here *tava* comes into play (30.6/1182) which is said to consists of two varieties, namely external and internal, each of which consists again of six sub-varieties, for instance fasting and meditation respectively. The remainder of the chapter is devoted to descriptions of all these varieties of *tava*.

Chapter 31 provides a list of ways and means through which a monk will be able to escape quickly from *saṃsāra*. This might explain its position in this section, after a chapter defining *tava*. If, however, we look at the list, which besides ascetic practices includes, for instance, mastering the 23 lectures of the *Sūyagaḍa*, one may wonder why the chapter is found here at all. To this point I will return below.

With the thirty-second chapter the topic switches to *kamma* and more specifically to the causes of *kamma*. The latter include in particular love, hate and bewilderment (*rāga*, *dosa* and *moha*). Love of beauty, for instance, makes one want to possess the thing of beauty, while dislike, on the other hand, makes one to want to destroy it (32.22/1256ff.). This is repeated for the different objects of the senses, each paragraph ending with the refrain in which it is stated that a man whose mind is blurred by the desire for such things as beauty and sound accumulates *kamma* (*paduṭṭhacitto ya ciṇāi kammaṃ*).[19] At the end the chapter turns to *tava* again, in particular that of the "internal" variety: "At the end of his life, free of the influx of [new] *kamma*, by meditation and concentration and being pure he reaches liberation", *aṇāsave jhāṇasamāhijutte āukkhae mokkhaṃ uveti suddhe* (32.109/1343).[20]

The topic of *kamma* is pursued in Chapters 33 and 34, with 33 defining the various types of *kamma* and 34 dealing with the *lesā*s, which is the colouring effect of *kamma* on the soul. With Chapter 35, however, we go back again to ways and means to liberate oneself from the pain of human existence. It starts with leaving home (*gihivāsaṃ pariccajja pavvajjām āsio muṇī*, 35.2/1433) and ends with *tava* proper, which consists of both meditation (*sukkajjhāṇaṃ jhiyāejjā*, 35.19/1450) and fasting to death (20/1451):

nijjūhiūṇa āhāraṃ kāladhamme uvaṭṭhie
caiūṇa māṇusaṃ boṃdiṃ pahū dukkhā vimuccaī.

The final chapter, Chapter 36, is clearly divided into two parts. The first contains an elaborate enumeration of the many categories of beings with and without a soul. This is followed by 19 verses (36.250–268/1702–1720) dealing with *tava*, and more specifically fasting to death. According to both Charpentier and Alsdorf this second part has no relationship with the first part.[21] Alsdorf characterizes it as an appendix, which had been pieced together by verses taken from the two other texts dealing with fasting to death, namely the *Āurapaccakkhāṇa* and *Maraṇasamāhi*. In denying any relationship between the two parts of this chapter, Charpentier and Alsdorf ignore the text itself, which does establish a connection in the very first verse ("In order to be successful in performing austerities one has to know the division of the *jīva*s and *ajīva*s") as well as in the conclusion of the first part in 249/1701:

> *iti jīvam ajīve ya soccā saddahiūṇa ya*
> *savvanayāṇa aṇumae ramejjā saṃjame muṇī,*

If *savvanaya* may be taken to refer to aspects of right conduct (*naya* = *caritta*?), we have here again a variant of the list of four steps, with *soccā* corresponding to *suī*/*nāṇa*, *saddahiūṇa* to *saddhā*/*daṃsaṇa*, *savvanaya* to *caritta* and *saṃjame* to *saṃjama*. *māṇusatta* of the first list seems to be included in the first element, or *nāṇa*, as the object of the knowledge acquired. After this the text continues with the practice of fasting to death, which can be spread out over twelve years, one year or six months (250–255/1702–1707). The chapter closes with one's behaviour or attitude at the time of death and the different destinations after death arising from this (256/1708). With this chapter we have as it were come full circle: we are back at the very first topic, that of human existence, placed here in the totality of existences. As expected, the text is mainly concerned with ways of ending life here, a topic which, however, was also clearly present in the *māṇusatta* section. Interestingly, the chapter, and the text as such as a whole, ends with the "warning" that if one is not careful enough during one's life, one runs the risk of having to start all over again (267/1719):

> *satthaggahaṇaṃ visabhakkhaṇaṃ ca jalaṇaṃ ca jalapaveso ya*
> *aṇāyārabhaṃḍasevā jammaṇamaraṇāṇi baṃdhaṃti,*
>
> Those who use weapons, eat poison, throw themselves into fire or kill themselves by drowning, who behave badly or use insulting language, such persons will suffer to be born and die again and again.

As said, the text in the final section goes back and forth from *tava* to *kamma* to *tava* again. Apart from the irregular internal order, however, the individual chapters all revolve tightly around the main theme of *tava-kamma*.

As indicated above, the odd one out seems to be Chapter 31, which deals with topics without any direct relationship with *tava* or *kamma*. It contains a list of topics ordered according to the number of their constituent elements. Thus, the study of the *Sūyagaḍa*, with its 23 lectures (31.16/1229), is mentioned after steadfastness in the face of the 22 *parīsaha*s (16/1228). The only direct connection of this chapter with those surrounding it may well be the very first item of the list, namely *saṃjama* mentioned in 31.2/1215, which constitutes the very topic of the preceding chapter. If this is indeed what has determined the presentation of 31 after 30, 31 may well be construed as a comment or correction on 30. For, while in the latter chapter *tava* is explicitly said to be twofold, namely involving internal as well as external practices, in 30 *saṃjama*, by being the first item enumerated, is presented as an undivided concept which by implication consists of both internal and external practices.

The preface

Chapters 30 and 31 show that the connection between chapters may be a matter of detail of an almost accidental nature. Something like this we have already seen in the case of Chapter 9: its position in (or at the end of) the *māṇusatta* section can be understood only by giving extraordinary weight to its very first sentence. A similar type of linking may be at stake at the beginning of the *Uttarajjhāyā* between Chapters 1 and 2 as well.

As I have tried to show above, the third chapter outlines the programme for the remainder of the text. As such, Chapter 1 and 2 are left to stand more or less on their own. The contents of the first chapter is quite clear. It emphasizes the importance of showing respect (*viṇaya*) to the teacher, thus forming a fitting introduction or preface to a text which is labelled a lesson (*ajjhāyā*), one presumably received from a teacher, or *āyariya* or *guru* (1.20/20). Chapter 2 deals with something completely different. It provides a list of the 22 so-called hardships (*parīsaha*s) which a monk has to put up with in the course of his ascetic life. For instance, however hungry he may be, he should withstand the temptation to cut or break things in the attempt to collect food (2.4/52). One may wonder what this chapter has to do with the preceding one about the teacher. I think a possible connection may be found in the very last *parīsaha* mentioned, which tells a monk to resist the fear of being lied to by one's teachers: "A *bhikkhu* should not think 'they lied to me when they said that there were, are and always will be Jinas'".[22] With this we are back at the teacher, his reliability or usefulness, and the respect due to him.

Conclusion

The above study has shown that, in contrast to Charpentier's claim about its lack of order, the *Uttarajjhāyā* is a text which was planned from beginning to end. There is, moreover, no evidence to support Charpentier's assumption of a neat and slender *Ur-Uttarajjhāyā* which in the course of time increased in size through the accumulation of additional related material. For all we know, the *Uttarajjhāyā* as we now have it is the result of a one-time process of composition, though of course minor later additions cannot be ruled out. All this is not to say that the result is a systematic, uniform and transparent treatise. For instance, the plan identified so far basically functioned as a skeleton. How the individual chapters were placed within this frame is not yet clear and still has to be investigated. The few peculiarities mentioned above in the order of the chapters within the sections are by their nature difficult to generalize. At the micro level the *Uttarajjhāyā* is "just" a compilation of independent chapters each of which would also make perfect sense when standing on their own.[23] In this connection it is to be noted that in the process of compilation anomalies were not avoided. A case in point is the occurrence side by side of the rarely attested list of four terms, namely *māṇusatta*, *suī*, *saddhā* and *saṃjamammi vīriya* in Chapter 3 and a partly overlapping and functionally equivalent list of three, which is instead quite common in Jaina texts, *nāṇa*, *daṃsaṇa* and *tava*, in Chapter 28.

Except for the frame identified here, the *Uttarajjhāyā* is a somewhat messy text, which contains a bit of everything: mere enumerations besides poetry and stories. In this connection one may ask what might have been the function of this text. Unfortunately its title *Uttarajjhāyā*, "final Lesson", and its inclusion among the four Mūlasūtras, or "basic *sūtras*",[24] are not really helpful in this matter. On the basis of its "preface", however, it would appear that we are dealing with a text containing the essence of the teachings which one might expect from a teacher. Maybe the *Uttarajjhāyā* is meant to reflect the full range of this teacher's wisdom and teaching method – in other words, not just dry dogmatics with exhaustive lists, not just poetry and not just stories, but precisely a bit of everything.

Notes

1 See, e.g. Alsdorf 1966.
2 Charpentier 1922: 40ff.
3 On this point the traditional interpretation of the text is unfortunately not very helpful either. Thus, while Devendra in his *ṭīkā*-commentary at the beginning of each chapter of the *Uttarajjhāyā* indicates how the chapter is related to the preceding one, one does not get a clear idea as to how, to give an extreme example, the thirty-sixth chapter is related to the first one. Since Charpentier (1922), the question of the composition of the *Uttarajjhāyā* has not been taken up in any detail again. Bruhn, for instance, mentions the *Uttarajjhāyā* together with the *Āyāraṃga*, *Sūyagaḍa* and *Viyāhapannatti* as an example of a Jaina canonical text which can be split into two parts. Thus, while both the *Āyāraṃga* and *Sūyagaḍa* are formally divided into two parts, the *Viyāhapannatti* into a nucleus and accretions, in the *Uttarajjhāyā* one can distinguish between early and late chapters and between text passages in early and late (*āryā*) metre (Bruhn 1993: 20). Bruhn wants to distinguish this "broad" division from attempts at identifying detailed textual strata, though in some cases the two types of distinctions seem to coincide. For instance, the second part of the *Āyāraṃga* as well as the *Sūyagaḍa* is generally held to be younger than the first (Bollée 1977: 1). However, when Folkert refers to the "later, more systematic portion of the *Uttarādhyanana*", implying that the first part is not systematic, or not strikingly so, he is merely repeating what Charpentier said about the last nine chapters (Folkert 1993: 120). Typically, both Bruhn and Folkert base themselves only on formal criteria. Investigations into the coherence in the presentation of the contents in texts are rare in Jaina studies, a recent exception being Caillat 2008. This is all the more strange as the problem of the coherence is often quite obvious. For instance, what is the relationship between the first and the second part in the *Āyāraṃga* and *Sūyagaḍa*?
4 3.11/107:

māṇusattammi āyāo jo dhammaṃ socca saddahe
tavassī vīriyaṃ laddhuṃ saṃvuḍo niddhuṇe rayaṃ.

5 3.12/108: *nivvāṇaṃ paramaṃ jāi.*
6 For *daṃsaṇa* as synonymous to *saddhā*, see 28.35/1099, quoted below.
7 In this list, *māṇusatta* of the other list is included in *nāṇa*, or "knowledge of existence(s)"; see further below, at the discussion of Chapter 36.
8 Jacobi 1895: 156–157.
9 *natthi carittaṃ sammattavihūṇaṃ daṃsaṇe u bhaiyavvaṃ*
sammattacarittāiṃ jugavaṃ puvvaṃ va sammattaṃ.
10 See in this connection 30.3/1179:

paṃcasamio tigutto akasāo jiiṃdio
agāravo ya nissallo jīvo bhavai ṇāsavo,

and 6/1182:

bhavakoḍīsaṃciyaṃ kammaṃ tavasā nijjarijjaī.

11 Note 21.11/774, which provides the table of contents of the chapter:

jahittu saṃgaṃ tha mahākilesaṃ mahaṃtamohaṃ kasiṇaṃ bhayāvahaṃ
pariyāyadhammaṃ ca'bhiroyaejjā vayāṇi sīlāṇi parīsahe *ya,*

Having abandoned attachment, the great distress, the great delusion and everything which causes fear [of rebirth] one should adopt the laws of the mode of life [as a monk] and the vows [*vayāṇi*] that come with it, as well as the types of conduct [*sīlāṇi*] and the hardships [*parīsahe*].

12 See Jacobi 1895: 104, n. 2.

13 See 18.33/583:

kiriyaṃ ca royae dhīre akiriyaṃ parivajjae
diṭṭhīe diṭṭhisaṃpanne dhammaṃ cara suduccaraṃ.

14 25.38/990:

na kajjaṃ majjha bhikkheṇaṃ khippaṃ nikkhamasū diyā
mā bhamihisi bhayāvatte ghore saṃsārasāgare.

15 25.43/995:

khavettā puvvakammāiṃ saṃjameṇa taveṇa ya
jayaghosavijayaghosā siddhiṃ pattā aṇuttaraṃ.

16 It is said that once in hell or born as an animal it is very hard to get back on the right track again, taking a long time to do so (7.18/196).

17 It should in this connection be noted that while in the *māṇusatta* section as a whole the reward of human existence is final bliss, at a certain point in Chapter 7 instead of bliss, heaven is mentioned (7.19/197ff.). Heaven, however, here obviously has the meaning it has in ordinary, non-Jaina, parlance, namely that of a higher aim to be realized through living a careful life.

18 We are dealing with a formula here. The same line is also found in 25.43/995, quoted above in n. 15.

19 e.g. 32.32–34/1266–1268):

[rūvā]ṇurattassa narassa evaṃ katto suhaṃ hojja kayāi kiṃci
tatthovabhoge vi kilesadukkhaṃ nivvattae jassa kae ṇa dukkhaṃ
emeva [rūvammi] gao paosaṃ uvei dukkhoghaparaṃparāo
paduṭṭhacitto ya ciṇāi kammaṃ jaṃ se puṇo hoi dukkhaṃ vivāge
[rūve] viratto maṇuo visogo eeṇa dukkhoghaparaṃpareṇa
na lippaī bhavamajjhe vi saṃto jaleṇa vā pukkhariṇīpalāsaṃ.

20 *Tava* of the physical type may well be hidden in the words *kayasavvakicca* in the preceding verse (32.1081342):

sa vīyarāgo kayasavvakicco *khavei nāṇāvaraṇaṃ khaṇeṇaṃ*
taheva jaṃ daṃsaṇam āvarei caṃtarāyaṃ pakarei kammaṃ,

Having shed his likes [and dislikes] and having done everything there is to be done he destroys in a second the *kamma* obstructing knowledge, the *kamma* which obstructs right faith and the *kamma* which prevents one's entrance on the path leading to liberation.

21 Charpentier (1922: 408) and Alsdorf (1966: 163 ff).

22 2.47/95:

abhū jiṇā atthi jiṇā aduvā vi bhavissaī
musaṃ te evam āhaṃsu ii bhikkhū na ciṃtae.

23 Some chapters, in their turn, are themselves compilations. A clear example is Chapter 36, which, as shown by Alsdorf, was pieced together with materials borrowed from various sources (Alsdorf 1977: 163ff.). In this process sometimes "new" sentences were produced to connect the various parts with one another. This can also be seen in the story chapters, in which we find old dialogue stanzas in a Pāli-like language, framed by stanzas in another, later, dialect providing the context of the dialogue (see Tieken 1998).

24 For the use of the term *sūtra* in Mūlasūtra we may have to go back to the Buddhists' use of the term rather than the one current in Sanskrit literature.

References

Alsdorf, Ludwig, *The Āryā Stanzas of the Uttarajjhāyā. Contributions to the Text History and Interpretation of a Canonical Jaina Text.* Abhandlungen der geistes- und sozialwissenschaftlichen Klasse. Jahrgang 1966. Nr. 2. Wiesbaden, 1966.

Bollée, Willem B., *Studien zum Sūyagaḍa. Die Jainas und die anderen Weltanschauungen vor der Zeitwende. Textteile, Nijjutti, Übersetzung und Anmerkungen.* Schriftenreihe des Südasien-Instituts der Universität Heidelberg 24. Wiesbaden, 1977.

Bruhn, Klaus, "Sectional Studies in Jainology II". *Berliner Indologische Studien* 7 (1993), 9–58.

Caillat, Colette, "On the Composition of the Śvetāmbara Tract *Maraṇavibhatti-/ Maraṇasamādhi-Paiṇṇayaṃ*". In: Colette Caillat and Nalini Balbir (eds), *Jaina Studies. Papers of the 12th World Sanskrit Conference* Vol. 9. Delhi 2008, 1–32.

Charpentier, Jarl, *The Uttarādhyayanasūtra. Being the First Mūlasūtra of the Śvetāmbara Jains.* Edited with an Introduction, Text, Critical Notes and a Commentary. Upsala 1922. First Indian Edition New Delhi 1980.

Folkert, Kendall W., *Scripture and Community. Collected Essays on the Jains.* Edited by John E. Cort. Atlanta 1993.

Jacobi, Hermann, *Jaina Sūtras. Translated from the Prākrit. Part II: The Uttarādhyayana Sūtra, The Sūtrakritāṅga Sūtra.* Oxford 1895. Reprint New Delhi 1973.

Tieken, Herman, "The Distribution of the Absolutive in *–ūṇaṃ* in *Uttarajjhāyā* ". *Asiatische Studien/Études Asiatiques* LII/1 (1998), 261–286.

Uttarajjhāyā, *Dasaveyāliyasuttaṃ Uttara[j]jhayaṇāiṃ and Āvassayasuttaṃ.* Muni Shri Puṇyavijayaji and Pt. Amritalāl Mohanlāl Bhojak (eds). *Jaina-Āgama-Series* No. 15. Bombay 1977.

2 A rare manuscript of the *Bhagavatī Ārādhanā*

Prem Suman Jain

The *Bhagavatī Ārādhanā* (BhĀ) is one of the most valuable ancient works belonging to the Digambara Jaina tradition. It was composed by Śivarāya or Śivakoṭī (hereafter Śivarāya)[1] in the second century AD[2] and contains some 2170 verses in Śaurasenī Prākṛt. According to its author the title of the work is *Ārādhanā*, *°bhagavatī* being an honorific designation added to qualify the practice of *ārādhanā*. Later Jaina authors, such as Prabhācandra and Āśādhara, designated the text *Mūlārādhanā*, in order to glorify its subject matter.[3] The BhĀ deals mainly with the different types of *ārādhanā*, including the practice of the three jewels (*ratnatraya*), asceticism (*tapas*) and *samādhimaraṇa* or voluntary peaceful death. BhĀ is the most complete treatise devoted to the latter subject.[4] According to Jaina thought, *samādhimaraṇa* is not only a process of giving up the breath by undertaking fasting, but a systematic practice to shed spiritual flaws, such as attachment and aversion. The BhĀ also includes descriptions of hellish miseries as well as of the eternal bliss of final liberation. Stressing the importance of death in a state of equanimity, Śivāraya states: "One who dies a peaceful death in a state of equanimity (*samādhi*), even once, will be liberated within a maximum of seven or eight births."[5] The practice of *samādhimaraṇa* enables a person to maintain equanimity of mind both in life and death.[6] The purpose of the four *ārādhanās*, including the practice of three jewels and asceticism, is to develop detachment, forbearance, self-restraint and mental equipoise at the critical hour of death, and finally to attain spiritual purification and liberation. Śivāraya has divided the subject matter of BhĀ into four main topics: (i) correct faith (*darśana*), (ii) knowledge (*jñāna*), (iii) conduct (*cāritra*) and (iv) asceticism (*tapas*); the text emphasizes the necessity of practicing twelve types of penance – external and internal – in order to attain spiritual purity. Śivāraya also deals with other aspects of Jainism, such as the five supreme divinities (*pañcaparameṣṭhin*), the life of Digambara Jaina monks, the six indispensable duties (*āvaśyaka*), the six karmic stains (*leśya*), service (*sevā*) to the fourfold congregation, the five great vows (*mahāvrata*), the four kinds of meditation (*ārta-*, *raudra-*, *dharma-* and *śukladhyāna*) and the twelve types of reflection (*anuprekṣā*).

Editions and translations of the *Bhagavatī Ārādhanā*

BhĀ, including a commentary by Pt. Sadāsukhadāsa, was published for the first time in 1909. The text was then edited together with three commentaries, and translated into Hindi by J.P. Phadakule in 1935. Later, in 1978, Pt. Kailāśacandra Śāstrī published a Hindi translation of BhĀ (fourth reprint 2006). A critical edition of BhĀ, based on available manuscripts, is still awaited. I am not aware of any translation of BhĀ into English or any other European language or research papers or dissertations on BhĀ.

Commentaries on the Bhagavatī Ārādhanā

Due to its importance to Jaina monks and laymen, later Jaina writers composed comprehensive commentaries on the BhĀ. The earliest and most exhaustive is the *Vijayodayā Ṭīkā* of Aparājita Sūri written between the fifth and tenth century AD. Other commentaries include the *Mūlārādhanādarpaṇa* of Āśādhara, the *Ārādhanāpañjikā* (unknown author) and the *Bhāṣāvacanikā* of Pt. Sadāsukhadāsa. Āśādhara repeatedly refers to a Ṭīkā on BhĀ, but the name of its author is not mentioned, and no manuscript of this text is known to us. The impact of this Prākṛt commentary is, however, seen in works of later authors of *ārādhanā* texts.

Bhagavatī Ārādhanā *and* Kathākośas

The Prākṛt *gāthās* of BhĀ refer to didactic, legendary, edificatory and ascetic tales which served as the source for later writers of kathākośas composed in Prākṛt, Sanskrit and Apabhraṃśa.[7] Śrīcandra (eleventh century) quotes thirty-nine *gāthās* from BhĀ in his Apabhraṃśa *Kahākosu*. First he explains their literal meaning in Sanskrit and then he gives short and long tales elucidating their doctrinal content. Śrīcandra remarks that just as there cannot be a painting without a frame, the reader cannot grasp a story without word-to-word explanation of the basic *gāthā*:

> *saṃbandha vihūṇu savvu vi hīṇu rasu na dei guṇavantahaṃ* |
> *teṇiya gāhāu payaḍivi tāu kahami kahāu suṇantahaṃ* ||
>
> bhaṇidaṃ ca –
>
> *jiha kuḍḍeṇa vihūṇaṃ ālekkhaṃ natthi jīvaloyammi* |
> *tiha pavayeṇa vihūṇaṃ pāvanti kahaṃ na soyārā* ||[8]

Another *kathākośa* quoting from the BhĀ is the *Vaḍḍhārādhane* composed by an unknown Kannaḍa poet.[9] The nineteen stories found in the *Vaḍḍhārādhane* are based on nineteen verses (1539–1557) from the thirty-fifth chapter of the BhĀ. The author first quotes the BhĀ *gāthā*, then gives its literal meaning in

Kannaḍa followed by a narration of the story. The thirty-nine Prākṛt *gāthā*s quoted by Śrīcandra (see above and Table 2.6 below) and the nineteen Prākṛt *gāthā*s quoted by the author of *Vaḍḍhārādhane* form the basis of establishing the original Śaurasenī Prākṛt reading of the *gāthās* of BhĀ. A critical edition of BhĀ may thus be prepared on the basis of these fifty-eight (thirty-nine plus nineteen) Prākṛt *gāthās*. There may be a relation between these fifty-eight *gāthā*s and the hitherto unknown Prākṛt commentary mentioned by Āśādhara.

The Pune manuscript – a rare manuscript of the *Bhagavatī Ārādhanā*

The present author has embarked upon a project of collecting information on available manuscripts of the BhĀ. Hitherto, thirty-nine manuscripts from different places in India have been identified.[10] These manuscripts are most useful in critical editing the BhĀ. In the following, I would like to describe one rare manuscript of the BhĀ kept in the Bhandarkar Oriental Research Institute, Pune.[11] This rare paper manuscript contains 135 folios, with 9–10 lines on each folio. The script is *devanāgarī*, the scribe Brāhmaṇika, pupil of Bhaṭṭāraka Jainacandra, the date 1539 VS and the place Kāsilinagar, an unknown location in Rajasthan. In Tables 2.3 and 2.4 below, the Pune manuscript is compared with the edition of Pt. Kailāśacandra Śāstrī and Aparājitasūri's *Vijayodayā Ṭīkā*. The material contained in the BhĀ belongs to the time of early Jainism when the division of Śvetāmbara and Digambara did not exist. The subject matter of the BhĀ became popular in both the traditions of the Jaina Saṃgha and some *gāthā*s are found in texts in both traditions. It thus seems that there must be a common source of Prākṛt verses from where later authors might have derived those verses (see Table 2.7).

Sanskrit Ṭippana on the Pune Manuscript

The Pune Manuscript has been provided with glosses by an expert scholar or *muni*. Some examples are given below:

Some extra *gāthās*

The number of total Prākṛt *gāthās* given on folio No. 134A is 2157. It does not tally with the *gāthā* number as given in the printed edition of the BhĀ edited by Pt. Kailāśacandra Śāstrī (2164).

Colophon and *praśasti*

A *praśasti* is found on the last folio of the Pune MS. It gives some information about the tradition of Bhaṭṭārakas and the name of the scriber with date and place.[12] The concluding portion of the colophon runs: *evaṃ bhagavadī ārādhanā sammattā* ||. Scribal remarks in the Pune MS are given in the following way: *Saṃvat 1539 varṣe Poṣasudi 5 Śanaiścara vāre Dhaniṣṭhā nakṣatre Kāsilīnagare Śrī Kundakundācārya anvaye … Śrī Jinacandra devā tatśiṣya Brahmanikama* ||

Table 2.1 Sanskrit Ṭippana on the Pune manuscript

Gāthā No. 33 on folio No. 2B

Words of the gāthā	*Gloss in Sanskrit*
tao	• tataḥ
taṃ	• niścayārthaḥ
mandacārittaṃ	• mandacārittaṃ
sadhdahadi	• śraddhādātavya

Gāthā No. 34 on folio No. 2B

Words of the gāthā	*Gloss in Sanskrit*
patteyabudhada	• pratyekabuddha
aruhā gaṅthaṃ gathanti	• āptavacanabalena
jahā jarido	• yathā jūrirogī

Svakarmakṣayārthaṃ svapaṭhanārthaṃ edaṃ granthaṃ svahasteṇaṃ likhitam. The scribe has rendered his teacher's tradition as follows:

> In the tradition of Śrī Kundakunda, in the Balātkāragaṇa of the Sarasvatīgaccha:
>
> Bhaṭṭāraka Śri Ratnakīrtideva
> ↓
> Bhaṭṭāraka Prabhācandradeva
> ↓
> Bhaṭṭāraka Śri Padmanandideva
> ↓
> Bhaṭṭāraka Śri Jinacandradeva
> ↓
> His disciple Brāhmaṇikāma has copied this text.

The scribe advises the readers that they should protect the text from water, fire and oily hands, since, for scholars, it represents the state of omniscience:

> *nīrāgnipāṇisnehebhyo rakṣaṇiyaṃ prayatnataḥ* |
> *jñānibhiḥ pustakaṃ yasmāt sarvajñapadavācakam* ||

Table 2.2 Manuscripts of BhĀ

Sl. No	*Manuscript centre or catalogue*	*Commentary*	*Remarks*
1	Vijayadharma Lakṣmī Jñānamandir, Belanganj, Agra. List of K.H. Jhaveri (1938), no. 1121	Not found	Collection shifted at Ahmedabad
2	The 4th Bhandarkar Collection Report (1887–1897), BORI, no. 1024	Vijayodayā Ṭīkā	–
3	Candraprabha Digambara Jain Mandir, Bhuleshvar, Bombay. Elaka Pannalāl Digambara Jain Sarasvatī Bhavan, Bandal, no. 46	Not known	–
4	Catalogue of Jesalmer Bhaṇḍāra, G.O.S., Baroda (1923), p. 32	Not known	–
5	Lalith Kīrti Bhaṇḍāra, Ajmer, in the list of Sarasvatī Bhavan, Bombay, no. 127	Not known	–
6	Report of the A. B. Khathavate Collection of 1835–1902, BORI, no. 1112	Original *gāthās* with Sanskrit Ṭippana	135 pages, dated 1539 V.S. Xerox copy obtained by Dr P.S. Jain
7	Report of the A.B. Khathavate Collection of 1835–1902, BORI, no. 1113	With Dīpikāvṛtti of Śivajidāruṇa	403 pages, dated 1818 V.S. Xerox copy obtained by Dr P.S. Jain
8	Report of the A.B. Khathavate Collection of 1835–1902, BORI, no. 1114	Vijayodayā Ṭīkā	–
9	Report of the A.B. Khathavate Collection of 1835–1902, BORI, no. 1115	Vijayodayā Ṭīkā	–
10	The Sixth report by Dr Peterson in the collection of the 1895–1898, BORI, list S.N. 679	Ārādhanā Pañjikā Ṭīkā	436 pages, dated 1416 V.S. by Brahmadeva Nathu. Xerox copy obtained by P.S. Jain
11	Pannalāl Jain Sarasvatī Bhavan, Bhuleshvar, Bombay, no. 1163	Vijayodayā Ṭīkā	–

continued

Table 2.2 Manuscripts of BhĀ

Sl. No	*Manuscript centre or catalogue*	*Commentary*	*Remarks*
12	Pannalāl Jain Sarasvatī Bhavan, Bhuleshvar, Bombay, no. 1266	Vijayodayā Ṭīkā	–
13	Pannalāl Jain Sarasvatī Bhavan, Bhuleshvar, Bombay, no. 2419	Darpaṇa Ṭīkā of Āśādhara	–
14	Pannalāl Jain Sarasvatī Bhavan, Bhuleshvar, Bombay, no. 2718	Darpaṇa Ṭīkā of Āśādhara	–
15	Pannalāl Jain Sarasvatī Bhavan, Bhuleshvar, Bombay, no. 2640	Maraṇakāṇḍikā of Amitagati	–
16	Strassburg Library List of E. Leumann, published in the *Vienna Oriental Journal* XI (1897):279–298.	Vijayodayā Ṭīkā	–
17	Terāpanthī Digambara Jain Mandir, Bombay. List of Grantha Bhaṇḍāra obtained from Sarasvatī Jain Bhavan, Bandal, no. 1704	Bhagavatī Ārādhanā	Four copies, details not known
18	Catalogue of Sanskrit and Prakrit MSS in C.P. and Varar, Nāgpūr 1926, no. 682	Darpaṇa Ṭīkā of Āśādhara	–
19	Vimalagaccha Upāsarā, Hajpatelpole, Ahmedabad. List of Grantha Bhaṇḍāara, Dabba, no. 26, pothī 1	Nandigani Ṭīkā	Details not known. Dr P.S. Jain visited this Upasara five years ago, but its Bhandar has shifted to Samvegino Upasara in Ahmedabad
20	Bhaṭṭārakīya Grantha Bhaṇḍāra, Nāgaur (Raj). Grantha S.N. 211/1781	With Commentary	Folio pages copied in 1518 V.S.
21	Bhaṭṭārakīya Grantha Bhaṇḍāra, Nāgaur (Raj). Grantha S.N. 299/820	May be original *gāthās* only	130 folios, copied in 1568 V.S.
22	Bhaṭṭārakīya Grantha Bhaṇḍāra, Nāgaur (Raj). Grantha S.N. 300	With Commentary	448 folios, copied in 1664 V.S.
23	Bhaṭṭārakīya Grantha Bhaṇḍāra, Nāgaur (Raj). Grantha S.N. 301	With Commentary	283 folios, copied in 1877 V.S.

24	Bhaṭṭārakīya Grantha Bhaṇḍāra, Nāgaur (Raj). Grantha S.N. 3966	With Commentary	235 folios
25	Bhaṭṭārakīya Grantha Bhaṇḍāra, Nāgaur (Raj). Grantha S.N. 1742	With Commentary	322 folios, copied in 1831 V.S.
26	Bhaṭṭārakīya Grantha Bhaṇḍāra, Nāgaur (Raj). Grantha S.N. 211/1781	With Hindi Vacanikā of Pt. Sadāsukhadāsa	630 folios 630, copied in 1908 V.S.
27	Digambara Jain Mandir Baḍī Pañcāyata, Ding Village (Raj.). Jain Grantha Bhaṇḍāras of Rajasthan, Kaslival, P 74, Vestean, no. 24	Prākṛt Verses 2170	65 folios copied in 1511 V.S. in Mandalgarh
28	Jain Siddhant Bhavan, Arraha, no. 177	With Hindi Vacanikā	410 folios
29	Amera Sastra Bhandara, Jaipur	With Commentary	498 folios, copied in 1760 V.S. Used by Pt. K.C. Śāstrī in his edition
30	Amera Śāstra Bhaṇḍāra, Jaipur		Incomplete, copied in 1514 V.S.
31	Todarāj Sṅngh Granth Bhaṇḍāra, Ajmer		379 folios, copied in 1999 V.S.
32	Digambara Jain Mandir Bhaṇḍāra, Dharampura, Delhi		312 folios, copied in 1863 V.S.
33	Digambara Jain Bhaṭṭāraka Bhaṇḍāra, Nāgaur		281 folios, copied in 1911 V.S.
34	Choṭe Divānjī Jain Temple Granth Bhaṇḍāra, Jaipur, S.N. 1	With Hindi Vacanikā of Sadāsukhadāsa	630 folios, copied in 1908 V.S.
35	Digambara Jain Mandir, Laskar, Jaipur, Veston, no. 57	May be original *gāthās*	123 folios, copied in 1732 V.S.
36	Digambara Jain Pañcāyatī Mandir, Bharatpur (Raj.), Veston, no. 286	With Commentary	514 folios, copied in 1794 V.S.
37	Digambara Jain Agravāl Mandir, Udaipur (Raj.), Veston, no. 175	May be original *gāthās*	248 folios, copied in 1786 V.S.
38	Digambara Jain Mandir, Karauli, (Raj.), Veston, no. 14	May be original *gāthās*	282 folios

Table 2.3 Comparative various readings

	Pune MS		*Śāstrī's edition*		*Vijayodayā Ṭīkā*	
1	ārāhanā	ārāhaṇaṃ	ārāhaṇaṃ	vucchaṃ	vocchaṃ	vocchaṃ
2	ṇitharṇaṃ	ṇiccharaṇaṃ	ṇistaraṇa			
3	bhaṇiyā	bhaṇiyā	bhaṇidā			
4	bhave	have	have			
6	ārāhio	ārāhio	ārādhido	tao	tavaṃ	tavo
7	hoe	hodi	hodi			
9	ṇāūṇa	ṇāūṇa	ṇādūṇa	hoe	hoi	havadi
13	kāyavvā	kāyavvā	kādavvā			
18	jadijjadi	jadi jadadi	jadi jadadi			
20	bhavissahidi	bhavissadi hi	bhavissadi			
21	bhavissahidi	bhavissahadi	bhavissanti			
24	khaṇṇuya˚	khaṇṇuga˚	khaṇṇuga˚			
	ṇihi diṭṭhantaṃ	khaṇṇugadiṭṭhaṃto	khaṇṇugadiṭṭhaṃto	khaṇṇugadiṭṭhaṃto	˚diṭṭhanto	

Table 2.4 Chart No. 3

Gāthā No.	*Pune MS*	*Śāstrī's edition*	*Vijayodayā Ṭīkā*
28	jahuttacarissa	jahuttacārissa	jadhuttacārassa
65	suttapadāem	suttapadāem	suttapadāni
65	neyāem	neyāim	neyāī
67	anusaṭṭhi	asasiṭṭhi	anusiṭṭhi
67	padicchā	padichā	padichā
Note: padikkhā or parikkhā. Reading is correct			
101	paridi	parīdi	parīdi
Note: the word parie is used in Uttarādhyayana Sūtra 27.13			
202	sajjādi	sajjai	sajjādi
Note: Sajjāe is used in Uttarādhyayana Sūtra 25.20			

Table 2.5 Chart No. 4

Gāthā No.	*Pune MS*	*Śāstrī's edition*	*Vijayodaya Ṭīkā*
4	°ārāhiyam arahamteṇa	°ārāhiyam arahamteṇa	°ārādhidam aradhamteṇa
7	hodi and hoe	hodi	hodi
9	nāūṇa	nāūṇa	nādūṇa
120	kāia° vāia° manasio°	kāiya° vāia° manasio°	vāiga° kāiga° manasigo°
1358	nasedūṇa jadhā kodha jadhā	nasedūṇa jadhā kodho jadhā	No commentary No commentary No commentary jahā
1344	vigadadehada huṃti	videhada huṃti	videhada huṃti
1351	sudakevali ārādhanāṃ	sudakevali ārādhanāṃ	No commentary No commentary

Table 2.6 Chart No. 5

Reference	*Prākṛt Verse A*	*Remark*
(A) Bhagavatī Ārādhanā, *gāthā* 48. Quoted in Śrīcandra's Kahākosu (5.1)	saddahayā pattiyayā rocaya phāsaṃtayā pavayaṇassa | sayalassa je narā te *sammattahaya honti* ||	
Pune MS Folio No. 3-A	*identical reading*	
Śāstrī's edition (1978)	This verse is not included in the original text. It is given as an example in the commentary. One reading differs: *jena edete instead of je narā te*	
Bombay edition (1992) and Solāpur edition (1935)	*The same reading as in Śāstrī's edition*	The reading *je narā te* is correct.
Reference	*Prākṛt Verse B*	*Remark*
(B) Bhagavatī Ārādhanā, *gāthā* 747. Quoted in Śrīcandra's Kahākosu (21.1)	*vijja vi bhattimantassa* *siddhim uvayadi hodi safala* | *kaha punu nibbudivijja* *sijjhihidi abhattivantassa* ||	
Pune MS Folio 43A	Different readings in these words: *vijjahi – vijja vi* *kiha – kaha* *bijaṃ – vijja* *sijjhihadi – sijjhihidi*	
Śāstrī's edition (1978)	Same reading as Pune MS *Exception: sijjhahidi is given for sijjhahadi*	The readings *bija* and *sijjhahidi* are correct
Reference	*Prākṛt Verse C*	*Remark*
(C) Bhagavatī Ārādhanā, *gāthā* 903. Quoted in Śrīcandra's Kahākosu (31.1)	*niccaṃ pi kundadi kamma* *kuluttadugumchidaṃ vigadamāno* | *varattao vi kammaṃ* *akāsi jahā laṃkhiya heduṃ* ||	
Pune MS, folio 52 B	Same *gāthā* (903) with the following different readings: *nicaṃ* for *niccaṃ* *laṃghiya* for *laṃkhiya*	The readings *nicam* and *laṃkhiya* in the Pune MS are correct.

Table 2.7a Chart No. 6A

Reference	*Gāthā quotes*
Pune MS, folio 120 B, verse 1976	jatto disāya gāmo tatto sīsaṃ karittu sovadhiyaṃ | uṭṭhantā rakkhanatham vosaridavvaṃ sarīraṃ taṃ ||
Śāstrī's edition, verse 1980, p. 865	jatto disāe gāmo tatto sīsaṃ karittu sovadhiya uṭṭhaṃtārakkhaṇaṭṭha vosaridavvaṃ sarīraṃ taṃ ||
Āvaśyakacūrṇi and -niryukti, verse 52. Ratlām 1928, p. 112	jae didāe gamo jatto sīsaṃ tu hoe kayavvaṃ uṭṭhenta rakkhanattha eva hi se samasenaṃ ||
Bṛhatkalpabhāṣya, verse 5531. Bhāvnagar 1938, p. 1465	jatto disāe gamo tatto sīsaṃ tu hoe kayavvaṃ uṭṭhentarakkhanttha amangalaṃ loga gariha ya ||

Note
The 1st and 3rd lines of the *gāthā* have no difference. 2nd and 4th lines differ in wording, but not in meaning. Only the Bṛhatkalpabhāṣya says new things in the 4th line.

Table 2.7b Chart No. 6B

Reference	*Gāthā quoted*
Pune MS, folio 120 B, verse No. 1964	jaṃ velaṃ kālagado bhikhu taṃ velaṃ evaiharanaṃ | *jaggana-vandhana-chedana* vidhi abelaya kādavva ||
Śāstrī's edition, verse 1968, p. 862	same readings
Āvaśyakacūrṇi and -niryukti, verse 1928, p. 110	jaṃ velaṃ kālagao karne bhave niroho | cheyana-vandhana-jaggana kaiyamatte ya hatthaude ||
Bṛhatkalpabhāṣya, verse 5518. Bhāvnagar 1938, p. 1463	jaṃ velaṃ kālagato nigaraṇa-karaṇe bhave nirodho | jaggana-vandhana-chedana etaṃ tu vihiṃ tahiṃ kujjā ||

Note
1st and 3rd lines of the verse are almost the same. The differences are clear regarding Kālagado (Śaurasenī), Kālagao (Mahārāṣṭrī) and Kālagato (Ardhamāgadhī).

Table 2.7c Chart No. 6C

Reference	*Gāthā quoted*
Pune MS, folio 121 B, verse 1981	asadi taṇe cuṇṇehiṃ va kesaracharidikādi cuṇṇehiṃ | kādavvotha kakāro uvare hiṭṭhā takāro se ||
Śāstrī's edition, verse 1986, p. 867	asadi taṇe cunnehiṃ ca kesaracchāriṭṭīyādicuṇṇehiṃ | kādavvotha kakāro uvariṃ hiṭṭhā takāro se ||
Āvaśyakacūrṇi and -niryukti verse 38. Ratlām 1928, p. 110	jathā ya natthi tanaiṃ cunnehiṃ tatthā kesarehiṃ va | kāyavvotha kakaro hettha takaraṃ ca bandhejja ||
Bṛhatkalpabhāṣya, verse 5535. Bhāvnagar 1938, p. 1466	same readings

Notes

1 From the text itself we learn that the author's name is Śivāraya with the epithet *pani-dal-bhoi:* "[the monk who ate his] food in the cavity of his palms". Śivarāya or Śivakoṭī has been referred to as its author in works by later Jaina *ācāryas*. However, we are not aware of any epigraphic reference to the author of BhĀ. Premi (1956: 50–60) and other scholars have discussed the authorship of BhĀ in detail.

2 On the date of the BhĀ, see Premi (1956: 50–60); Jain (2006). Upadhye (1943: 55) states that the BhĀ belongs to the earliest stratum of the Digambara proto-canon. It is quite likely that Śivāraya might be senior even to Kundakunda, but we have to await further research.

3 See Velankar (1944: 31ff.): "ārādhanā". The concept of *ārādhanā* covers a wide range of dogmatic and ethico-religious discussions.

4 See Baya (2007: 180f.).

5 *egammi bhāvaggahaṇe samādhimaraṇeṇa jo gado | ṇahu so hiṃḍadi bahuso sattaṭṭhabhave pamattūṇa* ||. *Bhagavatī Ārādhanā*, Gāthā 681. For details, see Tukol (1976).

6 See Jain (2006).

7 The names of writers of *kathākośa*s are given by Prof. A.N. Upadhye (1943) in his introduction to the *Bṛhatkathākośa*. These writers include Śrīcandra (*Kahākosu*), Hariṣeṇa (*Bṛhatkathākośa*), Prabhācandra (*Ārādhanākathāprabandha*), Nemidatta (*Ārādhanā-sār kathā-prabhandha*) and the unknown author of *Vaḍḍhārādhane*.

8 *Kahākosu*, Saṃdhi 1–8–9.

9 Khadabadi (1969).

10 Velankar (1944); Table 2.2.

11 Work No. 1112 in A.B. Khathavate's collection of 1895–1902.

12 See copy of the *praśasti* folio of the MS.

Bibliography

Primary sources

Bṛhatkathākośa of Ācārya Hariṣeṇa. The Sanskrit Text Authentically Edited for the First Time with Various Readings, With a Critical Introduction, Notes, Index of Proper Names, etc., by Ādinātha Neminātha Upādhye. Bombay: Bharatiya Vidya Bhavan, 1943 (Siṅghī Jaina Granthamālā No. 17).

Bhagavatī Ārādhanā of Ācārya Śivārya

Ācāryaśrī Aparājita Sūri racita Vijayodayā Ṭīkā tathā Tadanusārī Hindī Ṭīkā sahita. Saṃpādaka evaṃ Anuvādaka: Paṇḍit Kailāśacandra Siddhānta Śāstrī. Solāpur: Jaina-Saṃskṛti-Saṃrakṣaka-Saṃgha, 1978 (Jīvarāja Jaina Granthamālā, Hindī Vibhāga No. 36–37).

Bhagavatī Ārādhanā.

Edited by Prem Suman Jain. Jaipur: Bhagavāna Ṛṣabhadeva Granthamālā, 2006.

Kahākosu of Śrīcandra. Sampādaka: Hīrālāla Jain. Ahamadābāda: Prākṛta Grantha Pariṣad, 1969.

Secondary sources

Baya, D.S. 'Śreyas'. *Death with Equanimity: The Pursuit of Immortality*. Jaipur: Prakrit Bharati Academy, 2007.

Jain, Hiralal. 1969. See *Kahākosu.*

Jain, Prem Suman. "Bhagavatī Ārādhanā Kī Pāṇḍulipiyāṁ." *Bhagavatī Ārādhanā Pariśīlana*. Jaipur: Bhagavāna Ṛṣabhadeva Granthamālā, 2006.

Khadabadi, Basavaraj Kallappa. *Vaḍḍārādhane – A Study*. Dharwad: Karnataka University, 1969/1979.

Premi, Nāthūrām. *Jain Sāhitya aur Itihāsa*, Bombay: Hindi Grantha Ratnākar, 1956.

Tukol, T.K. *Sallekhana is not Suicide*. Ahmedabad: L.D. Institute of Indology, 1976.

Upadhye, Adinath Neminath. 1943. See *Bṛhatkathākośa.*

Velankar, Hari Damodar. *Jinaratnakośa: An Alphabetical List of Jaina Works and Authors*. Vol. 1. Poona: Bhandarkar Oriental Research Institute, 1944 (Government Oriental Series Class C).

3 Śvetāmbara Āgamas in the Digambara tradition

Shin Fujinaga

In this chapter I would like to show that the attitude of a Jaina author in the Middle Ages towards the canon is somewhat different from what we suppose. The Śvetāmbaras claimed that the preaching of Mahāvīra had been preserved as the canon or at least as the books called *Aṅgas*, while the Digambaras proclaimed that what Mahāvīra taught was not kept in the *Aṅgas* and that little was known of Mahāvīra's original doctrine. Today, Digambaras and Śvetāmbaras view their respective sacred writings as authentic and deny the validity of each other's canon. However, to my knowledge, no one has clearly shown when this disagreement took place.[1] Our present study will contribute to solving this question. In the following we will study a work written by a Digambara author, paying special attention to quotations from different canonical texts serving as support of his own opinion. Thus we understand canon as writing or literature, a portion of which is quoted by other persons to support his or her opinion. Quotations appearing in a text for the mere purpose of refutation or grammatical explanation will, however, not be regarded as "canon".

The text of inquiry is the *Sarvārthasiddhi* of Pūjyapāda. This text was chosen for several reasons. First of all, it is the first Sanskrit work within the Digambara tradition that discusses topics such as ethics, epistemology, biology and cosmology. Its author therefore quotes from different texts on these specialized subjects. Second, the author and his work belong to the middle period of Jaina history, most probably the fifth or sixth century,[2] a time when the Śvetāmbaras may have compiled their Āgamas, and Digambaras produced some important works written in Prākrit. Pūjyapāda, then, was able to quote from these works when composing his commentary on Umāsvāti's or Umāsvāmin's *Tattvārthasūtra*, the *Sarvārthasiddhi.*

Pūjyapāda gives a detailed account of the Āgamas or Jaina canon.[3] The list of the names of the *Aṅga*s or *Aṅgapraviṣṭa*s, which constitutes the main part of the Āgamas, in the *Sarvārthasiddhi* corresponds completely to those which are traditionally admitted as authentic by the Śvetāmbaras. So we may conclude that, at the time of Pūjyapāda, the Digambaras had detailed information of the *Āgama*s or at least of the *Āṅgas.*[4]

In the *Sarvārthasiddhi*, we come across more than one hundred quotations from different sources. Some of them are from the *Tattvārthasūtra*, on which Pūjyapāda wrote his commentary, and some from a *vyākaraṇa* text attributed to

Pūjyapāda himself. Pūjyapāda also quotes textual passages to support his own opinion on various subjects. According to our tentative definition above, such phrases are regarded as a canon or part of it. The number of such quotations is about thirty, and most of them share a common feature: the quotation follows after the Sanskrit phrase *eva uktaṃ* or *uktaṃ ca* ("as it is said"). Pūjyapāda also quotes passages from authors of other schools merely to refute them. In such case, the quotations do not follow after the word *uktam*, instead they may be preceded by a verb. For example, at the very beginning of one of the quotes in the text, we come across the following sentence *caitanyaṃ puruṣasya svarūpam …*, preceded by the verb *parikalpayanti.* This sentence is quoted in order to refute a certain position and seems originally to stem from the *Yogabhāṣya*. Thus, in the *Sarvārthasiddhi*, the phrase *uktaṃ ca* or similar expressions may be used to indicate a quotation which belongs to an author and his work.[5]

The original sources of some of the mentioned thirty quotations still remain unknown to us. For example, in *Tattvārthasūtra* I.6, the concept of *naya* (viewpoint), which is unique to Jaina philosophy, is discussed. To give a definition of *naya*, Pūjyapāda quotes a Sanskrit sentence proceeded by *evaṃ hy uktaṃ*: *pragṛhya pramāṇataḥ pariṇativiśeṣād arthāvadhāraṇaṃ naya*. To our knowledge, this quote does not appear in any other extant texts, but it is clear that it is a quote and not Pūjyapāda's own composition. Consequently, it must be part of text which was written before him and does not exist anymore. In other cases, we know the original text of some of the quotations found in Pūjyapāda's text. Explaining the difference between an atom and a molecule, Pūjyapāda quotes the following verse from Kundakunda's *Niyamasāra*:

> *attādi attam ajjhaṃ attaṃtaṃ iṃdiye gejjhaṃ | jaṃ davvaṃ avibhāgī taṃ paramāṇuṃ viāṇāhi |*
>
> That substance which by itself is the beginning, the middle and the end, inapprehensible by the senses and indivisible, should be known as an atom.

Of course, we cannot rule out that the verse belongs to a work written by an author other than Kundakunda. It is, however, more likely that Pūjyapāda quotes this verse directly from Kundakunda's, since we find the same quotation in his text, and since Kundakunda is generally admitted to belong to an earlier period than Pūjyapāda.[6] In the same manner, we may identify some of the quotations found in the *Sarvārthasiddhi* as quotations from Kundakunda's works.[7]

Three verses from the *Sarvārthasiddhi* are worthy of special attention. The first one appears in the first chapter, which discusses the *prāpyakāritva* or moving out of the sense organs from the body, and the other two verses occur in the third chapter where the construction of Jambūdvīpa is the main topic. The first verse reads (V.1a):

> *puṭṭhaṃ suṇedi apuṭṭhaṃ ceva passade rūaṃ | gaṃdhaṃ rasaṃ phāsaṃ puṭṭham apuṭṭhaṃ viyāṇādi |*

> The ears apprehend both sounds that come and do not come in contact with them, but the eyes apprehend only colour which does not come into contact with them. In this manner, the sense organs of smell, taste and touch apprehend smell, taste and touch which do and do not come into contact with them.[8]

This verse does not have the set phrase *uktam ca* but instead *āgamatas tāvat*, which means "first of all due to [the authority] of Āgama." In the *Āvaśyakaniryukti* (V.1b) we find a similar verse:

> *puṭṭhaṃ suṇeti saddaṃ rūvaṃ puṇa pāsatī apuṭṭhaṃ tu | gaṃdhaṃ rasaṃ ca phāsaṃ ca baddhapuṭṭhaṃ viyāgare ||*

> They (i.e. the ears) apprehend sounds which come in contact with them. And smell, taste and touch are grasped when they come in close (*baddha*) contact with them.[9]

By comparison the two verses from the *Sarvārthasiddhi* and *Āvaśyakaniryukti*, respectively, are very similar but not identical. Let us have a close look at them.

In the *Tattvārtharājavārtika* written by Akalaṅka as a commentary on the *Sarvārthasiddhi*, verse V.1a appears with slight changes:

> *puṭṭhaṃ suṇedi saddaṃ apuṭṭhaṃ puṇa passade rūvam |*
> *gaṃdhaṃ rasaṃ ca phāsaṃ ca baddhapuṭṭhaṃ vijāṇādi* || V.1b

> They (i.e. the ears) apprehend sounds which come in contact with them, while the (eyes) apprehend colours which do not come into contact with them. Smell, taste and touch are grasped when they (i.e. the sense organs) come in close contact with them.

Here Akalaṅka also regards this verse as part of the Āgama, since he uses the phrase *āgamatas*. The editor of the *Tattvārtharājavārtika* shows that there is a variant reading, according to which *pāda* d reads *puṭṭhaṃ apuṭṭhaṃ*.[10] When we adopt this reading, the verse is identical to V.1a. As far as the Niryukti version is concerned, there are no variant readings. It is not difficult to assume that there was a common source from which the three variations of the same verse stem and that this source was regarded as authentic. Moreover, it is also possible to assume that Pūjyapāda quotes verse V.1a from a version of the *Āvaśyakaniryukti* which contained readings different from what we have now as part of the Śvetāmbara tradition.[11]

The second and third verse of the three verses from the *Sarvārthasiddhi* that were of special interest appear in the third chapter, where the main topic is cosmology, especially the size of the Jambūdvīpa. Pūjyapāda quotes:

> *puvvassa du parimāṇaṃ sadariṃ khalu koḍisadasahassāiṃ |*
> *chappaṇṇaṃ ca sahassā boddhavvā vāsakoḍīṇaṃ* ||[12]

vavahāruddhāraddhā pallā tiṇṇeve hoṃti boddhabbā |
saṃkhā dīvasamuddā kamaṭṭhidi vaṇṇidā tadie ||

A saviour (*tadi*) explained as *palla* is of three kinds; a common one, cutting one and temporal one. They are used in numbering, in measuring continents and oceans, and in showing duration of karma respectively.

The verse beginning with *puvvassa* is almost the same as verse 94 of the *Tiloyapaṇṇattī* composed by Yativṛṣabha, who is believed to have been a Digambara monk living in the fifth century. To our knowledge, there are, however, no texts which contain the same or similar passage as the second verse above, beginning with *vavahāruddhāraddhā*. A list of quotations (*uddhṛtavākyasūcī*) attached to the standard edition of the *Sarvārthasiddhi* tells us that these two verses are quoted from *Jambūdvīpaprajñapti* 13.12 and 13.36. We know of only one text which has the title *Jambūdvīpaprajñapti*, i.e. the second Upāṅga of the Śvetāmbara *āgama*s. But there we cannot find such verses.[13] If there were, our discussion will take another turn. As we have seen before, Pūjyapāda quotes the first verse adding the phrase *āgamatas*. This makes it clearly different from other quotations of the *Sarvārthasiddhi* that are quoted together with the words *uktaṃ ca* or the like. This type of quotation may be reliable as a source of argument, but not completely so, because they reflect the idea of a philosopher, such as Kundakunda, whose knowledge is not completely correct. On the other hand, the verses we focus on are regarded as *Āgama*. For Pūjyapāda the word Āgama means a highly reliable source of discussion or consideration. In other words, it works as criteria of our thinking and judgement. It is so because Āgama derives from the omniscient one. He observes:

sarvajñena paramārṣinā paramācintyakevalajñānavibhūtiviśeṣeṇa arthata āgama uddiṣṭaḥ tasya pratyakṣadarśitvāt prakṣīṇadoṣatvāc ca prāmāṇyaṃ.[14]

In reality, Āgama was taught by the Omniscient [Tīrthaṅkara], the supreme seer characterized by the glory of supreme and unimaginable perfect knowledge. The [Tīrthaṅkara] is an [absolute] authority, since he sees things directly and is bereft of errors.

Here we are faced with a question: within the Śvetāmbara tradition, the *Āvaśyaka Niryukti* is not regarded as part of *Āgama*, or at least it is not considered as the direct preaching of the Tīrthaṅkara, but a work belonging to a particular person, i.e. Bhadrabāhu. Pūjyapāda, as seen above, clearly mentions that the verse is part of *Āgama* derived from the omniscient one or Tīrthaṅkara. Thus we may conclude that Pūjyapāda ascribes higher authority to quotations including the word *āgamatas* than to other quotations including the phrase *uktaṃ ca* and the like.

Pūjyapāda's attitude of evaluating Śvetāmbara literature as highly as the literature of his own tradition, i.e. Digambara, reminds us of the Yāpanīya tradition. Thus, let us discuss the relationship between Pūjyapāda and Yāpanīya. Usually we understand the Digambaras and Śvetāmbaras as the two main sects of Jainism. This is correct as far as the present state of Jainism is concerned. Historically speaking, however, there once existed a third mendicant lineage that combined features from both traditions. In practice, the Yāpanīya monks followed the Digambara's way of living while in theory they mainly adhered to the doctrine of the Śvetāmbaras. They wear no clothes in remote place, supported the idea that women were able to obtain liberation, and agreed with the Śvetāmbaras that the omniscient ingested food.[15] In other words, they tried to harmonize the two different traditions, which had the same origin. The Yāpanīya lineage is believed to have existed by the fourteenth century and some authors, as well as works, are attributed to it, such as Siddhasena Divākara, the author of *Saṃmatitarka*, and the *Bhagavatī Ārādhanā*. In case of Siddhasena Divākara, the tendency to harmonize the two traditions is found in his discussions on the order of *darśana* and *jñāna* of a *kevalin*, and on the difference between *guṇa* and *paryāya*. So we can safely conclude that he belonged to the Yāpanīya tradition of Jainism.[16]

What about Pūjyapāda? Traditionally we understand that he belonged to the Digambara tradition, not to the Śvetāmbara. One of the facts that supports this opinion is that the Digambara philosopher Akalaṅka, as mentioned above, wrote a super-commentary on the *Sarvārthasiddhi*. So with high probability we can conclude that Pūjyapāda is a Digambara philosopher. However, two quotations in his *Tattvārthasūtra* stemming from the *Mūlācāra* of Vaṭṭakera may lead us to think that he knew some of the Yāpanīya writings. One of the quotations occurs in the commentary on *Tattvārthasūtra* II.32, when Pūjyapāda explains the classification of different types of births:

> *ṇiccidaradhādu satta ya taru viyaliṃgiesu chacceva* |
> *suraṇirayatiriya cauro coddasa maṇue sadasahassā* ||
>
> Nitya-nigodas, itara-nigodas, element-bodies (i.e. earth-, water-, fire-, air-bodies) are of seven lakh yonis, plants are of ten lakh yonis, those with two or three or four senses are of six lakh yonis, gods, hell beings and animals are of four lakh yonis. Human beings are of fourteen lakh yonis.

This verse is identical to verse 1106 of the *Mūlācāra*, the author of which is regarded as a Yāpanīya mendicant.[17] Pūjyapāda quotes the two verses from this work together with the phrases *uktaṃ ca* and *tathā coktaṃ* respectively.[18] This means that Pūjyapāda valued this work as reliable as that of Kundakunda, but not as Āgama.

From the above discussion, it is also possible that he may have had some tendency to harmonize Digambara and Śvetāmbara. More generally, we may argue that, by the time of Akalaṅka in the eighth century, Digambara thinkers did not completely deny the entire Āgama of the opposite sect and in this way they had a Yāpanīya-like attitude towards their own scriptures.

Notes

1 See Wiles (2006).
2 We assume that Pūjyapāda is senior to Samantabhadra, who belongs to the sixth or seventh century.
3 Fujinaga (2008).
4 Akalaṅka, who wrote a commentary on the *Sarvārthasiddhi*, gives a more exact description of the Āgamas than Pūjyapāda. See Fujinaga (2008).
5 Here we must remember that Schubring (1935: § 42, S. 58) regards the usage of the Prākrit phrase *ti bemi* as one of the features which show an archaic form in the Jaina Āgamas.
6 To determine the date of early Jaina philosophers, like Kundakunda, is difficult. However, Kundakunda seems to be senior to Umāsvāmi, the author of the *Tattvārthasūtra*, whereas Pūjyapāda is younger than Umāsvāmi, since he wrote a commentary on the *Tattvārthasūtra*.
7 One verse from *Pañcāstikāyasāra*, two from *Pravacanasāra*. Beside these verses, four verses in *Sarvārthasiddhi* are identical to those in the *Dvādaśānuprekṣā* or *Bārahaṇu- pekkhā*. However, we cannot decide whether or not the work belongs to Kundakunda.
8 This translation by S. A. Jain seems to follow the Hindi translation of *Sarvārthasiddhi*.
9 For the interpretation on this verse, I follow Maladhāri Hemacandra's commentary. It should also be noted that this verse appears as *gāthā* 75 of the *Nandīsūtra*.
10 *Tattvārtharājavārtika* (p. 67, n. 9).
11 Cf. Tatia (1951: 68, n. 2): "He [Pūjyapāda] quotes *Āvnir*, gāthā 5 in SSi on TSū, I. 19." Of course, here Pūjyapāda does not mention the specific author of the work, he only gives the reference as *āgamatas tāvat*.
12 The unit *pūrva* should be known as $70 \times 105 \times 107 + 56 \times 103 \times 107$.
13 It should be noted here that a verse similar to the first verse appears in the commentary by Śānticandra on *Jambūdvīpaprajñapti*. It reads:

> *puvvassa u parimāṇaṃ sayariṃ khalu huṃti koḍikkhāo/chappanaṃ sahassā boddhavvā vāsakoḍīṇaṃ //.*

See Jambūdvīpaprajñapti (p. 91).
14 Sarvārthasiddhi ad Tattvārthasūtra I.20 § 211.
15 Here I follow the description of Wiley (2004).
16 For the discussion of the temporal relation between *jñāna* and *darśana*, and the position of Siddhasena Divākara on this, see Tatia (1951: 70–80, especially p. 77).
17 See Wiley (2004), s. v. Yāpanīya.
18 S. A. Jain (1992) translates this verse with the phrase "To quote from the scriptures". But in the original text it only says *tathā coktam*.

Bibliography

Texts and translations

Jambūdvīpaprajñapti with Śānticandra's vṛtti. Ed. by Dīparatnasāgara. Ahmedabad, 2000 (Āgama Suttāṇi 13).

Mūlācara by Vaṭṭakera. Ed. by Pt. Kailash Chandra Shastri *et al.* New Delhi, 1992 (Second Edition) (Jñānapītha Murtidevī Jaina Granthamālā 19).

Niyamasāra by Kundakunda. Ed. and tr. by Uggar Sain. Lucknow, 1931 (Reprint New York 1974) (The Sacred Books of the Jainas 9).

Nandisuttaṃ. Ed. by Muni Puṇyavijaya *et al.* Bombay 1968 (Jaina Āgama Series No. 1).

Pañcāstikāyasāra by Kundakunda. Ed. and tr. by Sarat Chandra Ghoshal. Arrah, 1920 (Reprint New York 1974) (The Sacred Books of the Jainas 3).

Pravacanasāra by Kundakunda. Ed. by A. N. Upadhye. Agas, 1964 (Śrīmad Rājacandra Jaina Śāstramālā).

Saṃmatitarka by Siddhasena Divākara. With a Critical Introduction and Original Commentary by Paṇḍita Sukhlāl Saṅghavī and Paṇḍita Bechardās Doṣī. Ahmedabad, 2000 (Pt. Śrī Sukhalālajī Granthamālā 5).

Sarvārthasiddhi of Pūjyapāda. Ed. and Hindī Translation by Phūlcandraśāstrī. New Delhi: Bhāratīya Jñānapīṭha, n. d. (Mūrtidevī Jaina Granthamālā. Saṃskṛta Granthāṅka 8).

Sarvārthasiddhi of Pūjyapāda.2 See S. A. Jain 1992.

Tattvārtha Rāja Vārtika by Akalaṅka. Ed. and tr. by Mahendrakumār Jain. Second Edition. New Delhi, 1982 (Jñānapītha Mūrtidevī Jaina Granthamālā 10).

Tattvārtha Sūtra by Umāsvāti or Umāsvāmin. See *Sarvārthasiddhi.*

Tiloyapaṇṇattī by Yativṛṣabha. Ed. by Centaprakāś Pāṭnī. n. p., 1984.

Viśeṣāvaśyakabhāṣya by Jinabhadra with Maladhāri Hemacandra's vṛtti. Ed. by Vijayapremasūri. Ahamedabad, V.S. 2489.

Yogabhāṣyā by Vyāsa with Patañjali's *Yogasūtra.*
Bhavnagar: Bhāratīya Saṅskriti Vidyāpītha, 1982.

Secondary sources

Fujinaga, Shin. "Digambara Attitudes to the Śvetāmbara Canon." *International Journal of Jaina Studies* 1–3 (2008) 172–182.

Jain, S. A. *Reality*. English Translation of Śrī Pūjyapāda's *Sarvārthasiddhi.* Madras: Jwalamalini Trust, 1992.

Schubring, Walther. *Die Lehre der Jainas, nach den alten Quellen dargestellt.* Grundriss der Indo-Arischen Philologie und Altertumskunde. III Band, 7. Heft. Berlin und Leipzig: Walter De Gruyter & Co., 1935.

Tatia, Nathmal. *Studies in Jaina Philosophy.* Varanasi: Jain Cultural Research Society, 1951.

Wiles, Royce. "The Dating of the Jaina Councils: Do Scholarly Presentations Reflect the Traditional Sources?" *Studies in Jaina History and Culture. Dispute and Dialogues.* Ed. Peter Flügel, 107–116. London/New York: Routledge, 2006 (Routledge Advances in Jaina Studies 1).

Wiley, Kristi L. *Historical Dictionary of Jainism.* Historical Dictionary of Religions, Philosophies, and Movements, No. 53. Maryland, Toronto, Oxford: The Scarecrow Press, 2004.

Part II

Karman and ethics

4 What happened to Mahāvīra's body?[1]

Johannes Bronkhorst

Jainism has its *stūpas*, but their role is mysterious. Did they contain relics, of Mahāvīra or other saints? About relics in Jainism, Dundas (2002: 219) states the following:

> The origin of Jain holy places did not stem from the worship of relics, as seems to have been partly the case with early Buddhist pilgrimage sites. The remains of the Buddha's body were, after cremation, supposedly distributed throughout the Ganges basin, whereas the traditional accounts of Mahāvīra's funeral describe how his bone relics were collected together by Indra and taken to heaven where they were worshipped by the gods…

Dundas refers in this connection to Hemacandra's *Yogaśāstra* (1.8.67 = vol. I p. 40), a text composed some fifteen centuries after the event.[2] We learn from Schubring (2000: 26–27) – who refers in this connection to the canonical *Jambuddīvapannatti*, an Upāṅga text – that the cremation of the corpse of a *tīrthaṅkara*, any *tīrthaṅkara*, is performed by all godly princes under Sakka's, i.e. Indra's, leadership.[3] Schubring refers to the *Viyāhapannatti* (p. 502b) to add that the relics of *tīrthaṅkara*s enjoy adoration in the heavenly sphere. Elsewhere in his book (p. 49f.) he states:

> In the course of its most detailed description of a godly residence [the] Rāyap[aseṇaijja] refers to 4 sitting Jina figures … of natural size surrounding a stūpa towards which they turn their faces, adding that a special building … contains 108 [effigies of the Jinas] j[iṇa]-paḍimā. Their cult on the part of the god equals that of to-day consisting in the attendance of the figures by uttering devotional formulae. In the large hall (*sabhā*), however, there are spherical boxes (*gola-vaṭṭa-samugga*) containing the sacred remains (*j[iṇa]-sakahā*…) and hanging on hooks (*nāgadanta*) by means of cords (*sikkaga*). The whole description most certainly follows earthly examples.

What should we conclude from all this? Did the early Jainas worship relics, among these relics of Mahāvīra, or did they not? W. J. Johnson (2003: 224) thinks they did: "Although later Jaina tradition suggests that Mahāvīra's relics were whisked away by the gods, .. it is difficult to imagine that Jain stūpas were viewed simply as memorials, devoid of relics." Early Jaina literature frequently mentions *stūpas*, and archaeology has revealed an ancient *stūpa* in Mathurā which is identified as Jaina.[4] Dundas (2002: 291 n. 4), who decried the role of relics in Jainism in the passage considered above, is slightly embarrassed by the *stūpa* in Mathurā:

> The function of the stūpa at Mathurā has not been adequately explained, since relic worship has never been a significant component of Jainism, as it has in Buddhism. Nonetheless, it does seem that this early stūpa was in some way involved in commemoration of the dead.

A recent article by Peter Flügel (2008) sheds additional light on the tradition of *stūpas* and relic-worship in Jainism. Flügel states here (p. 18):

> [R]esearch in 2000–2001 produced the first documentation of two modern Jain bone relic *stūpa*s, a *samādhi-mandira* and a *smāraka*, constructed by the Terāpanth Śvetāmbara Jains. Subsequent fieldwork demonstrated that relic *stūpa*s are not only a feature of the aniconic Jain traditions…, but also of Mūrtipūjaka … and Digambara traditions. Hence, the initial hypothesis that the contemporary Jain cult of bone relics functions either as substitute or as a prototype for image-worship had to be amended.

This recent discovery does not solve the problem of the secondary role which *stūpas* and relic-worship play in Jainism; in a way it only deepens it. The inescapable question is: if *stūpas* played any role at all in Jainism, why then did *stūpa* and relic worship not develop here the way they did in Buddhism? In Buddhism, we all know, the tradition preserved in great detail the memory of what happened to the body of the Buddha, whereas in Jainism we only find late stories about the worship of the Jina's mortal remains by gods, preferably in heaven. Why this difference?

Until recently I might have given up at this point, recalling that our textual sources do not contain sufficient material to come up with a plausible answer. If, in spite of this, I now venture further ahead, this is because I have occupied myself with the Buddhist accounts of what happened to the body of the Buddha. Much to my initial surprise, I discovered that it is far from certain that the standard account is reliable as historical evidence. Numerous inconsistencies, alternative versions, as well as considerations about the place of Buddhism in the Indian traditions at large, led to the hypothesis that the corpse of the Buddha may not have been incinerated and divided, that the corpse may rather have been put, non-incinerated and non-divided, into one single *stūpa* built for the occasion. This possibility, which I arrived at on the basis of circumstantial evidence, is actually expressed in so many words in a version of the *Mahāparinirvāṇa Sūtra*, as I subsequently discovered. It must of course be admitted that this possibility is a hypothesis, but it is only fair to add that it is a hypothesis that is not less plausible than the alternative and widely accepted hypothesis according to which the body of the Buddha was incinerated and subsequently divided.

This is not the occasion to present the evidence in support of this view as to what happened to the dead body of the Buddha. This evidence is presented in an article that has recently come out (Bronkhorst 2009). Here it is important to emphasize that the presumed incineration and division of the Buddha's body constitute the necessary background for the cult of relics in *stūpas* that came to characterize Buddhism in all of its forms. In other words, if the story about what happened to the Buddha's body is indeed historically unreliable, it is clear why it had to be invented. Without widespread relics, there can be no widespread relic-worship.

Let us now turn to the oldest and paradigmatic account of the disposal of the body of the *tīrthaṅkara* Ṛṣabhadeva in the *Jambuddīvapannatti* (2.89–120; pp. 390–394). It is presumably applicable to all *tīrthaṅkara*s, including therefore Mahāvīra. It tells us that soon after his demise, Śakra and many other gods carried out a number of deeds, among them the following:

1 To begin with three funeral pyres (*ciyagā*) are built out of fragrant sandal wood: one for the *tīrthaṅkara*, one for the *gaṇadhara*s, one for other houseless monks (*aṇagāra*). (It is to be noted that these *gaṇadhara*s and houseless monks had died through *sallekhanā* at the occasion of the death of the *tīrthaṅkara*.) (2.95–96)
2 Milk-water (*khīrodaga*) is collected from the Milk-water Ocean and used to bathe the dead body of the *tīrthaṅkara*, which is subsequently anointed, wrapped in cloth and adorned with all manner of ornaments. The same happens to the dead bodies of the *gaṇadhara*s and houseless monks. (2.97–100)
3 A palanquin is constructed, the dead body of the *tīrthaṅkara* is lifted onto it, and the palanquin is put onto the funeral pyre. Two further palanquins are constructed, one for the *gaṇadhara*s and one for the houseless monks. (2.101–104)
4 Fire and wind are then made to do their job. The fire is subsequently extinguished. For each constituent event the *tīrthaṅkara*, the *gaṇadhara*s and the houseless monks are mentioned, altogether eight times. (2.105–112)
5 Different parts of the body of the *tīrthaṅkara* are taken by various gods, to begin with Śakra. No mention is made of *gaṇadhara*s and houseless monks. (2.113)
6 Three *stūpas* (*ceiyathūbha* = *cetiyastūpa*) are built: one for the *tīrthaṅkara*, one for the *gaṇadhara*s, one for the houseless monks. (2.114–115)
7 Having performed various festivals (*mahima*), the gods return home. Once back, they put the bones of the jina in round boxes (*golavaṭṭasamugga*), which they then worship. No *gaṇadhara*s and houseless monks are mentioned. (2.116–120)

What strikes the eye is that all but two of these seven episodes deal with one *tīrthaṅkara*, and several *gaṇadharas* and houseless monks who have taken their lives by way of *sallekhanā*. Two of the episodes do not include these *gaṇadharas* and houseless monks; these two, nos. 5 and 7, deal with bodily relics of the *tīrthaṅkara*. This suggests that these two episodes were inserted in a text that did not deal with bodily relics of the *tīrthaṅkara*. In other words, there may have been an account in which the *tīrthaṅkara* and his companions were cremated and put into *stūpas*, and no bodily relics were taken, neither by the gods nor by anyone else.

This impression is strengthened by the fact that the episodes that deal with all three types of saints end with the construction of *stūpas* for all of them: one for the *tīrthaṅkara*, one for the *gaṇadharas*, one for the houseless monks. What these *stūpas* were good for is not stated, and indeed, the presumably inserted episode reporting the disappearance of the bodily relics of the *tīrthaṅkara* to heavenly realms would make us think that these *stūpas* – or at any rate the *stūpa* built for the *tīrthaṅkara* – served no purpose whatsoever.[5] The plausible conclusion to be drawn is that there was an earlier account in which the bodily remains of the *tīrthaṅkara* were all put in a *stūpa*, one *stūpa*, those of the *gaṇadharas* in another, and those of the other liberated houseless monks in a third one. However, this original account was modified by the substitution of two episodes claiming that the bodily relics of the Jina had been taken to heaven.

Independent evidence that further strengthens this conclusion is constituted by the fact, pointed out by Flügel, that most Digambara accounts of Ṛṣabha's funeral differ from the *Jambuddīvapannatti* in that they do not mention bone relics, and omit the episode of the removal of the relics by the gods. Flügel refers in this connection to the Jaina *Harivaṃśa Purāṇa* (12.82) and *Ādi Purāṇa* (47.343–354).

The reason for the rather clumsy modification of the passage in the *Jambuddīvapannatti* is easy to see, and is the mirror image of the reason that presumably led the Buddhists to modify their story of the post-mortem destiny of the Buddha's body. In the case of Buddhism, the story of the large-scale distribution of relics from the Buddha's body justified the widespread *stūpa* worship that characterizes that religion. In the case of Jainism, the disappearance of the bodily relics of the Jina justifies the absence of their worship. In both cases we may guess that the whereabouts of the original relics were unknown to the later tradition. If so, both traditions were confronted with a similar problem. The way they resolved it was however quite different. Buddhism invented a story which allowed its followers to believe that there were authentic bodily relics in most if not all Buddhist *stūpas*. Jainism presented a story which convinced its followers that there were no authentic bodily relics of *tīrthaṅkaras* to be found on earth, because they had all be taken to heaven.[6]

One more question has to be dealt with. Even the "authentic" part of the story in the *Jambuddīvapannatti* maintains that the body of the Jina was cremated. In the case of Buddhism, we had been led to consider that the body of the Buddha had *not* been cremated, but had been put in a *stūpa* without undergoing this treatment. Should we not expect the same in the case of a Jina? Perhaps we should. It is therefore appropriate to remember that the *Jambuddīvapannatti* is not a very early text; Flügel dates it between the first and fifth century CE, and Bansidhar Bhatt, in a private communication, informs me that in his opinion it cannot be put earlier than the second century CE. What is more, Flügel (2010: 433) argues on the basis of the *Kappa Sutta* and the *Vavahāra Sutta* in particular, that

> the practice of cremating the discarded bodies of ascetics, which is only performed by laity or the general public, was either introduced not long after the composition of the early *Cheya Suttas* or, though less likely, always existed side by side with the monastic custom of abandoning the body.

In other words, it is possible that the body of the Jina was not cremated. Perhaps we should add that it may have been discarded the way the bodies of other Jaina ascetics were apparently discarded in the early Jaina tradition.

Returning now to the *Jambuddīvapannatti*, I would argue that it allows us to think of three succeeding periods:

1 We know nothing about what happened to the dead body of the Jina, except that it was probably not cremated; given that building *stūpas* and *stūpa*-like structures for at least certain dead people was a custom in Mahāvīra's region which is already attested in the *Śatapatha Brāhmaṇa*, it is possible that his corpse was put into a *stūpa*, but we cannot exclude that it was abandoned in nature.
2 For reasons that we do not know for certain but that we may plausibly guess (considerations of purity, newly acquired cultural propriety) the claim was made that the corpse of the Jina had been cremated before being put into a *stūpa*. This is recounted in the story of the *Jambuddīvapannatti*, minus its insertions.
3 Additions were made to this story, claiming that the relics had been taken away by the gods. This left an incoherent story and an empty *stūpa*, but presumably suited the tastes of those who made the changes. The practical consequence of these changes was that the worship of Mahāvīra's relics (or of the relics of any other *tīrthaṅkara* for that matter), though theoretically still respectable, was banished from the tradition.

Notes

1 This chapter has profited from the kindness of Dr Peter Flügel who, when told that I was planning to write a paper on the post-mortem fate of Mahāvīra's body, put at my disposal part of the work he had been doing on this topic. Dr Bansidhar Bhatt was subsequently kind enough to make further suggestions.
2 Flügel draws attention to the most famous depiction of Jaina relic-worship in the first book of Hemacandra's *Triṣaṣṭiśalākāpuruṣacaritra* (I.6.459–643) which, he points out, is largely based on earlier canonical accounts in the *Jambuddīvapannatti*, the

Jīvājīvābhigama and the *Āvassaya Nijjutti*, and their commentaries. It may be significant that Hemacandra uses the term *ratnastūpa* (v. 562) where the *Jambuddīvapannatti* has *stūpa* (*thūbha*).

3 Schubring refers here to p. 156b of the edition used by him, which is not accessible to me. See however below.

4 Smith (1900).

5 Calling them commemorative *stūpas* is of course only a trick to avoid the issue.

6 The bones of Jinas (*jiṇa-sakahā*), kept in globular diamond reliquaries (*gola-vaṭṭa-samugga*) in a *stūpa* (*ceiya-khambha*) in heaven (or more precisely, in the residence of the god Camara) are also mentioned in the *Viyāhapannatti*. See Deleu (1970: 171).

Bibliography

Primary sources

Ādi Purāṇa of Jinasena. Part II. Edited, with Hindi Translation, Introduction and Appendices, by Pannalal Jain. Tenth Edition. New Delhi: Bharatiya Jnanpith, 2005.

Harivaṃśa Purāṇa of Jinasena. Edited, with Hindi Translation, Introduction & Appendices, by Pt. Panna Lal Jain. Kashi: Bhāratīya Jñānapītha, 1962 (Jñānapītha Mūrtidevī Jaina Granthamālā, Sanskrit Granth 27).

Jambuddīvapaṇṇattī. In: *Uvaṅga Suttāṇi* IV (Part II). Ed. Yuvācārya Mahāprajña. Ladnun: Jain Vishva Bharati, 1989, pp. 357–588.

Triṣaṣṭiśalākāpuruṣacaritramahākāvya of Hemacandra. Part 1. Ed. Śrīcaraṇavijaya. Ahmedabad, 1990.

Viyāhapannatti (Bhagavaī). Viyāhapannatti (Bhagavaī): The Fifth Anga of the Jaina Canon. Introduction, Critical Analysis, Commentary & Indexes by Jozef Deleu. Delhi: Motilal Banarsidas, 1970/1996 (Lala Sundar Lal Jain Research Series 10).

Yogaśāstra of Hemacandra. Ed. Muni Jambūvijaya. 3 Vols. Bombay, 1977–1986.

Secondary sources

Bronkhorst, Johannes. "Hendrik Kern and the Body of the Buddha." *Asiatische Studien/ Études Asiatiques* 63, 1 (2009) 7–27.

Deleu, Jozef. See *Viyāhapannatti (Bhagavaí).*

Dundas, Paul. *The Jains.* Second Edition. London & New York: Routledge, 2002.

Flügel, Peter. "Jaina Relic Stūpas." *Jaina Studies.* Newsletter of the Centre of Jaina Studies, SOAS, University of London Issue 3 (2008) 18–23.

Flügel, Peter. "The Jaina Cult of Relic Stūpas." *Numen* 57, 3 (2010) 389–504.

Johnson, William J. "The 'Jina Experience': A Different Approach to Jaina Image Worship." *Jainism and Early Buddhism.* Essays in Honor of Padmanabh S. Jaini. Part I. Ed. Olle Qvarnström, 217–230. Fremont, California: Asian Humanities Press, 2003.

Schubring, Walther. *The Doctrine of the Jainas: Described after the Old Sources.* Translated from the Revised German Edition by Wolfgang Beurlen. With three Indices enlarged and added by Willem Bollée and Jayandra Soni. Delhi: Motilal Banarsidas, 1962/2000 (Lala Sundarlal Jain Research Series 15).

Smith, Vincent A. *The Jain Stûpa and Other Antiquities of Mathurâ.* Varanasi & Delhi: Indological Book House, 1900/1969.

5 The *Niyatidvātriṃśikā* ascribed to Siddhasena Divākara

Olle Qvarnström

Introduction

The majority of medieval Indian texts reviewing different systems of contemporary thought – so called doxographies – belong to the Śvetāmbara, Madhyamaka and Advaita Vedānta traditions of Jainism, Buddhism and Brāhmaṇism. Irrespective of ideological affiliation, these texts provide us with accounts of a wide spectrum of religious and philosophical thought. Their historical value is occasionally difficult to assess, but they are nevertheless of great interest to the historian of religion. This is especially due to the fact that they sometimes furnish us with testimonies, which must be ranked as primary sources, from a period of which our knowledge is scarce or even inexisting.[1]

One of the earliest Jaina doxographical texts known to us form part of a set of minor texts, which by the Jaina tradition has been labelled *Dvātriṃśikā* and ascribed to the sixth century philosopher Siddhasena Divākara.[2] This author has been extolled by the Jaina tradition primarily for his contributions to Jaina logic and philosophy, as manifested in the *Nyāyāvatāra*[3] and *Sanmatitarka*. But his poetical and encyclopaedic talent, as displayed in the *Dvātriṃśikā*, is also greatly appreciated by the Jainas and is held to have served as an inspiration for later prominent Jaina doxographers, such as Haribhadrasūri.[4] Originally, the *Dvātriṃśikā* is said to have comprised 32 texts of which 22 are still extant, including the *Nyāyāvatāra*. The doctrinal content of the *Dvātriṃśikā* ranges from Jaina philosophy and religion to doxographical accounts of non-Jaina systems, labelled by the copyists in the colophons as *Vedavāda-* (IX), *Nyāya-* (XII), *Sāṃkhya-* (XIII), *Vaiśeṣika-* (XIV), *Bauddha-* (XV) and *Niyatidvātriṃśikā* (XVI).[5]

The scholarly community has likewise acknowledged the accomplishment of the author of the *Nyāyāvatāra*, but has been unwilling to ascribe the *Dvātriṃśikā* and its various texts to the same author, despite the traditional inclusion of the *Nyāyāvatāra* among the latter.[6] Indeed, there is nothing which disproves the contention that the accomplished logician and author of the *Nyāyāvatāra* also could have had an encyclopaedic talent, including knowledge of various Brāhmaṇical systems, especially since he is said to have been a Brahmin convert. But the lack of any cross-references between the *Nyāyāvatāra* (and *Sanmatitarka*) and the various doxographical texts constituting the *Dvātriṃśikā* rule out the theory of a common authorship. Moreover, the references to the *Dvātriṃśikā* as a homogenous text are late and occur first in hagiographies on Siddhasena Divākara.[7]

In fact, internal and external criteria also negate the assumption that the *Dvātriṃśikā* and its doxographical texts were written by a single author. Leaving aside the question of authorship, an intriguing possibility is that these texts instead constitute emic accounts that were merely edited (and possibly altered) by one or several individuals serving as transmitters rather than authors of accounts of non-Jaina knowledge systems within the Jaina tradition. Such a hypothesis applies to at least two texts: the *Vedavādadvātriṃśikā* and *Niyatidvātriṃśikā.* Apart from possibly being emic accounts, these two texts also aroused my interest since they presumably stem from a period of which our historical knowledge is fragmentary or simply lacking. Their style and content suggest that they may date from the fifth/sixth century CE, even though this assumption rests on weak grounds.[8] Accordingly, they may furnish us with more or less well-informed accounts of early Vedānta and Ājīvika philosophy and thus promise to be a welcome addition to our present knowledge of these traditions.[9]

Even though I agree with Sanghavi and Doshi as to the extremely incorrect text of the Bhavnagar edition (my main source) of the *Dvātriṃśikā*, including many doubtful readings,[10] I nevertheless decided to undertake the risky project of studying the *Niyatidvātriṃśikā* and in so doing honouring Professor Wilhelm B. Bollée for his brilliant contributions to the study of Jainism. It must be emphasized though that the following study is incomplete and highly tentative.[11]

Niyatidvātriṃśikā

The Ājīvika tradition still fascinates indologists and historians of religion, despite the limited possibility of discovering material that would contribute substantial new information to Basham's seminal study.[12] Persistent scholarly interest ranges from investigations into the early history of the Ājīvika tradition to questions of textual transmission and interpretation respecting available source material.

For dedicated Jaina scholars, the study of the Ājīvika tradition is made even more intriguing by the documented closeness between the two traditions – a closeness that is conveyed in the well-known relationship between Gośāla and Mahāvīra[13] and exemplified by common views on such matters as ascetic and nutritional practice, classification of beings (*abhijāti/leśyā*),[14] omniscience, Tīrthāṅkaras, as well as deterministic elements in Jainism.[15]

Statements about similarities and difference, however, must remain ever qualified since no primary Ājīvika source appears to have survived, and what we do know comes mainly from Jaina and Buddhist literature. Apart from the fact that these texts are secondary sources, they suffer from a further (obvious) complication: the Ājīvikas were the principal rivals of the Jainas and Buddhists and thus their descriptions of Ājīvika thought are most likely tainted by a diversity of underlying, and presumably biased, motives.[16]

At the same time, a number of medieval Jaina works include various quotations and altered versions of Sanskrit verses that they attribute to the Ājīvika tradition, at least some of which are most probably genuine. As noted by Basham,[17] this indicates the likelihood that in later times the Ājīvikas adopted Sanskrit for the writing of religious and philosophical texts that delineated a fully elaborated doctrinal system whose logic and epistemology resembled that of the Jainas.

As to the possibility of discovering new relevant material on the Ājīvika tradition, it is made likelier by the fact that the Jaina tradition highly prized the knowledge of other doctrines and that medieval Jaina monks educated themselves far beyond their own specialty, as evidenced in the richness of information on non-Jaina religions embodied in Jaina texts.

The *Niyatidvātriṃśikā* may be turn out to be such an Ājīvika Sanskrit text, i.e. an emic portrayal of Ājīvika doctrine – including certain polemical elements – reflecting a fully elaborated doctrinal system whose logic and epistemology resembled that of the Jainas.

Reading the *Niyatidvātriṃśikā* one discerns a number of central Ājīvika doctrines. As would be expected, the underlying and frequently recurring theme of the work is the notion of predestination or *niyati*, which is said to apply to humans and all other living beings: from one-sense beings (*ekendriya*) to gods (*sura*),[18] as well as to the greater cosmic processes. No one transmigrates caused by himself, someone else or both.

In this regard, all living beings (*sattva*) are divided into different classes (*abhijāti*) according to their predetermined (*niyata*) intrinsic nature (*svabhāva*), and no one exists – neither man nor god – that is superior to (*adhyakṣa*) this intrinsic nature.[19]

Those beings that belong to the same class are thought to possess a fixed degree of both happiness (*sukha*), suffering (*duḥkha*), knowledge (*jñāna*) and passion (*rāga*); they are also thought to possess a certain hue, e.g. blackish (*kṛṣṇa*), reddish (*rakta*), etc.[20] Each class or *abhijāti* corresponds to a particular level of reality, and all of these are progressively revealed, without the need of learning, as one automatically traverses the predetermined path of rebirths from one *abhijāti* to another – just as a lotus flower, when exposed to the sun, continually unfolds its petals until it is fully bloomed.[21]

In all of this, the Self or *puruṣa* is not conceived as an independent agent capable of directing the conduct of the body and mind.[22] Rather, the body and mind are seen as being moved along a set path by various causes and conditions, such as [time] and place,[23] which are themselves governed by the principle of *niyati*. Along similar lines, good (*sat*) and bad (*asat*) are seen to appear without a cause (*nimitta*) rather than as a result of the Self's own efforts (*puruṣakāra*),[24] and neither human volition (*yatna*), nor knowledge (*jñāna*), nor asceticism (*śrama*) are considered capable of eradicating conditions such as ignorance and passion,[25] caused by karma.[26] As such, the transmigration of the human being is caused neither by itself nor by others – nor by a combination of the two (*svaparobhaya*).[27] Instead, it is the fixed order of everything that predetermines birth in a particular class (*abhijāti*), level of knowledge, etc. When a human being comes to the point of understanding that the Self is not an agent and that nature's *guṇas* act out of necessity, it is no longer in doubt (*sampramugdha*) about the eventual attainment of insight (*jñāna*) and detachment (*vairāgya*).[28] It is only when the unborn Self mistakenly identifies with the actions of the *guṇas* that the notion of an independent agent (*kartṛ*) arises.[29]

The principal features of the doctrine thus far presented in the *Niyatidvātriṃśikā* resemble those found in Buddhist and Jaina depictions of the early Ājīvika tradition, namely: (1) the principle of absolute determinism (*niyati*); (2) the denial of human effort or volition (*puruṣakāra*); and (3) the division of living beings into different classes (*abhijāti*). In other words, there is no cause (*hetu*) of the happiness and suffering of living beings and no effort on their part (virtuous or otherwise) can change their course – i.e. the predetermined course of the Self. *Niyati* is the factor that moves the universe and the exclusive agent of all change; all is governed by the cosmic law of *niyati*, operating through the intrinsic nature (*svabhāva*) of all living beings. The *Niyatidvātriṃśikā* incorporates non-humans (*ajana*), such as gods (*sura*), into the Ājīvika classificatory system of *abhijātis*.[30] Moreover, the particular class represented by the blackish hue is said to lack distinctive characteristics because it is formless (*arūpa*).

Concerning the notion of predestination as applied to the cosmic processes, the *Niyatidvātriṃśikā* seems to introduce two principal cosmologies, one of which appears to have been embraced by the author himself. In this version, the different substances (*dravya*) and their qualities (*guṇa*), such as earth (*pṛthivī*), are conceived as being subject to effortless (*aprayatna*) predetermined transformations (*pariṇāma*), unlike the Self (*puruṣa*), which is separate from the *guṇas* and remains always the same.[31]

In contrast to this dynamic view of the cosmos, the *Niyatidvātriṃśikā's* alternate theory declares the utter non-existence of ether (*vyoman*) and space (*avakāśa*), time (*kāla*) and substance (*dravya*), life (*jīva*) and death (*ajīva*).[32]

The first of these two cosmologies seems to show some similarities with that which is presented in the Buddhist work *Samaññaphalasutta*, the second may reflect the cosmology presented in the *Nīlākeśi*, the ninth century Jaina religio-philosophical text together with its commentary by Vāmanamuni.[33]

According to the *Nīlākeś*'s classic formulation of this theory, the notion of a dynamic process in which living entities gradually develop according to the law of *niyati* is contrasted with the doctrine of a completely changeless reality – *avicalitanityatva* – in which time (along with all the motion, development and change that takes place within it) is ultimately illusory. With respect to the first cosmological theory, the *Niyatidvātriṃśikā* hints at an idea of the cosmos that allows for the gradual attainment of higher *abhijātis* through meditation.

The *Niyatidvātriṃśikā* also contains another noteworthy piece of information about Ājīvika doctrine: an apparent twofold epistemology that draws a distinction between conventional truth on the one hand and absolute truth on the other. From the absolute perspective, belief in an agent is *dhīmātra*,[34] or mere thought, and the division of reality into categories such as time and space, cause and effect, substances (*dravya*), qualities (*guṇa*) and modes (*paryāya*), is merely the working of the mind (*manovṛtti*),[35] which generates a conventional view of reality or *vyavahāraviniścaya.*[36]

The author of the *Niyatidvātriṃśikā* also seems to say that the discursive operations of the mind[37] – which are related to causality and the division of time into past, present and future – are the inevitable basis of mistaken conceptions of reality (*mithyātva*) and, in extension, of the process of transmigration or *saṃsāra*. Only the one who is detached (*ayojita*),[38] and has eradicated all desires realizes the truth (*tattva*) and may then be called *siddhārtha.*[39] Only the enlightened person (*pratibuddha*) has a valid understanding of reality (*samyagdarśana*).[40]

The conversation between Mahāvīra and the Ājīvika layman Saddālaputta, as recounted in the *Uvāsagadasāo*, highlights two contradictory Ājīvika views of reality: the one presuming the existence of free will (*puruṣakāra*) and the other presuming the predetermined nature (*niyati*) of all things. From his reading of this and other textual passages, Basham[41] felt that the Ājīvika tradition must have been aware of these two ways of viewing reality. From this he concluded that if the Ājīvikas had developed an epistemological theory that incorporated both a practical/empirical (*vyavahārika*) and an absolute (*pāramārthika*) notion of reality, this would have enabled them to resolve the inherent contradictions that naturally arise between a staunchly held determinism on the one hand and the inner conviction of free will on the other; in this way, he thought, they would have avoided certain aspects of the critique levelled at them by Jaina and Buddhist opponents. Unfortunately, Basham never came across the *Niyatidvātriṃśikā*, which may have afforded him some comfort in this regard.

The very existence of the *Niyatidvātriṃśikā* possibly indicates that during the sixth century CE the Ājīvikas were still engaged in polemics with Jainas and Buddhists, and that the philosophical discourse was conducted in the Sanskrit idiom. Moreover, a preliminary read of this work suggests that the Ājīvika tradition of the sixth century may have encompassed alternate understandings of the *abhijāti* classificatory system (e.g. the existence of non-human categories) as well as alternate theories of cosmology (e.g. the notion of a changeless reality), previously thought to have been of later date. Finally, the *Niyatidvātriṃśikā* appears to propound some sort of doctrine of two truths, drawing a distinction between a conventional (*vyavahāra*) and an absolute perspective (*tattva*). The foundational notion of *niyati* or absolute predestination appears to be valid only from the perspective of absolute truth, whereas notions of causality, etc. – which are thought to be creations of the mind (*manas/dhī*) – appear to be valid only from the perspective of conventional truth. Such an epistemological device is also found in early Jaina philosophy,[42] notable in the writings of Kundakunda, who advocates some kind of deterministic doctrine, according to which the infinite modifications (*paryāya*) of any given substance (*dravya*), such as the Self, are fixed in sequential order (*kramabaddhaparyāya*), as viewed from a pure vantage point (*śuddhaniścayanaya*).[43]

The study of texts such as the *Niyatidvātriṃśikā* thus encourages a comparative perspective that may enhance our understanding of this vanished Indic religion as well as the relationship between Jainism and the Ājīvika tradition on matters related to ontology and epistemology.

Appendix: materials for the study of the Dvātriṃśikā ascribed to Siddhasena Divākara

Manuscripts

Koba (K)

A manuscript belonging to the Śrī Māhāvir Jain Ārādhana Kendra, Koba Tīrth, Gandhinagar, Gujarat. Originally, the manuscript was located in the Vijaya-Dharma-Lakṣmī-Jñānamandira of Agra, Belanganj,[44] but was recently moved to Koba. It was made available to me through the kindness of Pu Ācārya Śrī Śilacandrasūrijī, through his secretary Shailesh Mehta. Later on, Jitendra B. Shah of the L. D. Institute, Ahmedabad, brought me in contact with Ācārya Śrī Kailaś Sagarsūri Gyan Mandir of Koba Tirth, who provided me with scanned copies of the manuscript (no. 13010). The manuscript is without signature or number. It contains 22 folios (15 lines recto/verso) covering 21 Dvātriṃśikās (i.e. not the *Nyāyāvatāra*). Its colophon runs as follows: "*miti āṣāḍha vadī 1 bhaumavāsare śrīsaṃvat 1961 hastākṣareṇa paṃḍita bālājī vaidyasya* //". The *Niyatidvātriṃśikā* occupy folios 16b, l.5–17a, l.14, and end with the sub-colophon *niyatidvātriṃśikā ṣoḍaśamī (ṣoḍaśī)*. The manuscript is dated V.S. 1961 (=1904).

Poona (P)

A manuscript from the Bhandarkar Oriental Research Institute, Poona. It is catalogued as "Dvātriṃśikāviṃśātiḥ, Siddhasenadivākara, manuscript no. 1189 of 1891–95 of the Government Manuscripts Library of the Bhandarkar Oriental Research Institute, Poona". The manuscript is undated and without colophon. It contains 27 folios (11 lines recto/verso) covering the first 20 Dvātriṃśikās. The *Niyatidvātriṃśikā* occupy folios 21a, l.11–22a, l.11, and end with the sub-colophon *niyatidvātriṃśikā ṣoḍaśamī samāptā*. I obtained a transcript of the manuscript through the courtesy of the Assistant Curator, Shreenand L. Bapat at BORI.[45]

Printed editions

Bhavnagar (Bh)

In addition I have made use of two printed editions.[46] The first stems from Bhavnagar and is entitled "Śrī-Siddhasena-Divākara-kṛta-granthāmāla (Ekaviṃśati-Dvātriṃśikā, Nyāyāva-tāra, Sanmatisūtra Mūla)". It was published in the Śrī-Jaina-Dharma-Prasāraka Sabhā, Ser. 10, Bhavnagar, V.S. 1965 (1908). The sub-colophon read: *iti niyatadvātriṃśikā ṣoḍaśī.*

Muni Bhuvanacandra (G)

The third printed edition contains only the *Niyatidvātriṃśikā* and was edited by Muni Bhuvanacandra. According to the foreword in Gujarati, the textual material used in preparing the edition included three handwritten manuscripts and two printed editions. The handwritten manuscripts derived from Vīravijayajī Bhaṇḍāra, Ahmedabad; Jainānanda Pustakālaya, Surat; and Mahua Bhāṇḍāra, Mahua. The printed editions used by the editor include Bhavnagar (Bh) and another edition not specified by the author. Since the handwritten manuscripts were not entirely reliable, according to the editor, the edition is largely based on the Bhavnagar edition.

Notes

1 This introduction is partly based on Qvarnström (1999, 2003).

2 On biographies of Siddhasena, see Granoff (1989, 1990).

3 The *Nyāyāvatāra* seems to be the earliest Jaina compendium written in Sanskrit on logic and epistemology under the impact of the Buddhist *pramāṇa*-school established by Dignāga, Dharmakīrti, etc. Besides the arguments proposed by Upadhye and others as to the dating of the *Nyāyāvatāra*, one may consider the following circumstances. In the eighth-century commentary on Dharmakīrti's *Pramāṇavārtika* (II.5), Śākyabuddhi or Śākyamati quotes the second verse of the *Nyāyāvatāra* and claims that this verse is the object of Dharmakīrti's critique. Furthermore, the *Nyāyāvatāra* (28) uses the signature element of Dignāga, namely "*pramāṇaphala*" (Dreyfus and Lindtner 1989). Though tentative, these notices tend to place the *Nyāyāvatāra* in between Dignāga (CE 480–540) and Dharmakīrti, who according to Krasser's (2012) working hypothesis was active during the middle of the sixth century CE. Balcerowicz (2000) questions the traditional attribution of the *Nyāyāvatāra* to Siddhasena Divākara, instead suggesting that Siddhasena Mahāmati authored the *Nyāyāvatāra* between 620/660 and 800 CE. The *Nyāyāvatāra* were known to Haribhadrasūri, who quotes it in his *Aṣṭakaprakaraṇa* and *Ṣaḍdarśanasamuccaya* (*Aṣṭakaprakaraṇa* XIII.5 quotes the *Nyāyāvatāra* 2, and *Ṣaḍdarśanasamuccaya* 56 the *Nyāyāvatāra* 4). See Kapadia (1947: xcviii). There are at least two testimonies to the effect that Haribhadrasūri – like his pupil Siddharṣi – wrote a *vṛtti* to the *Nyāyāvatāra*, though it does not seem to have survived to the present day.

4 Kapadia (1947: 98ff.); Qvarnström (1999).

5 On the content, style, etc., of the *Dvātriṃśikā*, see Sanghavi and Doshi (1939: 130–154); Upadhye (1971: *3–*72 *passim*); Krause (1999: 127f.).

6 Cf. Velankar (1944: 183); Kapadia (1947: cxix); Upadhye (1971: xxi, xxv, cf. 7, 18f., 27, 36f., 41, 51f., 56).

7 According to Krause (1999: 127, 169 n. 96), these references are found in the thirteenth century *Prabhāvakacarita* of Prabhacandra (1.1, p. 59, St. 142); the *Vividhatīrthakalpa* (1.1, p. 88); the *Prabandhacintāmaṇi* (1.1, p. 7); the *Prabandhakośa* (1.1, p. 18). Even scholars, such as Kapadia (1947: cxix), Velankar (1944: 183) and Upadhye (1971: xxv), as well as scholar-pandits, such as Sukhalal Sanghavi and Bechardas Doshi (1939: 130), ascribe the entire *Dvātriṃśikā*, or parts of it (Upadhye), to Siddhasena Divākara.

8 See Qvarnström (1999: 177–179) with notes. Pūjyapāda or Devanandin in his sixth century *Sarvārthasiddhi* (VII.13) quotes [*Pramāṇa*]*dvātriṃśikā* III.16a. The [*Pramāṇa*]*dvātriṃśikā* is, according to Kapadia (1947: II, xclx), also quoted by Siddhasena Gaṇi (ninth century CE; Williams 1963: 7) in his commentary (p. 71) on *Tattvārthasūtra* I.10. Furthermore, Pūjyapāda or Devanandin, who also authored the

Jainendravyākaraṇa (see Pathak 1883, cf. Kielhorn 1881), in his *sūtra* "*vetteḥ siddhasenasya*" (V.1.7) most likely refers to the form "vidrate" in verse 22 of the *Vedavādadvātriṃśikā*.

9 For a critical edition and annotated English translation of the *Vedavādadvātriṃśikā*, see Qvarnström (2003).

10 Sanghavi and Doshi (1939: 131).

11 Only a small number of manuscripts and printed texts have been available to me, despite prolonged efforts to acquire manuscripts from itinerant Jaina monks, various monastic libraries and institutions of higher learning in India and elsewhere. Furthermore, these manuscripts (and in extension, the editions based on these and other manuscripts) unfortunately seem to a great degree to depend on one another and do not reflect separate lines of textual transmission. In addition, they are quite corrupt.

12 Basham (1951).

13 Jaini (2000: 29f.) points to the lack of research on the connection between Jainism with Makkhali Gosāla and the Ājīvikas in Digambara texts, notably the *Bhāvasaṃgraha* and the *Darśanasāra* by Devasena (eleventh century).

14 On the relationship between the *leśyā* theory of the Jains and the *abhijāti* theory of the Ājīvika, see Charpentier (1910), Edholm (1988) and Wiley (2000).

15 On tendencies, or perhaps even strict determinism in Jainism, see Jaini (1977, 2000: 29f.); Bronkhorst (2000, 2002, 2007: 15ff.).

16 Cf. Dundas (2002: 29).

17 Basham (1951: 220ff., 274f.).

18 *niyatāntaram avyaktisukhaduḥkhābhijātayaḥ /*
svabhāvaḥ sarvasattvānāṃ payaḥkṣīrāṅkurādivat //1//
[niyatāntaram (G): nityānantaraṃ Bh]
ekendriyāṇām avyakter ajātyantarasaṃgatau /
vyaktānāṃ ca tadādau kā rāgādipravibhaktayaḥ //17//

19 *sudūram api te gatvā hetuvādo nivartsyati /*
na hi svabhāvān adhyakṣo lokadharmo 'sti kaścana //10//

20 *sparśaikaviṣayatvāditattvāntāḥ kramajātayaḥ /*
arūpād anabhivyaktabhedāḥ kṛṣṇābhijātayaḥ //22//
yathā duḥkhādi nirayas tiryakṣi puruṣottamāḥ /
raktāyām ajanāyāṃ tu sukhajā na guṇottarāḥ //23//
[tiryakṣi: tiryakṣu Bh]

21 *na copadeśo buddheḥ syād ravipaṅkajayogavat /*
tattvaṃ ca pratibudhyante tebhyaḥ pratyabhijātayaḥ //25//

22 *dharmādharmātmakatve tu śarīrendriyasaṃvidām /*
kathaṃ puruṣakāraḥ syād idam eveti neti vā //2//
śarīrendriyaniṣpattau yo nāma svayam aprabhuḥ /
tasya kaḥ kartṛvādo 'stu tadāyattāsu vṛttiṣu //3//

23 *dharmādharmau tadānyonyanirodhātiśayakriyau /*
deśādyapekṣau ca tayoḥ kathaṃ kaḥ kartṛsaṃbhavaḥ //4//

24 *yat pravṛttyopamardena vṛttaṃ sadasadātmakam /*
tad vetaranimittaṃ vety ubhayaṃ pakṣaghātakam //5//

25 *bhaṅguraśravaṇādyarthasaṃvinmātre nirātmake /*
rāgādiśāntau yatnas te kathaṃ kasya kim ity ayam //14//

26 *karmajaḥ pratyayo nāma karma ca pratyayātmakam /*
tatphalaṃ nirayādyaś ca na ca sarvatra vismṛtaḥ //15//
jñānam avyabhicāraṃ cej jinānāṃ mā śramaṃ kṛthāḥ /
atha tatrāpy anekānto jitāḥ smaḥ kiṃ tu ko bhavān //16//

27 *na saṃsaraty ataḥ kaścit svaparobhayahetukam /18ab*

28 *pravartitavyam eveti pravartante yadā guṇāḥ /*
atha kiṃ saṃpramugdho 'si jñānavairāgyasiddhiṣu //11//

29 *pṛthivyā nāvarudhyeta yathā vā rājatakriyāḥ /*

guṇānāṃ puruṣe tadvad ahaṃ kartety adaḥ kṛte //9//
[ahaṃ kartety: adaḥ kṛte Bh]
30 Cf. Charpentier (1910: 27ff.).
31 *viśvaprāyaṃ pṛthivyādipariṇāmo 'prayatnataḥ /*
viṣayas tatprabodhas tau tulyau yasyeti manyate //7//
noktābhyāṃ saha nārambhāt samam adhyakṣasaṃpadi /
vināśānupapatteś ca bhojyabhakṣyavikalpataḥ //8//
sparśanādimano 'ntāni bhūtasāmānyajātimān /
mano 'haṃ niyataṃ dravyaṃ pariṇāmyanumūrti ca //21//
hiṃsāvidyābhicārārthaḥ pūrvānte madhyamaḥ śamaḥ /
samyagdarśanabhāvāntāḥ pratibuddhas tv ayojitaḥ //24//
32 *vyomāvakāśo nānyeṣāṃ kālo dravyaṃ kriyā vidhiḥ /*
sukhaduḥkharajodhātur jīvājīvanabhāṃsi ca //29//
33 Basham (1951: 235–238, 240–261).
34 *asato hetuto veti pratisaṃdhau ca vigrahaḥ /*
asaṃs tu hetur dhīmātraṃ karteti ca viśiṣyate //13//
35 *anumānaṃ manovṛttir anvayaniścayātmikā /*
traikālyāṅgādivṛttāntā hetur avyabhicārataḥ //30//
36 *saṃjñāsāmānyaparyāyaśabdadravyaguṇakriyāḥ /*
etenoktāḥ pṛthak ceti vyavahāraviniścayaḥ //31//
37 See verse 30, *supra.*
38 *hiṃsāvidyābhicārārthaḥ pūrvānte madhyamaḥ śamaḥ /*
samyagdarśanabhāvāntāḥ pratibuddhas tv ayojitaḥ //24//
39 *na nāma tattvam evaitan mithyātvāparabuddhayaḥ /*
na cārthapratiṣedhena na siddhārthaś ca kathyate //32//
40 See verse 24, *supra.*
41 Basham (1951: 229f.).
42 See Bhatt (1974).
43 Jaini (2000: 30).
44 See Krause (1999: 170 n. 99), who used this manuscript for her translation of the *Guṇavacanadvātriṃśikā.*
45 The manuscript is described in Upadhye (1971: 255f.) and quoted in NCC I: 467 as "BORI 1189 of 1891–1895".
46 Another available printed edition is that of Upadhye (1971: 155–157). Upadhye seems to have reproduced the Bhavnagar edition, but deviates occasionally from it and unannounced inserts variations of his own. In the same publication, Upadhye has listed alternative readings, which, according to himself, were based on a "bunch of sheets" given to him by Amritalalaji Doshi, who had received them from Muni Jambūvijaya, who in turn had them from a manuscript at BORI (Upadhye 1971: 255, 258f.). Upadhye studied these in comparison to the Bhavnagar edition and those which were found "useful" (my quotation marks) were selected and listed "with minor corrections here and there" (sic!).

Bibliography

Classical sources

Darśanasāra of Devasena. Critically edited by A. N. Upadhye. *Annals of the Bhandarkar Oriental Research Institute* (ABORI) XV/3–4: 198–206.

Dvātriṃśikā ascribed to Siddhasena Divākara. The *Vedavādadvātriṃśikā.* Edited by Jina Vijaya Muni and translated into Gujarati by Sukhalālajī Saṃghavī. Bombay, 1945 (Bhāratīyavidyā Granthāvalī 7). Edited with the *Nyāyāvatāra* and *Saṃmatitarka* by

Anandasagara. Bhavnagar: Jainadharmaprasāraka Sabhā (JDPS), 1909. Text with slight alterations and variant readings from a manuscript preserved in the Bhandarkar Oriental Research Institute by A. N. Upadhye. In Upadhye 1971: 111–169, 241–257, 255–259.

Niyatidvātriṃśikā. Gujarati Translation and Glossary by Muni Bhuvanacandra. Gandhidham (Kutch): Jain Sahitya Academy, 2002.

Jainendravyākaraṇa of Pūjyapāda/Devanandin. Edited with the commentary of Abhayanandin by Sambhunātha Tripāṭhī and Mahādeva Caturvedī. Jaina Granthamālā 17. Varanasi: Bhāratīya Jñānapīṭha Kāśī, 1956.

Modern works

Balcerowicz, Piotr. "On the Date of the Nyāyāvatāra." *On the Understanding of Other Cultures. Proceedings of the International Conference on Sanskrit and Related Studies to Commemorate the Centenary of the Birth of Stanislaw Schayer (1899–1941)*. Ed. Piotr Balcerowicz and Marek Mejor, 331–370. Warsaw: Studia Indologiczne 7, 2000.

Basham, Arthur Llewellyn. *History and Doctrines of the Ājīvikas: A Vanished Indian Religion.* London: Luzac, 1951.

Bhatt, Bansidhar. "Vyavahāra-naya and Niścaya-naya in Kundakunda's Work." *Zeitschrift der Deutschen Morgenländischen Gesellschaft* (1974) 279–291.

Bronkhorst, Johannes. "The Riddle of the Jainas and Ājīvikas in Early Buddhist Literature." *Journal of Indian Philosophy* 28, 5–6 (2000) 511–529.

Bronkhorst, Johannes. 2002. "Ājīvika Doctrine Reconsidered." *Essays in Jaina Philosophy and Religion.* Edited by Piotr Balcerowicz, 153–171. Delhi: Motilal Banarsidass.

Bronkhorst, Johannes. *Greater Magadha: Studies in the Culture of Early India.* Handbuch der Orientalistik. Abteilung 2, Indien. Band 19. Leiden: E.J. Brill, 2007.

Charpentier, Jarl. "The Leśyā-theory of the Jainas and Ājīvikas." *Festskrift tillegnad Karl Ferdinand Johansson*, 20–38. Göteborg: Wald. Zachrissons Boktryckeri A.–B, 1910.

Dreyfus, Georges B. and Christian Lindtner. "The Yogācāra Philosophy of Dignāga and Dharmakīrti." *Studies in Central & East Asian Religions* 2 (1989) 27–52.

Dundas, Paul. *The Jains.* Second revised edition. London: Routledge, 2002.

Edholm, E. af. "The Colours of the Soul and the Origin of Karmic Eschatology." *On the Meaning of Death: Essays on Mortuary Rituals and Eschatological Beliefs.* Ed. S. Cederroth, C. Corlin and J. Lindström, 95–111. Uppsala: Acta Universitatis Upsaliensis, 1988.

Granoff, Phyllis. "The Biographies of Siddhasena: A Study in the Texture of Allusion and the Weaving of a Group-Image (Part I)." *Journal of Indian Philosophy* 17, 4 (1989) 329–384.

Granoff, Phyllis. 1990. "The Biographies of Siddhasena. A Study in the Texture of Allusion and the Weaving of a Group-Image (Part II)." *Journal of Indian Philosophy* 18/4: 109–125.

Jaini, Padmanabh S. "Bhavyatva and Abhavyatva." A Jaina Doctrine of 'Predestination'." *Bhagavān Mahāvīra and His Teachings: 2,500 Nirvāṇa Anniversary Volume*, 95–111. Bombay: Mahāvīr Jaina Vidyālaya, 1977.

Jaini, Padmanabh S. "The Jainas and the Western Scholar." *Collected Papers on Jaina Studies*, 23–36. Delhi: Motilal Banarsidass, 2000.

Kapadia, Hiralal Rasikdas. *The Anekāntajayapatākā of Haribhadra Sūri. With his own Commentary and Municandra Sūri's Supercommentary.* Volume II. Baroda: Oriental Institute, 1947.

Kielhorn, Franz. "On the Jainendra-Vyākaraṇa." *The Indian Antiquary* 10 (1881) 75–79.

Krasser, H. "Bhāviveka, Dharmakīrti and Kumārila." *Devadattīyam, Johannes Bronkhorst Felicitation Volume*. Ed. F. Voegeli, V. Eltschinger, D. Feller, M. P. Candotti, B. Diaconescu and M. Kulkarni, 535–594. Bern/New York: Peter Lang, 2012.

Krause, Charlotte. "Siddhasena Divākara and Vikramāditya." *German Jaina Śrāvikā Dr. Charlotte Krause. Her Life & Literature*. Compiled by Hazarimull Banthia and Luitgard Soni, 114–178. Varanasi: Pārśvanātha Vidyāpīṭha, 1999.

NCC = *New Catalogus Catalogorum*. Ed. V. Raghavan, K. Kunjunni Raja *et al*. Madras: University of Madras, 1949.

Pathak, K. B. "Pūjyapāda and the Authorship of the Jainendra-Vyākaraṇa." *The Indian Antiquary* 12 (1883) 19–21.

Qvarnström, Olle. "Haribhadra and the Beginnings of Doxography in India." *Approaches to Jaina Studies: Philosophy, Logic, Rituals and Symbols*. Ed. Olle Qvarnström and N. K. Wagle, 169–210. South Asian Studies Papers 11. Toronto: University of Toronto, 1999.

Qvarnström, Olle. "Early Vedānta Philosophy Preserved by the Jain Tradition: The Vedavādadvātriṃśikā of Siddhasena Divākara." *Jainism and Early Buddhism: Essays in Honor of Padmanabh S. Jaini*. Parts 1–2. Ed. Olle Qvarnström, 575–594. Fremont: Asian Humanities Press, 2003.

Sanghavi, Sukhalal and Bechardas Doshi. *Sanmatitarka of Siddhasena Divākara*. Pandit Shri Sukhalalji Granthamala 5. Ahmedabad: L. D. Institute of Indology, 1939.

Upadhye, Adinath Neminath. *Siddhasena's Nyāyāvatāra and Other Works (With a Bibliographical Review)*. Bombay: Jaina Sahitya Vikasa Mandala, 1971.

Velankar, Hari Damodar. *Jinaratnakośa: An Alphabetical List of Jaina Works and Authors*. Vol. 1. Poona: Bhandarkar Oriental Research Institute, 1944.

Wiley, Kristi L. "Colors of the Soul: By-Products of Activity or Passions?" *Philosophy East & West* 50 (2000) 348–366.

Williams, R. *Jaina Yoga. A Survey of the Mediaeval Śrāvakācāras*. Oxford: London Oriental Series, Vol. 14, 1963.

6 Bee and mendicant

The two different versions in the extant Jaina Āgamas

Kenji Watanabe

The chapter is in three parts. The first part deals with the simile of bee and mendicant in the *Dasaveyāliya-sutta* and its textual problems. The second part concerns another example in the *Dasaveyāliya-sutta*, and the last part relates to the Aśoka inscription on this matter.

The *Dasaveyāliya-sutta* forms part of the Āgamas or Siddhānta, i.e. the canon of the holy scriptures of the Śvetāmbara Jainas, and belongs to the oldest part of the Āgamas. The *Dasaveyāliya-sutta* is one of the four *mūla-sūtra*s of the Āgamas and consists of sayings pertaining to monastic life and rules for monastic discipline, some of which remind us of the sayings in the Buddhist *Dhammapada* and *Suttanipāta*. This *sutta* consists of ten chapters and two appendices. The oldest nucleus consists of valuable poems, a series of gnomic aphorisms, which belong to the ascetic poetry of ancient India, and also have their parallels in Buddhist literature. The present survey of the extant Jaina-Āgamas will be limited to the *Dasaveyāliya-sutta*.

In the *Dasaveyāliya-sutta*, Ernst Leumann's (1892) edition,[1] which is regarded as a standard, shows locative plural endings *-esu* in the text and in Haribhadra's commentary that is followed by the modern editions.

But the *Agastyasiṃha-cuṇṇi*[2] has several times the oblique plural endings *-ehiṃ* where the rest of the tradition shows *-esu*. The *Cuṇṇi* seems to favour the oblique plural ending *-ehi(ṃ)* of the eastern dialect in the texts.

In the opening chapter of the *Dasaveyāliya-sutta*, we can see the simile of a bee and mendicant. The behaviour of the bee in the flower is simply an analogy for the calm, uninvolved obtaining of alms by mendicants.

(I) *pupphesu* and *pupphehiṃ* will be considered first. *Dasaveyāliya-sutta* I, 2–4 inform us of the behaviour of the bee delicately taking nourishment at random and without violence to those who give. In the well-known verses edited by E. Leumann (1892: 613), who was a pioneer of Jainology, the verses read:

jahā dumassa pupphesu bhamaro[3] *āviyai rasaṃ* |
na ya pupphaṃ kilāmei so ya pīṇei appayaṃ ||2||
em ee samaṇā muttā je loe santi sāhuṇo |
vihaṃgamā va pupphesu dāṇa-bhatt'esaṇe rayā ||3||
vayaṃ ca vittiṃ labbhāmo na ya koi uvahammaī |
ahāgaḍesu rīyante pupphesu bhamarā jahā ||4||

W. Schubring (1932/1977: 81/199) translated the above passages as follows:

2 As the bee sucks honey in the blossoms of a tree without hurting the blossom, and strengthens itself.

3 So those pious monks, who are without attachment in the world are content with searching their outfit and food like unto the flying [bees] in the blossoms.

4 [They say:] "We earn our living and no one [of the almsgivers] is hurt [by our doing so]." They go where they [may] meet with accidental alms as the bees do at blossoms.

This text describes proper monastic conduct of the begging round by taking a hint from the bee that strengthens itself by sucking honey in the blossoms of a tree without hurting the blossoms. Here is a good example of an ancient scriptural idiom which could inform modern ecological ethics. When we humans see something beautiful or useful in nature, we take it until it is depleted and exhausted. If we were to follow the way of the bee, we would learn to take only a little from nature and be content. We have to learn from nature. Look at the bee go from flower to flower taking only small amounts of nectar from each flower; a flower has never complained that a bee came and took all of its nectar away. Both the bee and the flower seem to be in agreement with one another. In the same way, a mendicant should go from door to door and from household to household, begging for his food, always taking just a little.

As for the text, there are two different readings in the extant manuscripts. *Dasaveyāliya* I.4 (Leumann's edition) reads:

> *vayaṃ ca vittiṃ labbhāmo na ya koi uvahammaī* |
> *ahāgaḍesu rīyante pupphesu bhamarā jahā* ||*4*||

> They go where they [may] meet with accidental alms, as the bees do at the blossoms (Schubring's translation).

But the text of *Cuṇṇi* I.4 reads:

> *vayaṃ ca vittiṃ labbhāmo na ya koti uvahammati* |
> *ahāgaḍehiṃ rīyante pupphehiṃ bhamarā jahā* ||*4*||

The *Cuṇṇi* variant *ahāgaḍehiṃ rīyaṃti pupphehiṃ bhamarā jahā* means:

> They separate from the place where they [may] meet with accidental alms, as the bees do at the blossoms (Watanabe's tentative translation).

Here the verb "*riyante*" from root √*ri* means "to release…, RV.; … detach from (abl.)" in Monier-Williams' (1899: 881) *Sanskrit-English Dictionary*, a root √*ri* taking the ablative, but not "to go" in Haribhadra's interpretation[4] in his *Bṛhat-vṛtti* (*rīyaṃti gacchanti*) and in Schubring's translation. So the reading in the *Cuṇṇi* "*pupphehiṃ*" means "from blossoms" and one can translate the text "the bees detach from the blossoms". What is the difference between the reading "*pupphesu*" and "*pupphehiṃ*"? The most likely explanation is that the original form of the verse had ablative plural forms with the Eastern dialect ending *-ehiṃ*. Some retained it, either recognizing it was a locative which was also *-ehiṃ* in the Eastern dialect and replaced it by *-esu*. The word form "*pupphehiṃ*" is the Eastern dialect form, someone believing it to be an instrumental as for similar ending forms replaced it by *-esu*.

About this *Dasaveyāliya-sutta*'s expression of a bee and mendicant, two passages come to our attention, which convey the same idea. This *Dasaveyāliya-sutta* I.4 (Leumann's text) is to be compared with a passage in the *Dhammapada* 49 as mentioned by P. L. Vaidya (1934) in the notes to his translation of the *Dhammapada*.

Generally speaking, formerly Buddhist and Jaina scriptures were studied independently of each other. But, if we come to take note of the fact that there are many common elements in them, we will be able to take a wider scope of both religions. As Buddhism came into existence in the same period and in the same social context, it is quite natural that there are many common elements in both religions. Buddhism underwent quite a great deal of change in the lapse of time.[5] The earlier stage of the development of this religion was, the clearer Jaina influence can be noticed. In the scriptures of both religions, especially in the *gāthā* portions of both scriptures, common phrases can be noticed. This means that these phrases were derived from the same spiritual atmosphere of the earlier period in which both religions were not distinctly separated.

We can say that comparison with parallel passages in early Buddhist scripture is quite helpful in clarifying the meanings of terms and phrases and the purport or thought of passages of Jaina scriptures which would otherwise be doubtful or difficult to understand.

Dhammapada 49 informs us of the behaviour of the bee, delicately taking nourishment at random and without violence to those who give. In von Hinüber and K. R. Norman's new edition the verse reads:

Dasaveyāliya-sutta I, 4	*Dhammapada* 49
(Text of *Cuṇṇi*)	(Ed. von Hinüber and Norman) 1994)[6]
vayaṃ ca vittiṃ labbhāmo	*yathāpi bhamaro puppham*
na ya koti uvahammati |	*vaṇṇagandhaṃ aheṭhayaṃ*
ahāgaḍehiṃ rīyaṃti	*paleti rasam ādāya*
pupphhehiṃ bhamarā jahā ||	*evaṃ gāme munī care* |
"We earn our living" and	As a bee without harming the flower,
"no one is hurt".	its colour or scent flies away,
As the bees separate from flowers	collecting only the honey,
where collecting the honey	even so should the sage wander
So should mendicants wander	in the village.
(in the village).	(Tr. by Narada Thera)
(Tr. by K. Watanabe)	

The *Dhammapada* 49 seems to be a concentrated form of the *Dasaveyāliya-sutta* I, 3–4. These verses indicate "begging in the manner of a bee".

The comparison with the bee and the begging mendicant is instructive at least in two ways. A bee gathers nectar from many flowers and does not injure them in the process. Likewise, an ascetic does not become a burden on any single householder by begging a little food from several houses. If we were to follow the way of the bee, we would learn to take only a little from flowers and be content.

Now we turn to the language problem, which L. Alsdorf (1936: 321) discovered: ablative singular *-aṃ*. In *Dhammapada* 49a, Alsdorf takes the word "*pupphaṃ*" as ablative in the sense of "from the flower", the same as *pupphehiṃ* in the *Cuṇṇi* of the *Dasaveyāliya-sutta*. Hence, Alsdorf (p. 331) translates *Dhammapada* 49 as follows:

> And as the bee, having take the juice,
> flies away *from* the flower (*puspāt*!)
> without damaging its colour and smell, even so…

Usually, scholars understand "*pupphaṃ*" as accusative here. Yet, our passage is repeated in a Sanskrit version of the Sarvāstivāda tradition. The Sanskrit text *Udānavarga* XVIII. 8 reads "*pupphaṃ*" as "*puṣpāt*, as indicted by Alsdorf. Around this verse, I can point to further Eastern dialect characters. For example, the commentary glosses "*ahāgaḍehiṃ*" in pāda c as "*yathākṛtaḥ*" and represents it as a borrowing from a dialect where the relative pronoun lacked the initial *y*-, such as the Eastern dialect of the Aśoka inscriptions.[7] Also the change of dental *t* into a cerebral *ḍ* in the Eastern dialect in past passive participles of certain roots in *ṛ*, and the change of *ka* into *go* occurs in Māgadhī. The declension *-ehiṃ* is the Eastern dialect form.

In *Dhammapada* 49, the *-aṃ* ending of *pupphaṃ* is an ablative form in the Eastern dialect. The "*l*" in *paleti* is a Magadhism: usually it is "*r*" in Pāli.

The behaviour of the bees referred to in the *Dasaveyāliya-sutta* and in the *Dhammapada* is simply an analogy for the calm, uninvolved method of obtaining alms practiced by mendicants. It is an expression found also in the Epic (for example *Mahābhārata* 12. 171) and in the Hindu tradition, with no evidence for it having been borrowed from the Jaina source.[8] The way of begging named *mādhūkara* (a large black bee) in the Hindu tradition, the scriptures say, signifies the begging of food in the manner of a bee: by going to three, five and seven houses that have not been deliberately selected. Like a bee moves from blossom to blossom in the flower, the mendicant moves from house to house in the village.

(II) On the other hand, we can find an example of the same phenomenon in the extant text of the *Dasaveyāliya-sutta*. The *Cuṇṇi* has the oblique plural ending *-ehiṃ*, where the rest of the tradition show *-esu*. In Leumann's edition it reads:

> *evaṃ karenti sambuddhā paṇḍiyā paviyakkhaṇā* |
> *viṇiyaṭṭanti bhogesu jahā se puris'uttamo* || *tti bemi* ||
> (Dasaveyāliya-sutta II, 11)

Although there would seem to be no difficulty in translating pāda c, *viṇiyaṭṭanti bhogesu*, as "they turn away from [sensual] pleasure", Schubring (1932/1977: 82/200) apparently follows the commentary, which takes the locative in the sense of ablative. In his note on the translation "They turn away from the [sensual] pleasures", Schubring (p. 122/240) states that the locative of "*bhogesu*" is in the sense of the ablative. This interpretation agrees with the *Cuṇṇi*'s reading "*bhogehiṃ*", i. e. plural ablative which is not seen in the edition of Leumann. It would seem that Schubring's translation is based upon Haribhadra's explanation in his *Vṛtti*; "[*vi-*]*nirvartante bhogebhyo*". Here *bhogebhyo* is plural ablative. Monier-Williams' (1899: 971) *Sanskrit-English Dictionary* takes "*viniyattanti*" as a verb root *vi-ṇi-√vṛt* which means "to turn back, turn away, cease from (abl.)" and mentions that this verb is used with ablative.

In the text of the *Cuṇṇi* the verse reads:

evaṃ kareṃti saṃpaṇṇā paṃditā paviyakkhaṇā |
viṇiyaṭṭaṃti bhogehiṃ jahā se purisuttame ||11|| tti bemi ||

Schubring (1932/1977: 82/200) translates the equivalent verse *Dasaveyāliya-sutta* II, 11 as follows:

"Thus act awakened, wise and far-sighted [men]. They turn away from the [sensual] pleasures like that hero. Thus I say."

We can see next the same expression as in *Dasaveyāliya-sutta* II, 11, belonging to the same category *bhogesu* and *bhogehiṃ* in *Dasaveyāliya-sutta* VIII, 34, which reads:

adhuvaṃ jīviyaṃ naccā siddhimaggaṃ viyāṇiyā |
viṇiyaṭṭejjā bhogesu āusaṃ parimiyamappaṇo ||34||

The *Cuṇṇi* version has "*bhogehiṃ*" in the place of "*bhogesu*" in Leumann's text, which might be the same phenomena as *Dasaveyāliya* II, 11 mentioned above.

Schubring (1932/1977: 107/225) translates *Dasaveyāliya-sutta* VIII, 34 as:

Knowing that life is transient and the span of life allotted to him is limited, and having realised the path to perfection, he should turn away from worldly enjoyments.

(III) Another passage comes to our attention, which has the ending *-esu* in the Leumann's text while *Cuṇṇi* has *-ehiṃ*.

Dasaveyāliya-sutta V, 1, 57 in Leumann's edition reads:

asaṇaṃ pāṇagaṃ vā vi khāimaṃ sāimaṃ tahā |
pupphesu hojja ummīsam bīesu hariesu vā ||57||

In the *Cuṇṇi* the verse reads:

> *asaṇaṃ pāṇagaṃ vā vi khādimaṃ sādimaṃ tahā |*
> *pupphehiṃ hojja ummissaṃ bīehiṃ hariehiṃ vā ||68||*

The translation by Schubring (1932/1977: 91/209) has:

> Food of any kind might be mingled with blossoms, seeds, and plants.

AMg. *ummissa* is *unmiśra* in Skt. which means "mixed with (inst.)". Here, syntactically the instrumental is necessary, but not the locative.

Conclusion

I would like to conclude with a few general remarks on the *Agastyasiṃha-Cuṇṇi*; several times it has the oblique plural ending *-ehiṃ*, where the rest of the tradition shows *-esu* in the *Dasaveyāliya-sutta*.

All these examples testify to the fact that *Cuṇṇi*'s readings are better and more original than the readings in the extant text represented by Leumann's edition.

It is interesting to mention that the readings which are accepted by the *Cuṇṇi* are not available in any other manuscript traditions in the extant Jaina Āgamas. The version which we now find in different mss. is mostly in consonance with the tradition of readings which are followed by the author of the *Vṛtti*.

The word-form "*pupphehiṃ*" is the Eastern dialect form, someone who believed it to be an instrumental as for similar ending forms replaced it by *-esu*. According to Professor H. Lüders's (1954 § 223: 155) hypothesis, there must have been a similar "transposition" in the scriptural traditions of the Jaina Siddhānta as in the early Eastern Buddhist dialects. In the Pāli canon, Lüders collected many examples of instances which clearly show that difficulties in the understanding of Pāli can be removed if we understand that they are based upon mistranslation of passages which were originally in an Eastern dialect.

Examples of the same kind of phenomena we can find not only in the *Dasaveyāliya-sutta*, but also in other old Āgamas: in the first Śrutaskhandha of *Āyāraṅga-sutta*, the first part of the *Sūyagaḍaṅga* and in the *Uttarajjhāyā*. It is also interesting that exactly the same distribution of case forms is found in Aśoka's Rock Edict VI, where the Eastern dialects have *mahāmāttehi*, "to the ministers", in Dauli. This form is replaced by *mahāmātresu* at Girnar in the West.[9]

It is likely that at the time of the compilation of the Jaina canon, either in the council held at Valabhī under Devardhigaṇin or in the council of Mathurā under Skandilācārya, the original dialect assumed a western colouration. Particularly at Valabhī the influence of Māhārāṣṭrī might have been quite considerable.

Notes

1 Leumann (1892: 613ff.). Japanese Translation and Notes: Matsunami (1968). For studies of the *Dasaveyaliya-sutta*, see Collette Caillat (1980–81, 1982). [Leumann 1892: 596 also offers a German translation of the passage discussed in the following. The Editors.]

2 In: *Sayyambhava's Dasaveyāliysuttaṃ with Bhadrabāhu's Niryukti and Agastysiṃha's Cūrṇi*. Edited by Muni Puṇyavijayajī. Varanasi-Ahmedabad: Prakrit Text Society Series 17, 1973.

3 This *bhamra* (Skt. *bhramara*) means, as is explained by Apte's (1890/1965: 1215) *Sanskrit-English Dictionary*, "a bee, a large black bee". The *bhamara* in original sense of the word means a large black bee, but I here translate the *bhamara* simply as a bee.

4 *"rīyante" gacchanti, varttante ity arthaḥ: Hāribhadrīya.* Haribhadra's commentary, in: *Śrī Daśavaikālikaṃ, with Niryukti and Bṛhadvṛtti.* Devacandra Lalabhai Jainapustakoddhara Granthankaḥ 47. Bombay 1917.

5 Nakamura (1983).

6 Cf. *Dhammapada* translated with notes by Narada Thera and John Murray (1954), and Japanese Translation by Nakamura (1978) (this is the best Japanese translation of the *Dhammapada* and translation's notes).

7 See Alsdorf (1980/1998: 826, 1965: 16f.).

8 *Mahābhārata* 12.17 (MBh. Cr. 12. 475, ll. 7–8: P. 12. 178.11); *Bhāgavata-Purāṇa* XI. 8. 9–10; *Nārada-Parivrājika-Upaniṣad* 7. *Saṃnyāsa-Upaniṣad* 2. 59. See Olivelle (1995/1997).

9 Bloch (1950: 107). See also Norman (1977).

Bibliography

Primary sources

Dasaveyāliya-sutta. In: Leumann (1892). Translated by Schubring (1932/1977), Matsunami (1968).

Dasaveyāliyasuttaṃ Uttarājhayaṇāiṃ and Āvassaysuttaṃ. Edited by Muni Śrī Puṇyavijayajī and A. M. Bhojak. Jaina-Āgama Series No. 15. Bombay: Mahāvīra Jaina Vidyālaya, 1977.

Dhammapada. Text in Devanāgarī with Notes, Introduction and Translation by Parasurama Lakshmana Vaidya. Second Revised Edition. Poona: Oriental Book Agency, 1934.

Dhammapada. Translated with Notes by Narada Thera and John Murray. With a Foreword by Bhikkhu Kassapa and an Introduction by E. J. Thomas. London: John Murray, 1954.

Dhammapada and Udānavarga. Japanese Translation by Hajime Nakamura. Tokyo: Iwanamibunko, 1978.

Dhammapada. Edited by Oscar von Hinüber and Kenneth Roy Norman. With a Complete Word Index Compiled by Shoko Tabata and Tetsuya Tabata. Oxford: The Pali Text Society, 1994.

Mahābhārata. Critical Edition. Volume III. Poona: The Bhandarkar Oriental Research Institute, 1974.

Sayyambhava's Dasaveyāliysuttaṃ with Bhadrabāhu's Niryukti and Agastysiṃha's Cūrṇi. Edited by Muni Puṇyavijayajī. Varanasi-Ahmedabad: Prakrit Text Society Series 17, 1973.

Śrī Daśavaikālikaṃ, with Niryukti and Bṛhadvṛtti. Bombay: Devacandra Lālabhāī Jainapustakoddhāra Granthaṅkaḥ 47, 1917.

Secondary sources

Alsdorf, Ludwig. "The Vasudevahiṇḍi, A Specimen of Archaic Jaina Māhārāṣṭrī." *Bulletin of the School of Oriental and African Studies* 8, 2–3 (1936) 319–333 (Reprint: *Kleine Schriften.* Herausgegeben von Albrecht Wezler, 56–70. Zweite Auflage. Wiesbaden: Franz Steiner Verlag, 1974/2001 (Glasenapp-Stiftung Band 10)).

Alsdorf, Ludwig. "Ardha-Māgadhī." *Kleine Schriften, Nachtragsband.* Herausgegen von Albrecht Wezler, 824–830. Wiesbaden: Franz Steiner Verlag, 1980/1998 (Glasenapp-Stiftung Band 35).

Alsdorf, Ludwig. *Les études Jaina: état présent et tâches futures.* Paris: Collège de France, 1965.

Alsdorf, Ludwig. *Jaina Studies: Their Present State and Future Tasks.* Translated from the Original French into English by Bal Patil. Revised and Edited by Willem Bollée with Editor's Preface. Pandit Nathuram Premi Research Series Vol. 1. Mumbai: Hindi Grantha Karyalaya, 2006.

Apte, Vaman Shivram. *The Practical Sanskrit-English Dictionary: Containing Appendices on Sanskrit Prosody and Important Literary and Geographical Names in the Ancient History of India.* Third Revised and Enlarged Edition. Delhi: Motilal Banarsidas, 1890/1965.

Bloch, Jules. *Les Inscriptions d'Asoka. Traduites et commentées.* Collection Emile Senart. Paris: "Les Belles Lettres", 1950.

Caillat, Collette. "Notes sur les variantes dans la tradition du *Dasaveyāliya-sutta.*" *Indologica Taurinensia* 8–9 (1980–81) 71–83.

Caillat, Collette. "Notes sur les variantes grammaticales dans la tradition du *Dasaveyāliya-sutta.*" *Indological and Buddhist Studies: Volume in Honour of Professor J. W. de Jong on his Sixtieth Birthday.* Edited by L. A. Hercus, F. B. J. Kuiper, T. Rajapatirana and E. R. Skrzypczak, 69–94. Canberra: Faculty of Asian Studies, 1982.

Leumann, Ernst. "Daśavaikālika-sūtra und -nirjukti nach dem Erzählungsgehalt untersucht und herausgegeben." *Zeitschrift der Deutschen Morgenländischen Gesellschaft* 46 (1892) 581–663 (Reprint: *Kleine Schriften.* Herausgegeben von Nalini Balbir, 207–259. Wiesbaden: Franz Steiner Verlag, 1998 (Glasenapp-Stiftung Band 37)).

Lüders, Heinrich. *Beobachtung über die Sprache des Buddhistischen Urkanons.* Berlin: Akademie-Verlag, 1954.

Matsunami, Seiren. "*Dasaveyāliya-sutta* (a Jain Text)." *Memoirs of Taisho University* 53 (1968) 100–150 (1)–(51).

Monier-Williams, Monier (Comp.). *Sanskrit-English Dictionary.* New Edition, Greatly Enlarged and Improved. Oxford: Oxford University Press, 1899.

Nakamura, Hajime. "Common Elements in Early Jain and Buddhist Literature." *Indologica Taurinensia* 11 (1983) 303–329.

Norman, Kenneth Roy. "Kāvilīyaṃ: A Metrical Analysis of the Eighth Chapter of the Uttarādhyayaṃ-sūtra." *Mahāvīra and His Teachings.* Edited by Adinath Neminath Upadhye *et al.*, 9–19. Bombay: Bhagavān Mahāvīra 2500th Nirvāṇa Samiti, 1977.

Olivelle, Patrick. *Rules and Regulation of Brahmanical Ascetics: Yatidharmasamuccaya of Yādava Prakāśa.* Albany: State University of New York Press, 1995 (Indian Edition: Sri Garib Dass Oriental Series No. 208. Delhi: Indian Book Centre, 1997).

Schubring, Walther. *The Dasaveyāliya Sutta: Introduction, Text and Variants.* English Translation. Ahmedabad: Managers of Sheth Anandji Kalianji, 1932 (Reprinted in Walther Schubring, *Kleine Schriften.* Herausgegeben von Klaus Bruhn, 110–248. Wiesbaden: Franz Steiner Verlag, 1977 (Glasenapp-Stiftung Band 13)).

7 Lay atonements

Investigation into the Śvetāmbara textual tradition[1]

Nalini Balbir

§ 1. The topic selected for this contribution could be an adequate homage to Prof. Bollée, since he illustrates with such brightness the German *guruparamparā* of scholars who did extensive work on the Śvetāmbara branch of canonical literature known as Chedasūtras, walking along the path initiated by Ernst Leumann (1859–1931) and Walther Schubring (1881–1969). In France, this tree produced an offshoot with the works of Colette Caillat (1921–2007), a student of Schubring, whose *Atonements in the Ancient Ritual of the Jaina Monks* (1965, 1975) has become a classic. In India, work in this area has been the apanage of Jain mendicants, who have provided editions of texts and commentaries: Muni Caturvijaya and Muni Puṇyavijaya have been the pioneers with their edition of the *Bṛhatkalpabhāṣya* (1933ff.); Muni Jinavijaya has published the *Jītakalpasūtra* (1926). Today Ācārya Vijayamunicandrasūri follows this line, providing re-editions (2010), whereas Samaṇī Kusumpragyā of the Terāpanth has made an extremely significant contribution with editions (VyavBh (K) 1996) and Hindi translations (JKBh (K) 2010).

§ 2. Śvetāmbaras have produced a large body of texts dealing with atonements (Pkt. *pacchitta*, Skt. *prāyaścitta*) meant to compensate all possible transgressions occurring in monastic life. A large part of the works coming under the heading "Chedasūtras", whether the *Kalpa-*, the *Niśītha-* or the *Vyavahāra-sūtra* deals with this subject which is central to the regulation of monastic life.[2] But it seems that the necessity was felt for having a specific work systematically devoted to monastic atonements with a high degree of technicalities and conciseness. This is the *Jītakalpa* corpus. It consists of a *sūtra* which is unlike other Śvetāmbara *sūtra*s for two reasons: first, it is not in prose, as expected, but in verse, which is, normally, the form of a *bhāṣya*; second, it is not anonymous, but authored by Jinabhadragaṇi Kṣamāśramaṇa, one of the most famous Śvetāmbara scholars in the field of exegesis, philosophy and cosmology. Thus it can be dated with some likeliness to the sixth century CE. The sūtra-verses, which number 103, are expanded upon in a large *bhāṣya*, also in verse. Both are in Ardhamāgadhī Prakrit. The *bhāṣya* is, in turn, commented upon in a *cūrṇi*, which, as expected for this type of commentary, is in Māhārāṣṭrī Prakrit and in prose. It was written by Siddhasenasūri. This *cūrṇi* gave birth to a Sanskrit commentary composed in V.S. 1227 (=CE 1170) by Śrīcandrasūri, pupil of

Dhaneśvara, pupil of Śīlabhadrasūri, the *Bṛhaccūrṇi-viṣamapada-vyākhyā*. Another (still unpublished) commentary was written by Tilakācārya in V.S. 1274 (1217 CE; below § 5.2). Reasons which led to include the *Jītakalpa* among the Chedasūtras, although it is a text with a well-identified author, are not fully clear.[3] *Jīta* (Pkt. *jīya*) refers to "custom" as one of the five sources of knowledge for the procedure to be taken towards a transgressor. The other four are based on the Canon (*āgama*), on tradition (*sua*), on order (*āṇā*) or on charge/memorization (*dhāraṇā*). The first two can be resorted to only by religious teachers of certain categories, who master nine or ten Pūrvas and the full scriptural tradition. The third may be used in particular circumstances where a mendicant gets an atonement sent to him through an intermediary because he is far from his teacher. The fourth consists in applying an atonement which one remembers (*avadhārya*) having seen it earlier applied to an identical trangression. The concept of *jīta* is supposed to include both what has been established or experienced (*ācīrṇam, ācaritam*) by earlier teachers and to take into consideration changing circumstances which may lead to modify an earlier usage. It makes use of lists of atonements providing various alternatives: if the first one is not applicable, the next one is considered, etc. In this process the teacher who is the ultimate source for atonements clearly plays a crucial part.[4]

§ 3. The *Jītakalpa* was first treated one century ago by the pioneer of Jain studies, Ernst Leumann, in his contribution "Jinabhadra's Jītakalpa, mit Auszügen aus Siddhasena's Cûrṇi" (1892), but was otherwise rather neglected in the West. Leumann's interest in the *Jītakalpa* was probably due in part to the fact that it is ascribed to Jinabhadra, the author of the *Viśeṣāvaśyakabhāṣya* which was central to Leumann's investigations of the so-called "Āvaśyaka literature". Leumann's article consists in the edition of the 103 stanzas that make the *Jītakalpa*, based on a palm leaf manuscript kept in Pune, followed by extracts from the beginning of the Cūrṇi thereupon with translation. The five pages of notes supply additional extracts from the Cūrṇi and references to parallel passages in other Chedasūtras. The introduction gives a brief presentation of the text, but does not unfold its many mysteries. In one sentence, Leumann refers to the contents:

> Der Text ist eine Bussenliste für Jaina-Mönche. In neuerer Zeit, seitdem nämlich eine ähnliche Bussenliste für die frommen Laien (Śrâddha-Jîtakalpa) hergestellt worden ist, heisst die unsrige zum Unterschied von dieser in der Regel Yati-Jîtakalpa, so z.B. in dem saṃvat 1456 von Sâdhuratna dazu verfassten Skt-Commentar.
>
> (1892, p. 1195)[5]

In brief, Leumann's contribution to this corpus provides materials, and stimulates curiosity. His statements provoke questions. For instance, what is meant exactly by "in more recent times" as the period when a system comparable to the *Jītakalpa* was elaborated for application to the laity? Leumann probably meant that this elaboration was post-canonical. As will be seen below, the *Jītakalpa* provides the general frame and pattern for further elaboration applied to the area of the layman's life.

As connected with the notion of fault, transgression, violations of conduct and compensations for it, the concept of atonements should be central to the Jain laity's (*śrāvaka, śrāddha*) daily life, as it is to the mendicant's (*yati, sādhu*). The present chapter will deal with the kinds of literature dealing with this topic and the variety of responses which are given in the texts at our disposal.

§ 4.

> All the failures of conduct . . ., when they are practised intentionally and out of crookedness, are of the form of an utter violation of the *vrata* concerned and hence are in fact the cases of misconduct; on the other hand, when they are practised out of carelessness which in its turn is born of forgetfulness they are the cases of failure-of-conduct proper.[6]

This quotation from Pandit Sukhlalji's commentary on the *Tattvārthasūtra* shows that whatever is connected with the definition and understanding of "failure", "mistake", "transgression", etc. is complex and subject to discussion in the Jain tradition. This is of course central to any discussion of atonement too.

As can be expected in a system such as Jainism, the semantic area of transgression is rather rich. The main terms are *doṣa, bhaṅga, aticāra, virādhanā* and *khaṇḍita*. The last two occur, for example, in the layman's Pratikramaṇa: *bārasa-vihassa sāvaga-dhammassa jaṃ khaṇḍiyaṃ jaṃ virāhiyaṃ tassa micchā mi dukkaḍaṃ*.[7] Whether it is "intellectual hair-splitting", as Williams wants it,[8] these terms have produced discussions in the tradition. The difference between them can be of degree or intensity: according to Hemacandra, *khaṇḍita* means "partially broken", whereas *virādhita* means "intensely broken, but not totally".[9] In the *Uvāsagadasāo*, the word *aticāra* occurs in connection with the vows taken by the layman Ānanda, first applied to "right faith", the basis of lay conduct: *sammattassa panca aiyārā peyālā jāṇiyavvā na samāyariyavvā*:[10] "Five typical violations of right faith should be known but not practised". *Aticāra* seems to distinguish itself from *bhaṅga* in the following way: *aticāra* is a theoretical frame giving instances of possible ways in which a given vow could be violated. The phrase of the *Uvāsagadasāo* emphasizes this point, in my opinion. In order not to do wrong one should know how far he can go. The set of five *aticāras* per vow, which has become a well-established category, and follows in the *Uvāsagadasāo* is meant to draw these limits. At the same time, some of the terms which refer to the transgressions are vague enough to allow various contents as is clear from comparative readings of the *śrāvakācāra*s. Thus, the description of *aticāra*s combines strictness with a flexibility that is typical of any prescriptive frame in the Indian context. *Bhaṅga*, on the other hand, is a concrete word, which refers to actual violations of the vow. Thus the tendency is to consider that an *aticāra* is a partial *bhaṅga* or "half a *bhaṅga*" – in other words, a virtual violation and not an act as such. Such distinctions, however, are attempts by Jain teachers to differentiate shades of meanings, but they are not necessarily prevalent. In the tracts dealing with lay atonements, *aticāra*s are violations for which a compensation is required if they are committed.

Another term, which seems to be less frequent, is *vrata-mālinya*, “dirtying the vow”. It is used, for example, in Kīrtivijayagaṇi’s *Hīrapraśna* (seventeenth century) about the *deśāvakāśikavrata*, the second of the four *śikṣāvratas*:

> With regard to this vow somebody has kept it for an area of 100 yojanas. Is there “dirtying of the vow” in case a letter is sent to a distance superior to that, when a matter has arisen, or not? This is the question. The answer is: It should be known that there *is* dirtying of the vow if a letter is sent to an area which is superior to the one that has been fixed, because the same has been said in the *Yogaśāstra* commentary and other sources.[11]

Comparing this passage with Hemacandra’s work, the impression is that *vrata-mālinya* is an euphemistic designation for *vrata-bhaṅga*, rather than a designation for a less serious violation of conduct. This is supported by Hemacandra’s commentary where *mālinya* is a gloss for *aticāra*.[12]

§ 5. Specific treatises devoted to lay atonements are not many and they form an area that has not been much explored so far. Their language is Prakrit or Sanskrit.

Prakrit verse tracts

§ 5.1. Cataloguing work of the British Library Jain manuscripts brought to light one manuscript containing a short tract on this topic. This tract is the *Sāvayapacchitta* (= SPAn), as it is named in the London manuscript, which is now accessible in digital form on the JAINpedia website (Figure 7.1; see below References). To the best of my knowledge, the only other manuscript to have this text is one Bhandarkar Oriental Research Institute manuscript which was used by Leumann for the unpublished transcription he provided. This is Notebook No. 128, which is part of the “Nachlass” kept at the Indian and Tibetan

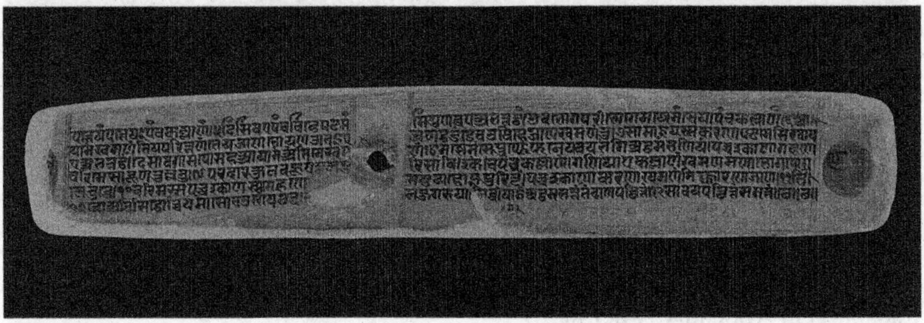

Figure 7.1 Folio 9v of the British Library palm-leaf manuscript Or. 1385 showing the anonymous *Sāvayapacchitta*, here labelled SPAn. © The British Library. All rights reserved.

Figure 7.2 Ernst Leumann's transcription of the Pune manuscript of the anonymous *Sāvayapacchitta*, here labelled SPAn. Notebook 128 in Leumann's Nachlass.

Studies Institute in Hamburg (Figure 7.2a–b). This text is critically edited and translated in Appendix A below.

Both manuscripts are palm leaf. It is significant that in both cases the tract is not a text copied independently. It is appended at the end of the *Jītakalpa* and forms the second text. The Pune manuscript has 16 verses, the London

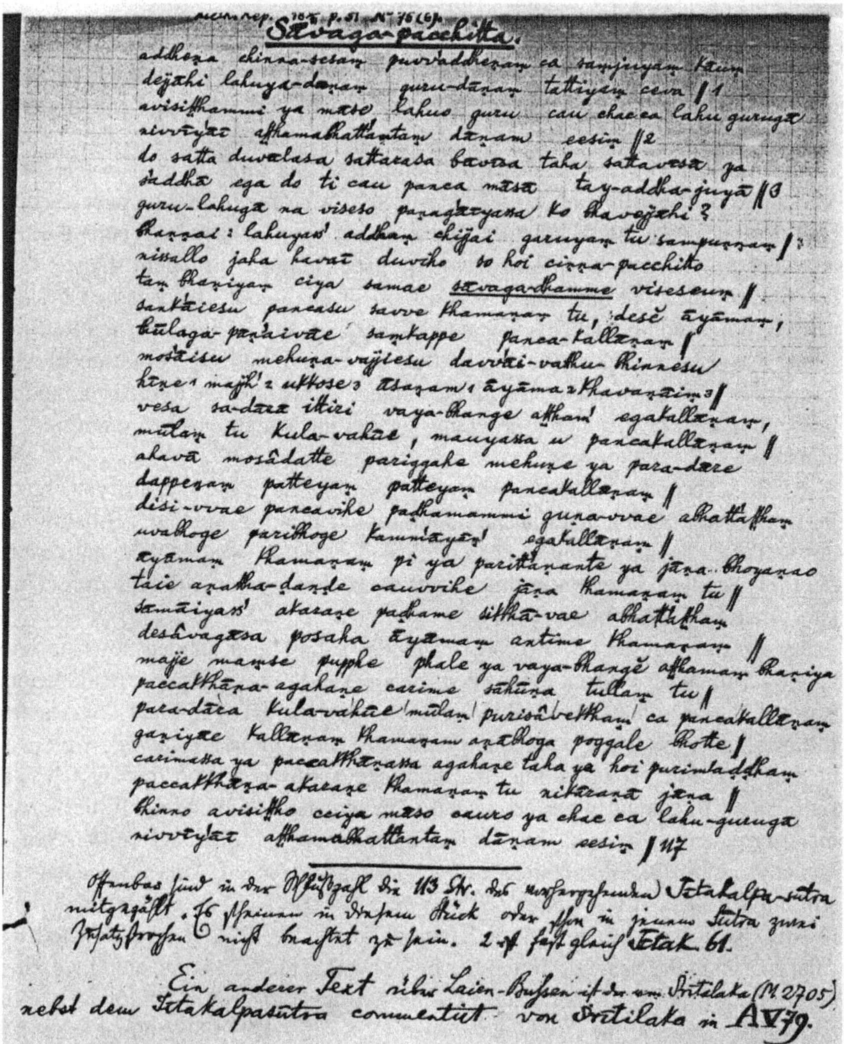

Leum. Rep. 18[illegible] p. 51 N° 76(6).

Sāvaga-pacchitta.

addhesa chinna-sesaṃ puvvaddheṇaṃ ca saṃjuyaṃ kāuṃ
dejjāhi lahuya-dāṇaṃ guru-dāṇaṃ tattiyaṃ ceva || 1
avisiṭṭhammi ya māse lahuo guru cau chacca lahu guruga
nivvīyāī aṭṭhamabhattantaṃ dāṇam eesiṃ || 2
do satta duvālasa sattarasa bāvīsa taha sattavīsā ya
saddhā ega do ti cau panca māsā tay-addha-juyā || 3
guru-lahugā na viseso pāṇagāiyāsu ko bhavejjāhi ?
bhaṇṇai : lahuyāo addhaṃ chijjai guruyaṃ tu saṃpuṇṇaṃ | 4
nissallo jaha hoi duviho so hoi ciṇṇa-pacchitto
taṃ bhaṇiyaṃ ciya samae sāvaga-dhamme visesenaṃ |
saṃkāiesu pancasu savve khamaṇaṃ tu, desē āyāmaṃ,
kulaga-pāsaiyāe saṃkappe panca-kallāṇaṃ |
mosāisu mehuṇa-vajjesu davvāi-vatthu-bhinnesu
hīṇe1 majjh'2 ukkose3 āsaṇam1 āyāma2 khavaṇāiṃ3 |
vesa sadāra ittiri vaya-bhange aṭṭhamaṃ egakallāṇaṃ,
mūlaṃ tu kula-vahūe, mannyassa u pancakallāṇaṃ |
ahavā mosādatte pariggahe mehuṇe ya para-dāre
dappeṇaṃ patteyaṃ patteyaṃ pancakallāṇaṃ |
disi-vvae pancavihe paḍhamammi guṇa-vvae abhattaṭṭhaṃ
uvabhoge paribhoge kammāyāṃ egakallāṇaṃ |
āyāmaṃ khamaṇaṃ pi ya pariṭṭhaṇante ya jāṇa bhoyaṇao
taie aṇattha-daṇḍe cauvvihe jāṇa khamaṇaṃ tu ||
sāmāiyassa akaraṇe paḍhame sikkhā-vae abhattaṭṭhaṃ
desāvagāsa posaha āyāmaṃ antime khamaṇaṃ ||
majje maṃse pupphe phale ya vaya-bhange aṭṭhamaṃ bhaṇiya
paccakkhāṇa-agahaṇe carime sahuṇa tullaṃ tu |
para-dāra kula-vahūe mūlaṃ purisābbhatthaṃ ca pancakallāṇaṃ
gaṇiyāe kallāṇaṃ khamaṇam aṇābhoga poggale bhotte |
carimassa ya paccakkhāṇassa agahaṇe taha ya hoi purimaḍḍhaṃ
paccakkhāṇa-akaraṇe khamaṇaṃ tu nikkāraṇā jāṇa |
bhinno avisiṭṭho cciya māso caüro ya chac ca lahu-guruga
nivvīyāī aṭṭhamabhattantaṃ dāṇam eesiṃ | 117

Offenbar sind in der Handschrift die 113 Str. des vorhergehenden Jītakalpa-sutra mitgezählt. Es [illegible] in diesem Stück oder aber in jenem Sutra zwei [illegible] nicht [illegible]. 2 ist fast gleich Jītak. 61.

Ein anderer Text über Laien-Bußen ist der von Śrītilaka (M. 2705) nebst dem Jītakalpasutra commentiert von Śrītilaka in A V 79.

Figure 7.2 Continued

manuscript 12. The Pune manuscript starts with four stanzas which are not in the London document. But all the remaining verses are common. Thus, although the two texts are not fully identical, they surely represent the same work. Leumann was attracted by the *Sāvayapacchitta* precisely in the course of his work on the *Jītakalpa*. A footnote in this contribution remarks:

> Ein Sâvaga-pacchitta in bloss 16 Pkt-Âryâs folgt in unserm MS. dem Jîtakalpa als eine Art Appendix (1892: 1195 n. 1).[13]

The *Sāvayapacchitta* is anonymous. It is impossible to know when it was composed. The fact that it is preserved at the end of two palm-leaf manuscripts which contain the sūtra but also the cūrṇi of the *Jītakalpa* shows that it was considered as a component of the full corpus on the topic at least in the early Middle Ages (twelfth century) when palm leaf was in use, and perhaps earlier. On the other hand, the fact that the text does not seem to have been copied often and does not seem to be known from any paper manuscript would suggest that its tradition died out and that it was a kind of dead end. The versified Prakrit tract is not accompanied by any commentary in any of the two manuscripts where it is preserved. Its style is extremely concise, to the verge of obscurity, for a reader who is not acquainted with the subject and is not able to read behind the lines. It is clearly meant for providing an outline which can be committed to memory.

§ **5.2.** A second work is the *Sāvayapacchitta* (= SPT) by Tilakācārya (Figure 7.3). A critical edition and translation are provided in the Appendix B below, as this text does not seem to have been published so far. In some of the manuscripts the title *Sāmāyārī* is given to this tract, which, however, is different from Tilaka's prose *Sāmācārī* (below § 5.5).

Its transmission has been more sustained. It has been handed down in one palm-leaf manuscript from Patan (P, used here) and in several paper manuscripts (three being used here: A, B, C; see below Appendix B). The Prakrit verses are followed by a Sanskrit commentary also by the author (*svopajña*), which is helpful. It is interesting to note that, here again, this is a short tract which is a supplement to a main work connected with monastic atonements. In the Patan manuscript and in ms. A, this *Sāvayapacchitta* comes after the Sanskrit commentary on the *Jītakalpa* composed by Tilakācārya himself. This commentary is still unpublished. It was composed in V.S. 1274 (= CE 1217), as the concluding *praśasti* indicates (our ms. A or Kielhorn 1881: No. 79). It is also listed by Tilakācārya in the *praśasti* of another of his works, the *Sāmācārī*, along with his other compositions, a commentary on the *Daśavaikālika* (V.S. CE 1304 = 1247), and another one on the *Āvaśyakaniryukti* (V.S. CE 1286 = 1229; unpublished).[14]

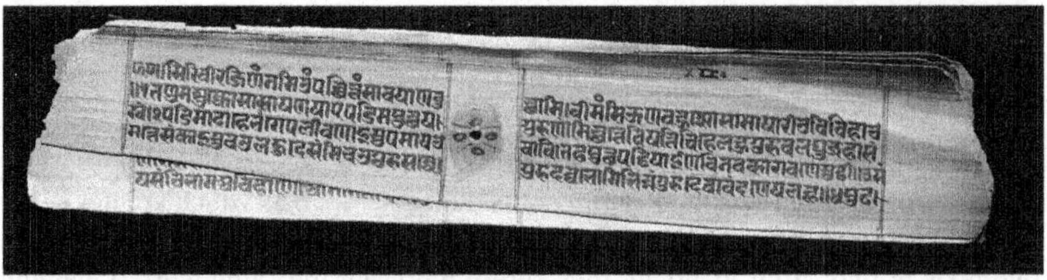

Figure 7.3 Folio 150r of the Patan palm-leaf manuscript F 18 showing the beginning of Tilakācārya's *Sāvayapacchitta*, here labelled SPT.

The *praśasti* of the *Sāmācārī* refers to the composition of the JK commentary as already achieved. Thus the *Sāmācārī* was written after V.S. 1274.

Tilakācārya's spiritual affiliation is detailed in the *praśasti* of his works in identical terms:

Candraprabhasūri (Dundas 2011: 191–192)
Dharmaghoṣasūri
Cakreśvarasūri
Śivaprabha
Tilaka (*tadīya-śiṣya-leśo 'haṃ sūriḥ śrīTilakābhidhaḥ*) = Tilakaprabha or Tilakācārya

In our *Sāvayapacchitta* only the names Cakkasūri and Sivapahasūri occur (verse 20). The name of the *gaccha* is not given explicitly, only the affiliation to the Candraprabhasūri-vaṃśa appears, but these teachers belong to the Pūrṇimāgaccha (Tripuṭī 1960: 500).

The transmission of the SPT is stable enough. The nucleus common to all the consulted manuscripts is made of 20 *āryā*s. Alone among them, ms. A has three more verses: two between v. 4 and 5, and one after v. 7. They can be regarded as amplifications, partly summarizing what has been said earlier, partly adding specifications, influenced by other works on the same topic (see notes *ad locum*). Moreover, SPT also has a set of stanzas (*gāthā*) relating to transgressions of the *poṣadha*, which is attested by mss. P and A. In P they are treated as an independent tract located after the SPT: first come ten stanzas, numbered from 1 to 10, then their Sanskrit commentary. In A, they number 13, are located after the commentary on 18 and numbered continuously (23–35). Hence in this manuscript, the SPT has a total of 36 continuously numbered stanzas.

§ 5.3. Slightly better known, although hardly used, is Dharmaghoṣa's *Saḍḍhajīyakappa*, which has been published in India (1960)[15] and is available through manuscripts found in various libraries, in India and outside. It is also written in Prakrit, but is much longer than the two SPs, having 142 stanzas. Dharmaghoṣa, pupil of Devendrasūri, was a well-known leader of the Tapāgaccha who was active between the second half of the thirteenth century and the beginning of the fourteenth century CE. The composition of this work probably took place between 1271 and 1300.[16] In the West, only brief remarks have been made about it:

> Das entspräche den Ausführungen im Saḍḍhajīyakappa (141 G.) des Dharmaghoṣa (13 Jh.), einem späten Seitenstück zu dem oben erwähnten Jīyakappa.
>
> (Schubring 1935 § 164; see also Williams 1963: 13)

The SJK was the starting point of various commentaries for which precise chronological indications are lacking. The printed one (apparently not by Dharmaghoṣa himself) is rather extensive and often quotes earlier works. It could have been written after V.S. 1456 (= CE 1399) which is the date of a commentary on Somaprabhasūri's *Yatijītakalpa* quoted by the SJK commentator (Introduction: 8). The commentary available in the British Library manuscript (Or. 2105 G) consists of selective notes. The commentator of the printed commentary might have known and consulted Tilaka's SPT. Although he never mentions his name, he quotes Prakrit stanzas which correspond to what Tilaka writes.

Apart from explaining the Prakrit verses, the commentary on Dharmaghoṣa's work has an interesting characteristic. The commentator often refers to divergent opinions and variants of the atonements prescribed in the verses themselves, introduced by the standard phrases *anye tu*, *kecit*, *matāntareṇa*, etc. (e.g. on SJK 63, 88, etc.). He does not, however, discuss them or decide. They are only recorded as such. Such a tendency is, indeed, in tune with the concept of *jīta*, i.e. custom as the basis for atonements. Since custom, as it is understood in such contexts, takes into account parameters of change such as time, place, social factors, etc., it underlines more the aspect of evolution than that of permanence, especially when compared to other terms such as *āgama*, and *sua*. It leads, however, to a curious impression: how to reconcile an apparently seemingly extremely precise or even minute account and conflicting opinions? How is such a work to be used in practice? What is the rule to be followed?

Commentaries on the Prakrit verse tracts and Tilakācārya's Sāmācārī

§ 5.4. A commentary on SPAn could have been a useful tool, but none could be traced so far.

The commentary on SPT, in Sanskrit, is an auto-commentary by Tilakācārya as stated right away:

> *prāyaścittaṃ sva-gāthôktaṃ vyākhyāmi sukha-buddhaye*
>
> I explain the atonements stated in my own verses for understanding and happiness

The largest part of it is identical in all the manuscripts. The palm-leaf manuscript P and the paper manuscript C written by a modern hand share common peculiarities or mistakes suggesting their filiation. The paper manuscript A, on the other hand, has some differences: in its version of the commentary on SPT 1 the initial dialogue between the culprit and the teacher (see below § 9) is missing. In manuscript B more details on the possible lapses are found in the form of sentences in mixed Sanskrit and Gujarati in the commentary of SPT 2, 4, 6 and 7. They betray the influence of vernacular *Pākṣika Aticāra* manuals (see below § 18).

§ 5.5. Tilakācārya was a kind of specialist of atonements. To his commentary on the *Jītakalpasūtra* and to the SPT (verses and commentary), should be added section 16 of his *Sāmācārī* (pp. 19b–21a; = ST). The work in general deals with monastic conduct, but this section deals with lay atonements. It is written in Sanskrit prose but the initial sentences are in Gujarati. The presence of Gujarati phrases at the beginning of both SPT commentary and of ST suggests that they go back to the author's time (end of twelfth–beginning of thirteenth century), and do not form later interpolations born in the manuscript tradition. They thus illustrate how Sanskrit and the vernacular language started coexisting especially in liturgical contexts or performances. The sequence, contents and wording of this *Sāmācārī* section are very close to the SPT commentary, so that reading it is like reading the SPT commentary without the verse text. The *Sāmācārī* section confirms two observations presented above: (1) the additional stanzas of ms. A have no corresponding contents in the *Sāmācārī* and thus can be described as interpolations; (2) in the *Sāmācārī* the atonements for *poṣadha* come after the atonements for violations of *pratyākhyāna* (p. 20b), the last topic of SPT, showing that the *poṣadha* stanzas which are treated as an independent tract following the SPT in the palm-leaf ms. P, are part of the exposition of lay atonements.

Sanskrit tracts

§ 5.6. In Vardhamānasūri's *Ācāradinakara* (ĀD), said to have been written in the fifteenth century and often quoted because it gives detailed information on *pūjā* and Jain deities (see, for instance, Williams 1963: 15), there is a long section on atonements (*prāyaścitta-vidhi*, pp. 250b–272). It is made of successive sets of verses in Sanskrit, and contains numerous quotations, some of which are in Prakrit. The atonement section of the work is a kind of cumulative collection of tracts on the topic. The last sub-section dealing with transgressions, like contacts with *caṇḍāla*s, for which prescribed atonements consist in baths (*snāna*, p. 270a), is in tune with the author's general tendency to go to the borders of Hindu practices, but takes us outside the world of Jain lay atonements and is out of scope here.

After a discussion of the qualities required from the religious teacher (p. 251b), of the necessity and conditions of confession (*ālocanā*, p. 252a) both for monastic and lay atonements (p. 252b), the following topics are considered in sets of verses of various sizes: transgressions where the atonement is confession (*ālocanārham*), repentance (*pratikramaṇārham*), restitution (*vivekārham*), rejection of the body (*kāyotsargārham*), fasting (*taporham*, p. 254b and following). As expected, this sub-section is longer. The technical names (*saṃjñā*) of fasts are the subject of several stanzas which list a variety of synonyms for each of the basic terms (on which see below § 11). It includes a set of equivalences between fasts and other modes of compensations, such as recitations of the *namaskāramantra* (pp. 254b–255b). Then comes a group of 95 Sanskrit verses (pp. 254b–258b) spelling out transgressions in the field of knowledge (*jñānāticāra*), conduct (*cāritrāticāra*), penance (*tapaḥ*) and energy (*vīrya*). They concern the mendicant, and are placed under the sign of the *jītakalpa* (p. 257b verse 68), a recurring characteristic of this part of the ĀD. The next subsection (pp. 258b–259a) also deals with monastic atonements, relating successively to partial reduction of seniority (*cheda*), total reduction amounting to reinitiation (*mūla*), demotion (*anāvṛtta*; usual Prakrit term *aṇavaṭṭhappa*), exclusion (*pārāñcika*). Again the *jītakalpa* is mentioned as the source in conclusion. Then comes a new set of 32 Sanskrit verses dealing with lay atonements, also ending with a similar reference:

> *saṃkṣepāt kathitaḥ pūrvo jītakalpo 'nagāriṇām*
> *atha saṃśrāvakāṇāṃ tu kathyate tapasaiva hi* (p. 259b)
> *iti prāyaścittādhikāre Śrāvakajītakalpaḥ saṃpūrṇaḥ* (p. 260b).

As much as to the text corpus, *jītakalpa* here refers to the customized procedures it contains.

The next set of verses (146; up to p. 265a) again turns to the mendicant, starting with *atha laghu-jītakalpa-vidhinā yati-prāyaścittam* and ending with *iti laghu-jītakalpa-vidhinā yati-prāyaścittaṃ sampūrṇam* (p. 265a).

Yet another group of 92 verses is introduced as *atha vyavahāra-jītakalpa-krameṇa yati-śrāvaka-prāyaścitta-vidhiḥ* (pp. 265a–268a) and, differently from the other subsections, is not anonymous. It ends:

> *jānann api hi sarvaṃ yo vrataṃ darpān nikṛntati* (89cd)
> *tasyeva śuddhaye proktāḥ pratyekaṃ dvādaśāntimāḥ*
> *prāyaścitta-vidhiś cāyaṃ śrāddhānām upadarśitaḥ* (90)
> *yati-śrāvaka-vargasya prāyaścittaṃ viśuddhi-dam*
> *Vyavahāra-Jītakalpaṃ yathā-śodhi padād api* (91)
> *paṭo 'yaṃ likhito vīkṣya śiṣyaiḥ sva-para-hetave*
> *śrīYaśobhadrasūrīṇāṃ śrīPṛthvīcandrasūribhiḥ* (92)
>
> It is precisely for the purification of the one who, although he knows, breaks all the vows out of arrogance, that (these atonements) have been stated one by one up to the twelfth vow. And this is the procedure of atonements prescribed for laypeople. Atonements for mendicants and laypeople bestow purification This tract (? *paṭa*) has been written by Pṛthvīcandrasūri, pupil of Yaśobhadrasūri, for the benefit of himself and others, after having examined the *Vyavahāra-Jītakalpa* which has been corrected accordingly word after word.

The conjunction in the same *praśasti* of Pṛthvīcandrasūri and Yaśobhadrasūri supports the identification of the former as the author of a *Kalpasūtraṭippaṇa* (edited in Puṇyavijaya 1952: 1–23). Both belong to the Dharmaghoṣagaccha of the Rājagaccha. Pṛthivīcandrasūri's direct predecessor was Devasenagaṇi who is known to have restored the Neminātha temple at Girnar in V.S. 1215 (CE 1168). His successor was Jayacandrasūri who is responsible for a *pratiṣṭhā* in V.S. 1343 (CE 1286). He would thus have been active in the thirteenth century. His tract on atonements has not been traced independently. It seems to belong to those texts which survived only because they were quoted. It is possible that this tract is a counterpart to Pṛthvīcandra's *Yatiśikṣāpañcāśikā* (Velankar 1944: 317) but this cannot be proved until this work can be consulted.

Finally the ĀD continues with a "miscellany" subsection on atonements (*prakīrṇaka-prāyaścitta*, pp. 268a–269a, 31 verses), where, in particular, the symmetry between atonements of male and female mendicants and of laymen and laywomen is emphasized (v. 26) and where the titles of treatises on the topic are listed (*Mahāniśītha*, *Niśītha*, *Jītakalpa-dvayam*, v. 27).

Like the SJK, the ĀD section occasionally states divergent opinions on atonements (e.g. p. 265b verse 6 *kecid atra*; verse 14 *kecid āhuḥ*; p. 268a verse 84 *matāntare*).

§ 5.7. The *Śrāvakaprāyaścitta* promulgated by Āc. Tulsi of the Terāpanthin in 1944 is an illuminating example of how lay atonements are treated in the twentieth century.[17] There are several features conforming to the traditional pattern. First, it comes after a section on monastic atonements, both together forming a *Prāyaścitta vidhi*. The lay section is much briefer (20 paragraphs) than the monastic counterpart. The language is Rajasthani, and more marked as such than in the part devoted to monastic atonements. The vocabulary is a combination of Prakrit or Sanskrit terms with vernacular technical terms. It is in prose, but in the way it favours elliptic juxtaposition rather than full sentences it amounts to notes recalling the Bhāṣya style. In its presentation and its attempt to cover a wide range of transgressions, this tract continues the tradition of the *Chedasūtra-bhāṣya*s. For instance:

> If a householder pulls out a thorn (out of his clothes) during one *sāmāyik*, then (s/he should) recite fifteen *Navkār*. If this occurs in two (consecutive) *sāmāyik*s, then forty. In this way twenty-five *Navkār* are added for each thorn in every further *sāmāyik*.
>
> (No. 1; Flügel's translation, forthcoming)

The pattern followed is that of one to one: trangression A/atonement A, transgression B/atonement B, etc. In the hierarchy of atonements, fasts are meant for the most serious ones, recitations of the Namaskāra mantra or of Sāmāyika, in varying numbers, are another type of compensation considered.

Beside this document, there is another current list of nine lay atonements which was codified in 1989. It is a simplified version with nine headings (quoted in Flügel forthcoming, n. 116):

1	*sāmāyik meṃ kāṇṭā nikle* if a thorn is pulled out during *sāmāyik*	*25 navkār*
2	*varṣā kī būnde lag jāe* if rain drops fall	*1 navkārvālī*
3	*sāmāyik kam pār le baiṭhā rahe* if one has reduced the time of sitting for *sāmāyik*	*2 yā 3 navkārvālī*
4	*sāmāyik bhang ho jāe* if *sāmāyik* is interrupted	*1 sāmāyik*

5	*pauṣadh cau praharī* (transgressing rules) in a 12-hour *pauṣadh*	*2 (3) sāmāyik*
6	*pauṣadh cha praharī* (transgressing rules) in an 18-hour *pauṣadh*	*4 sāmāyik*
7	*pauṣadh aṣṭa praharī* (transgressing rules) in a 24-hour *pauṣadh*	*5 sāmāyik*
8	*pauṣadh meṃ pānī pī le* if one drinks water during *pauṣadh*	*1 belā* One continuous fast of two days
9	*tyāg meṃ rātri bhojan ādi kar le* if one practices eating at night, etc. while having renounced (it)	*1 upavās yā 1 mās miṭhāī choṛnā* One day fast or giving up sweets for one month

The existence of two versions, one more detailed, another simplified, shows how technical manuals or directions are meant for mendicant specialists but, how, to some extent, they need to be adjusted for actual practice (see below § 20).

§ 5.8. Among the Digambaras, the *Prāyaścittagrantha* ascribed to "Akalanka" (not the well-known philosopher) is addressed to the Jain laity (*prāyaścittaṃ pravakṣyāmi śrāvakāṇāṃ viśuddhaye* 1cd). It quotes various Digambara sources such as the *Jñānārṇava,* but is a curious text. It is obviously influenced by Hindu practices, when it says, for instance, that the gift of one cow or more is an atonement for a transgression. These Digambara texts require a study of their own.

§ 6. SPAn and SPT follow the trend illustrated in the *Jītakalpa* corpus. The fact that the *Jītakalpa* provides the pattern and is the implicit reference of the SPAn is clear from the arrangement of the manuscripts, where this short work follows the longer one as a supplement. The same holds true for the SPT which follows Tilaka's *Jītakalpa* commentary in ms. A. In the Patan palm-leaf manuscript, the *Jītakalpasūtra* comes after the SPT.

This reference is also transparent in the title of Dharmaghoṣa's work, the *Saḍḍhajīyakappa.* The colophons of the SPT manuscripts also have *jītakalpa* in their titles. Initial homage to the Teaching in the first verse is nothing extraordinary, but it is certainly not by chance that SPAn, SPT and SJK all use the compound *kaya-pavayaṇa-ppaṇāmo* as their first word, exactly like the JKS. Although Dharmaghoṣa's purpose is to deal with lay atonements, the scope of his work is wider. In the first part (1–54), he deals at length with "confession", which is the necessary preliminary to the prescription of any atonement, whether to a mendicant or a layman, and with the conditions required for an adequate procedure. But when he comes to the contents of what should be confessed, the terms used refer only to transgressions relating to the mendicant's life (*mūla-guṇas* and *uttara-guṇas*). And it becomes obvious that trying to separate the layman and the mendicant with regard to this topic is untenable and artificial. This is the reason adduced by the commentator to justify his account of faults relating to the mendicant's search for alms: both parties are concerned.[18] It is the second part of Dharmaghoṣa's work (55ff.), which can be closely compared with the SPs as it deals strictly with the details of lay atonements, following the same order of exposition in often very close terms.

§ 7. SPAn 5 expresses in its own way the common idea that atonements are meant to extract thorns, and implies that atonements are not useless even if one is without thorn. It claims that the topic has been addressed specifically for what concerns the layman:

> A person without thorn is twofold, one of them being the person who has performed atonements. This is precisely what has been said in the doctrine, with specification to the layman's code of conduct.

The commentary on the *Saḍḍhajīyakappa* quotes a verse from the *Jītakalpa* where the two possible "popular" etymologies of Pkt. *pacchitta* underline the value of atonement for those who are guilty, and for others too:

> Because it cuts off the evil it is called *pāyacchitta*. Or, because, generally speaking, it purifies the mind, therefore it is called *pacchitta*.[19]

The pattern and method of exposition followed in the *Sāvayapacchitta*s and in the *Saḍḍhajīyakappa* are highly indebted to those found in exegetical literature. The style of their verses reminds of that of *niryukti* and *bhāṣya* verses by its brevity and the prevalence of nominal sentences. The verses are meant to be learnt by heart by somebody who is familiar with the topic and would be able to understand what hides behind the words.

§ 8. The exposition of the transgressions and of their corresponding atonements follows a similar path in all the texts of the SP corpus. In the Prakrit verse SPs they are stated rather abruptly, as the style imitates the *bhāṣya* style on the Chedasūtras. The underlying structure is explicit in the transitional sentences found in the commentary on SPT. Their headings define five fundamentals of Jain lay life as:

I Behaviour relating to right knowledge (*jñānācāra*) and transgressions amounting to wrong knowledge. They relate to misuse of or offences to the objects relating to knowledge (manuscripts, images, etc.) or manipulations and inappropriate recitations or readings of texts.

II Behaviour relating to right faith (*darśanācāra*) and transgressions amounting to wrong faith.

III Conduct (*cāritra*), namely the 12 minor vows (*aṇuvrata*) of lay Jains. Transgressions and atonements relating to each of them in turn are described:

- five *aṇuvrata*s: (1) *ahiṃsā* – (2) *satya* – (3) *asteya* – (4) *brahma* – (5) *aparigraha*
- three *guṇavrata*s: (1) *dig* – (2) *bhogopabhoga* in its two aspects, namely food and professions – (3) *anarthadaṇḍa*

- four *śikṣāvratas*: (1) *sāmāyika* – (2) *deśāvakāśika* – (3) *poṣadhopavāsa* – (4) *atithisaṃvibhāga.*

IV *Tapas* deals with atonements for lapses in the practice of penances.
V Energy (*vīrya*) deals with atonements for lapses in the practice of *pratyākhyāna.*

The various types of dietary restrictions combined with various possible durations (see below § 11.3) are applied to all these areas of lay life. The course of exposition is exactly the same in the Sanskrit tract of lay atonements in 32 verses preserved in ĀD (pp. 259b–260b) and in the second one in 92 verses (pp. 265a–268a). The contents of the situations considered and the atonements prescribed are similar to SPT, and could be compared in all details. Ultimately, the model is the one delineated in JKS 15 *daṃsaṇa-nāṇa-caraṇāvarāhesu* for the mendicant.

§ 9. Tilaka's commentary on SPT as handed down in all manuscripts except A and B underlines at the start that atonements take place in an interactive process and involve a ceremonial. It implies the presence of two persons, the layman and the teacher who is the only one qualified to prescribe the atonements. This part of the commentary emphasizes an important point: atonements depend on the teacher, in accordance with his monastic pratice (*guruḥ sāmācāry-anusāreṇa prāyaścittaṃ dadāti*). It begins with a preliminary codified Prakrit dialogue and the ritual of confession (*ālocanā*) which is a necessary prerequisite:[20]

> In accordance with the proper moment, an atonement is accepted in the presence of a teacher who is provided with distinguished knowledge, faith and conduct. Then, first of all, the candidate to confession, on the day of purification, when the moon is strong (*candra-vala* = °*bala*), says after a *kṣamāśramaṇa-sūtra*:[21] "Kindly give us purification". – "We give it", says the teacher. Having said "I wish, forbearing monk, kindly allow us to pay homage to the temples in order to give purification". – "We allow you with the hand of the forbearing monks, the great teachers Goyama etc.". Having said "I wish, forbearing monk, venerable Lord, kindly give the permission voluntarily. Shall I pay homage to the temples?". – "Do it", the teacher says. Having said "I wish", after having uttered the homage formula to the Jina Mahāvīra, after having recited the praise in honour of Śakra, having said "forbearing monks" to the teachers, to the preceptors and to all the mendicants, he recites "of two and a half islands and oceans", etc. Then after having said "forbearing monks", following the teacher's instructions, he inspects the mouth-cloth, performs the full ritual of homage and says: "Kindly give the permission voluntarily, shall I be instructed in purity?". – "Get instructed", says the teacher. Having said "I wish", forbearing monk, kindly give the permission voluntarily, shall I get purity?". – "Get it", the teacher says. Having said "I wish, forbearing monk, kindly give the permission voluntarily, shall I be instructed to take the seat?"[22] – "Get instructed", the teacher says. – "I wish, forbearing monk, kindly give the permission voluntarily,

> Lord, shall I be standing on the seat?" – "Be", the teacher says. Squatting, or sitting, he remembers or confesses whatever transgressions he has committed in whatever ways. And having considered them the teacher gives an atonement according to practice. The atonement would relate to transgressions in matter of the five areas of conduct: knowledge, practice, etc.[23]

Such is the method used here to emphasize straight away that the well-known centrality of confession in the context of atonements applies to the layman as well: the topic cannot be avoided but does not enter the tract itself, differently from what happens in Dharmaghoṣa's SJK (above § 6). This centrality easily explains how SP manuscripts can come to be supplemented by additional tracts dealing more specifically with *ālocanā*. Our ms. B illustrates this process of expansion through connected tracts (below Appendix B). As already demonstrated by Leumann, Jain liturgy represented in the large body of Āvaśyaka literature needs to be approached not as fixed and closed texts, but rather as made of units which can be assembled in different ways. In the case of lay atonements, there are at least three textual units: the transgressions and compensations themselves, the *pauṣadhika* stanzas and the confession.

§ 10. Like the monastic treatises, SPAn and SPT make use of special categories and terms. Meant for specialists in atonements who are experts in manipulating them, and deliberately brief, they are taken for granted and not defined. Dharmaghoṣa's SJK is more systematic in this respect.

The discussion of lay atonements makes use of the same categories of understanding as those used in the *Chedasūtra*s. There are series of set factors which regulate the seriousness of the transgression as they enable to "appreciate exactly the responsibility of the offender" (Caillat 1975: 108) and the ensuing scale of atonements. They are expressed by recurring terms. These factors define the motivation or the origin of the transgression (see JKS 64 *paḍisevaṇāo* and 74). A list of ten terms is given in Dharmaghoṣa's SJK 41 and defined in the commentary. They are adverbial ablatives or instrumentals, meaning "out of", "because of". Among them those used in SPAn and SPT are:

sahasā: action done without thought, done suddenly, rashly (SPT 6)
aṇābhogao: involuntarily, unknowingly or out of forgetfulness (SPT 6; SPAn 14 *–e*), cf. *sahasā 'ṇābhogeṇa va*, JKS 11, 44, etc. opposed to *ābhogeṇa* or *ābhogao*.
pamāyā: out of carelessness (SPT 17)
dappā: out of "presumption" (Caillat 1975: 109) or arrogance (SPT 7; SPAn *dappeṇaṃ*), cf. *dappeṇaṃ*, JKS 57.
saṃkappā: intentionally (SPT 7; SPAn 6 *saṃkappe*).

An additional term occurring in JKS 74 and briefly explained in JKBh 2265 is *āuṭṭiyāe* "in full consciousness", which determines an extremely serious transgression. It is not used in the verses of the SPs, but once in SPT commentary (on 15, under its Sanskritized form *ākuṭṭikayā*, with reference to meat eating; see also SJK 117). In the ĀD (p. 258a verse 76), the Sanskrit form corresponding to this term is *āvṛtti*, which, along with carelessness (*pramāda*), arrogance (*darpa*) and exercice of the Rule (*kalpa*; or "intention" = *saṃkalpa*) form the four sources of transgression.

To this can be added the adverb *akāraṇe* (or *akāraṇa*) "in the absence of a (valid) cause", which is used to qualify the non-observance of a rule of conduct. Valid causes are all the special situations where somebody is authorized not to observe a rule, such as cases of illness, external situations of emergency, etc. If there is no such cause, the non-observance becomes a transgression, eligible for atonements.

The opposite pair *ṇāe/aṇāe*, "when known" versus "when unknown" is another category (SPT 11, 12). According to the commentary on Dharmaghoṣa's SJK 83, this does not refer to the agent of the transgression. It refers to the existence or non-existence of public knowledge about the transgression: *ajñāte – lokāprasiddhe* versus *jñāte – loka-prasiddhe*. Thus the parameter is whether there is a risk of scandal going beyond the culprit himself and spoiling the reputation of the Jain society as a whole. This concern, which is cental to the Chedasūtras (Jyväsjärvi 2010: 137; Granoff forthcoming) is expressed in particular in the case of adultery, where, moreover, the social status of the lady is an element which is taken into account (below § 15).

The violation of the vow can be total (*savva*) or partial (*desa*); SPAn 6 (cf. JKS 27).

Degrees of intensity in seriousness are expressed through the well-known adjectives *jahanna* (or *taṇu*, SPT 2) "inferior", *majjha* "medium", *ukkosa* "maximum" (SPT 2, 8).

§ 11. The SP Prakrit verse corpus (SPAn, SPT and SJK) is marked by the coinage of a codified terminology relating to the atonements prescribed for transgressions. These technical terms are occasionally called *saṃjñā* in commentaries. Lists summarizing them are found at the beginning (SPAn), or, more unexpectedly, at the end of the texts. This is the case in Dharmaghoṣa's SJK (137ff.). Such a list is available in ms. A of SPT, but not in the other ones. Applied to the layman's atonements, these terms are borrowed from the texts dealing with monastic atonements as they appear in the exegetical tradition on the *Vyavahāra*-, the *Bṛhatkalpa*- and the *Niśītha-sūtras*, as well as in Jinabhadra's *Jītakalpa*, their most direct reference. The criterion of "seniority", valid in the hierarchy of the mendicant's community, having no relevance for laypeople, fasts and dietary restrictions are the main form of compensation. They form a sophisticated system where fasts are combined with durations, following the one elaborated in the *Bhāṣya*s. This system has come to replace other types of atonements which are said to have been lost in the transmission and became either unknown or obsolete. The development of this system has produced new terms not found in the *sūtra*s themselves.

§ 11.1. For the duration scale, the pattern is JKBh 1802–1803 on JKS 61.[24] The minimal duration is five days, the maximal is six months. The lowest durations, namely 5, 10, 15 and 20 days are not used in the SP corpus, where the first level is the *bhinna-māsa*: divided or incomplete month, equivalent to 25 days.

Whereas the notion of *bhinna-māsa* is not subject to qualification (Pkt. *a-visiṭṭha*), from *māsa* onwards each duration is subjected to a further division into *lahu* "light" and *guru* "heavy". The full list is thus:

bhinna-māsa: incomplete month
lahu-māsa: one light month
guru-māsa: one heavy month
cau-lahumāsa: four light months
cau-gurumāsa: four heavy months
cha-lahumāsa: six light months
cha-gurumāsa: six heavy months (compare in Sanskrit, ĀD p. 257b, verses 68–72: *Jītakalpānusārataḥ*).

All these terms are normally abbreviated as *bhinna, lahu* (or *la°*), *guru, cau-lahu, cau-guru, cha-lahu, cha-guru.* In treatises dealing with lay life, the last category (*cha°*) is in use only for the most serious offences, that which relate to the first and the fourth *aṇuvrata*s (ex. below § 14; SPT 10). Further, there are the additional terms *lahuga* and *guruga* which are not always mere synonyms of *lahu* and *guru*: *lahuga* may mean four light, and *guruga* four heavy (e.g. SPT 13 notes below Appendix B; commentary on SJK 59; SJK 71ab and commentary). A further division, not attested in the SPs, is between "unreduced" (*anudghātika*) and "reduced" (*ghātika*) penance, respectively considered as equivalents for "heavy" and "light" (e.g. SJK 62 and commentary).

§ 11.2. The main form of atonements in use in the SPs and in the SJK is fast. The list of fasts comes from the Bhāṣyas. It is taken for granted and is not subject to any definition. There are five kinds of fasts, enumerated in increasing order of their difficulty:

nivvīya: consuming food without the *vikṛti*s
purim'-aḍḍha: abstaining from food during the first half of the day
egāsaṇa: taking only one meal a day
āyāma: rendered into Sanskrit as *ācāmāmla* or *ācāmla*, it is in this context the usual form for what is well-known as *āyambila*, i.e. taking only "sour food", i.e. boiled rice or cereal unmixed with any other thing, not even salted (Deo 1960: 46).
khamaṇa or *khavaṇa*: this word, rendered into Sanskrit by the commentaries as *kṣapaṇa* or *kṣamaṇa*, becomes the generic term for all complete fasts where only water is consumed. A more common equivalent, also met with in our texts, is Skt. *upavāsa*.

The sequence of fasts is significant and determines a hierarchy which is to be understood implicitly in abbreviation devices such as *ādi*, *kameṇaṃ* "in succession", etc.: e.g. *purimaḍḍhādi* = *purimaḍḍha, egāsaṇa, āyāma, khamaṇa.*

These are the most common terms. For each of them a number of equivalents considered as techinical terms (*tapasaḥ saṃjñā*) are recorded in the ĀD

(p. 254b). Some of them are rare in practical use, except for the Sanskrit tracts preserved in the ĀD itself.

§ 11.3. Atonements are based on the combination of durations and fasts. The pattern of their association and equivalences is stated, for instance, in JKBh 1804–1806:[25]

incomplete month or smaller duration	food without dainties (also *paṇaga* SJK 65; SPT 3 (Poṣadha section)
one light month	abstaining from food in the first half of the day
one heavy month	eating only once a day (JKBh *bhatt'ekkaṃ*)
four light months	eating only sour food
four heavy months	full fast, only water, for one day (JKBh *abhatt'-aṭṭhaṃ*)
six light months	two day and a half continuous fast (JKBh *chaṭṭha*, Jain Hindi/Rajasthani. *belā*)
six heavy months	three day and a half continous fast (JKBh *aṭṭhamaga*, SPAn *aṭṭhama* or *aṭṭhama-bhattaṃ*; Jain Hindi/ Rajasthani *telā*, or *aṭṭham tap*; SPT *panca-kallāṇa*)

This is what is meant in the very concise phrasing of SPAn 2 (see below Appendix A). SPT mostly uses the system of durations, but can also combine both systems in the same verse (SPT 6). A similar list of equivalences is given in SJK 137 with reference to the *Jītakalpa* (*Jīta-paribhāṣayā ucyante*, comm.).

§ 11.4. Pkt. *kalla* or *kallāṇa* is used as a generic term designating one complete set of the five fasts listed above (§ 11.2). It is Sanskritized into *kalya* or *kalyāṇa(ka)*. Occurrences are SPAn 8, 9, 10, 14, SPT 6, 7, 9, 10, 11, 12, 15, 16 and corresponding commentary, SJK 72 and 74 (*paṇa-kallaṃ*). Again there is no definition in the verses, but only in prose commentaries. Thus, for instance *pañca tapāṃsi nirvikṛtika-purimārddhaikāśanācāmāmlopavāsa-rūpāṇi samuditāni pañca-kalyāṇam ucyate* (SJK comm. on 137), or in an abridged form *kalyaṃ*: *ni° pu° e° āṃ° u°- rūpam* (SJK comm. on 74 p. 59 or JKCūrṇi Sanskrit annotations on JKS 32, ed. Jinavijaya p. 45). As a technical term (*saṃjñā*), *kallāṇaṃ* is defined as the sum of these five in the list available in SPT ms. B (fol. 7v). "Multiplied by five it is *pancakallāṇaṃ*" (ibid. fol. 8r).

The term *kalla/kallāṇa* in this usage is typical of the *Chedasūtra-bhāṣya*s in the context of atonements, and goes back to them. When used along with a number, it means that the full set of fasts is repeated:

> *cau-tiga-duga-kallāṇa egaṃ kallāṇagaṃ ca kārenti* (JKBh 306ab = VyavBh (M) 4187ab = VyavBh (K and T) 4207ab).
>
> "They perform four, three or two sets of the five fasts, and one".

These are offered as alternatives in decreasing order of difficulty. Atonements have to be prescribed in accordance with the culprit's capacity: if he is not able to perform the first in the list, the second becomes a possibility, and so on until the level proper to his situation is found. This is part of the *jīya* system, which can be called "customized".

As for the compound *paṇa-kalla, panca-kallāṇa*, it refers to the highest atonement where each of the five types of fast is repeated five times (JKS 58). But occasional ambiguity in the interpretation comes from the fact that *kalla* can be used as *kalla* or as an abbreviation for *panca*°, especially in verses. This is the case in JKBh 305 (= VyavBh (M) 4186 = VyavBh (K and T) 4206), which forms a pair with 306 (see above). The exposition goes from the highest to the lowest: the maximum atonement that can be given and is logically expected, as the commentator's explanation implies, are "five *kalla*s". Only if the culprit is unable to cope with them, should the lower possibilities be considered, namely "four, three, two or one *kalla*" (306). In another verse (BKBh1971ab = NiśBh 3072ab), which deals with the atonement for an ill monk who has been cured and for the one who attended to him, only *kallāṇagaṃ* is used:

> *pauṇaṃmi ya pacchittaṃ dijjai kallāṇagaṃ duveṇhaṃ pi*

The corresponding commentaries (NiśC III p. 12 and BKBhṬ II p. 574) make it clear that the term has two different contents, "even if it is stated undifferenciately" (BKBhṬ): for the cured monk five sets are prescribed, one for the attendant.

As the following example will show, misunderstanding can arise if the technical term is not recognized as such. At the beginning of the *Vyavahārabhāṣya*, we read a verse which is meant to illustrate what is meant by the word *jīya* "custom, usage" as the source for atonements:

> *daddura-m-ādisu kallāṇagaṃ tu vigal'-indiesu 'bhatt'-aṭṭho* [read so, = *abhatt'*, not *bhatt'*°]
> *pariyāvaṇa e(t)esiṃ cauttha-m-āyambilā honti* (VyavBh (M) and (T) 10)

Bollée translates (2006: 6):

> For beings such as frogs, whose organs of sense are defective, food is good fortune. For them fourth meals (only, i.e. after skipping three meals) consisting of sour gruel (show) are austerities.

This misses the point. One should understand:

> For frogs and other (five-sensed beings deprived of life): (the atonement is) *kalyāṇaka* (i.e. each of the five types of fasts); for beings with less sense organs deprived of life: no food; inflicting suffering on these means (respectively) a fast up to the fourth meal or sour food only.

The verse is based on two structuring oppositions. There is the opposition between two groups of living beings: those with five sense-organs and those with less than five (*vigalendiya*). There is then a distinction to be made between depriving of life and inflicting suffering, which are two actions not having the same degree of gravity. The intention is to underline the fact that the system of atonements depends on the seriousness of the offence: the more serious the offence, the more serious the atonement. In decreasing order, the scale is here:

murdering five-sensed animals	one set of the five fasts
murdering two-, three- and four-sensed animals	full fast
inflicting suffering on five-sensed animals	full fast
inflicting suffering on two-, three- and four-sensed animals	sour food only

The commentary lists further atonements for rubbing against (*saṃghaṭṭana*), depending on the number of senses of the beings concerned. This is precisely the point of *jīta-vyavahāra* to adjust atonements to circumstances from a given general pattern.[26]

The connotations of the etymological meanings of Skt. *kalya* "sound, healthy" and *kalyāṇa* "salutary, good" seem to have merged in this word which, used in the neuter as a substantive, could be rendered as "good thing, salutary way", or a "way to become healthy". It is in tune with the general vocabulary and images in use in the context of atonements, which often refer to the sphere of medicine (see above § 7), considering the teacher as the equivalent of a doctor.[27] In modern times the term *kalyāṇaka* "auspicious action" has been introduced by the Terāpanth leader Āc. Tulsi in connection with the individual recordings of achievement (*kalyāṇaka-patra*) of each mendicant (Flügel 2003: 186ff.).

It is worthy of note that the terms for the five fasts, and the generic term *kalla* are attested also in specialized Digambara sources for the mendicants, showing the existence of a common Jain vocabulary:

nivviyaḍī purimaṇḍalam āyāmaṃ eya-ṭhāṇa khamaṇam idi
kalyāṇam egam edehiṃ paṃcahiṃ panca-kallāṇaṃ (*Chedapiṇḍa* 5).
āyambila nivviyaḍī purimaṇḍalam eya-ṭhāṇa khamaṇāṇi
eyaṃ khalu kallāṇaṃ panca-guṇaṃ jāṇa mūla-guṇaṃ (*Chedaśāstra* 5).[28]

§ 11.5. Apart from words which are provided with a special meaning in a given context, the SP commentaries and Dharmaghoṣasūri's SJK also make use of a metalanguage which recalls the one used, for instance, by Indian grammarians, at a much narrower scale though. These are meaningless syllables which have to be understood as conventional designations of a given notion whose validity is limited to the context. The system of equivalences is:

ṇka: four light months
ṇkā: four heavy months (e.g. comm. on SJK 81)
phra: six light months (e.g. comm. on SJK 81)
phrā: six heavy months (e.g. comm. on SJK 81).

Despite their phonetic form which is not so easy to handle, such syllables may be inserted within a Prakrit *āryā* (SJK 138cd).

These designations in the form of letters are themselves optional terms for the same thing referred by numbers, detailed in the prose commentary:

1: light
4: four light
6: six light.

The same followed by a long "ī" (*1ī, 4ī, 6ī*) mean *guru, catur-guru* and *ṣaḍ-guru* (see examples in ms. A, variant in the comm. on verse 8 of the Poṣadhasāmācārī unit, below Appendix B; comm. on SJK 81 or 91). Finally the syllable *nā* designates refraining from food with dainties in connection with an "incomplete" month of atonement, that is 25 days. All the system, which also combines the use of small circles, empty for "light", full for "guru", is summed up in SJK 138:

> *iga cau cha sunna lahu guru ritta bhariya keval' ī-sarā aṃkā*
> *cau cha lahū ṇka*[29] *phra gurū sāgārā bhinne* (short e) *paṇaga nnā*
>
> The number 1, 4, 6 alone, empty circles: light; the number with *ī*, full (circles): heavy. Four and six light (respectively) *ṇka* and *phra*; heavy, with *ā*; for an incomplete (month the number) 5 (or the symbol) *nnā*.

Such abbreviated symbols are relevant because synthetic vizualisation in the form of tables (*yantra*s) of what has earlier been described in words and verses is a component of atonement literature. Such tables are often found in manuscripts (Figure 7.4). At the end of the lay atonements section of his *Sāmācārī*,

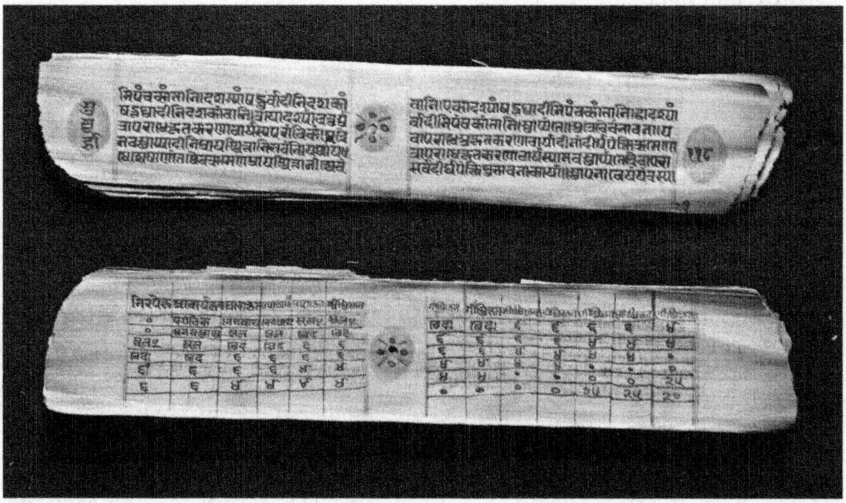

Figure 7.4 Metalanguage and visualization: table in the Patan manuscript F 18, fol. 119r.

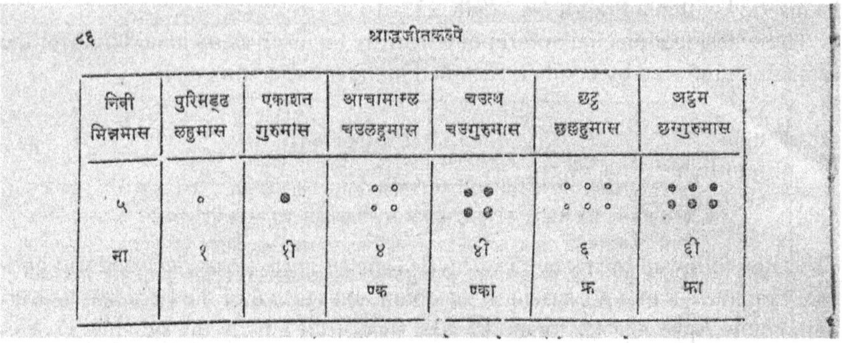

८६ श्राद्धजीतकल्पे

निवी भिन्नमास	पुरिमड्ढ लहुमास	एकाशन गुरुमास	आचामाम्ल चउलहुमास	चउत्थ चउगुरुमास	छट्ठ छल्लहुमास	अट्ठम छग्गुरुमास
५	°	●	° ° ° °	● ● ● ●	° ° ° ° ° °	● ● ● ● ● ●
ना	१	१ी	४	४ी	६	६ी
			ण्क	ण्का	ष्क	ष्का

Figure 7.5 Metalanguage and visualization: table on p. 86 of the 1960 edition of Dharmaghoṣasūri's *Saḍḍhajīyakappa* (SJK).

Tilaka refers to them (*yantrakāṇi*, p. 20b) for details of the concordances between kinds of fasts and durations writes. One is reproduced at the end of the printed edition of Dharmaghoṣa's SJK (Figure 7.5), but the British Library manuscript, for instance, does not have any, as such charts are by no means compulsory.

As can be expected, this type of system with symbolic letters has not been invented by Tilaka or Dharmaghoṣa. It is used in the *cūrṇi* on the *Niśītha-bhāṣya* at several places. Where the verses have the full words (*cau-lahu*, etc.), the *cūrṇi* uses symbolic abbreviations (e.g. on 6630, 6632, 6636, on sūtras 20.47–53):

°: light month
ṅka: four light
ṅkā: four heavy
rphu or *phru*: six light
su: pure.[30]

Syllables referring to "4" or "6" are also those which are found commonly among the letter-numerals used to number folios in palm-leaf manuscripts. Those of the *Niśītha* tradition and those handed down by Dharmaghoṣa are variants, also traced in manuscripts, where several syllables for the same numerical value may be found (chart in Punyavijaya 1969: 49, reproduced in Balbir *et al.* (2006) vol. 2: 490–491; Kapadia (1937)). Their presence in bhāṣyas and cūrṇis is evidence for the antiquity of these symbolic syllables, even more than the manuscripts, which do not go beyond the eleventh–twelfth centuries.

§ 12. Apart from fasts, recitations are another mode of compensation. In Tilakācārya's original works (SPT and ST), this is expressed by the term *sajjhāya-lakkha* (Skt. *svādhyāya-lakṣa* "100 000", SPT 9 and ST p. 20a) or the number alone (*lakkhaṃ*, SPT 11a and 12; *asiī lakkhaṃ* SPT 12 "180 000"; ST p. 20a). This refers to the recitation of *gāthā*s as quickly as possible, without controlled breathing or in a specific number of breaths. In SPT 19, on the other hand, "108" refers to the number of recitations of the *namaskāra-mantra.* Other types of equivalents between fasts and recitations are detailed in ĀD (pp. 254b–255a).

§ 13. There are numerous parallels between the SPs and the second half of Dharmaghoṣa's SJK, which deals strictly with the layman's atonements following similar lines.

The anonymous *Sāvayapacchitta* (SPAn) is an extremely concise version which leaves certain things unclear. Conciseness often confines to obscurity, either because the verses are meant only for mnemonic use, or, perhaps, deliberately because they have to be understood only by a selected audience of specialists, namely the competent religious teacher who is qualified to prescribe the atonement to the lay culprit. Tilakācārya's version (SPT) does not differ much in this regard. Dharmaghoṣa, on the other hand, goes into more detail and, in several cases, appears as a kind of elaboration of SPT, although no explicit reference is made to it. Without mention of the source, the Sanskrit commentary of Dharmaghoṣa's work quotes two verses borrowed from SPT.[31] Dharmaghoṣa's work, on the other hand, tends to emphasize the importance of some of the vows by expanding their treatment. This is the case particularly with the first and the fourth *aṇuvratas*, i.e. transgressions against *ahiṃsā* and against the *brahmavrata.* The special situation of these two *vrata*s is in tune with the general tendency of the *śrāvakācāra*s, where they are always considered to be fundamental.

§ 14. Modes of the transgressions to the first vow, non-violence, are expressed in SPT 5–6 and SJK 70–71 with a common vocabulary. This vocabulary comes from the JKBh, which forms their common source:

> *egiṃdi'-ṇaṃta-vajje ghaṭṭaṇa aṇagāḍha gāḍha-paritāve*
> *nivvigatigam ādiyaṃ jā āyāmaṃ tu uddavaṇe* (683)
> *vigaliṃd'-aṇanta ghaṭṭaṇa tāvaṇāṇagāḍha gāḍhe taheva uddavaṇe*
> *purimaḍḍhādi kameṇaṃ nāyavvaṃ jāva khamaṇaṃ tu* (684)
> *paṃciṃdiya ghaṭṭaṇa tāvaṇāṇagāḍha gāḍhe taheva uddavaṇe*
> *ekkāsaṇa āyāmaṃ khavaṇaṃ taha paṃca kallāṇaṃ* (685)[32]

> Harming one-sense bodies except living beings with numerous organisms, not serious or serious hurting: food without dainties, etc. respectively, up to sour food in case of killing (683). Harming of beings with two to four senses, serious or not serious hurting, and also killing: no food during the first half of the day, etc. in succession, up to full fast (684). Harming five-sense bodies, serious or not serious hurting, and also killing: one meal a day, sour food, full fast and the set of five (685).

Pkt. *uddavaṇa* here refers to the most serious form of aggression. It is replaced in the corresponding SJK (70) by the more straightforward *vaha.* The JKBh deals with the mendicant, the SPs and SJK with the layman. Still, the categorization of living beings differentiates between one-sensed, except *anantakāya*s, two- to four-sensed and *anantakāyas*, and five-sensed, and the scale of atonements depends both on the category of beings and the gravity of the aggression. These have been established in the JKBh. They remain identical in the SPT and in the SJK. Whereas SPT follows JKBh in prescribing "one set of five" for the most serious offence, this is called "six lights" (*cha lahu*) in SJK 71.

This being said, both Tilakācārya and the commentator on SJK state in identical words and without ambiguity that "for a householder violence with a purpose to a gross living being is not forbidden; violence without purpose is forbidden" (see below Appendix B on 5).The commentary on SJK elaborates that in lay life, destruction of the higher forms of life (*sthūla-hiṃsā*) which is intentional is the only area eligible for atonements. There is no embarrassment in acknowledging the fact that (1) the layman does not have to bother about the destruction of one- or two-sensed living beings, and (2) that he does not have to be worried about violence implied by an activity such as agriculture.

SPT and SJK thus follow the pattern of exposition and use the vocabulary of their model, the JKBh, and remain chained to it. It is in the commentaries that the more particular situation of the layman intrudes. In that they differ from SPAn – where transgressions relating to the first vow are treated in half a verse and only consider gross living beings:

> *thūlaga-pāṇ'aivāe saṃkappe panca-kallāṇaṃ*
>
> For intentional violence against a gross living being: one set of five (see below Appendix A).

§ 15. In SPAn 7 the compound *mehuṇa-vajjiesu* "except for the sexual intercourse (vow)" in a verse dealing with the global treatment of transgressions to the third and fifth vows underlines the necessity of a special treatment for the fourth vow. This verse goes back to the JKSūtra (33), applied to the monk. Similarly in SPT atonements for the breaking of the third and of the fifth vow are treated together (SPT 8–9) and the fourth vow is dealt with separately (10–12ab). In SPAn, the subject comes twice, first at the expected place in the sequence of vows (5), then, for an unknown reason, again after the treatment of the twelfth vow in the middle of that of *pratyākhyāna* which has just started (14). Indeed, breaking this vow is the fault that requires the highest level atonements (from "four heavy" to "radical reduction", SPT 10). The main issue is the quality and status of the woman with whom adultery has been committed: one's own wife, a woman taken as temporary wife, a prostitute, a married wife of high family, or another man's wife of a low status are those listed in SPT 10–11. The commentary and SJK add the cases of a widow or a spinster. The issue of the publicity of the fault is also a determining factor. In all texts, the atonement for breaking this vow with a lady from a good family is the most serious one (including ĀD p. 260a, verse 18 and again p. 267a verse 57 or p. 268a verse 86). It is designated as *mūla* (e.g. SPT 10). In the case of a mendicant, *mūla* means "radical suppression of religious seniority" (Caillat 1975: 177; SJK comm. on 46: *mūlaṃ:*

yasyāṃ cāsevanāyāṃ sarva-paryāyam apanīya punar mahāvratāropaṇaṃ kriyate tan mūlārham), taking the vows again and starting monastic life all over again at the beginning. The only available explanation in the lay treatises is that of the SJK commentary: *punaḥ śrāvakadharmāropaḥ kriyate, ṣāṇmāsikaṃ vā tapo deyam* (p. 62 on 82): "the lay law should be imposed on him once again, or a six month penance should be given". This can be reduced to "a set of five" if a factor of fragility (*mauya, mauyā*) is taken into account, as SPAn 8, SPAn 14, SPT 10 and SJK (commentary on 82) indicate.

The prescriptions of the SPs and SJK can be compared with the corresponding item in the Terāpanthin lay code of conduct (above § 5.7):

> If someone renounces [sex with] the wife of another lifelong and breaks [this vow], then for each time at least one three-day fast. If it is done with a widow or a virgin etc. in a way which will cause enormous disrespect in the eyes of the public, then an atonement for this is taken from the *ācārya*.
>
> (No. 15, Flügel's translation, forthcoming)[33]

§ 16. One of the main features of Dharmaghoṣa's work and the commentary thereupon is the fact that the atonements are not seen from the man's angle only. In the offences to the *brahmavrata*, for instance, atonements of various kinds are prescribed for adulterous women too, that is when they are those who are responsible for the transgression (82 and comm.). The equality of men and women (SJK 116) with respect to atonements is explicitly stated: the same ones can be given to both. The important criterion, that atonements should be given to any individual only after having assessed his capacities, otherwise they are without any use and will do no good, which is applied to members of the monastic community as well, is repeated in this case too. But the criterion is not of gender. The place given to the female component of the Jain community in this system could be a way to take into account a sociological reality, and to translate practical concerns, as well as a manner to stress the Śvetāmbara Jain identity.

Similarly, the final section of the lay atonements tract preserved in Sanskrit in the ĀD, after having dealt with the atonements for the 12 vows, introduces a set of verses specially meant for laywomen:

> *ayam eva śrāvikāṇāṃ prāyaścitta-vidhiḥ smṛtaḥ*
> *viśeṣaḥ ko 'pi tāsāṃ tu punar eva prakīrtyate.*
>
> (p. 260b verse 26)

For example, 25 recitations of the *namaskāra* are prescribed for a woman who would have rubbed against a man while she is standing for *sāmāyika* or *poṣadha*. If she breaks a given type of *pratyākhyāna* she should perform again the same type.

In the areas of daily life where laypeople interact with mendicants, it is interesting to observe that, in case of a transgression which amounts to a mendicant breaking a rule, the layman has "to pay" for him, and to pay the high price (SJK 60–61).

§ 17. In order to assess the impact of such works, one factor should be taken into account: the fact that works relating to atonements have always been considered as a special category which cannot be read by everybody without discrimination. This holds true primarily for those dealing with atonements for the mendicants, the *Chedasūtra*s of the Śvetāmbara tradition. The general idea is that only those who are fairly advanced in knowledge and religious life can have access to them. Such mendicants are referred to as *gītārthas*. The apparent motivation for such precautions seems to be the insisting statement that an atonement will do no good, or can even be harmful, if it is given by somebody who is unable to take into consideration all the parameters necessary for an adequate treatment. Thus, junior monks are excluded from the reading of the *Chedasūtras*. The seventeenth century *Senapraśna* raises the question about who has the right (*adhikārin*) to read them and answers very clearly on the basis of statements found in Haribhadra's *Pañcavastuka* that only mendicants are qualified, not laypeople.[34] On the other hand, it is known that among certain *gaccha*s nuns are not entitled to have access to *Chedasūtra*s. Lay counterparts to the *Chedasūtras*, although they do exist in the form of the works analysed above, seem to be also subjected to limitations of some type. The result is that the classical *śrāvakācāra*s (such as those studied by Williams, for instance) do not contain anything similar to our tracts in their technical aspects: the varieties of atonements, the technical terms referring to them and the complete chart are not found. What remains, however, is occasional quotations from Dharmaghoṣa's verses connected with the discussion of *ālocanā*. Ratnaśekharasūri, the author of the *Śrāddhavidhiprakaraṇa* in the fourteenth century, who also belonged to the Tapāgaccha, is one case in point.[35] The verses he quotes are borrowed from the beginning of Dharmaghoṣa's work. They express general considerations on the topic of confession. Such observations could tend to suggest that religious teachers of the Middle Ages continued to regard Dharmaghoṣa's work as a standard reference on the subject of lay atonement. The idea that a given transgression has to be compensated by a specific atonement in a system of correspondence of the type 1 to 1, however, seems to have generally fallen into disuse or felt to be unpractical.

§ 18. The technicalities of the SPs or the SJK remained in the hands of specialists. The metalanguage, sophisticated terminology and full system of atonements were not widely used. However, the idea that lay Jains should repent for transgressions relating to the specific areas of their lives in the sequence delineated in the SPs was continued all along. In medieval times, it is part of the *Ṣaḍāvaśyakasūtra* and their commentaries, especially in Gujarati (*bālāvabodha*s), where stories illustrating the transgressions are often included (e.g. Jayavijaya: Nawab 1977). In modern times it forms the contents of *Pākṣika Aticāra* manuals published as independent booklets in use among Śvetāmbara lay communities (e.g. Sādhvī Mokṣarasāśrījī 2010; Gaṇivīrya Arihantasāgarjī 2005, Muni Amitayaśavijaya n.d.; Kuṃvarjī Āṇandjī 2011) or sections inserted within the larger framework of Pratikramaṇa manuals (e.g. Nirvāṇa Sāgara 1986).

They consist of various textual components combining Prakrit verses and prose explanations in Gujarati, with some amount of variations depending on the versions.

1 A set of eight Prakrit *āryā*s known as *Aticāra gāthā sūtra* or *Pancācāra aticāra* starts with listing the same five areas of conduct as the SPT: knowledge, faith, practice, penance and energy:

nāṇammi daṃsaṇammi a, caraṇammi tavammi taha ya viriyammi
āyaraṇaṃ āyāro, ia eso paṃcahā bhaṇio.

Conduct in knowledge is then described as eightfold (2. *kāle viṇae*°): proper time, proper respect, reverence, *upadhāna*, absence of concealment, letter, meaning, both. Conduct in right faith is equally described as eightfold (3. *nissaṃkia nikkaṃkhia*°): absence of doubt, desirelessness, absence of repugnance, unswerving orthodoxy, edification, strengthening, kindness, spreading. Conduct in practice is eightfold as well (4. *paṇihāṇa-joga-jutto*°): fully intent on activities with the five *samiti*s and the three *gupti*s. Conduct in penance means observing the twelvefold penances, external and internal, without regret and without making a living of them (5. *bārasavihammi vi tave*°). External (6. *aṇasaṇam*°) and internal forms (7. *pāyacchittaṃ viṇao*°) are then spelled out with the usual list (e.g. Williams 1963: 238). Conduct in energy consists in practicing sincerely and according to one's own abilities (8. *aṇiguhia-bala-virio*°). At this stage, conduct is described positively in its various aspects with keywords.

2 Another set of Prakrit verses, usually referred to only by their incipits, relates to conduct in practice (*caritrācāra*) and lists the transgressions (*aticāra*) of *samyaktva*, followed by those relating to each of the 12 lay vows, to which *saṃlekhanā* is added. This is a notable difference with the Prakrit verse SPs, which deal with *pratyākhyāna* as such or with the "final" one, but not with fasting unto death strictly speaking. The transgression verses are found in full form in the *Vandittu sūtra* (*vandittu savva-siddhe*, etc.). They are lists of notional terms.

3 The Prakrit verses are good for memorization, but they need spelling out to make their meaning more concrete with reference to daily life contexts. This is the task of the prose commentary in vernaculars, which for their contents are the equivalents of the SPs Sanskrit commentaries. They enumerate all sorts of situations, using a specific vocabulary when it comes, for instance, to religious implements. The Gujarati of these parts is an old form of the language which does not seem to be so easy to grasp today, as prefaces to twenty-first century *Pākṣika Aticār* manuals underline. Thus they require extensive explanations (Shah 2011), and may be accompanied by glossaries (Kuṃvarjī Āṇandjī 2011: 114–128). This Gujarati is even more difficult for Jain speakers in Hindi, and has justified the publication of a new Hindi translation of the *Pākṣik Aticār*, ending with notes on difficult words (Arihantasāgara 2005: 19–23).

In such manuals, there is no prescription of atonement. Their conclusive sentence is:

> *evaṃkāre śrāvaka taṇe dharme śrī samakita-mūla bāra vrata, eka so covīśa aticāra māṃhi anero je koi aticāra pakṣa divasa māṃhi sūkṣma-bādara, jāṇatāṃ-a jāṇatāṃ huo hoy, te savi huṃ mana vacana kāyae karī micchā mi dukkaḍaṃ.*
>
> Such are the twelve vows founded in orthodoxy of the Jain lay law. Whatever of these hundred twenty four transgressions has taken place in this fortnight, whether gross or subtle, knowingly or unknowingly, all of them I recognize as wrong in mind, speech and act.[36]

Finally, comes a specification that such manuals are valid for quarterly (*cāturmāsika*) transgressions and those repented on the day of the annual *pratikramaṇa* (*sāṃvatsarika*).

§ 19. Highly technical tracts such as the *Sāvayapacchitta* or Dharmaghoṣa's work were probably considered irrelevant precisely because the lay Pratikramaṇa ritual (*Śrāddhapratikramaṇa*) provides a ready and global answer for the compensation of transgressions. *Ālocanā*, "confession", *pratikramaṇa*, "repentance", and *kāyotsarga*, "giving up the operations of body and speech", are components of this procedure, but they are also three items of the traditional list of ten *prāyaścittas*. Thus Pratikramaṇa can be regarded as a kind of large-scale atonement which encompasses all that makes lay life. The *aticārālocanā*, the preliminary step of the *pratikramaṇa* ritual, reads:

> *icchā-kāreṇa saṃdisaha bhagavaṃ devasiyaṃ āloiuṃ (the guru: āloaha) icchaṃ āloemi jo me devasio aiyāro kao kāio vāio māṇasio ussutto ummaggo akappo akaraṇijjo dujjhāyo duvvicintio aṇāyāro aṇicchiyavvo asāvaga-pāoggo nāṇe daṃsaṇe cārittācāritte sue sāmāiye tiṇhaṃ guttīṇaṃ cauṇhaṃ kasāyāṇaṃ paṃcaṇhaṃ aṇuvvayāṇaṃ tiṇhaṃ guṇavvayāṇaṃ cauṇhaṃ sikkhāvayāṇaṃ bārasavihassa sāvagadhammassa jaṃ khaṇḍiyaṃ jaṃ virāhiyaṃ tassa micchā mi dukkaḍaṃ.*
>
> Instruct me, lord, at my own desire to make *ālocanā* for the day. (*The guru*: Do so.) I wish to make *ālocanā*: whatever fault has been committed by me during the day in body, speech, or mind, in contravention of the scriptures and of right conduct, unfitting and improper to be done, ill meditated and ill conceived, immoral and undesirable, unbecoming for a layman, in regard to knowledge and philosophy and the lay life and the holy writ and the *sāmāyika*, and whatever transgression or infraction I may have committed in respect of the three *guptis* and four *kaṣāyas*, and the five *aṇu-vratas*, three *guṇa-vratas*, and four *śikṣā-vratas*, that is to say, the layman's twelvefold rule of conduct – may that evil have been done in vain.[37]

Thus it covers all the areas of lay life in one stretch. As the preface of a modern booklet (written by a lay Jain) admits straightaway:

> Man does continue to commit garlands of bad actions, but he lacks time for atonements of bad actions. But in order to keep purity performing *pratikramaṇa* morning and evening, fortnightly, quarterly or at least once a year *pratikramaṇa* is necessary.
>
> (in Gaṇivarya Arihantasāgarajī 2005)

Pratikramaṇa is thus an adequate substitute for specific atonements. Yet, the latter can be resorted to on request: when a layman is aware that he has committed an important violation of the code of conduct, he can visit a religious teacher who will give him the right answer relevant to his own case, for which a specific treatise may be useful, or superfluous. During a conversation, Ācārya Vijayaśīlacandrasūri Mahārāj (Godhra, January 2014) took out notebooks where monks from his lineage had copied old folios showing charts in the line of SPs, suggesting that they may be referred to in case of need. He also specified that not every mendicant is authorized to decide for atonements, and that reference has to be made to the leading authority in one's own *gaccha*. This was confirmed by other mendicants too.

§ 20. To sum up: the *Sāvayapacchitta*s and the *Saḍḍhajīyakappa* are attempts to provide a symmetrical counterpart to the monastic treatises dealing with atonements. They are modelled after these treatises. Such attempts are not surprising given the parallelisms between the mendicant's code and the layman's code that are central to the Jain system. The corpus of texts on lay atonements provide an instance of strong intertextuality. But, on the other hand, they appear more as intellectual exercises meant to complete a theoretical frame than as tools for actual compensation of transgressions and they are meant to be read by mendicants only, although they deal with areas of the layman's life. The prevailing tendency with regard to atonements is to stress the difference between monastic and lay situations. For the latter's requirements the performance of Pratikramaṇa is the best way – the panacea – for remedying any failure in conduct. The *communis opinio* is thus expressed by Ratnaśekharasūri: "Pratikramaṇa should be performed by the layman every day, and also at both junctures in order to purify all the transgressions of right faith and others, and also for practice." Under these circumstances, the texts which describe a full system of specific fasts and fasts of various durations for each and every transgresssion tend to become obsolete. They are compensated by daily practice and personal encounters with the religious teachers who are the ultimate source for prescribing atonements in the form of fasts or recitations.

Appendix A

Anonymous Sāvayapacchitta (= SPAn)

Critical edition and translation

The following edition is based on:

- BhORI: Second text ("75(b)/1880–81") in a manuscript centring on the *Jītakalpa* corpus, described in BhORI 17.2 No. 591. Accessible through its transcription by Ernst Leumann, Notebook No. 128 belonging to his Nachlass kept in Hamburg (see Figure 7.2a–b): 16 Āryās.
  This is the second text in a manuscript having three:

1	Jītakalpasūtra	1b–12a
2	SPAn (not described in printed parts of BhORI)	12a–13v
3	Jītakalpa-cūrṇi-gata-siddhatthety-ādi-vivaraṇa (BhORI 17.2 No. 597)	13v–18v

- BL: British Library palm-leaf manuscript Or. 1385, Manuscript A, Text 2, fol. 9A3–9B (Figure 7.1) = Cat. No 161 in Balbir *et al.* (2006). See Cat. No. 158 for the material description of the manuscript, which is digitized on jainpedia.org: 12 numbered verses. The text ends: *Sāvaya-pacchittaṃ samattaṃ* // Here also the SPAn follows the text of the *Jītakalpasūtra*.

We use the Pune manuscript as the basic document as it is more complete. The British Library manuscript lacks four verses at the beginning and has some inconsistencies, which are collected in footnotes.

addheṇa chinna-sesaṃ puvv'addheṇaṃ ca saṃjuyaṃ kāuṃ
dejjāhi lahuya-dāṇaṃ guru-dāṇaṃ tattiyaṃ ceva //1
a-visiṭṭhammi ya māse lahuo guru cau chac ca lahu-gurugā
nivvīy'āī aṭṭhama-bhatt'antaṃ dāṇaṃ eesiṃ //2
do satta duvālasa sattarasa bāvīsa taha sattavīsā ya
s'addhā ega do ti cau panca māsā tay-addha-juyā //3
guru-lahugāṇa (?) viseso paṇag'āīyassa ko bhavejjāhi?
bhaṇṇai: lahuyass' addhaṃ chijjai guruyaṃ tu sampuṇṇaṃ // [4]
[1]nissallo jaha havaī duviho so hoi cinna-pacchitto
taṃ bhaṇiyaṃ ciya samae sāvaga-dhamme viseseuṃ // [5]
sankâiesu pancasu savve khamaṇaṃ[2] tu, desĕ[3] āyāmaṃ
thūlaga-pāṇ'aivāe saṃkappe panca-kallāṇaṃ // [6]
mosâisu mehuṇa-vajjiesu davvâi-vatthu-bhinnesu
hīṇe majjh'-ukkose āsaṇaṃ āyāma khavaṇāiṃ[4] // [7][5]
vesa sa-dārā ittiri vaya-bhange aṭṭham' ega-kallāṇaṃ
mūlaṃ tu kula-vahūe, mauyassa u[6] panca-kallāṇaṃ // [8]

ahavā mosâdatte pariggahe mehuṇe ya para-dāre
dappeṇaṃ patteyaṃ patteyaṃ panca-kallāṇaṃ // [9]
disi-vvae[7] pancavihe paḍhamammi guṇa-vvae abhatt'aṭṭhaṃ
uvabhoge paribhoge[8] kamm'āyāṇ' ega-kallāṇaṃ[9] // [10]
āyāmaṃ khamaṇaṃ pi[10] ya paritt'aṇante ya jāṇa bhoyaṇao
taie aṇattha-ḍaṇḍe cauvvihe jāṇa khamaṇaṃ tu // [11]
sāmāiyass' a-karaṇe paḍhame sikkhā-vae abhatt'aṭṭhaṃ
desâvagāsa posaha āyāmaṃ antime khamaṇaṃ // [12]
majje maṃse pupphe phale ya vaya-bhangĕ[11] aṭṭhamaṃ bhaṇiyaṃ
paccakkhāṇa-a-gahaṇe carime sāhūṇa tullaṃ tu // [13]
para-dāra kula-vahūe mūlaṃ purisâvekkhaṃ ca[12] panca-kallāṇaṃ
gaṇiyāe kallāṇaṃ khamaṇam aṇ-ābhoga poggale bhutte[13] // [14]
carimassa ya paccakkhāṇassa a-gahaṇe[14] taha ya hoi purim'aḍḍhaṃ
paccakkhāṇa-akaraṇe[15] khamaṇaṃ tu nikkāraṇā jāṇa // [15]
bhinno a-visiṭṭho cciya māso cauro ya chac ca lahu-gurugā[16]
nivvīyâī aṭṭhama-bhatt'antaṃ dāṇam eesiṃ[17] // [16][18]

Notes: 1. The London manuscript starts here. – 2. Same beginning as JKS 28–3. desi, BL. – 4. Leumann's transcription has "guru-lahugā na", which we do not follow; -ukkose egāsaṇayāma khamaṇāiṃ, BL. – 5. This stanza, which is identical to JKSūtra 33, is quoted in the commentary on Dharmaghoṣa's SJK 79 with the same wording as the Pune ms. – 6. ya, BL. – 7. disivae, BL 6. – 8. uvabhoga parībhoge, BL. – 9. The second part of this stanza seems to have suffered in the BL ms. which has: majje maṃse ya panca-kallāṇaṃ, both unmetrical and unsatisfactory from the point of view of the contents, since alcohol and meat are dealt with later in the text. – 10. ti, BL – 11. bhaṃgi, BL. – 12. purisāvikkhaṃ ca, BL, although two signs above "kkhaṃ" seem to indicate that it is a mistake; purisâveṭṭhaṃ (Leumann) is enigmatic. – 13. bhutte, BL; bhotte (Leumann) – 14. carimassa paccakkhāṇassāgahaṇe – 15. paccakkhāṇākaraṇe khamaṇaṃ nikkāraṇā jāṇa, BL. – 16. garuyā, BL – 17. dāṇa-pacchittaṃ, BL – 18. In the Pune ms. the last verse of the text is numbered 117. Leumann observes: "Offenbar sind in der Schlusszahl die 113 der vorhergehenden Jītakalpa-sūtra mitgezählt. Es scheinen in diesem Stück oder schon im jenem Sūtra zwei Zusatsstrophen nicht beachtet zu sein. 2 ist fast gleich Jītak. 61" (Notebook No. 128).

Translation

1 One should give a light atonement after having cut half and again joined half. But giving a heavy (atonement) can be only that.

2 And in a month with no specification, one light, one heavy, four and six – light or heavy, food without dainties, fast up to the eighth meal are what should be given to them.

3 Two, seven, twelve, seventeen, twenty-two and twenty-seven with their halves; one, two, three, four, five months along with their halves (?).

4 What would be the difference between five etc. for heavy and light? It is said: for a “light” half is cut off, while a “heavy” one is complete.

5 A person without thorn is twofold, one of them being the person who has performed atonements. This is precisely what has been said in the doctrine, with specification to the lay code of conduct.

6 As for the five (transgressions), doubt and the others: for a complete one, a complete fast, and only sour food for a partial one. For intentional violence against a gross living being, five sets of five.

7 For false (speech) and other (*vrata*s) – sexual intercourse excluded – which are divided according to their object and other (parameters, i.e., time, place, mental behaviour), depending on whether it is inferior, medium or high, there is (respectively) (one) meal a day, sour food or full fast.

8 A harlot, one’s own wife, a temporary wife for breaking the vow: (fast up to) the eighth (meal), one set of five. But the radical (atonement) if it concerns a married woman from a good family; however, for a fragile person, five sets of five.

9 Or for false (speech) and for (taking what) has not been given, for attachment to possession and for sexual intercourse with a woman other (than one’s own wife), if done out of arrogance: five sets of five for each of them.

10 For the vow relating to the area (of one’s own action), fivefold, the first *guṇavrata*: no food up to the eighth meal. For objects of consumption, of enjoyment, for engaging in the (fifteen forbidden) activities: one set of five.

11 Sour food and full fast, know it, for having consumed (respectively) elementary (living beings) or (living beings) with an infinity of organisms. But for the third (*guṇavrata*), harmful activity with no purpose, which is fourfold: full fast, know it.

12 For not performing *sāmāyika*, the first *śikṣāvrata*, without valid cause: no food up to the eighth meal. For (the vow relating to) occasional restriction of space, for ritual fasting: sour food. For the last (vow): full fast.

13 For alcohol, meat, flower and fruit: in case of breaking of the vow, fasting up to the eighth meal has been told. But for not taking *pratyākhyāna* at the last hour: identical to monks.

14 A woman other (than one’s own wife): for a married woman of a good family: the radical (atonement), and, depending on the man, five sets of five. For a harlot, a set of five. A full fast for meat having been consumed involuntarily.

15 For not taking the final *pratyākhyāna* there is similarly no food in the first half of the day. But for not performing *pratyākhyāna*: full fast, know it, if there is no valid reason.

16 An incomplete month has no specification, one month, four and six – light or heavy, food without dainties, and the others up to fast up to the eighth meal are what should be given to them.

Remarks

1. Not fully clear. The idea seems to be that a light atonement can be adjusted, while a heavy cannot be. The same idea is expressed in 4cd. – 2. See above § 11.1 to § 11.3. – 3. Not clear. The Patan ms of SPT (below Appendix B) has a table at the end which clearly refers to what is said here, but does not help (me) to understand what it means exactly. – 7–9. See above § 15. – 10. For the five transgressions of the *dig-vrata*, which are not spelled out here, see Williams (1963: 99–102). – 11ab. Close in contents to SJK 91ab with more brevity in wording; *paritta* is the antonym of *aṇanta* and is the same as what is otherwise called *pratyeka-vanaspati*. – 11cd. Four types of *anarthadaṇḍa* "are listed in the canon and maintained by the Śvetāmbaras" (Williams 1963: 123). They are: evil brooding (*apadhyāna*), purposeless mischief (*pramādacarita*), facilitation of destruction (*hiṃsāpradāna*), harmful counsel (*pāpopadeśa*), faulty reading (*duḥśruti*). – 12. The "last" vow, not referred to here by its technical name, is the *atithisaṃvibhāga-vrata* "giving alms to the Jain mendicants", compare below SPT 14: the atonement prescribed for not having observed the vow is the same: full fast, here = four heavy (SPT). – 13. The second part of the verse refers to fasting unto death and the practice of *santhāra*. In front of this situation monks and laypeople are equal. – 14ab. This return to adultery interrupts the course of the exposition on *pratyākhyāna* just started. Is it an interpolation? See above § 15. I understand *purisāvekkhaṃ* "depending on the man" as another way of phrasing that an alleviated atonement is possible, like in 8 *mauyassa* … – 14cd. I understand Pk. *poggala* as a designation of "meat", which is well-attested. The consumption of meat has already been treated very generally in 13. But here it is qualified as "involuntarily". The atonement prescribed is in agreement with SPT 15 and comm. – 15ab. The same atonement, expressed as "one light" (*laghu*), is prescribed in SPT 18 and SJK 104cd, for not having performed the last day of *pratyākhyāna*. – 15cd. Similar wording and same atonement in SPT 18ab. – 16. See above § 11.1.

Appendix B

The Sāmāyārī or Sāvayapacchitta by Tilakācāryasūri (= SPT) and its auto-commentary

Critical edition with translation of the verse text

Manuscripts used for this edition are:

- P: Palm-leaf manuscript F 18 *Jitakalpasutra-adi Cha Grantho* kept at the Hemachandracharya Jain Jnan Bhandar, Patan, 175 folios.

Preliminary description in Dalal and Gandhi (1937: 404).

Foliation indicated by letter-numerals in the left-hand margin, by numbers in the right-hand margin. A few folios seem to be missing; folio 171 is a replacement.

The "six works" (*cha grantho*) are:

1	Tilakācārya's *Jītakalpasūtra-vṛtti*	1–149v	unpublished
2	Tilakācārya's Śrāvakasāmācārī or °prāyaścitta (= SPT), 20 Pkt. verses	150r–152r	edited and translated here (Fig. 7.3)
3	Tilakācārya's Sanskrit commentary on SPT	152r–160r (fol. 159 missing, commentary of verses 19–20 missing)	edited and analysed here
4	Tilakācārya's Poṣadhaprāyaścittasāmācārī, 10 Pkt. verses	160r–161r	edited and translated here
5	Sanskrit commentary on Poṣadha°	161r–163r (163v blank)	edited and analysed here
6	*Jītakalpasūtra*	164r–175v	see bibliography

I am extremely thankful to Prof. Shin Fujinaga: he was the one who suggested, after a preliminary version of this essay was given at the London Jain Workshop in March 2009, that benefit could be taken from Muni Jambuvijaya's presence in Patan to get the full manuscript photographed. It was done on 4–5 April 2009 by Hiroko Matsuoka (Hiroshima University) who was kind enough to send excellent digital photographs. I am thankful to Mr Yatin Vrajlal Shah (Patan), who kindly double-checked that fol. 159 is actually missing in the manuscript.

- A: Paper manuscript No. 26344 kept at the L.D. Institute of Indology, Ahmedabad; 66 folios; date of copy indicated at the end of the JKV (fol. 61v): *saṃ° 1590* (CE 1533) *varṣe Yeṣṭa vadi 11 dine ravivāraḥ*; from another hand at the end of the ms. (fol. 66r): *saṃvat 1628* (= CE 1571) *varṣe Paṃjābī guru śrīPremavijayajī ma° nā śiṣya muniLābhavinayajī hetave śrīr astu*.

1	Tilakācārya's *Jītakalpasūtravṛtti*	1v–61v, copied V.S. 1590 = 1533 CE
2	Tilakācārya's SPT and its commentary 36 verses numbered continuously, including the *poṣadhasāmācārīgāthā*s (= Units 4 and 5 in ms. P)	61v–66r, date by a second hand as V.S. 1628 = 1571

- B: Paper manuscript, shelfmark No. 2213 kept at the L.D. Institute of Indology, Ahmedabad; eight folios, undated, but fairly old script.

1	Tilakācārya's SPT, 20 verses Does not include the *poṣadhasāmācārīgāthā*s	1r–1v, *iti śrāvaka-jītakalpaḥ samāptaḥ*

2	Tilakācārya's commentary on SPT	1v-5r8, *śrāvaka-jītakalpa-vṛtti samāptā*
3	*Ālocanāvidhi*	5r8–6r11
4	*Ālocanāvidhi*, Pkt. 25 verses	6v1–7v9
5	No formal title: list of Prakrit technical terms on atonements, ritual of confession for the layman	7v9–8v

- C: Paper manuscript No. 27898 kept at the L.D. Institute of Indology, Ahmedabad; five folios, undated, but fairly modern.

1	Tilakācārya's SPT, 20 verses Does not include the *poṣadhasāmācārīgāthā*s	1v–2r
2	Tilakācārya's commentary on SPT	2r–5v

Reproductions of the Ahmedabad manuscripts were sent through the good offices of Dr Jitendra B. Shah, Director, L.D. Institute of Indology.

Mitra (1886): Another paper ms. of SPT and commentary, which could not be consulted, is recorded in Mitra (1886): No. 2705 *Prāyaścittasāmācārī, vyākhyāsahitaḥ*, eight folios, nāgarī, described as "Prâyâshcitta-sâmâchâri. A treatise on expiations according to the ordinance of the Jains. By Tilaka Âchârya". Extracts from beginning and end are quoted and confirm that this is the same text as the one edited here. The existence of this manuscript was noted by Leumann (Notebook No. 128): "Ein anderer Text über Laien-Bussen ist der vom ŚrīTilaka (M 2705), nebst dem Jītakalpasūtra commentirt von ŚrīTilaka in AV79".

Preliminary remarks

In manuscripts P, B, C, the Prakrit verse text comes first, followed by the Sanskrit commentary. In manuscript A, each verse is immediately followed by its commentary. We have followed this pattern here, adding the translation and the notes after each verse as well.

In ms. P the *Poṣadhasāmācārīgāthā*s form a unit separate from the SPT *stricto sensu*. The ten Prakrit verses of the *Poṣadha*° come after the SPT. Then comes their commentary.

Manuscript A shows a slightly expanded version of the verse (three additions within the set of 20) and takes the *Poṣadhasāmācārīgāthās* with commentary as a part of SPT, included in between verse 18 and verse 19 of the 20 verse version; not as a distinct unit. All verses are numbered continuously, amounting to 36.

Manuscripts B and C do not contain the *Poṣadhasāmācārīgāthā*s and their commentary.

For sake of convenience we first give the SPT unit *stricto sensu* on the basis of mss. P, A, B, C, and then the *Poṣadhasāmācārī* unit on the basis of mss. P and A.

SPT stricto sensu

1. siriVīra-jiṇaṃ namiuṃ pacchittaṃ sāvayāṇa vucchāmi
vīmaṃsiūṇa bahuso sāmāyārīu vivihāo.
Having paid homage to the Jina Lord Vīra, I will tell the lay atonements, after having examined in various ways the various codes of conduct.

siri-Vīrajiṇaṃ ityādi sugamā.

So in P, B, C. A: spaṣṭā.

praṇipatya Jinaṃ Vīraṃ śrāvakāṇāṃ viśuddhi-kṛt
prāyaścittaṃ sva-gāthôktaṃ vyākhyāmi sukha-buddhaye

This stanza not in A; °buddhaye B; °vudhaye P, C.

tatrêyaṃ namaskārâbhidheyâbhidhāyikâdyā gāthā.

This sentence not in A.
[1]iha samayânumānena viśiṣṭa-jñāna-darśana-cāritravatāṃ gurūṇāṃ pārśve prāyaścittam aṃgī-kriyate. tatra prathamam evâlocanā-grāhī viśuddhi-divase praśaste caṃdravale vijanaṃ kṛtvā kṣamāśramaṇaṃ datvā bhaṇati "icchākāreṇa tubbhe[2]amha sodhi deaha" – "demo" iti gurûkte. "iccham" ity uktvā kṣamāśramaṇaṃ datvā "icchākāreṇa tubbhe amhe sodhi-dāṇ'-atthaṃ ceiyāiṃ vaṃdāvaha". – "vaṃdāvemo khamāsamaṇāṇaṃ Goamâīṇaṃ mahā-muṇīṇaṃ hattheṇaṃ" ti gurūkte, "iccham" ity uktvā, "kṣamā° icchākāreṇa bhagavan saṃdisaha caitya-vaṃdanā karauṃ". – "kareha" tti gurûkte. "iccham" ity uktvā śrīVīraJina-namaskārān uccārya, Śakra-stavaṃ bhaṇitvā, ācāryôpādhyāya-sarva-sādhūnāṃ kṣamā° 3 datvā "aḍḍhāijjesu" ityādi bhaṇati. tataḥ kṣamāśramaṇa-pūrvaṃ gurûpadeśena mukha-vastrikāṃ prati-likhya dvādaśâvartta-vaṃdanaṃ vidhāyâbhidhatte "icchākāreṇa bhagavan saṃdisaha sodhi saṃdisāvauṃ". – "saṃdisāvaha" tti gurûkte. "iccham" ity uktvā, "kṣamā° icchākāreṇa bhagavan saṃdisaha, sodhi leauṃ". – "leaha" tti gurûkte. "itthaṃ kṣamā°, icchākāreṇa bhagavan saṃdisaha kaṭṭhâsaṇauṃ saṃdisāvauṃ". – "saṃdisāvaha" tti gurûkte. "icchaṃ kṣamā° icchākāreṇa bhagavan saṃdisaha kaṭṭhâsaṇai ṭṭhāuṃ". – "ṭhāyaha" tti gurûkte utkaṭikaḥ upaviśya vā, yathā yathā kṛtāḥ smarati vâticārās, tathā tathâlocayati. tāṃś câvadhārya guruḥ samācāry-anusāreṇa prāyaścittaṃ dadāti. tac ca jñānâcārādy-ācāra-paṃcakâticāra-gocaraṃ syād.

1 All this paragraph neither in A nor in B; only in P and C, see translation above § 9; 2. From here up to *tubbhe* text added in the right-hand margin of B.

ataḥ prathamaṃ jñānācārâticāra-viṣayam āha.

So in P, B (*iha* instead of *ataḥ*), C; pūrvaṃ jñānācāra-viṣayaṃ prāyaścittam āha A.

2 taṇu-majjh'-ukkosâsāyaṇayāe paḍima-putthaya-gurūṇaṃ
micchatte vi ya tivihe lahu guru cau lahu jahā-saṃkhaṃ.
A °ukkosāsāyaṇāsu; A paḍimāṇa P guruṇaṃ; P ttivihe; P *ca* instead of *cau*; laghu P, B, C. – The metrical structure of cd is comparable to that of SJK 58cd, with the fourth and fifth gaṇas both made of four short syllables.
For minimal, medium and maximum offences to image, manuscript, teacher, and also for threefold (i.e. minimal, medium and maximum) wrong faith (atonement is): light, heavy and four light, respectively.

Commentary

taṇu-gāhā.

(*This paragraph only in* B:) ṭhavaṇī, kamalī, dorā ūtarī, pāṭhāṃ vīṃṭaṇāṃ jñāna kāla-velāṃ paḍhiuṃ, viparīta-kathana, utsūtra-prarūpaṇā, aśraddadhāna artha bhaṇatāṃ, jñāna-dravya bhakṣita upekṣita, nukaravālī paga lāgu //

pratimāyā vāsakuṃpikā-sphālana[1], adhauta[2] -potikayā pūjana-pramādato bhūmi-pātanâdyāḥ, pustaka-paṭṭikā-ṭippanâder[3] vadanôttha-niṣṭhīvana-lava-sparśa[4], caraṇa-ghaṭṭana[5] niṣṭhyūtena paṭṭikâkṣara-mārjana, bhūmi-pātanâdyāḥ guroḥ[6] sthāpanācāryasyânutthāpitasya cālana, bhūmi-pātana-praṇāmanâdyāḥ[7]. athavā guror ācāryasya jaghanya-madhyamôtkṛṣṭā āśātanās tāsu kṛtāsu, tathā pustaka-bhaṇanāt, akāla-pāṭhâdike aṣṭa-vidhe 'pi jñānācārâticāre jaghanya-madhyamôtkṛṣṭe[8] mithyātve ca tri-vidhe jaghanyâdau laghu, guru, catur-laghūni, purimārddhaikāśanā cāmāmlāni[9] yathā-saṃkhyaṃ prāyaścittāni dīyaṃta[10] iti bhāvârthaḥ. ca-śabdāt sūtrârthâśātanāyāṃ[11] catur-laghu catur-guruke/2

1. sphalana P; 2. adhota A; 3. ṭippanakāder A; 4. sparśāt B; 5. ghaṭṭanā A; 6. from guroḥ up to the end of the sentence, not in A; 7. bhūmipātapraṇāśanādyāh B; 8. °otkṛṣṭaḥ A; 9. cāmlāni A, B; 10. dīyante A and sentence ends; 11. krameṇa added A.

Remarks

Parallels: SJK 55–56 (offences to the "manuscript") + 64ff. (offences to the "image"). – For c see SJK 58cd.

The commentary expands on the three terms "image, manuscript and teacher", with more emphasis on the first and provides more concrete instances than it usually does. We give them in translation:

- Making burst out the small bags containing scented powder for an image (cf. *kumpikā: vāsa-karpūrādi-bhājana-viśeṣaḥ*, comm. on SJK 64).
- Making an image fall on the ground out of carelessness in worship with a mouth-cloth that has not been cleaned.

- Contact of a manuscript, the wooden plank (on which it is placed) or a page with drops of sputter having come out of the mouth.
- Rubbing these objects with the feet.
- Erasing letters with saliva.
- Making the teacher's *sthāpanācārya* fall down.
- With the word "manuscript" it is referred to reading at improper time (for instance in case there is a reason for forbidding study, technically called *anadhyāya* or *asvādhyāya*).

But despite these explanations, Tilaka's verse and his commentary remain somewhat elusive, especially in the case of "wrong faith" for they do not clearly connect the cases for transgression and the corresponding atonement. In this regard, Dharmaghoṣa is clearer:

hīṇ'akkharâi lahu putthiyâi-pāḍaṇa-payâi-thukkâī
caulahu guru a-kālāi niṃda-paḍiṇīyayâīsu (56)

For a missing syllable etc.: one light; for making a manuscript and others fall down, for (touching them) with the feet etc. and for spitting etc.: four light. A heavy for (reading or performing) at the wrong moment, for blame and for opposition etc.

The beginning of the commentary has a very close parallel in Gujarati in ST section 16: *jñānācāre vāsakuṃpī āphalī, adhotī devapūjā pramādi pratimā pāḍī, pāṭī pothī ṭīpaṇaiṃ thuṃka lāgaiṃ, paga lāguṃ, thuṃkai akṣara māṃjiu, pothī bhūmi pāḍī, ṭhavaṇāriu cāliu pāḍiu, bhūmi hāraviu, akāla pāṭhādika, aṣṭavidhajñānāticāra, guru āśātanā kīdhī* (p. 19b).

The situations of offences described in the commentary of SJK are partly similar to those mentioned above, as are those described in the Sanskrit tracts preserved in ĀD (p. 259b–260a; p. 265b).

The additional paragraph available in B lists offences to the mishandling of various objects which come under the heading *jñānopakaraṇa*, under their Gujarati names: the stand of the *sthāpanācārya* (*ṭhavaṇī*), the small stick of bamboo used in wrapping on a book (*kamalī* or *kavalī*; Shah 2011: 13), the rosary bead for counting *namaskāra*s (*nukaravālī*).

tathā (missing in A)

3. paḍimā-dāhe bhaṃge palīvaṇâisu pamāyao vā vi
taha puttha-paṭṭiyâīṇa vi nava-kārāvaṇe suddhī.
(paṭṭiyāṇa A; kāravaṇe havai A)

In case of burning of an image, on the occasion of fire or other circumstances or also out of carelessness, and in case of breaking of a book, of a wooden plank, etc.: purification through having new ones made.

Commentary

paḍimā-dāhe bhaṃge palīvaṇâisu pamāyao vā vi. taha puttha-paḍiyâīṇa vi nava- kārāvaṇe suddhī // 3 spaṣṭa (= P, C).

[*paḍimā-dāhe bhaṃge* ityādi gāthā spaṣṭā, B; spaṣṭā A].

Remarks

Parallel: SJK 67.

atha darśanācārâticāra-viṣayam āha //

4. saṃmatte saṃkâisu cau lahu desaṃmi cau guru savve
guru-davva-bhogi bhinnaṃ guru-devâvaṃdaṇe ya lahū.

Regarding orthodoxy, in case of doubt and other transgressions: four light ones for partial (transgression), four heavy ones for total (transgression). For using an object belonging to a monk: one incomplete month. And for not paying homage to the teacher or to the Jina: one light.

Commentary

samatte-gāhā. samyaktve śaṃkâdiṣu paṃcasv aticāreṣu

(*This paragraph only in* B:) deva-guru-dharmma-saṃdeha, para-darśanābhilāṣa, sva-darśana-niṃdā, mithyādṛṣṭi-praśaṃsā yāga, bhoga śrādha-saṃvatsarī-lokīka-tithi-vāra māṃnyāṃ huiṃ, anumata dīdhuṃ hui, kīdhāṃ huiṃ

upalakṣaṇatvād darśanâcārâticārāṣtake[1] aticāra-sāmyāt. dvādaśa-vratâticāreṣv api sarveṣu deśataś catur-laghu, sarvataś catur-guru,[2]guru-dravya-bhoge bhinna-māsaḥ, guru-devâvaṃdane laghu- māsaḥ. ca-kārāt[3] pārśva-sthâdiṣu mamatve vātsyālye[4] ca māsa-guru (guruḥ A) // 4

1. pi A B. 2. mukhavastrikādi A; 3. va-kārā P; 4. vātsalye A B.

Remarks

Parallels: ab, cf. SJK 57–58. – c: cf. SJK 68 (*jai-davva-bhogi*). The expression is rather vague. Tilaka's commentary does not make it more precise. The commentary on Dharmaghoṣa's SJK indicates that it may refer to a monk's implement (mouth-cloth, seat), but also to a substance meant for a monk, like food or drink, used as medicines. – d: cf. SJK 62.

The five transgressions of orthodoxy as listed in the additional paragraph available in B are: doubt on the doctrine of the Jinas and of the teacher, inclination towards other faiths, blaming one's own faith, praising wrong faith, sacrifice, (offering) food (to folk deities; Shah 2011: 53), celebrating commemorative funeral rituals, annual rituals, non Jain festival days, authorizing their celebration, organizing their celebration. In modern lay *Pākṣika aticāra* manuals in Gujarati (or Hindi), names of contemporary holy days are given (e.g. Holi, Pretatīj, Gaurītrīj, Nāgapancamī, etc.: Sādhvī Mokṣarasāśrījī 2010: 10; Shah 2011: 50–52).

Addition in ms. A:

jiṇa-nāha-davva-bhoge bhuttaṃ jaṃ tattha 'nnattha vā dei
hīṇe majjh'-uccamae cau lahu cau guru a cha lahugā //5
guruga jaīṇam agāḍhe diṃte kammâi lahuga mīsâi
ajjhoarâi gurugo, lahu uddisie, paṇaga ṭhavie/6 = SJK 59
ms. jaiṇam; hiṃte; lahu u uddisiaṃ paṇag' uṭṭhaviaṃ
spaṣṭe.

For an object of consumption meant for the Lord Jinas which one consumes or gives to some other destination – for the lowest, the medium or the superior (type): four light, four heavy and six light (respectively).

Four heavy, if giving, without emergency reason, food implying violence and other faults; four light for combined food and other faults; one heavy for food increased (by additional material) and other faults; one light for food prepared specially; one incomplete month for food that has been put aside.

Remarks

The contents of verse 5 is the same as SJK 69 with several common words:

> *sāhāraṇa-jiṇadavvaṃ jaṃ bhuttaṃ asaṇa-vattha-kaṇagāī*
> *tatth' annattha va dinne cau lahu cau gurua cha-llahugā.*

The phrasing of ms. A, however, is more allusive. One should understand that "lowest, medium and superior" refer, respectively, to foodstuff, cloth and gold, as made clear in SJK and its commentary: *deva-dravya vā trividhe jaghanya-madhyamôtkṛṣṭa-rūpe 'śanâdau vastrâdau kanakâdau ca.*

Verse 6 deals with atonements in the context of almsgiving to mendicants. Laypeople are responsible for the food, as they are the ones who prepare it. Hence they have to compensate for transgressions that form the sixteen *uggama-dosa*s (Skt. *udgama-doṣa*). Some of their technical names are explicitly mentioned in the verse: *kamma* (Skt. *karma*) is an abbreviation for the first, Pkt. *ādhākamma* (Skt. *ādhākarma*), *mīsa* (Skt. *miśra*) is the fourth, *ajjhoyara* (Skt. *adhyavapūraka*) is the sixteenth, *ṭhavia* (Skt. *sthāpita*) is the fifth, *uddesia* (Skt. *auddeśika*) is the second. Others are implied through the use of *ādi* as the commentator on SJK explains. The situation is complicated by the fact that most of the sixteen faults have further subdivisions which have varying degrees of seriousness. Thus, for instance, a given fault may imply "four heavy" or "four light" depending on which subdivision is meant: two types of the *miśra* fault imply "four heavy", the third one "four light". See the extensive SJK commentary for details of the complex distribution (pp. 49 and pp. 39–41), and Deo (1956: 288–295) for a convenient description of the sixteen *uggama-dosa*s for which the ultimate source is the *Piṇḍa-niryukti*.

cāritrâcāra-prathamâṇuvrata-viṣayam āha.

> 5. puḍhavâīṇam a-kāraṇa saṃghaṭṭā'gāḍha gāḍha-pariyāve
> udavaṇe ya kameṇaṃ bhinnâī jāva cau lahuyaṃ.
> Numbered 7 in A; akāraṇaṃ A; pariāve A; uddavaṇe a A;
> For rubbing against earth bodies and other (kinds of bodies) without cause, for not serious or serious hurting and killing: respectively, an incomplete month and the others (namely, a light month, a heavy month) up to four light.

Commentary

puḍhavâī-gāhā. iha niṣiddhasyâcaraṇe tāvat prāyaścittaṃ. gṛhiṇaś ca sârthikā sthāvara-kāya-hiṃsā na niṣiddhā, nir-arthikā punar niṣiddhaiva *[identical to the first sentence of the commentary on Dharmaghoṣa's SJK 70].* tato a-kāraṇe kāraṇâbhāve niḥ-prayojanaṃ bhū-jala-jvalanânila-pratyeka-vanaspatīnāṃ saṃghaṭṭâgāḍha-paritāpa-gāḍha-paritāpôpadraveṣu krameṇa bhinna-māsa, laghu-māsa, guru-māsa, catur-laghūni (*add.* A prāyaścittāni) dīyante/5

Remarks

Pkt. *udavaṇa* is perhaps slightly archaic. It is used in the corresponding development of the *Jītakalpa*, Bhāṣya 1072 as *uddavaṇa.* In the *Sāmācārī* Tilakācārya uses *upadrava* (p. 19b), as well as one of the Sanskrit tracts preserved in ĀD (p. 265v verses 17 and 18); SJK has Pkt. *vaha* in the verse and *upadrava* in the Sanskrit commentary.

Parallel: SJK 70.

> 6. tah' aṇaṃta-kāiyāṇa vi sahasâṇābhogao va vigalāṇaṃ
> purimâī khavaṇ'-aṃtaṃ paṇ'-iṃdi gurugâi kallaṃ taṃ.
> Numbered 8 in A.
> And also for the plants with an infinite number of living organisms and for those with two, three or four organs of senses, (in case of rubbing against, not serious hurting, serious hurting and killing) out of harshness or involuntary: respectively (the series) starting with no food during the first half and the others (namely one meal a day, sour food) and ending with full fast. For those with five organs of senses (in case of rubbing against, not serious hurting, serious hurting and killing): respectively heavy and the others (namely four light, four heavy) and one full set in the list.

Commentary

tah' aṇaṃta-gāhā. tathêty aupamye. yathā pṛthivy-ādīnām evam[1]

(*This paragraph only in* B:) ādraka, nīlī haladra, āṃbilī kuṃlī ityādi kaṃda anaṃtakāya ṣādhāṃ huiṃ: thohari, kuṃyāri, guggali galo, bhagga aṃkura, kisalaya, paṇagā, sevāla, bhūmi-phoḍā ya allaya tti, gajjara, muttha, vattha-laya, thega, pallaṃgā

aṇaṃta-kāyikānām api niḥ-prayojanaṃ saṃghaṭṭâdiṣu, tathā caṃdanikā-kīṭikā-nagara-śuṣira-vṛty-ādiṣu snāna-jaloṣṇâvasrāvaṇâder[2] vahane[3], saṃkhārakasya[4] ccharddane śoṣe vā, agalita-jala-vyāpāraṇe, galyamānasya vā kiyato pi chardane. aśodhitêṃdhanasyâgnau kṣepe, keśa-viralī-karaṇe śiraḥ-kaṃḍūyane vā, śara-leṣṭv-ādeḥ, krīḍârtham[5] anyataḥ kṣepe 'pi, sahasākārād anābhogād vā vikalānāṃ dvi-tri-catur-iṃdriyāṇāṃ saṃghaṭṭâdiṣu, purimārddhaikāśanā cāmāmla[6]- kṣapaṇāni prāyaścittāni; paṃceṃdriyāṇāṃ tu vikaleṃdriya-nyāyenaiva saṃghaṭṭâdiṣu guru-māsa, catur-laghu, catur-guru, eka-kalyāṇikāni yathā-saṃkhyaṃ // 6

1. eva A B. 2. avaśravaṇāder A. 3. vāhane. 4. saṃskārakasya A. 5. krīḍā artham A. 6. cāmla B. 7. kalyāni A.

Remarks

Parallels: SJK 71–72. The commentaries are largely identical, the variations pertaining mostly to the sequence of statements. The contents of stanza 72, not in Tilaka's work, is a Prakrit rendering of the special situations listed in the Sanskrit commentaries.

The additional paragraph from B lists some of the *anantakāya*s, i.e. plants inhabited by an infinite number of living organisms (Williams 1963: 113ff.; Shah 2011: 82–83). From *aṃkura* to *pallaṃgā*, the text is almost a quotation of Śāntisūri's *Jīvavicāra* verse 9.

7. saṃkappā dappā vā thūla-vahâīsu paṃca kallāṇaṃ
egâi das'-aṃtesuṃ taṃ taṃ parau ya dasagaṃ tu.
(Numbered 9 in A; dappā, om. A = mistake; taṃ ta parao saṃkhadasaṃga tu A)

For killing and other (transgressions of the *aṇuvrata*s) relating to gross (living beings) out of purpose or out of arrogance: five sets of five. For (harming, etc. of) one up to ten: the same with one more (each time; = two to ten full sets); and beyond: ten sets indeed.

Commentary

saṃkappā-gāhā. saṃkalpataḥ prayojanaṃ saṃkalpa-darpād[1] vā mattatayā, trasa-jīvānāṃ dvi-tri-catuḥ-paṃcêmdriyāṇāṃ vadho. ādi-śabdān mṛṣâdattamaithuna-parigraha-vrateṣu virādhiteṣu[2] paṃca-kalyāṇaṃ. ekâdi daśānteṣu tat tat. ekasya dvîndriyâder vadhe ekaṃ sva-prāyaścittaṃ, dvayor dve, trayāṇāṃ trīṇi yāvad daśānāṃ vadhe daśa. parataś caikādaśâdiṣu yāvad asaṃkhyeṣv api. daśakaṃ tu[3]. tur eva-kārârthe daśakam eva prāyaścittam ity arthaḥ. ca-śabdāj

(*This paragraph only in* B:) saṃkha, mehara, alasīyāṃ, śaramīyā, māṃkaṇa, jūā, jū, maṃkoḍā, ūdehī, ghīmeli, cūḍeli, gāḍhara, ḍāṃsa, masā, māṣī, tīḍa, vīṃchī <rā> bhramarīyā, kolīyā, bhamarī-ghara bhāṃjyāṃ, dhanerīyā, maccha dūhivyā, dvipada, catuppada, savasi dūhavyā laṃghavyā ura-pari(sappa), bhuja-parisarppa, panara karmmādāna, jalacara, thalacara,

jalaukasāṃ mocane catur-laghu //7

1. saṃkalpāt darpād vā A. 2. not in A. 3 not in A. 4. ms. laṃghyāvā.

Remarks

Parallels: SJK 73 and, for pādas cd, the Prakrit verse quoted in the commentary on 59 and again on 70:

egāi-dasaṃtesu egāi-dasaṃtayaṃ sa-pacchittaṃ
teṇa paraṃ dasagaṃ ciya bahuesu vi sagala-vigalesu.

It refers to the special atonement called *sapacchitta* (Skt. *svaprāyaścitta*), which is said to be explained in the monastic Jītakalpa. The number of atonements is the same as the number of beings who have been hurt, with a maximum of ten.

The additional paragraph from B lists various small animals or kinds of insects (spiders, varieties of ants, insects found in corn, lice, etc.), following the line of Śāntisūri's *Jīvavicāra* 15–21 with which it shares several names. Even more, it exhibits the influence of *Pākṣika Aticāra* manuals in Gujarati, where, in the same context, such living beings and others are listed (Sādhvī Mokṣarasāśrījī 2010: 13; Shah 2011: 59–60). Towards the end the list is interrupted by a mention of the "fifteen prohibited activities" (*panara karmmādāna*; see below verse 15).

In ms. A the Sanskrit commentary is followed by the following stanza:

[agaliya-jalassa p<i>āṇe tāvaṇa aṃgholi-m-āi aṭṭhamayaṃ
kolia puḍa saṃkhāraya kīḍiya-nagarāi paṇa kallaṃ//10]

In case of drinking unfiltered water, or warming (it), a bath, ?, cobweb, remaining water, (destruction) of worms' houses etc. (= cocoons, beehives, etc.): five complete sets.

Without commentary, it is an expansion, also related to the first *aṇuvrata*, following the line of *Pākṣika Aticāra* manuals in Gujarati (Mokṣarasāśrījī 2010: 14; Shah 2011: 60–61). This verse is close to Dharmaghoṣa's SJK 72:

agalia-jala-chaḍḍaṇa-ṇhāṇa-pāṇa dhua-tāvaṇâi cha gguruaṃ (read so with BL ms.; Ed. *tāvaṇa-ghaṭṭaṇâi cha guruaṃ*, unmetrical)
paṇa-kallaṃ saṃkhāraya kolia-kīḍia-gharâīsu

Drinking, wasting or bathing with unfiltered water, washing (clothes), warming, injuring, etc. (with such water): six heavy. Five complete sets for water remaining, for houses of spiders (= cobwebs) and of worms (= silkworms' cocoons) (having been broken).

Aṃgholi in ms. A is a variant form of Pkt. *aṃgaholi* and Guj. *aṃghola*, "bathing, bath", and thus a semantic equivalent of SJK *ṇhāṇa* (Skt. *snāna*).

(*This paragraph only in* B:) mṛṣāvāda-vrati sahasātkāri, kūḍua padosa, kūḍī sāṣi kanyā, go, bhūmi, ṭhavaṇī mosu delagani (?) rāulagani (?) kūḍī sāṣi, adattādāni coryuṃ corāvyuṃ.

mṛṣâdatta-parigraheṣv āha:

8. taṇu-majjhima-ukkose mosaṃmi parigahe ya gurugâī
niya-gehaṃmi adinne lahū jahanne, garū majjhe.
9. nāe ya cau lah', ukkosae a-nāe vi paṃca kallāṇaṃ.
nāe ŏ jāya-kalahe taṃ vi ya sajjhāya-lakkha-juyaṃ.
Numbered 11 and 12 in A; pariggahe a A; nia geha ti adinne A; 9 taṃ cia A; °jayaṃ P.

For wrong speech and possession, depending on whether they are minimal, medium or maximum: heavy and the others in the series. For taking of what has not been given in one's own house: light when minimal, heavy when medium. And when it is known, four light; when maximal, even if unknown, a full set of five; if known, in case a quarrel has come up, the same, together with hundred thousand recitations.

Commentary

taṇu-majjhima-gāhā. *nāe*-gāhā. jaghanya-madhyamôtkṛṣṭe mṛṣāvāde parigrahe[1] ca gurukâdi-ekāśanâcāmāmla-kṣapaṇa-svarūpaṃ[2] prāyaścittaṃ. ca-kārāt[3] sarva-parigraha-pramāṇa[4]-bhaṃge utkarṣataḥ svādhyāya-lakṣaṃ sahasrâdhikaṃ. sva-gṛhe jaghanye 'dattādāne laghukaṃ, madhyame gurukaṃ/8

madhyame 'pi ca jñāte catur-laghu, utkṛṣṭe punar a-jñāte pi paṃca kalyāṇaṃ, jñāte punar utkṛṣṭe[5] jāta-kalahe[6] tad eva paṃca kalyāṇaṃ. svādhyāya-lakṣa-yuktaṃ[7] dīyata ity arthaḥ // 9

1. parigraha cau A. 2. kṣapaṇaṃ rūpaṃ A. 3 cakārā bhūsarva A. 4. parimāṇa A. 5. A adds rājakulaparyaṃte ca. 6. kalahe jāte A. 7. yutaṃ A, B.

Remarks

Parallels: SJK 80 and 79 (*kalahe*).

The initial paragraph, available only in B, is, in Gujarati, a list of the transgressions of the *satyavrata*, according to the traditional divisions of its application: untruth relating to a girl, a cow, land, a deposit (*ṭhavaṇī*), false witness. It also includes false accusation made without required enquiry (compare Shah 2011: 63ff.) and ends with a definition relating to the third vow, since both are treated together in the stanza that follows.

maithuna-viṣayam āha /

10. cau guru cha lahu cha guru sa-dāra ittariya vesa-vaya-bhaṃge
mūlaṃ tu kula-vahūe, mauyāe paṃca kallāṇaṃ.
11. nāe lakkham a-nāe paṇa kallāṇaṃ tu hīṇa-paradāre
asiī lakkham a-nāe, nāe puṇa uttame mūlaṃ.
Numbered 13 and 14 in A; cha llahu cha gguru A; asii A; lakham P; nāe in 11d missing P, C.

Four heavy, six light, six heavy: for breaking the vow (involuntarily) with regard to one's own wife, with a temporary wife, with a prostitute. But with a lady from a good family, "radical". In case of softness, five sets of five. If it becomes known publicly, hundred thousand (recitations), if it does not become known, a set of five in case the adulteress lady is of low extraction. However, hundred eighty thousand (recitations) if it has not been known, in case the adulteress lady is of an excellent family, "radical" (if it becomes known).

Commentary

cau-guru-gāhā. *nāe*-gāhā. sva-dārêtvara-parigṛhīta-veśyāsv anābhogān niyama-bhaṃge catur-gurv-ādīni, jānatas tu tisṛṣv api paṃca kalyāṇaṃ, kula-vadhvā saha maithune mūlaṃ, mṛta-patikayā punas tayāpi[1] bṛhat-kumārikayā vā paṃca kalyāṇaṃ //10 jñātvā hīna-jātīyān para-dārān tad-āsevane svādhyāya-lakṣaṃ. ajñātvā tu tad-āsevane paścāt jñāte paṃca kalyāṇaṃ. uttame rājany-āmātya-dārâdike[2] ajñātvā āsevite[3] aśīti-sahasrâdhikaṃ lakṣaṃ. jñātvā tv āsevite mūlaṃ //11

1. From here onwards A is quite different: tayā vṛha tvāsevite mūlaṃ //14 uttamakula-para-kalatre vrata-bhaṃge mūle 'pi samāgate 'priti (*sic*-prasiddha-pātrasya tu paṃca)-kalyāṇam eva deyaṃ na mūlam iti. The nonsensical sequence *vṛha tvāsevite mūlaṃ* is the result of an error: the scribe has skipped over several lines in the copy which was before him: *vṛha* is the beginning of *vṛhat* = *bṛhat-kumārikayā* and *tvāsevite mūlaṃ* is the end of the commentary on the two verses. 2. uttame rājakanyādikānyadārādike B. 3. ārovite P is probably the result of a misreading of the manuscript from which it was copied.

Remarks

Parallels: SJK 81–84 and 85+87.

mauyāe is here understood as the oblique case of *mauyā*, feminine abstract noun on *mau* < Skt. *mṛdu*. This interpretation is supported by SPAn 8 *mauyassa*, gen. of *mauya* < Skt. *mṛduka* referring to a person. The SJK 82 does not use this word, but conveys a similar idea with *sāsaṃka* explained in the commentary as referring to the adulterous couple. Further, the commentary on SJK says: *mṛdu-svabhāvasya tu pañca-kalyam eva, "jai saṃtappai to paṃca-kallaṇammi" ti vacanāt*, "but for the person who has a soft nature, only five sets, on the basis of the saying 'if he has remorse, then five sets'", using Skt. *mṛdu* as in SPAn or SPT. This would be in tune with the fact that in order to be efficient atonements have to be adjusted to the strength and abilities of the culprit. The commentary on SPT, however, goes in another direction and may have understood Pkt. *mauyāe* in Skt. *mṛtapatikā* (which, however, in SJK 84 has the expected form Pkt. *maya-paiyā*).

12. sīlassa balā bhaṃge lakkhaṃ itthīi sa-paṇa-kallāṇaṃ
paṃcuṃbari-mahu-bhogo khavaṇam a-nāe cha guru nāe.
Numbered 15 in A; °bhogo P, C; °bhoge A,B.

For breaking the honour of a lady forcibly: hundred thousand (recitations) with five sets of five. Eating the five *udumbara* fruits or honey: a full fast if done unknowingly; six heavy, if done knowingly.

Commentary

sīlassa-gāhā. striyāḥ śīlasya balāt-kāreṇa bhaṃge[1] svādhyāya-lakṣaṃ, paṃca kalyāṇaṃ ca tapaḥ.[2] paṃcoḍuṃvara-phalānāṃ[3] madhunaś ca ajñātvā bhoge kṣapaṇaṃ. jñātvā tu bhoge ṣaḍ-gurukaṃ/12

1. jaghanyataḥ is added in A. 2. karakarmmaṇi ṣaḍ guru/asaikae paṃcakalyaṃ/ mūā vaḍiā vaḍiāe paṃcakalyaṃ is then added in A. 3. paṃcobaraphalānāṃ A.

Remarks

Parallels: ab are quoted in the commentary on Dharmaghoṣa's SJK 85, with the introductory remark: *anye tu striyaṃ praty evam āhuḥ* – cd, cf. SJK 90 (in connection with the second *guṇavrata*). According to Dharmaghoṣa the atonement for eating unknowingly is *guruga*, that is "four heavy", and the comm. records varying opinions on the topic.

13. cau lahu para-parivāy'-abbhakkhāṇâsabbha-rāḍi-pesunne
saṃḍa-vivāhe kanā-hale ya lahugaṃ ḍhiullīṇaṃ.
Numbered 16 in A; kannāhale A.

Four light for scandal on others, false charge, indecent talk, shout and back-biting. For marrying a eunuch and for (accepting) a dowry four light – (for making) dolls out of rags.

Commentary

cau lahu-gāhā. para-parivādâbhyākhyānâsabhya-rāṭi-paiśūnya-ṣaṃḍa[1]-vivāha-kanyā-phala-grahaṇeṣu catur-laghu, ḍhiullikānāṃ[2] ca krīḍârthaṃ karaṇe māsa laghu //13

1. śaṃḍha A. 2. ṭiullikānāṃ P, C.

Remarks

Parallels: ab = SJK 79ab; cd: cf. SJK 63ab. The present commentary is briefer than the one on Dharmaghoṣa's SJK, which is helpful to assert three points:

1 *lahugaṃ* here, *lahugā* in SJK, is a technical term different from *lahu*, and is the same as "four light". Tilaka's commentary also understands it that way, and the commentary on SJK gives the definition: *laghukāḥ – catur-laghu-prāyaścittaṃ bhavatîty arthaḥ.*

2 The commentary on SJK has a gloss for Pkt. *ḍhiullī*: *ḍhiullikānāṃ – vastra-khaṇḍa-nirmita-puttalikānāṃ tu vivāhe krīḍârthaṃ vā karaṇe laghu-māsaḥ 1*. This refers to the use of dolls made out of rags as sex toys.

3 There is a discrepancy in the atonement prescribed for using these dolls between Tilaka's verse and his commentary. The verse has no other term than *lahuga*, which means "four light", whereas the commentary prescribes "a light month". This is a reflection of two different opinions in the tradition about this atonement, as is made clear by the commentary on Dharmaghoṣa's SJK: he prescribes "one light month" (see the quotation under 2) just above), but adds: *matântareṇa tv atrâpi catur-laghava eva.*

14. disivaya-aṇattha-bhaṃge sāmāiya-saṃvibhāga-avihāṇe
a-nimittaṃ nisi-bhutte aṇaṃta-asaṇe ya cau guruyaṃ.

Numbered 17 in A. Each item followed by a serial number from 1 to 6 in A. For breaking the vow of spatial limitation and that of violence without aim, for not performing the equanimity vow or that of alms-giving to mendicants, for having eaten at night when there was no valid reason (to do so), and for eating plants having an infinite number of living organisms: four heavy.

Commentary

disivaya-gāhā. digvratânartha-daṃḍayor bhaṃge, sāmāyikâtithisaṃvibhāgayor akaraṇe, niḥ-kāraṇaṃ niśāyāṃ bhojane. niṣiddhasya cânaṃtakāyasyâśane catur-gurukaṃ // 14

Remarks

Parallels: a = SJK 88a; b: cf. SJK 93 ab and 103a; c: cf. SJK 88b; d: cf. SJK 91a: *cau guru 'ṇante*.

Tilakācārya has a synthetic presentation, dealing together with all the vows for which violation is to be compensated by the same atonement. Dharmaghoṣa treats each vow independently.

15. patteya-bhogi cau lahu taha desavagāsa posahâkaraṇe
kammādāṇe (short e) cha lahu sura-maṃse (short e) khavaṇa paṃca-kallāṇe.
Numbered 18 in A; desavagāsi A; cha llahu A; °kallāṇaṃ A
For consuming elementary (living beings): four light, and also for the vow relating to the scope of space of action and for not performing *poṣadha*. For practice of the (fifteen forbidden) activities: six light. For alcohol and meat: full fast or five sets of five.

Commentary

patteya-gāhā. niṣiddhasya[1] pratyeka-vanaspati-puṣpa-phalâder[2] bhoge. tathā deśāvakāśikasya yathā pratijñāta-poṣadhasya câkaraṇe catur-laghu. paṃcadaśasu karmādāneṣu niṣiddhâseviteṣu ṣaḍ laghu. madya-māṃsayor anābhogād bhoge kṣapaṇaṃ. ākuṭṭikayā ca bhoge paṃca kalyāṇaṃ // 15

1. niṣiddhasyâmrādiṣu A. 2. So read with A,B; puṣpakalāder P, C.

Remarks

Parallels: SJK 91 to 93 for similar contents.

One of the most serious transgressions is the consumption of meat and alcohol. The wording of SPT "for alcohol and meat: full fast or five sets of five" is extremely concise. The type of atonement does not depend on whether it is meat or alcohol. One should follow the commentary, in agreement with SJK 91cd, and understand that "full fast" (here *khamaṇa*; *cau guru* in SJK) is to be prescribed in case consumption is involuntary (*anābhogād*), and "five sets of five" (*panca-kallāṇe* SPT; *cha-ggaru* SJK) in case it is done in full consciousness (*ākuṭṭikayā*, SPT comm.; *ābhogataḥ*, SJK comm.).

For more details on the fifteen forbidden trades see, for instance, Williams (1963: 117ff.); Shah (2011: 94).

16. kohe pakkhâīe pagāḍha-māyā-maesu cau garuyaṃ.
vimhariy'-annāya-kae pai-varisaṃ paṃca kallāṇaṃ.
Verse not in A, only comm. – numbered 19.

For anger, for going beyond the fortnight, for strong treachery or arrogance: four heavy. For something forgotten or not known: every year five sets of five.

Commentary

kohe-gāhā. krodhe pakṣâdy-atīte, pakṣaṃ cātur-māsakaṃ vâtikramyâpi kṛtâvasthāne.[1] pragāḍha-māyāyāṃ ati[2]-lobhāt paravaṃcanâtmikāyāṃ māyāyāṃ[3] kṛtāyāṃ madeṣu ca jāti-madâdiṣûtkaṭeṣu catur-gurukaṃ. vismṛtâjñāta-kṛte ālocanīyasyâticārasya kurvadbhir ajñātasyâkaraṇânaṃtaraṃ vā vismṛtasya kṛte, sarvasyâpy etasya śodhanāya[4] śodhana-nimittaṃ prati-varṣaṃ yāvadbhyo varṣebhya ālocanāṃ gṛhṇāti tāvaṃti paṃca kalyāṇāni vitīryaṃta[5] ity arthaḥ // 16

1. vātikramyātikṛtāvasthāne P, C. 2. iti A. 3. māyāyāṃ not in A. 4. vismṛtasya śodhanāya nimittaṃ prativarṣaṃ A, B. 5. vitīryaṃta B; vaṃtīryaṃta P, A; dīyaṃte A.

Remarks

Parallels: ab = cf. SJK 88cd (following what relates to breaking of the *digvrata*, the *anarthadaṇḍavrata* and not observing the prohibition to eat at night, which all are compensated by an identical atonement) – cd: cf. SJK 108cd, where this point is treated towards the end of the work because it concerns all types of transgressions, and relates to confession. The commentary records several different opinions about how this should be compensated. SPT comm. also refers to the context of confession.

Here the author's purpose is to contrast transgressions which have been done under the power of a passion, treachery or concealing, and that which has been done without deliberation, which is less serious.

vīryâcāra-viṣayam āha /

17. cau guru cau lahu a pamāyā 'paḍikamaṇe vaiṭṭha-paḍikamaṇe
evaṃ vaṃdaṇagassa vi dāṇâdāṇesu lahu guruge.

Numbered 20 in A; the avagraha conveying the privative prefix a- is noted only in A.

Four heavy, four light (respectively) for non-performing of repentance out of carelessness, and for repentance (performed) sitting carelessly. Similarly in exchanges for paying homage: light or heavy.

Commentary

cau guru-gāhā. pramādād ālasyād a-pratikramaṇe catur-guru[1] 17.
[2]śaktasyopaviṣṭasya[3] pratikramaṇe catur-laghu. evaṃ vaṃdanakasyâpy upaviṣṭe na dāne māsa laghu, sarvathâpy adāne māsa guru.

1. caturlaghu A; 2. This paragraph of the commenatry is available only in A and B. 3. śaktisyāpy ālasyād upaviṣṭasya B.

Remarks

Parallel: SJK 106, with a less concise and more transparent wording:

paḍikamaṇassâkaraṇe cau guru, cau lahu baiṭṭha-paḍikamaṇe
guru vaṃdaṇagâkaraṇe baiṭṭha-karaṇe a lahu-māso.

Tilaka's *dāṇâdāṇesu* seems to be expanded in the commentary on SJK as referring to errors relating to the stereotyped sentences exchanged by the performer of the homage and his teacher, which have to be compensated by *bhinnādi*. Hence the full scale would be:

non-performing of homage: one heavy month
transgressions in the way of sitting: one light month
errors in verbal exchanges: one incomplete month and other atonements.
In mss. P and C the commentary only translates into Sanskrit the first statement.
tapa-ācāra-viṣayam āha //

18. khavaṇam a-paccaṣāṇe akāraṇe purima-carimagâkaraṇe
lahugaṃ dava sacitte ahige ahiga vigaie paṇagaṃ.
Numbered 21 in A; khamaṇam B; apaccakkhāṇe A; davva A; ahiga gahia vigaie paṇayaṃ A; C ahigehiga vigaie paṇagaṃ; B ahigehigavigaie paṇagaṃ – Metre of cd not satisfactory.
Full fast: for not putting into effect taken resolutions if there is no valid reason (for not doing so). For not performing the first or the last (days of *pratyākhyāna*): one light. For a substance with life in excess, for derived products in excess: five.

Commentary

khavaṇa-gāhā. parva-tithau mayâmukaṃ pratyākhyānaṃ kartavyaṃ[1] śeṣa-tithiṣu câmukam ity abhigrahaṃ kṛtvâpi niḥ-kāraṇaṃ[2] glānatvâdikāraṇâbhāve 'pi[3]pratyākhyānâkaraṇe kṣapaṇaṃ. carama-pratyākhyānâkaraṇe ca laghukaṃ.[4] dravye sacitte vâbhigṛhītād adhike bhukte laghukaṃ, vikṛtau câdhikāyāṃ bhuktāyāṃ paṃcakaṃ, śeṣâbhigraheṣu cābhogāt khaṃḍiteṣu[5] bhinna-māsaḥ. [6]anābhogâdinā punaḥ khaṃḍitānāṃ dvādaśa-vrata-satkānāṃ mayy abhigrahānāṃ deśavirati-ṭippane ya ekāśanādir[7] daṃḍo likhyate sa-bhayârthaṃ yenêdṛśād[8] daṃḍād bhīto 'bhigrahāt vismārya na bhanakti // 18

1. karttavyaṃ B and in the same sentence in the comm. on SJK; kāryaṃ A; kathaṃ P, C. 2. Followed by tat pratyākhyānā'karaṇe kṣapaṇaṃ/akāraṇe gl. A. 3. prathama-carimākaraṇā namaskāra-sahita-divasa-carima-pratyākhyānâkaraṇe laghukaṃ, dravye etc. in A. 4. So P, C; caturlaghukaṃ B. 5. So P (cābhogā with t added above the lines); cānābhogāt kh. A, B; vābhogā na kh. C. 6. All this paragraph not in A. 7. So P, C (with spelling °ṭṭipane); ṭippane yad B. 8. yenadṛśād P and yanedṛśād C are errors.

Remarks

Parallels: SJK 103–104.

19. gaṃṭhi-sahiyassa bhaṃge aṭṭha-sayaṃ sesa-paccakkhāṇassa
bhaṃge taṃ ceva tavo cha-mmāsaṃ bahuya-pāve vi.
Numbered 22 in A; gaṃṭha A; paccakhāṇassa A

For breaking of (a *pratyākhyāna*) associated with a knot: hundred and eight (*namaskāras*). For breaking of remaining *pratyākhyānas* the same penance (corresponding to that *pratyākhyāna*). Six months for serious evil.

Commentary

gaṃṭhi-gāhā. graṃtha-muṣṭy-ādi sahitasya upalakṣaṇatvān namaskāra-sahitasya bhaṃge[1]<pānâhāreṇa namaskārâṣṭottaraṃ śataṃ, svādyâhāreṇa dve śate aṣṭottare, khādyâśanābhyāṃ tu bhaṃge purimārddhaṃ. śeṣa-pratyākhyāna-bhaṃge tu tad eva pratyākhyānaṃ. ko 'rthaḥ? purima-bhaṃge> purimam eva yāvat kṣapaṇa-bhaṃge kṣapaṇam eva. bahuke pi ca pāpe mūlânavasthāpya yogye iha śrīVīra-tīrthe ṣaṇ-māsikam eva prāyaścittaṃ[2] śrāvakāṇāṃ śrāvikāṇāṃ ca śakty-ādikaṃ vicārya dātavyam ity arthaḥ //19

Missing in P due to lack of fol. 159. – 1. < > only in B and C, not in A. – 2. dīyate ity arthaḥ, A ends.

Remarks

(*Pratyākhyāna*) "with a knot" refers to the third type of *saṅketa-pratyākyāna*, which is based on a symbolic convention. For instance, *granthi-pr.* means "I will refrain from taking food as long as I don't loosen this knot" (Williams 1963: 208). *Muṣṭi*° (comm.) refers to the second type: "as long as I do not unclench my hand". The penance for the violation of other *pratyākhyānas* should be the same as the type of *pratyākhyāna* which one has committed to, going to a full fast, if this was the commitment.

The six months atonement is the maximal one. It is reserved for transgressions viewed as very serious. Compare the phrase *cha-mmāsaṃ bahuya-pāve vi* quoted in SJK comm. on 82 p. 62 about the vow of celibacy.

samāpti-gāthā (in B)

20. siri-Cakkasūri-paṭṭâhiva-siriSivapahasūri-sīsa-lesehiṃ
esā Sāmāyārī raiyā siri-Tilayasūrīhiṃ.
Numbered 36 in A; Cakasuri P.

This code of conduct has been composed by Tilakasūri, the humble pupil of Śivaprabhasūri, the master of the lineage of Cakreśvarasūri.

Commentary

B: spaṣṭā. – C: *siri-Cakkasūri*-gāthā. spaṣṭā //20 – A: no commentary; P ends with: āloyaṇāe diṇṇā icchāmo sāraṇa-vāraṇa-coyaṇāu iti guruṇā bhāṇaitavyaḥ (sic)/svayaṃ ca aham api sāraṃyavvo/vāriyavvo voiyavvo iti vācyaṃ //. The beginning of this sentence also appears at the very end of ms. B, fol. 8v.

P: iti śrī śrīTilakācārya-gumphitaḥ Śrāvaka-prāyaścitta-samācārī-vidhiḥ // X//
B: Śrāvaka-jītakalpa-vṛtti samāptā //X//

C: Śrāvaka-jītakalpa-vṛtti samāptêti.
A: iti śrīTilakasūri-gumphita-śrāddha-Laghujītakalpa-vṛttiḥ // sa-sūtrā samāptāḥ.

Poṣadhasāmācārī unit (only in mss. P and A)

Prakrit verses

pauṣadhika-prāyaścittam āha (A)

1 posahio na kareī āvasiyaṃ vā nisīhiyaṃ vā vi
kuṇai ya mutt'-uccāre thaṃḍila-paḍilehaṇāi viṇā
2 kuḍḍâi-avaṭṭhaṃbhe kaṭṭhāsaṇagâi-gahaṇa-nikkheve
vār'-ugghāḍaṇa-pihaṇe a-pamajjiya kāya-kaṃḍuyaṇe [cf. SJK 95]
3 uvahiṃ na ppaḍilehai n'iriyaṃ paḍikamai vasahi na pamajje [cf. SJK 94]
pāḍiya-puttī-lābhe paṇagaṃ, cau guru a-lābhaṃmi [cd: cf. SJK 93cd]
4 sajjhāyassâkaraṇe bhinnam a-pāriya jime jalaṃ ca pive
no uddharei puṃjaṃ nâsaja-bhaṇiro pamajjae lahuyaṃ [cf. SJK 96]
5 vamaṇe nisi vosiraṇe jimiūṇaṃ vaṃdaṇe asaṃvaraṇe
animitta diyā suyaṇe vigahā sāvajja-bhāsāe [= SJK 101]
6 sāgārâpaccakkhāṇe saṃthārâsaṃdisāvaṇe taha ya
saṃthāraya-gāhāo (short o) ṇuccariuṃ suyai cau lahuyaṃ [cf. SJK 102]
7 gurugaṃ jahanna alie cau lahu majjhaṃmi cau gur' ukkose
uvaviṭha-paḍikamaṇe lahugaṃ jaha bhaṇiya ceiyâ-namaṇe
8 purisass' itthī-phāse cau lahu, itthīi hoi cau gurugaṃ
lahugaṃ saṃtara-phāse, aṃcala-tiri-phāsaṇe bhinnaṃ [= SJK 97]
9 ti-viha jala-jalaṇa-phusaṇe vijju-pphusaṇe ya bhinna lahu gurugā
cau lahu vagghāraṃmī taṃ ciya daga-maṭṭi-gamaṇe ya 9 [almost = SJK 98]
9bis nava-vāsa-vuṭṭhi kisalaya-virāhaṇā jattāṇi divasāṇi
tāvaiā cau gurugā dasagaṃ chapiāla-sui-nāse [= SJK 99]
10 puḍhavâi-ghaṭṭaṇâisu bhinnâi aṇaṃta vigala lahugâi
paṃc'iṃdisu gurugāi dasagaṃ savvesu nava-parao/10 [= SJK 100]
10bis bhinna-māsa 1 lahua māse 2 guru-māse 3 cau-lahua 4 caugurugā 5
cha-mmāsa lahua cha-mmāsa garua 7 nivviāīṇaṃ sannā.
10ter Hatthuttara Savaṇa tigaṃ Revai Rohiṇi Puṇavvasūṇa dugaṃ

Aṇurāha samaṃ bhaṇia solasa āloaṇā rikkhā

etāḥ pauṣadhika-prāyaścitta-sāmācārī-gāthāḥ (P).

These verses are numbered 23 to 35 in A – Verse 2. vārugghāḍaṇe A; kaṃḍūyaṇe A – 3. niriyaṃ A; nariyaṃ P; pāḍiaputtialābhe A – 4. apārīya P; nāsajabhamiro A; lahua A – 6. sāgāra A; taya P – 7. uvaviṭṭha A; jahanne A; lahuaṃ jai ceiānamaṇe A – 8. lahuaṃ A – 9. maṭṭia-game a A = SJK 98d – 9bis. Only in A where it is numbered 32 – 10. gurugāī A; parao P, A, against purao

SJK ed. and BL ms. Or. 2105G – 10bis and 10ter. Only in A where they are numbered 34 and 35 and not commented upon; 10ter. Also in Mitra (1886) according to extracts.

Sanskrit commentary

1 āvaśyikīṃ na karoti, naiṣedhikīṃ na karoti, a-pratilekhita-sthaṃḍile prasravaṇam uccāraṃ vā karoti,

2 a-pramṛjya kuḍyâdāv avaṣṭhambhaṃ karoti, a-pramṛjyâsana-paṭṭâdikaṃ gṛhṇāti nikṣipati vā, a-pramṛjya dvāram udghāṭayati pidhatte vā, a-pramṛjya kāyaṃ kaṃḍūyate,

3 upadhiṃ na pratilekhayati, vasatiṃ na pramārjayati, iryāṃpathas tyāgâdau na pratikrāmati, pātayitvā mukhāvastrikāṃ labhate, sarveṣv eteṣu pratyekaṃ paṃcakaṃ, pātita-mukhavastrikāyās tv a-lābhe 'rdha-namaskārâvalikā, nāśane māsa guruḥ.

4 prātaḥ svādhyāyaṃ na karoti 25, a-pārite bhuṃjīta payaḥ pibed vā 25, puṃjakaṃ nôddharati laghu, rātrāv āsajjêti bhaṇan pramārjayaṃś ca na hiṃḍate la° (= *abbreviation for* laghu).

5 vāṃtiṃ karoti 4, rātrau saṃjñām utsṛjati 4, bhojanânantaraṃ vaṃdanakaṃ datvā pratyākhyānaṃ na karoti 4, a-nimittaṃ divā svapiti 4, vikathāṃ karoti 4, sāvadyaṃ bhāṣate 4,

6 saṃstārakaṃ a-saṃdeśya 4, sākāram a-pratyākhyāya 4, saṃstāra-gāthā anuccārya śete 4.

7 a-satyaṃ vakti jaghanyaṃ guru, madhyamaṃ 4, utkṛṣṭaṃ 4, a-śaktyā upaviṣṭaḥ pratikrāmati la°, yathā-bhaṇitāś caitya-vaṃdanā(ṃ) na karoti la°.

8 puruṣasya strī-saṃghaṭṭe ca 4, striyāḥ puruṣa-saṃghaṭṭe gu° 4, sāṃtara-saṃghaṭṭe la°, aṃcala-saṃghaṭṭe 25, tiryak-saṃghaṭṭe ca 25,

9 jala-jvalana-sparśane vidyut-sparśane ca jaghanye 25, madhyame la°, utkṛṣṭe gu°, vaghāre punaś catur-laghu, udaka-mṛttikā-gamane 4,

9bis nava-varṣā-vṛṣ-ṭoyāni kiśalayāni anaṃtakāya-rūpāṇi syus, teṣāṃ virādhanā yāvaṃti dināni syus tāvantaś catur-gurukāḥ prāyaścittaṃ. ayaṃ bhāvaḥ: varṣāsu prathama-vṛṣṭau trīṇi dināni aṃtarmuhūrtaṃ yāvad anaṃtakāya-rūpāḥ prāyaḥ sarvatra pratikṣaṇaṃ prādur-bhavaṃti. tad-virādhanā-tyāgāya dina-trayaṃ sādhavo yataṃte. yatamānānām api teṣāṃ navāṃkura-virādhanāni tāvaṃti catur- gurūṇi syuḥ. tathā ṣaṭpady-ālayo yūkā-gṛhaṃ sūcī-sūcikâlayas tayor nāśe pratyekaṃ daśakaṃ pratyāsatteś catur-gurukāṇām iti.

10 pṛthivy-āp-tejo-vāyu-pratyeka-vanaspati-saṃghaṭṭâdiṣu bhinnâdīni, anaṃta-vanaspati-vikaleṃdriya-saṃghaṭṭâdiṣu laghukâdīni, paṃceṃdriya-saṃghaṭṭâdiṣu gurukâdīni, navâdhikeṣu vâsaṃkhyeṣv api sakaleṣu vikaleṣu vā daśakam eva prāyaścittaṃ dīyate, nâdhikam api. pauṣadhikasya prāyeṇaitāny ālocanīya-padāni saṃbhavaṃti. teṣām eṣā prāyaścitta-sāmācārī.

iti śrīśrīTilakācārya-gumphitaḥ Pauṣadhika-prāyaścitta-samācārī-vidhiḥ //

Comm. on verse 2. avaṣṭhambhe P – 3. °vastrikāyās tv alābhe caturguru namaskārāvalikā – 4. prātaḥ not in A; paṃcakaṃ A, instead of the first '25' and laghumāsaḥ instead of the second '25'; puṃjaṃ A; āsajjetti A – 7. guru om. P; caturlaghu A, instead of the first '4', caturguru instead of the second '4' – 8. striyāḥ P; catur guru 4ī A, instead of 'gu° 4' (see above § 11.5 for symbols such as '4ī'); aṃcalasaṃghaṭṭe tiryaksaṃghaṭṭe ca bhinnaṃ A – 9. bhinnaṃ A, instead of '25' – 10. °ap-tejo° A; the last sentence as in P, with pauruṣadhikasya; etat pauṣadhika-prāyaścittam A; prāyeṇaitāny, etc. also in Mitra (1886) according to extracts.

Translation

1 The performer of poṣadha does not perform *āvaśyakā* or *niṣidhikā*. But he urinates or defecates without having inspected a proper place.

2 For leaning on a wall, for taking or placing back wooden seats and other objects, for opening or closing a door, for itching the body, without having cleaned (them before).

3 He does not inspect the implements, he does not repent in relation with his own movement, does not clean the monastic place. For finding a mouth-cloth that he had made fall down: five; four heavy in case he does not find it.

4 For not performing study: an incomplete month. If he would eat or even drink water without having broken the fast, if he does not pick up what has been cleaned, (and), saying '?' does not clean (the *upāśraya*): one light.

5 For vomiting, for liberating excreta at night, for paying homage after having eaten without having observed (*pratyākhyāna* up to its final stage), for sleeping during the day without having a valid cause to do so, (for) forbidden kind of talk, for blamable speech,

6 for no *pratyākhyāna* with contingencies, as well as for not asking authorization for bed, he sleeps without having uttered the "bed verses": four light.

7 One heavy for a minimal lie, four light for a medium one, four heavy for a maximal one. For repentance performed seated, for not paying homage to temples as prescribed: one light.

8 For a man in case of contact with a lady: four light; (for) a lady (in case of contact with a man) it is four heavy. A light in case of contact with interruption; in case of contact of the border (of the clothes) and in case of horizontal (contact), an incomplete month.

9 Three varieties in case of contact with water and fire, and in case of contact with lightning (respectively): incomplete, light, heavy. Four light in the case of uninterrupted rain; exactly the same in case of going in water or earth.

9bis Offence to sprouts (born from) rain in the new rainy-season: as many four heavy as the number of days. Ten in case of destruction of bees' and tailor-birds' homes.

10 For harm to earth-bodies and the others, incomplete and the others in the series; for plants with infinite number of living organisms and for beings with two, three or four organs of senses: light and the others in the series. For beings with five organs of senses: heavy and the others in the series. Beyond nine, for all (light, etc.) ten (not more).

10bis (1) Incomplete month, (2) light month, (3) heavy month, (4) four light, (5) four heavy, (6) six light months, (7) six heavy months are the technical names for food without dainties and the other (respectively).

10ter Hastottara, the three Śravaṇa, Revati, Rohiṇī, the two Pūrṇavasu, and the (eight) Anurādhas are the sixteen constellations for confession.

Remarks

For a Sanskrit version very similar to this exposition see ĀD p. 267b. About the violations of the *poṣadhopavāsa-vrata*, which is the eleventh of the twelve lay vows, see, for instance, Williams (1963: 147ff.), and the contemporary manuals (e.g. Mokṣarasāśrījī 2010: 29–30; Shah 2011: 103ff.).

3cd Atonements regarding the mouth-cloth are subject to varying opinions. Tilaka's verse and Dharmaghoṣa's verse agree on "four heavy" as the atonement prescribed in case the mouth-cloth is completely lost. But the commentary on Dharmaghoṣa's SJK records another opinion (*matāntareṇa*) according to which it should be "four light". Tilaka and Dharmaghoṣa disagree on the atonement to be prescribed if the mouth-cloth is found again: "full set of five" for Tilaka, "a split month" for Dharmaghoṣa. Tilaka's verse and his Sanskrit commentary show a discrepancy. The opinion recorded in the commentary corresponds to what is stated in the commentary on Dharmaghoṣa's SJK with reference to "some source": *kvacin namaskārâvalikānāṃ nāśane ca māsa-guru.*

4 Note Pkt. *bhaṇiro*, with the typically Māhārāṣṭrī Prakrit suffix *–ira*, which forms primary derivatives on the basis of a verbal stem, and is rendered as a present participle in Sanskrit (see Schwarzchild 1962). – Pkt. *jime* and *pive* are third person singular optatives, differently from Dharmaghoṣa's verbal nouns in the locative (*a-pāriya jimaṇa-piyaṇe*, SJK 96). Such forms are more expected in this type of style, as verbs are rather rare. – The first transgression (not performing study) implies "an incomplete month" as atonement. This is expressed in the verse with the technical term *bhinna*, and in the commentary with the equivalent in number, i.e. "25", or with another variant (ms. A) *paṃcakaṃ* (see above § 11.3). The phrasing of the rest of the verse implies that the atonement for all other transgressions mentioned is "one light". This is also the case in the corresponding verse of SJK (96). But the commentary has two varying opinions in case one eat or drinks before having completed the *pratyākhyāna*: ms. A has "one light" but ms. P has "25" = "an incomplete month". Is it a real variant or a mere error?

5–6 The two verses form one syntactic unit, listing various transgressions which have to be compensated in an identical manner: by "four light", as stated at the end. – ab: text clear but metre puzzling? – The exact meaning of *asaṃvaraṇe* is not fully clear. It is explained as follows in the commentary on SJK 101: *asaṃvaraṇaṃ: pratyākhyānaṃ vandanaka-dāne 'pi caturvidhāhāra-pratyākhyāna-rūpa-divasa-carima-svarūpaṃ na vidhatte*. The comm. of our mss. A and P is more vague but seems to convey the same idea; Tilaka's *Sāmācārī* (p. 20b) has: *bhuktvôtthito vaṃdakena na pratyākhyāti*.

7 Part of the contents can be compared with SJK 106: *baiṭṭha-karaṇe a lahu-māso*. – Metre uncertain.

8 *Aṃcala-tiri-phāsaṇe* represent two distinct situations. The comm. on SJK 97 is not more explicit than the present one: *añcalena vastrântâdinā striyaḥ saṅghaṭṭe tiraścyāḥ sparśane ca bhinnaṃ bhinna-māsaḥ prāyaścittaṃ bhavati*.

9 Pkt. *vagghāra*, Skt. *vaghāra*, written as *vagghāra* in Dharmaghoṣa and explained thus: *vagghāraṃ nāma yā a-vicchinnā vṛṣṭiḥ, yad vā yasyāṃ vṛṣṭāv upari prāvṛtaṃ kambalâdikaṃ ścotati, yad vā uparitana-kambalâdikaṃ bhittvântaḥkāyam ārdrayati* (commentary on 98).

9bis Additional stanza in ms. A, identical to Dharmaghoṣa 99, in the same sequence as here, with an almost identical commentary as well.

10bis Unmetrical. See above § 11.3 for the correspondences between durations and kinds of fasts.

10ter Same stanza in SPT ms. B fol. 6v (*Ālocanāvidhi*, stanza 6). This is a stanza on atonements in respect with the *nakṣatra*s. There are similar ones for *tithi*s and *vāra*s as well. This one is not found in the *Gaṇivijjā*, which, however, has similar considerations.

Notes

1 Conversations with Ācārya Vijayaśīlacandrasūri Mahārāj, Sādhvī Kuladarśitā Mahārāj, Sādhvī Cāruśīlā Mahārāj and Pandit Rupendra Kumar Pagaria were helpful in the understanding of several points connected with the topic of this contribution. Needless to say, all errors or misunderstandings are mine.

2 For Digambara counterparts on monastic atonements, which would also require a study, see *Chedapiṇḍa* in Jaina Śauraseni Prakrit (361 verses) and *Chedaśāstra* in Māhārāṣṭrī Prakrit (94 verses).

3 Cf. Schubring (1935 § 114).

4 Based on SJK comm. pp. 3–4.

5

> The text is a list of penances for Jain monks. In more recent times, after a similar list of penances had been produced for the layman (*Śrāddha-Jītakalpa*), as a rule ours came to be known as *Yati-Jītakalpa* in order to be distinguished from the latter, for example in Sādhuratna's Sanskrit commentary from V.S. 1456.

The work Leumann has in mind is Somaprabhasūri's *Yatijītakalpa*, whose own commentary seems to be lost.

6 Sukhlalji (1974: 296).

7 Quoted, e.g. Williams (1963: 205).
8 Williams (1963: 63).
9 *Yogaśāstravṛtti* p. 684 (Williams 1963: 205): *yat khaṇḍitaṃ deśato bhagnaṃ, yad virādhitaṃ sutarāṃ bhagnam.*
10 *Uvāsagadasāo* chap. 1 (p. 10).
11 *Hīrapraśna* p. 23b: *deśāvakāśika-vrate kenacid yojana-śataṃ rakṣitam, kiñcit kāryam āpatitaṃ, tad-ūrdhvaṃ lekha-preṣaṇe vrata-mālinyaṃ na vā? iti praśno 'trottaram: niyamita-kṣetrād ūrdhvaṃ lekha-preṣaṇe vrata-mālinyaṃ bhavatîti jñāyate Yogaśāstravṛtty-ādau tathaiva darśanād iti.*
12 *Yogaśāstra* III.89: *vratāni sâticārāṇi su-kṛtāya bhavanti na/aticārās tato heyāḥ pañca pañca vrate vrate.*
13 "A *Sāvaga-pacchitta* in only 16 Prakrit Āryās follows the Jītakalpa in our manuscript, as a kind of Appendix".
14 A manuscript of this commentary kept in the Cambridge University Library was known to Leumann ('Add. 1775). This manuscript is part of the Cambridge University Library Sanskrit Manuscripts project, being digitized and described on the corresponding website.
15 I was informed by Ācārya Vijayaśīlancandrasūri Mahārāj that a re-edition (equivalent to a reprint) has been now published by Sādhvī Candanabālāśrījī but was unable to have access to the book or its bibliographical reference.
16 Cf. SJK ed., introduction p. 7 ("*Saṃ. 1328 ane Saṃ. 1357*"); but Velankar, *Jinaratnakośa:* "composed *in* Saṃ. 1357 by Dharmaghoṣa, pupil of Devendrasūri of the Tapāgaccha".
17 I am thankful to Peter Flügel who put the text and translation of this document at my disposal.
18 SJK p. 49.
19 SJK comm. p. 2 quoting JKBh 5. Compare Caillat (1975: 93).
20 Same type of codified dialogue in the confession tract available in SPT ms. B fol. 8r.
21 See similarly ĀD p. 252a for the mendicant: *śubha-nakṣatra-tithi-vāra-lagneṣu guru-śiṣyayoś candravale sādhuḥ sarva-caityeṣu caitya-vandanaṃ kuryāt.*
22 Etymologically *kaṭṭhāsaṇa* should refer to a wooden seat. But in common parlance it designates the rectagular mat, a piece of woollen cloth used by laypeople in the performance of *pratikramaṇa.* It is one of the four implements used in this context, together with the *sthāpanācārya*, the mouth-cloth, and the special broom for lay people (Guj. *caravalo*): see, for instance, *Vidhi sahit Paṃca Pratikramaṇa Sūtra* pp. 13–16.
23 See similarly ĀD p. 252b.
24 More or less clear descriptions of this system are found for instance in Schubring (1905: 14 n. 7) and Deo (1960: 46–47). The clearest is Samaṇī Kusumpragyā (2010: 142 (Introduction)).
25 See also Caillat (1975: 94) for similar lists in VyavBh 164f.
26 Compare another example of monastic atonements with reference to living beings in Jyväsjärvi (2010: 157).
27 Needless to say, this expression does not have anything to do with the meaning which is obvious to all Jains, i.e. the "five auspicious events" of the Jinas' lives.
28 See also Gurudāsa, *Prāyaścitta-cūlikā* in Sanskrit, verse 8.
29 There seem to be occasional hesitations between *ṇ* and *ṅ* in these symbolic designations.
30 See also JKBh (K): Introduction 63. Outside the context of atonements, just to indicate a number, a rare instance of this system is preserved in Agastyasiṃha's *cūrṇi* on the *Daśavaikālika-sūtra* (pp. 250–251, referred to in JKBh (K) introduction *ibidem.*
31 SJK commentary on vs. 79 p. 61 quotes *mosāisu mehuṇa-vajjiesu* ... and *ahavā mosādatte*...
32 Another passage discussing the same issues is JKS 31–32 with JKBh 1069–1074.

33 *jāvajīva parastrī kā tyāg bhāṅgai to jaghanya ek bār ko ek telo. tiṇ meṃ piṇ vidhvā kumārī ādi laukik bhārī avajñā ko kām huvai to tehno prāyaścitt ācāryādik ke pās meṃ leṇo.*
34 *Senapraśna* p. 25b.
35 Section 5 pp. 27–30 with two explicit mentions of the source: *Śrāddhajītakalpādau tad-vidhir evam*, p. 27; *iti Śrāddhajītakalpāttavṛtteś ca kiñcid uddhṛta ālocanā-vidhiḥ;* quotations of SJK vs. 6–8, 9, 13, 15.
36 The total of 124 is reached as follows:

Area	*Number of transgressions*
samyaktva	5
jñāna	8 × 3 = 24
12 *aṇuvrata*s	12 × 5 = 60
15 trades	15
saṃlekhanā	5
tapas	6 × 2 = 12
vīrya	3

See the illustration in form of a tree in Shah (2011).
37 William's translation (1963: 205).

Abbreviations and references

Primary sources

ĀD = *Ācāradinakara* by Vardhamānasūri. Reprinted by Āc. śrī Vijayanītiprabhasūri. Ahmedabad, 1981: section 4 pp. 250–271: *prāyaścittavidhiḥ*. Hindi translation: see below Sādhvī Mokṣaratnāśrī.

BhORI 17.2 = Hiralal Rasikdas Kapadia, *Descriptive Catalogue of the Government Collections of Manuscripts* deposited at the Bhandarkar Oriental Research Institute. Volume XVII Jaina Literature and Philosophy. Part II: (a) Āgamika Literature. Poona, 1936.

BKBh = *Bṛhatkalpabhāṣya* and BKBhṬ = *Bṛhatkalpabhāṣya-ṭīkā*: *Brihat Kalpa Sutra and Original Niryukti of Sthavir Arya Bhadrabahu Swami and a Bhashya by Shri Sanghadas Gani Kshamashramana thereon with a Commentary begun by Acharya Shri Malayagiri and Completed by Acharya Shri Kshemakirti*. Edited by Guru Shri Chaturvijaya and his Shishya Punyavijaya. Bhavnagar: Shri Atmanand Jain Sabha, 6 vols.; vol. 1: 1933; 2–3: 1936; 4–5: 1938; 6: 1942.

Chedapiṇḍa by Indranandiyogīndra in *Prāyaścitta-saṃgraha* ed. Pt. Pannalal Soni. Bombay, MDJGM 18, 1921: 1–75.

Chedaśāstra (anonymous in *Prāyaścitta-saṃgraha* ed. Pt. Pannalal Soni. Bombay, MDJGM 18, 1921: 76–103.

Hīrapraśna (*Praśnottarasamuccaya*), compiled by Kīrtivijayagaṇi. (No place, no date).

Jinaratnakośa. An Alphabetical Register of Jain Works and Authors. Vol. I. Works by H.D. Velankar. Poona, 1944.

JK = *Jītakalpa;* see also Leumann (1892).

Jinabhadragaṇikṣmāśramaṇa-viracitaṃ *Jītakalpasūtram svopañabhāṣyeṇa bhūṣitam*. Ed. Muni Puṇyavijaya. Ahmedabad, V.S. 1994 (=1937).

Jinabhadragaṇikṣmāśramaṇa-viracitaṃ *Jītakalpasūtram* (*viṣamapada-vyākhyālaṃkṛta-Siddhasenagaṇisandṛbdha Bṛhaccūrṇi-samanvitam*). Ed. Muni Jinavijaya. Jain Sāhitya Saṃshodhaka Samiti, Ahmedabad, V.S. 1983 (=1926).

JKBh (K) = *Jītakalpa sabhāṣya*. Editor/Translator (in Hindi) Samaṇī Kusumpragyā. Jain Vishva Bharati: Ladnun, 2010.

JKS = *Jītakalpa-sūtra*.

JKV = *Jītakalpa-vivaraṇa* or °*vṛtti* composed by Tilakācārya in V.S. 1274 (= CE 1167), unpublished. Available in mss. A and P (above Appendix A and § 5.2).

Manuscripts: see JKV, SJK, SPAn, SPT.

NisBh = *Niśītha-bhāṣya* and NisC = *Niśītha-cūrṇi* in *Nishith Sutram* (With Bhashya). Ed. by Upadhyaya Kavi Shri Amar Chand Ji Maharaj & Muni Shri Kanhaiya Lal Ji Maharaj "Kamal". 4 vols. Bharatiya Vidya Prakashan: Delhi, Varanasi & Sammati Gyan Peeth, Agra, 2nd rev. ed. 1982.

Pākṣik Aticār: see *Śrāvak Aticār*.

Prāyaścittagranthaḥ by "Akalanka" in *Prāyaścitta-saṃgraha* ed. Pt. Pannalal Soni. Bombay, MDJGM 18, 1921: 165–172.

Senapraśna (*Praśnaratnākara*)compiled by Śubhavijayagaṇi. Mumbaī: Śrī Jinaśāsana Ārādhanā Trust, 1988 (Vikrama saṃvat 2045).

SJK = *Saḍḍhajīyakappa* by Dharmaghoṣasūri. Tapāgaṇādhīśa-ĀcāryaśrīDharmaghoṣasūri-viracitaḥ sa-vṛttiḥ Saḍḍha-jīyakappo (Śrāddhajītakalpaḥ). Saṃśodhakaḥ: Munirāja Lābhasāgaragaṇiḥ. Kheda, V.S. 2027 (=1960) (Āgamoddhāraka Granthamālā 45).

British Library mansuscript Or. 2105G (Balbir *et al.* 2006 vol. 2: Cat. No., used to compare the mūla with that of the printed edition. Useful in order to correct occasional misprints and metrical errors.

SPAn = *Sāvayapacchitta* (anonymous): published and translated in Appendix A above, on the basis of E. Leumann's transcript and on the British Library palm-leaf ms. Or. 1385.

SPs = SPAN + SPT.

SPT = *Sāvayapacchitta* by Tilakācārya: published and translated in Appendix B above, on the basis of ms. P (palm-leaf from Patan) and mss. A, B, C (paper mss. from Ahmedabad, L.D. Institute of Indology).

Śrāddhavidhiprakaraṇa of Ratnaśekharasūri with auto-commentary. Revised by Paṃnyāsa Śrīvikramavijaya and Gaṇī Muniśrībhāskaravijaya. Surat: Śreṣṭhi-Devancanda-Lālbhāī-Jaina Pustakoddhara Fund No. 106.

Śrāvak Aticār: popular editions with Prakrit and Gujarati or Hindi: see Amitayaśavijaya, Arihantasāgarjī, Kuṃvarjī Āṇandjī, Mokṣarasāśrījī, Shah.

Śrāvakaprāyaścittavidhi prescribed by Āc. Tulsi in 1944, see Flügel (forthcoming).

ST = *Sāmācārī* by Tilakācārya. Prakāśaka: Śeṭh Ḍāhyābhāī Mokamcand. Panjrāpol, Amadāvād, Vīra san 2460; Vikrama saṃvat 1990.

Uvāsagadasāo. With Abhayadeva's commentary and Gujarati translation. Mumbai: Shri Mahavir Sahitya Prakashan, 1982 (Shri Mahavir Jain Sahitya Prakashan No. 3).

Vavahāra- und Nisīha-Sutta. Herausgegeben von Walther Schubring. Leipzig, 1918 (Abhandlungen für die Kunde des Morgenlandes, Band 15 – Nr. 1), reprint 1966.

Vidhi Sahit Paṃca Pratikramaṇa Sūtra. Jain Prakashan Mandir: Ahmedabad, no date.

VyavBh = *Vyavahāra-bhāṣya*.

VyavBh (K) = *Vyavahāra Bhāṣya* (Original text, variant readings, critical notes, niryukti, preface and various appendices). Editor: Samani Kusumprajna. Jain Vishva Bharati: Ladnun, 1996.

VyavBh (M) = *Śrīman-Malayagirisūri viracita vivaraṇa-yuta niryukti-bhāṣya-sametam śrī Vyavahārasūtram*. (Āgamaprabhākara Muni śrī Puṇyavijayajī sajjī-kṛta sāmāgrī-sahāyena. Ed. Āc. Vijaya Municandrasūri. Āc. śrī Oṃkārasūrijñānamandir, Surat, 2010, 6 vols.

VyavBh (T) = *Sānuvād Vyavahārabhāṣya*. Editor/Translator Muni Dularaj. Jain Vishva Bharati: Ladnun, 2004. (Hindi translation).

Yogaśāstra of Hemacandra, with *Svopajñavṛtti*. Ed. Muni Jambūvijaya. Three Volumes. Bombay: Jain Sāhitya Vikās Maṇḍal, 1977–86.

Secondary literature

Amitayaśavijayajī, Muni. *Śrī Pākṣik Aticār* (Gujarati). Ahmedabad, n.d.

Arihantasāgarjī, Parama Pūjya Gaṇivarya śrī. *Pākṣik Aticār (hindī)*. Bangalore, 2005.

Balbir, Nalini, Sheth, Kanhaiyalal, Sheth, Kalpana K., Tripathi, C.B. *Catalogue of the Jaina Manuscripts at the British Library*, 3 vols and a CD. London: the Brititsh Library, the Institute of Jainology, 2006.

Bollée, Willem B. *Bhadrabāhu, Bṛhat-Kalpa-Niryukti and Sanghadāsa, Bṛhat-Kalpa-Bhāṣya* [Text, glossary]. Stuttgart, 3 vols. (Beiträge zur Südasienforschung 181,1; 181,2; 181,3), 1998.

Bollée, Willem B. *Vyavahāra Bhāṣya Pīṭhikā*. Edited, translated and annotated. Hindi Granth Karyalay, Mumbai (Pandit Nathuram Premi Research Series vol. 4), 2006.

Caillat, Colette. *Les expiations dans le rituel ancien des religieux jaina*. Paris: De Boccard, 1965.

Caillat, Colette. *Atonements in the Ancient Ritual of the Jaina Monks*. Ahmedabad, L.D. Series 45, 1975.

Dalal, C.D. and Gandhi Lalchandra Bhagawandas. *A Descriptive Catalogue of Manuscripts in the Jain Bhandars at Pattan*. Vol. I. Palm-leaf MSS. Baroda: Oriental Institute, 1937.

Deo, Shantaram Bhalcandra. *History of Jaina Monachism from Inscriptions and Literature*. Poona, 1956.

Deo, Shantaram Bhalchandra. *Jaina Monastic Jurisprudence*. Banaras: Jaina Cultural Research Society, 1960.

Dundas, Paul. "How Not to Install an Image of the Jina. An Early Anti-Paurṇamīyaka Diatribe." *International Journal of Jaina Studies* 4–6 (2011) 187–208.

Flügel, Peter. "Spiritual Accounting. The Role of the *Kalyāṇaka Patra* in the Religious Economy of the Terāpanth Śvetāmbara Jain Ascetics." *Jainism and Early Buddhism*. Essays in Honor of Padmanabh S. Jaini. Ed. Olle Qvarnström, 167–204. Fremont California: Asian Humanities Press, 2003.

Flügel, Peter. "Atonements in the Rituals of the Terāpanth Śvetāmbara Jains." (With original text in Hindi and annotated translation of the text of the Terāpanth Prāyaścittavidhi), *Jaina Law and Society*. Ed. Peter Flügel. London: Routledge (2015).

Granoff, Phyllis. "Protecting the Faith: Exploring the Concerns of Jain Monastic Rules." *Jaina Law and Society*. Ed. Peter Flügel. London: Routledge (2015).

Jyväsjärvi, Mari. "Retrieving the Hidden Meaning: Jain Commentarial Techniques and the Art of Memory." *Journal of Indian Philosophy* 38 (2010) 133–162.

Jyaväsjärvi, Mari. *Fragile Virtue: Interpreting Women's Monastic Practice in Early Medieval India*. Harvard University PhD Thesis, 2011.

Kapadia, Hiralal Rasikdas. "Foliation of Jaina Manuscripts and Letter-Numerals." *Annals of the Bhandarkar Oriental Research Institute* 18, 2 (1937) 171–186.

Kielhorn, Franz. *Report on the Search for Sanskrit MSS. in the Bombay Presidency during the Year 1880–81*. Bombay, Government Central Book Depôt, 1881.

Kuṃvarjī Āṇandjī. *Śrāvak nā Pākṣik Aticār artha sahit*. Shri Jain Dharma Prasārak Sabhā, Bhavnagar, 2011.

Leumann, Ernst. Notebook No. 128 *Sāvaga-pacchitta* kept at the Institute for the Culture and History of India and Tibet, University of Hamburg (Plutat 1998): Transcript of the Pune manuscript of SPAn, n.d.

Leumann, Ernst. Jinabhadra's Jîtakalpa, mit Auszügen aus Siddhasena's Cûrṇi. *SPAW* 1892, Juni-December: 1195–1210. Reprinted in *Kleine Schriften* herausgegeben von Nalini Balbir, Stuttgart: F. Steiner, 1998, pp. 260–275.

Mitra, Rajendralala. *Notices of Sanskrit MSS ... for the year 1885–1886*, Calcutta, vol. VIII, Part 2, 1886.

Mokṣarasāśrījī, Sādhvī. *Śrāvak Dharm Aticār* (Prakrit and Gujarati). Sumativardhak Jain Sangh, Madhuvṛnda Society, Ghāṭloḍiyā, Amadāvād, 2010.

Mokṣaratnāśrī, Sādhvī. *Ācārya Vardhamānasūrikṛta Ācāradinakara caturtha khaṇḍa. Prāyaścitta, āvaśyaka, tapa evaṃ padāropaṇa vidhi*. (= Hindi translation). Samprerak Sādhvī Harṣayaśāśrījī, Anuvādak Sādhvī Mokṣaratnaśrī, Sampādak Dr. Sagarmal Jain. Prācyā Vidyāpīṭh Śājāpur (M. Pr.), A. Bhā. Śrī Jain Śvetāmbar Kharataragaccha Mahāsaṃgha, Mumbaī (Prācya Vidyāpīṭh Granthamālā 10), 2007.

Nawab, Sarabhai Manilal. Tapāgacchīya śrīVijayasenasūrisaṃtānīya muni śrīJayavijayajī viracita *Ṣaḍāvaśyaka Bālāvabodha* (Pratikramaṇa sūtra). Sūtra no mūlapāṭh, gujarātī bālāvabodha, kathāo tathā Mumbāi māṃ cītarāelāṃ ek so suḍatālīs citro sahita. Ahmedabad: Shree Jain Kala-Sahitya Shansodhan Series 17, 1997.

Plutat, Birte. *Catalogue of the Papers of Ernst Leumann in the Institute for the Culture and History of India and Tibet, University of Hamburg*. Franz Steiner Verlag: Stuttgart (Alt- und Neu-Indische Studien herausgegeben vom Institut für Kultur und Geschichte Indiens und Tibets an der Universität Hamburg 49), 1998.

Puṇyavijaya, Muni. *Kalpasūtra*. Ahmedabad: Sarabhai Nawab, 1952.

Punyavijaya, Muni. Āpaṇī adṛśya thatī lekhanakalā ane tenāṃ sādhano: *Jñānāṃjali*. Pūjya Muni Śrī Puṇyavijayajī Abhivādana Grantha. Mumbai, Mahāvīra Jaina Vidyālaya, 1969: 39–52.

Schubring, Walther. *Das Kalpa-sūtra*. Die alte Sammlung jinistischer Mönchsvorschriften. Einleitung, Text, Bemerkungen, Übersetzung, Glossar. Leipzig, 1905. Reprinted in W. Schubring, *Kleine Schriften*, herausgegeben von Klaus Bruhn. Wiesbaden: Franz Steiner Verlag, 1977, pp. 1–69.

Schubring, Walther. *Die Lehre der Jainas nach der alten Quellen dargestellt*. Leipzig, 1935.

Schwarzschild, L.A. (1962). *Ghummira, gholira* 'agité, branlant'. *Journal Asiatique* 250 (1962) 65–75. Reprinted in Royce Wiles (ed.), *Collected articles of LA Schwarzschild on Indo-Aryan 1953–1979*. Faculty of Asian Studies. Australian National University, 1991 (Faculty of Asian Studies Monographs: New Series No. 17), pp. 117–127.

Shah, Pandit Kamaleshbhai R. *Śrāvak Aticār Darpaṇ*. Arth-vivecan sahit. Ahmedabad, 2011 (1st edn 2009). [in Gujarati].

Sukhlalji, Pandit. *Pt. Sukhlalji's Commentary on Tattvārtha Sūtra of Vācaka Umāsvāti*. Translated by K.K. Dixit. Ahmedabad: L.D. Institute of Indology (L.D. Series 44), 1974.

Tripuṭī Mahārāj. *Jain Paramparā no Itihāsa*. Ahmedabad: Bhāg bījo, 1960.

Williams, Robert. *Jaina Yoga. A Survey of the Mediaeval Śrāvakācāras*. London, 1963; reprint Delhi, Motilal Banarsidass, 1983.

Part III

Aspects of philosophy

8 Aspects of philosophy in the *Ṣaṭkhaṇḍāgama*

Jayandra Soni

It is well-known that Nemicandra's *Gommaṭasāra* (ninth century) was considered to be the most sacred of available Digambara texts until the discovery of the *Ṣaṭkhaṇḍāgama* and the *Kaṣāyapāhuḍa* (the Scripture in Six Parts and the Treatise on Passions) in the late nineteenth century. The *Ṣaṭkhaṇḍāgama* (Chakkhaṇḍāgama) (ṢKhĀ) taught by Dharasena to the monks Puṣpadanta and Bhūtabali – approximately in the mid-second century CE – was first published in 16 volumes between 1939 and 1959 with the *ṭīkā* (commentary) called *Dhavalā* by Vīrasena (eighth century) and a Hindi translation[1] and then republished later (see the references below). The dramatic circumstances around the smuggling out and publication of the early portions of the text edited by the renowned Digambara academics Hīralāl Jain and A. N. Upādhye are also well-known, before the Mūḍbidrī temple authorities in south-west Karnataka "finally granted permission both for publication of the remainder of the text and direct consultation of the original manuscript by scholars".[2]

A debate has arisen about the antiquity of this text in comparison with the fourth Śvetāmbara *upāṅga*, the *Prajñāpanāsūtra* (*Paṇṇavaṇāsuttaṃ*).[3] In the second volume of this work, pp. 223–231, there is a section with the title "*Prajñāpanāsūtra* and *Ṣaṭkhaṇḍāgama*" and the editors conclude that the "*Prajñāpanā* is a work earlier than the *Ṣaṭkhaṇḍāgama*" (p. 231; similarly p. 235). The Digambaras, on their part, take up the point and in volume one of their publication of the ṢKhĀ there is a section called "*Ṣaṭkhaṇḍāgama and Prajñāpanāsūtra*" (pp. 4–10). Here the editors argue in conclusion that there is no "evidence to say that the Prajñāpana-sūtra was composed earlier than the Ṣaṭkhaṇḍāgama" (p. 9). This chapter can only point out the significance of the debate here.[4] Nonetheless, even Śvetāmbara scholars agree that "it [the ṢKhĀ] is doubtless the oldest available text containing a vast mass of details relating to the Karma doctrine," adding that this "masterpiece" supplies, "details of which there was no hint in the old Āgamic texts."[5]

The six parts of the voluminous ṢKhĀ, as conveniently divided in Vīrasena's commentary *Dhavalā*, are:

1 *jīvasthāna* (*jīvaṭṭhāṇa*), the stages of the soul containing eight *anuyogadvāras* (gateways to exposition): 1. *sat* (being), 2. *saṃkhyā* (number), 3. *kṣetra* (place), 4. *sparśana* (touch), 5 *kāla* (time), 6. *antara* (intermediate space or time), 7. *bhāva* (existing state of a substance), 8. *alpabahutva* (relative numerical

strength) (1, 1, 7, p. 156) and the following nine *cūlikā* (appendices): 1. *prakṛtisamutkīrtanā*, 2. *sthānasamutkīrtanā*, 3–5 three *mahādaṇḍaka*s, 6. *jaghanyasthiti*, 7. *utkṛṣṭasthiti*, 8. *samyaktvotpatti* and 9. *gati-āgati*.

2 *kṣullakhabandha* (*khuddhābandha*) or garments of a junior monk) with 11 *adhikāra*s.

3 *bandhasvāmitvavicaya* (*baṃdhasvāmitvavicaya*) discusses the *karmasambandhi* (karma-association) of a *jīva* or soul in 324 *sūtra*s.

4 *vedanā* (feeling) discusses the two *anuyogadvara*s: *kṛti* (actions, seven kinds of this: 1. *nāma* (name, naming), 2. *sthāpanā* (representation), 3. *dravya* (substance), 4. *gaṇanā* (calculation), 5. *grantha* (text), 6. *kāraṇa* (cause), 7. *bhāva* (actual state) and *vedanā* (with its 16 kinds of *adhikāra*: *nikṣepa, naya, nāma, dravya, kṣetra, kāla, bhāva, pratyaya, svāmitva, vedanā, gati, anantara, sannikarṣa, parimāṇa, bhāgābhāgānugama and alpabahutvānugama*).

5 *vargaṇā* (division) is discussed with four other *adhikāra*s: *sparśa, karma, prakṛti* and *bandhana*.

6 *mahābandha* (great bondage). The commentator Indranandi says that Bhūtabali composed this sixth part after Puṣpadanta's five. Among other things this part discusses in great detail the four *anuyogadvāra*s: *prakṛtibandha, sthitibandha, anubhāgabandha* and *pradeśabandha*, concluding everything related to *bandha* (bondage).

It must be pointed out that for a thorough study of the ṢKhĀ corresponding parts of it have to be compared with at least the following more than 11 works, as has been partially done by Śāstrī (1987: 143–336), from where this list and some information has been taken:

1 *Kaṣāyaprābhṛta* which, together with the ṢKhĀ and possibly older than it, is now regarded by the Digambaras as the only texts of the Jaina canon, both being regarded as containing direct elements of the lost *Dṛṣṭivāda*. These texts have to be compared, for example, regarding *samyaktva* (Śāstrī 1987: 149, also 148).

2 *Mūlācāra* attributed to Vaṭṭakera (*c.* second century CE), e.g. for the *guṇa* and *mārganāsthāna* (p. 154).

3 *Tattvārthasūtra* by Umāsvāti (*c.* fifth century CE), including the commentaries *Sarvārthasiddhi* by Pūjyapāda (fifth–sixth century CE) and *Tattvārthavārtika* by Akalaṅka (*c.* eighth century).

4 *Karmaprakṛti* by Śivaśarmasūri (fifth century, Vi. Saṃ).

5 *Ācārāṅgasūtra* of the Śvetāmbara canon.

6 *Jīvasamāsa* by an unknown author, an important Śvetāmbara canonical *gāthā* work.[6]

7 *Prajñāpanā* (*Paṇṇavaṇā*) by Śyāmārya, the fourth *Upāṅga* of the Śvetāmbara canon.

8 *Anuyogadvārasūtra*.

9 *Nandisūtra*.

10 *Pañcasaṅgraha.*
11 *Gommaṭasāra.*

Obviously this chapter cannot claim completeness because only a small section of one of the *sūtra*s is being studied here briefly. In Jaina philosophy *jñāna* and *darśana* are basic concepts used differently, depending on the context, namely, metaphysically as constituting the path to liberation (*mokṣamārga*) in the sense of *samyagjñāna* (proper knowledge) and *samyagdarśana* (proper faith), or in the sense of *jñānopayoga* or *darśanopayoga* (determinate and indeterminate cognitions), or epistemologically where *jñāna* is regarded as encompassing *matijñāna, śrutajñāna, avadhijñāna, manaḥparyāyajñāna* and *kevalajñāna* (sensory knowledge, scriptural knowledge, clairvoyance, telepathy and omniscience). Further, *jñāna* and *darśana* (together with *samyagcāritra* or proper conduct) are basic concepts in Jaina philosophy.[7] The task of obtaining their precise meaning is exacerbated by the adoption of these very terms in different contexts, e.g. epistemologically, metaphysically or ethically, as just indicated.

Ṣaṭkhaṇḍāgama 1, 1, 4 (p. 133, vol. 1) mentions 14 items (*jīvasamāsa*) that are associated with the *jīva* and many of these are significant to know about for the early history of Jaina philosophy in the mid-second century and for the role they play in later philosophical discourse: *gati* (class of animate being), *indriya* (sense organ), *kāya* (body), *yoga* (activity), *veda* (sexual behaviour), *kaṣāya* (vice), *jñāna* (determinate cognition), *saṃyama* (moral discipline), *darśana* (indeterminate cognition), *leśyā* (colouration, mental temperament), *bhavya* (capability of obtaining *mokṣa*), *samyaktva* (faith), *sañjñī* (possessing higher cognitive capacity) and *āhāra* (taking nourishment).

What is striking about this number "14" is that it is exactly the same as the number of *guṇasthāna*s, and also the 14 *mārgaṇāsthāna*s. Whatever reservations one might have about a simple enumeration of terms, in the history of Indian thought such a technique constitutes the basic structure of collecting items that belong together and preserving them in an authoritative way within a tradition, which the commentaries then explain in more or less detail. What is significant here in the lists of the ṢKhĀ is that they seem to have become standard items for both Digambaras and Śvetāmbaras. The point is noteworthy because the ṢKhĀ, as is now well-known, was discovered in the late nineteenth century. In this context it could be said that the discovery of the text has become a significant verifiable source of what has become traditional. Obviously much more needs to be done in analysing the work in greater detail and comparing it with other texts with, for example, the list of 20 *mārgaṇāsthāna*s.[8] Further, one needs a fine sieve to filter out the philosophically relevant items from among a vast amount of other details which might be sectarian and/or related to ascetic practices.

As already pointed out, out of the list of 14 items in the *sūtra* just quoted, the aim here is to see what the commentary exactly says about *jñāna* and *darśana*. Since the translation of these words depends on the context I shall retain these Sanskrit words.[9]

After explaining *kaṣāya* the commentary continues on pp. 143–145 saying:

bhūtārthaprakāśakaṃ jñānam | mithyādṛṣṭīnāṃ kathaṃ bhūtārthaprakāśakam iti cen na, samyaṅmithyādṛṣṭīnāṃ prakāśasya samānatopalambhāt | kathaṃ punaste 'jñānina iti cen na, mithyātvodayāt pratibhāsite 'pi vastuni saṃśay aviparyayānadhyavasāyānivṛttitas teṣām ajñānitokteḥ | evaṃ sati darś-anāvasthāyāṃ jñānābhāvaḥ syād iti cen naiṣa doṣaḥ, iṣṭatvāt | {144} *kāla-sūtreṇa saha virodhaḥ kin na bhaved iti cen na, tatra kṣayopaśamasya prādhānyāt |*

Jñāna is the manifestation of what really exists. If it is objected: how can incorrect views[10] be a manifestation of what really exists, then [we Jainas say] no [the objection does not apply], because correct and incorrect views yield generalities. If it is further objected with regard to these: how can there be one who does not know, then [we Jainas say] no, as a result of incorrectness, because even when objects are manifested [in incorrect views] they are called *ajñāna* through the non-cessation of doubt, error and misapprehension. If you now [in objection] say that this being the case there would be an absence of *jñāna* in the state of *darśana*, then [we Jainas say] this is not an error, because it is so desired.[11] If you [now] object: would this not go against the *Kālasūtra*s?,[12] then [we Jainas say] no, because there the destruction-cum-suppression [of certain types of *karman*] is important/foremost.

viparyayaḥ kathaṃ bhūtārthaprakāśaka iti cen na, candramasy upalabhyamānadvitvasyānyatra sattvatas tasya bhūtatvopapatteḥ | athavā sadbhāvaviniścayopalambhakaṃ jñānam | etena saṃśayaviparyayānadhyava sāyāvasthāsu jñānābhāvaḥ pratipāditaḥ syāt śuddhanayavivakṣāyāṃ tattvārthopalambhakaṃ jñānam | tato mithyādṛṣṭayo na jñānina iti siddhaṃ dravyaguṇaparyāyān anena jānātīti jñānam | abhinnasya kathaṃ karaṇatvam iti cen na, sarvathā bhede 'bhede ca {145} *svarūpahāniprasaṅgād anekānte svarūpopalabdher na tasya karaṇatvavirodha iti | uktaṃ ca— jāṇai tikāla-sahieṃ davva-guṇe pajjae ya bahu-bhee | paccakkhaṃ ca parokkhaṃ aṇeṇa ṇāṇaṃ ti ṇaṃ beṃti*[13] ||

If you ask: how can error manifest what really exists, then [we Jainas say] no [the objection does not apply], because it (the moon) really exists, since the duplication being perceived in the moon exists really elsewhere [as a single, real entity]. Or, *jñāna* is the certain perceiving of what really exists. Thereby, the absence of *jñāna* would be proved in the states of doubt, error and misapprehension; *jñāna* is the perceiving of reality in the sense (*vivakṣāyām*) of the pure standpoint. Therefore, with regard to incorrect views, there is no one who knows; it is established that *jñāna* is that through which (*anena*) one knows the substance, quality and modus [of an object]. If you now ask how can there be efficiency [in producing knowledge] of the non-difference [among the substance, quality and modus of an object], then no, because it would lead to a destruction of the intrinsic nature [of an object] when there is always difference and [always] non-difference; because one obtains the intrinsic nature [of an object only] in the manifold view, there is no contradiction with regard to it [i.e. an efficacy in producing knowledge].[14] And it has been said – *jñāna* is that through which in three-fold time a substance, its quality and its various modes are known directly or indirectly.

The term *darśana* is commented upon on pp. 146–150:

dṛśyate 'neneti darśanam | nākṣṇālokena cātiprasaṅgaḥ, tayor anātmadharmatvāt | dṛśyate jñāyate 'neneti darśanam ity ucyamāne jñānadarśanayor aviśeṣaḥ syād iti cen na, antarbahirmukhayoś citprakāśayor darśanajñānavyapadeśabhājor ekatvavirodhāt | kiṃ taccaitanyam iti cet, trikā lagocarānantaparyāyātmakasya jīvasvarūpasya svakṣayopaśamavaśena saṃvedanaṃ caitanyam | {147} svato vyatiriktabāhyārthāvagatiḥ prakāśa ity antarbahirmukhayoś citprakāśayor jānāty anenātmānaṃ bāhyam artham iti ca jñānam iti siddhatvāt ekatvam, tato na jñānadarśanayor bheda iti cen na, jñānād iva darśanāt prati karmavyavasthābhāvāt | tarhy astv antarbāhyasāmānyagrahaṇaṃ darśanam, viśeṣagrahaṇaṃ jñānam iti cen na, sāmānyaviśeṣātmakasya vastuno 'krameṇopalambhāt | so 'py astu na kaścid virodha iti cen na, 'haṃdi duve ṇatthi uvajogā' ity anena saha virodhāt | api ca na jñānaṃ pramāṇaṃ, sāmānyavyatiriktaviśeṣasyārthakriyākartṛtvaṃ praty asamarthatvato 'vastuno grahaṇāt | na tasya grahaṇam api, sāmānyavyatiriktaviśeṣe {148} avastuni kartṛkarmarūpābhāvāt | tata eva na darśanam api pramāṇam | astu pramāṇābhāva iti cen na, pramāṇābhāve sarvasyābhāvaprasaṅgāt | astu cen na, tathānupalambhāt | tataḥ sāmānyaviśe ṣātmakabāhyārthagrahaṇaṃ jñānaṃ, tathātmakasvarūpagrahaṇaṃ darśanam iti siddham |

Darśana is that through which [something] is seen. There is no unwarrantable stretch [in our definition] with regard to [both] the eye and seeing because these two are not the nature of the *ātman*. If you object: when you say *darśana* is that through which something is seen, is known, then there would be no difference between *jñāna* and *darśana*, then no, because the error is in taking as a single [entity] what has the designation *darśana* and *jñāna*, where the light of consciousness [of the first] is directed inwards and [of the second] outwards. If it is asked: what is this consciousness, then it is perceiving by means of destruction-cum-suppression [of certain types of *karman*] the intrinsic nature of the soul abiding in the three times and having the nature of endless modes (*paryāya*). If you now say: the light [of consciousness] is conceiving external objects different [in nature] from itself, [and] because of the internal and external lights of consciousness through which it knows objects external to itself is *jñāna*, since this established as being a single [activity], therefore there is no difference between *jñāna* and *darśana*, then [we Jainas say] no, because as with *jñāna* there is an absence of the respective *karman* with regard to *darśana*. If you now say: if this is so, then *darśana* is the grasping of internal and external universals and *jñāna* the particulars, then [we Jainas say] no, because the universal and particular nature of a thing is obtained without sequence. If you say: let it be so, there is no contradiction [at all], then [we Jainas say] no, because there is one with the statement "the two *upayoga*s do not take place simultaneously". Further, *jñāna* is not a means of knowing (*pramāṇa*), a particular devoid of a universal is not possible with regard to one who performs an act with a special purpose (*arthakriyakartṛtvam*) because it would be grasping a non-object [hence *jñāna* cannot serve as a *pramāṇa*]. Nor can it [the particular] be grasped when a non-substance is devoid of a universal, because there is no form of a deed for a doer. Therefore, *darśana* too is not a *pramāṇa*. If you now say: let it be so that there is no *pramāṇa*, then [we Jainas say again] no, because in the absence of a *pramāṇa* everything [related to it like objects to be known, the knowledge gained and the knower] would be absent. Then let it be so, if you say this, then no, because it [the absence of objects, etc.] is not perceived. Therefore it is established [for us Jainas] that *jñāna* grasps the nature of external objects which have the nature of universals and particulars, and *darśana* grasps their intrinsic natures.

{148/3} *tathā ca 'jaṃ sāmaṇṇaggahaṇaṃ taṃ daṃsaṇaṃ' iti vacanena virodhaḥ syād iti cen na, tatrātmanaḥ sakalabāhyārthasādhāraṇatvataḥ sāmānyavyapadeśabhājo grahaṇāt | tad api katham avasīyata iti cet 'bhāvāṇaṃ ṇeva kaṭṭu āyāraṃ' iti vacanāt | tad yathā, bhāvānāṃ bāhyārthānām ākāraṃ pratikarmavyavasthām akṛtvā yad grahaṇaṃ tad darśanam | asyaivārthasya punar api* {149} *dṛḍhīkaraṇārtham āha, 'avisesiūṇa aṭṭhe' iti, arthān aviśeṣasya yad grahaṇaṃ tad darśanam iti | na bāhyārthagatasāmānyagrahaṇaṃ darśanam ity āśaṅkanīyaṃ, tasyāvastunaḥ karmatvābhāvāt | na ca tadantareṇa viśeṣo grāhyatvam āskandati, atiprasaṅgāt | saty evam anadhyavasāyo darśanaṃ syād iti cen na, svādhya vasāyasyānadhyavasitabāhyārthasya darśanatvāt | darśanaṃ pramāṇam eva, avisaṃvāditvād, pratibhāsaḥ pramāṇañ cāpramāṇañ ca, visaṃvādāvisaṃvādobhayarūpasya tatropalambāt | ālokanavṛttir vā darśanam | asya gamanikā— ālokata ity ālokanam ātmā,* {150} *vartanaṃ vṛttiḥ, ālokanasya vṛttir ālokanavṛttiḥ svasaṃvedanaṃ, tad darśanam iti lakṣyanirdeśaḥ | prakāśavṛttir vā darśanam | asya gamanikā— prakāśo jñānam, tadartham ātmano vṛttiḥ prakāśavṛttiḥ prakāśavṛttis tad darśanam | viṣayaviṣayisaṃpātāt pūrvāvasthā darśanam ity arthaḥ | uktaṃ ca— jaṃ sāmaṇṇaggahaṇaṃ bhāvāṇaṃ ṇeva kaṭṭu āyāraṃ | avisesiūṇa atthe daṃsaṇam idi bhaṇṇade samae*[15] ||

And further, if it is objected that this would contradict the [Jaina canonical] statement "*darśana* grasps the universal", then no, because the *ātman*, which in a common way grasps the external object completely, is understood as part of a universal designation. Even so, if you ask: how is this to be understood, then [we Jainas say] in accordance with the statement: "without any distinction in the form of the object". In the same way, the apprehension (*bhāvanām*) which grasps the form of the external objects, without taking into account the absence of the respective karman, is *darśana*. Once again, in order to strengthen the meaning of this, it is said: "*avisesiūṇa aṭṭhe*", what grasps the objects without particularising them is called *darśana*. It is not to be doubted that *darśana* grasps the universal in the external object, because it [the universal without the particular] in the absence of any activity [that can know it alone] it is a non-object. And without it [the universal], the particular does not cover (*āskandati*) the grasping [of an object completely], because this would be an unwarrantable stretch [of a definition]. If you now object that this being so, *darśana* would be a non-apprehension [of an object], then no, because proper apprehension and not being ascertained entail having a *darśana* of an external object. *Darśana* is a *pramāṇa*, because it is not contradicted, the appearance (*pratibhāsa*) is both a *pramāṇa* and not a *pramāṇa*, because one perceives the form of both contradiction and non-contradiction. Or [in other words] the function/activity (*vṛtti*) of seeing/looking is *darśana*. A paraphrase of this is – seen/beheld means seeing/beholding, [viz.] the *ātman*, acting/doing is activity, the activity of seeing/beholding is seeing-activity/sight, [viz.] knowledge derived from one's self, this is called *darśana*, pointing out/indicating what is to be known (*lakṣhya*). Or the activity of illuminating/elucidating is *darśana*. A paraphrase of this is – illuminating/elucidating is *jñāna*, the activity of the *ātman* for the sake of that [*jñāna*] is the activity of illuminating/elucidating [and] this is *darśana*. The meaning is: the state [of knowledge] previous to the occurrence/the place of contact/the coming together (*saṃpāta*) of a property and what has the property (*viṣayaviṣayisaṃpātāt*) is *darśana*. And it has been said – (from the Hindi): Without distinguishing the external object in terms of its universal and particular nature, what grasps the universal or manifests only the intrinsic nature, this is called *darśana* in the supreme *Āgama*s.

Conclusion

By way of conclusion some points may be highlighted here in order to show how the commentary introduces some philosophically significant points. In the section on *jñāna* it is said: "even when objects are manifested [in incorrect views] they are called *ajñāna* through the non-cessation of doubt, error and misapprehension" (p. 143 of the ed.). This means that doubt, error and misapprehension prevail when one has an incorrect view. The point is interesting in itself, although a further clarification regarding how exactly this is so would be useful to know: how precisely can it be said that a person who has an incorrect view is not free of doubt, etc., how does the person realize that in fact doubt, etc.

prevail? What is intended here is perhaps the Jaina view that the person, namely the one who belongs to another school of thought, comes to realize the incorrect view only when the Jaina worldview is known and accepted. In other words, the prevalence of incorrect views is acknowledged in accepting that there are other schools of thought, with the option that they can correct their views in line with the Jaina thinking, as is being done in the text.

The point that is immediately raised after this is the objection: "If you now [in objection] say that this being the case there would be an absence of *jñāna* in the state of *darśana*, then [we Jainas say] this is not an error, because it is so desired." This significant statement would be baffling without knowing the Jaina concept of *upayoga*, even though the commentary itself does not use the word, only the free Hindi translation does so. The idea that *darśana* and *jñāna* correspond respectively to the general description in Indian epistemology between indeterminate perception (*nirvikalpakapratyakṣa*) and determinate perception (*savikalpakapratyakṣa*) has been dealt with elsewhere.[16]

In the second section on *jñāna* quoted above it is said, apart from reiterating the point already made, that *jñāna* is absent in doubt, error and misapprehension: "Therefore, with regard to incorrect views, there is no one who knows; it is established that *jñāna* is that through which (*anena*) one knows the substance (*dravya*), quality (*guṇa*) and modus (*paryāya*) [of an object]." These are well-known basic concepts which are effectively used by Jaina thinkers, enabling them to talk of change in a substance without the risk of its losing its substancehood; this applies for both the ontological categories of *jīva* and those which belong to *ajīva*. Indeed, these concepts are unique to the Jainas, when, for example, a change in the *jīva* is acknowledged. For more details see the discussion in note 13 above. The context in which *jñāna* is used here has to be seen together with the use of *darśana*; although *saṃyama* is briefly discussed because of the sequence in the enumeration of the 14 terms in this *sūtra* 1, 1, 4, for all intents and purposes they could be read together, something which the section on *darśana* also makes evident because the term *jñāna* appears there again.

The ṢKhĀ is a work on *karman*, which means that everything the commentary says has to be seen, in the first instance, in relation to its significance to this extremely complex karma theory in Jainism, starting with the basic distinction of eight karmas divided into the so-called four *ghātiya* (destructive) karmas and the four *aghātiya* (non-destructive) or secondary karmas.[17] Here it is significant that *karman* is seen as a form of *pudgala* or matter which needs to eradicated so that the *jīva* can manifest itself without any hindrance, something which strict ascetic practices can do. It is karma which determines every facet of human existence, until such time as it is destroyed. This means that, in our context here, *jñāna* and *darśana* are also affected, in whatever sense one uses the terms. The idea of obscuring or *āvaraṇīya karma*s is what has to be taken recourse to in the context here when talking about the details of *jñāna* and *darśana* and their obscuration, viz. the influence of *karman* in hindering their proper function, namely, as *jñānāvaraṇīyakarman* or as *darśanāvaraṇīyakarman*.[18]

When in the first section on *darśana* quoted above the opponent says: "there is no difference between *jñāna* and *darśana*" then the commentary says "no, because as with *jñāna* there is an absence of the respective *karman* with regard to *darśana*". The difference lies in the fact that for the Jainas *jñāna* and *darśana* serve different functions and although there is some kind of perception involved in both, each is a distinct category with a different, specific role. Here one would have to see both these functions as different *upayoga*s, as already explained. This interpretation is justified because the commentary immediately goes on to say: "If you now say: if this is so, then *darśana* is the grasping of internal and external universals and *jñāna* the particulars, then [we Jainas say] no, because the universal and particular nature of a thing is obtained without sequence." The point here is a technical one to meet with the opponent's objection: to see *jñāna* and *darśana* as separate entities, as separately yielding a perception respectively of the universal and the particular, would go against the Jaina view that these *upayoga*s are two stages of a single perception, they take place in sequence and only after the implementation of *jñānopayoga* is the object seen correctly as it is.

However, the opponent should not get the impression that there would be no contradiction in the functions of *jñāna* and *darśana,* in the way in which the opponent understands it, which is why the commentary makes the opponent raise another objection in order that the Jaina view may be clarified. The next statement is: "If you say: let it be so, there is no contradiction [at all], then [we Jainas say] no, because there is one with the statement 'the two *upayoga*s do not take place simultaneously' ". In other words, the opponent has to see that *jñāna* and *darśana* as *upayoga*s are presented in sequence.

The rest of this first section on *darśana* quoted above clarifies the point that the discussion on *jñāna* and *darśana* has not been one of means or instruments of knowledge (*pramāṇa*). In Jaina epistemology the word *darśana* does not feature at all and when *jñāna* is used it is in the sense of *matijñāna*, *śrutajñāna*, *avadhijñāna*, *manaḥparyāyajñāna* and *kevalajñāna*, as mentioned above. That is why the text says: *na jñānaṃ pramāṇaṃ (...) na darśanam api pramāṇam*, "neither *jñāna* nor *darśana* are used in this debate here as means or instruments of knowledge". The text makes it indirectly clear that the theory of knowledge is another theme and that the Jainas have their own views on the matter, namely, with *parokṣa* and *pratyakṣa* as the two basic means of indirect and direct knowledge.

The explanation above would seem to be contradicted by what the text says in the last section quoted above:

> *Darśana* is a *pramāṇa*, because it is not contradicted, the appearance (*pratibhāsa*) is both a *pramāṇa* and not a *pramāṇa*, because one perceives the form of both contradiction and non-contradiction. Or [in other words] the function/activity (*vṛtti*) of seeing/looking is *darśana.*

It seems that the word *darśana* is used in yet another context, namely to stand for sense perception as in *matijñāna.* The paraphrase that the text itself gives seems to justify the interpretation that *darśana* here is a synonym for the sense of seeing or looking, which would be sense perception. What is not contradicted, then, is that sense perception is indeed a *pramāṇa*.

Notes

1 See p. 2 of the "Editorial", volume 1.
2 Dundas (2002: 64f.). See also Jaini (1998: 50f.).
3 See the references for the details.
4 See also Dixit (1971: 78–83) and Dundas (2002: 63–65 and 79–81).
5 Dixit (1971: 78f.). It is interesting to note that in the same place, as Dundas (2002: 288, in note 66) also points out, Dixit develops the theory that during the period of the ṢKhĀ "Jaina authors had devised to compose such texts [as the ṢKhĀ] as would render superfluous a study of the old Āgamic texts…, and this was true of the Śvetāmbara as well as Digambara authors." The significance of Dixit's further statement concerning the Jaina canon in this context, ibid. p. 79, should not go unnoticed: "All this accounts for the so striking a similarity that obtains between the theoretical views of the Śvetāmbaras and Digambaras in spite of the fact that the former uphold and the latter repudiate the authority of the now current Āgamic texts."
6 See Śāstrī (1987: 222–228).
7 See *Tattvārthasūtra* 1, 1: *samyagdarśanajñānacāritrāṇi mokṣamārgaḥ*, where these terms constitute the path to liberation.
8 See Dixit (1971: 52) for this list from chapter three of the *Prajñāpanāsūtra*. See also his section "Gradual evolution of the various Anuyogadvāra lists, particularly Mārgaṇāsthānas, Jīvastānas, Guṇasthānas" (ibid., pp. 14–16). See also p. 30 where Dixit particularly notes the significance and contribution of the ṢKhĀ for our knowledge of the early, basic philosophical terms. In the tr. that follows I do not always follow the hints given in the Hindi tr. of the ṢKhĀ used here.
9 The terms could imply *samyagjñāna/samyagdarśana* (proper knowledge/proper faith), *jñāna* in the sense of *pramāṇa* (as a means or instrument of cognition), or in the sense of *jñānopayoga/darśanopayoga* (determinate or specific cognition/indeterminate or bare perception). See Soni (2007: 309).
10 The word *mithyādṛṣṭi* is also the name of the first *guṇasthāna*. See Jaini (1998: 141 and 272).
11 According to the Hindi tr. these words refer to *jñānopayoga* and *darśanopayoga* (determinate or specific cognition and indeterminate or bare perception), mentioned above in note 8.
12 The Sanskrit/Prakrit fn. to this word indicates that the *kālānuyogadvāra*s are to be understood here (*kālapadenātra kālānuyogadvāro boddhavyaḥ*, p. 144).
13 Fn. 2 of the ed. used, p. 145, says the stanza is from prā. paṃ. 1, 117 (this abbreviation is not in the list on pp. 80f.) and go. jī. (*Gommaṭasāra Jīvakāṇḍa*) 299.
14 If the non-difference here in fact refers to the non-difference among the substance, quality and modus of an object, then the logic behind this complex sentence, judging from the stanza quoted at the end of this section, might be the following: if there is always only the one or the other category then this would not do proper justice to the intrinsic nature of an object, which for the Jainas entail all three elements. Only when one accepts their *anekāntavāda*, their theory of manifold perspectives and standpoints, can the one or the other aspect be emphasized without ignoring the others and without harming the unity and essential nature of the object as a whole. The "If…" at the beginning here is because the Hindi translates the last sentence before the stanza in this way:

> *śaṅkā— jñāna to ātmāse abhinna hai, isaliye vaha padārthoṃke jānaneke prati sādhakatama kāraṇa kaise ho saktā hai? samādhāna— aisā kahanā ṭhīka nahīṃ*

> *haiṃ, kyoṃki, sādhakatama kāraṇarūpa jñānako ātmāse sarvathā bhinna athavā abhinna māna lene para ātmāke svarūpakī hānikā prasaṅgā ātā hai, aura kathaṃcit bhinna tathā abhinnasvarūpa anekāntake māna lene para vastusvarūpakī upalabdhi hotī hai, isaliye ātmāse kathaṃcit bhedarūpa jñānko jānanerūpa kriyāke prati sādhakatama kāraṇa māna lenemeṃ koī virodha nahīṃ ātā hai* |
>
> The doubt: *jñāna* is not different from the *ātman*, therefore how can it be the most effective cause with regard to knowing an object? Response: to say this is not all right, because to regard the most effective cause [namely,] *jñāna*, as always being different or non-different from the *ātman*, would lead to a destruction of the essential nature of the *ātman*, and by accepting the manifold perspective as having the nature of somehow being different and non-different, one obtains the essential nature of the object, therefore there is no contradiction in accepting *jñāna*, as somehow having a form of difference from the *ātman*, as the most effective cause with regard to the activity in the form of knowing.

After this, the Hindi gives the special meaning (*viśeṣārtha*) of the sentence here, explaining it in terms of *dharma* and *dharmin*. On *dravya, guṇa* and *paryāya* see Soni (1991).

15 Fn. 2 of the ed. used, p. 150, says the stanza is from prā. paṃ. 1, 135 (this abbreviation is not in the list on pp. 80f.) and go. jī. (*Gommaṭasāra Jīvakāṇḍa*) 482.

16 See Soni (2007, especially pp. 308f.).

17 See Jaini (1998: 111–115 and 131–133). See also Wiley (2004).

18

> It is important to note here that bliss is the only quality of the soul which can truly be defiled, that is, transformed into something of a different nature; other qualities can only be "obscured" or "blocked" (*āvṛta*) by so-called obscuring (*āvaraṇīya*) karmas.
>
> (Jaini 1998: 105)

See ibid. 131f. for the five types of *jñānāvaraṇīya-* and four types of *darśanāvaraṇīyakarman*. It is to be noted in the same place that *darśanamohanīya* is a different type of *karman* which deludes insight.

Bibliography

Primary sources

Gommaṭasāra by Nemicandra consisting of the *Jīvakāṇḍa* and *Karmakānda*, ed. A. N. Upadhye and published in two parts each in Delhi by Bhāratīya Jñānapīṭha, third reprints 2000 and 1999.

Prajñāpanāsūtra (*Paṇṇavaṇāsuttaṃ*) published in two volumes in 1971. Bombay: Shri Mahāvīra Jaina Vidyālaya.

Ṣaṭkhaṇḍāgama: see Puṣpadanta and Bhūtabali.

Secondary sources

Dixit, K. K. *Jaina Ontology*. Ahmedabad: L. D. Institute of Indology, 1971 (L. D. Series No. 31).

Dundas, Paul. *The Jains*. Second Revised Edition. London: Routledge, 2002 (first published in 1992).

Jaina, Hīrālāla, *Ṣaṭkhaṇḍāgama kī Śāstriya Bhūmikā*. Mujappharanagara: Prācya Śramaṇa Bhāratī, 2000.

Jaini, Padmanabh S. *The Jaina Path of Purification*. Delhi: Motilal Banarsidas, 1979/1998.

Kapadia, Hiralal Rasikdas. *A History of the Canonical Literature of the Jainas*. Ahmedabad: Shardaben Chimanbhai Educational Research Centre, 1941.

Puṣpadanta and Bhūtabali, *Ṣaṭkhaṇḍāgama* with Vīrasena's *Dhvavalā-ṭīkā* and Hindi Translation in 16 Volumes. Solāpura: Jaina Saṃskriti Saṃrakṣaka Saṅgha, 1992–1995.

Śāstrī, Paṇḍita Bālacandra. *Ṣaṭkhaṇḍāgama-Pariśīlana*. Dillī: Bhāratīya Jñānapīṭha, 1987.

Soni, Jayandra. "*Dravya, Guṇa* and *Paryāya* in Jaina Thought." *Journal of Indian Philosophy* 19 (1991) 75–88.

Soni, Jayandra. "*Upayoga*, according to Kundakunda and Umāsvāti." *Journal of Indian Philosophy* 35 (2007) 299–311.

Wiley, Kristi L. *Historical Dictionary of Jainism*. Lanham: Scarecrow, 2004.

9 Sensuous cognition – *pratyakṣa* or *parokṣa*?

Jinabhadra's reading of the *Nandīsūtra*

Anne Clavel

The epistemological tradition before the *Nandīsūtra*

1.1. The most ancient Jaina epistemological theory attained a first stage of development in the third *aṅga* of the Scriptures, namely the *Sthānāṅgasūtra* (SthSū). According to its tenets,[1] subsequently stated in Umāsvāmi's *Tattvārthādhigamasūtra* (TS),[2] the five kinds of cognition are integrated into two means of knowledge (cf. Figure 9.1 below):[3] whereas clairvoyance, telepathy and omniscience are put under the head of perception (*pratyakṣa*), sensuous cognition (called *abhinibodhikajñāna* in SthSū but *matijñāna* in TS) is recognized as a part of *parokṣa* – just like testimonial cognition (*śrutajñāna*) – insofar as only a cognition acquired by the mere soul belongs to *pratyakṣa*, but not cognition produced by sensory faculties (*indriya*) or understanding (*manas*).

1.2. Nevertheless, it is often admitted that external pressure, especially the meaning of the word *pratyakṣa* in use in Brāhmaṇical circles[4] compelled the

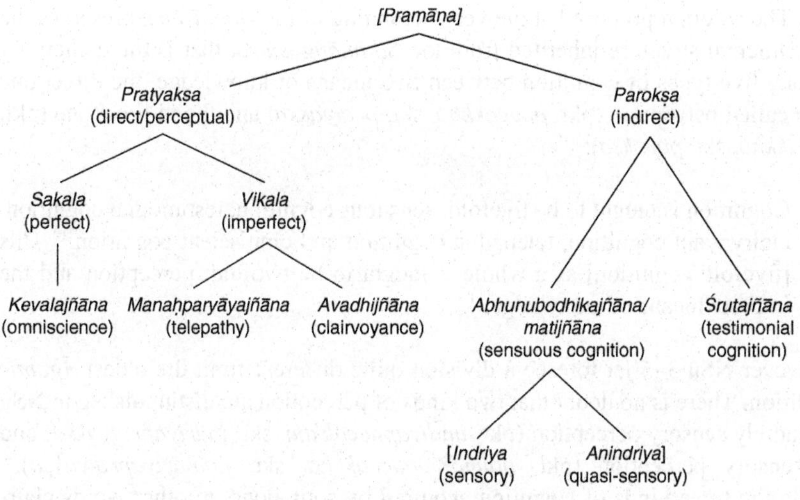

Figure 9.1 Classification of *pramāṇa* according to SthSū and TS.

Jaina philosophers to consider sensuous cognition as perception.[5] The *Anuyogadvārāṇi* (ADv) and the *Nandīsūtra* (NSū), which probably constitute the most recent stratum among the Jaina canonical texts,[6] reflect such an attempt.

1.2.1. The solution represented by ADv consists in dividing cognition into four types: perception (*pratyakṣa*), inference (*anumāna*), analogy (*upamāna*) and tradition (*āgama*). While doing so, ADv borrows the general framework from the Naiyāyika conception, since this fundamental tenet is expressed at the very beginning of the *Nyāyasūtra* (NS I.1.3). However, going further into detail, ADv links two different sorts of cognition within perception: while sensory perception (*indriyapratyakṣa*) corresponds to the cognition obtained thanks to one of the five sensory faculties (sight, hearing, smell, taste and touch), the three intuitive kinds of cognition, i.e. clairvoyance (*avadhi*), telepathy (*manaḥparyāya*) and omniscience (*kevala*), are put under the head of no-sensory perception (*noindriyapratyakṣa*).[7] No wonder this classification was doomed to fail: it associates two kinds of cognition that till then were absolutely separated in two distinct *pramāṇas* – sensory perception belonged to *parokṣa* but intuitive perception to *pratyakṣa*. In such a way, ADv integrates only a few Jaina ideas into the Naiyāyika structure[8] instead of preserving the traditional Jaina framework.

1.2.2. In contradistinction to this first attempt, the one proposed by the *Nandīsūtra* usually sinks into oblivion, even if it contains the seeds of the conception developed subsequently by great logicians, like Akalaṅka or Māṇikyanandin.[9] This oblivion may be partly explained by the fact that the view expounded in this canonical text, almost totally devoted to the theory of knowledge, may appear as inconsistent. The present chapter is an attempt to reconsider this problem of coherence.

A problem of coherence in the *Nandīsūtra*

2.1. The solution proposed at the very beginning of the *Nandīsūtra* preserves the fundamental structure inherited from the *Sthānāṅgasūtra*, that is the dichotomy among five types of cognition between two means of knowledge, the direct one also called perception (pkt. *paccakkha*, skt. *pratyakṣa*) and the indirect one (pkt. *parokkha*, skt. *parokṣa*):

> Cognition is taught to be fivefold: sensuous cognition, testimonial cognition, clairvoyant cognition, telepathic cognition and omniscient cognition.[10] This [fivefold cognition] as a whole is taught to be twofold: perception and the indirect means of knowledge.[11]

However NSū 3–5 let foresee a division quite different from the oldest *Āgamic* tradition. There is no doubt that two kinds of perception are distinguished in NSū 3, namely sensory perception (pkt. *iṃdiyapaccakkha*, skt. *indriyapratyakṣa*) and no-sensory perception (pkt. *ṇoiṃdiyapaccakkha*, skt. *noindriyapratyakṣa*),[12] while the three kinds of cognition acquired by soul alone, in other words clairvoyance, telepathy and omniscience, are included in this *noindriyapratyakṣa*.[13]

Moreover, if a subdivision called *indriyapratyakṣa* is mentioned, it implies that some cognition which was viewed as *parokṣa* before is now considered as a kind of *pratyakṣa*. Since the list of *jñānas* enumerated in NSū 1 is supposed to be exhaustive and since each of these *jñānas* has to be included either in *pratyakṣa* or in *parokṣa* – as the ablative case pkt. *samāsao* (NSū 2) let it think – one must elucidate which cognition(s), among the sensuous and the testimonial ones, has or have moved from *parokṣa* to *pratyakṣa*.[14] But nothing is clearly said about the place where each of them can be classified. The only clue is furnished in the fourth *sūtra*[15] where sensory perception is identified with the cognition produced thanks to one of the five sensory faculties (hearing, sight, taste, smell and touch); but this statement is not obviously conclusive, insofar as NSū 4, avoiding any generic term, does not use the same terminology as NSū 1.

Nevertheless, we can settle this difficulty thanks to a comparison with TS. For this text brings to the fore two different sources of sensuous cognition; in this way the cognition produced by sensory faculties (*indriyanimitta*) is distinguished from another one that depends on understanding (*anindriyanimitta*).[16] Thus, we may assume that *indriyapratyakṣa* should be identified with sensuous cognition (pkt. *abhiṇibohianāṇam*, skt. *ābhinibodhikajñāṇam*), or at least with a part of it, i.e. the one caused by sensory faculties. In Figure 9.2 that conveys this new classification, we use square brackets when the terms are not explicitly employed in NSū but result from our hypotheses.

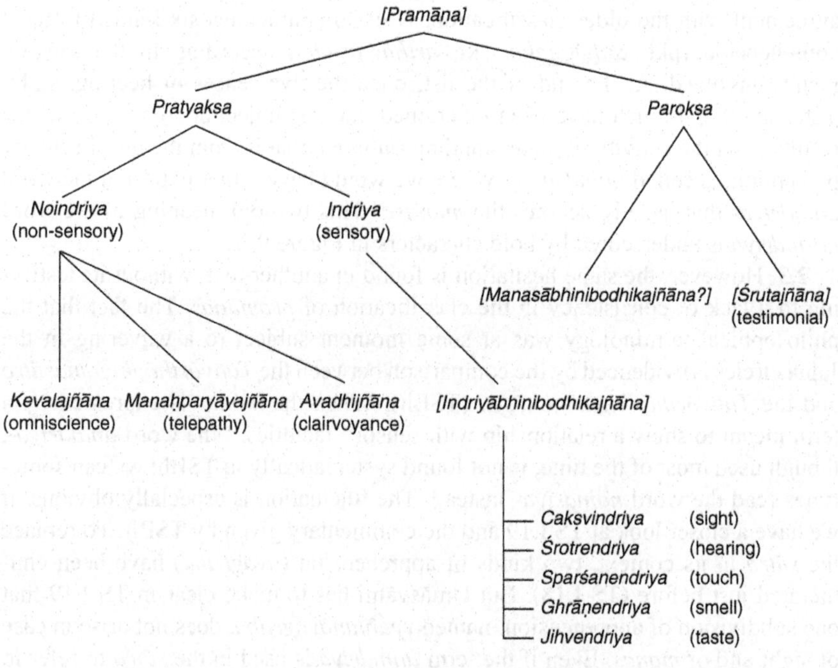

Figure 9.2 Classification of *pramāṇa* according to NSū 1–5.

2.2. But the remainder of the *Nandīsūtra* seems to follow the ancient classification adopted in the *Sthānāṅgasūtra*. Once the three kinds of non-sensory cognition set forth in the *sūtra* 5 have been explained in details (in NSū 6–23), a second investigation begins in the 24th *sūtra*: it concerns the two sorts of cognition mentioned in NSū 1, which have not been studied yet, that is sensuous cognition (pkt. *ābhiṇibohianāṇa*, skt. *ābhinibodhikajñāna*) and testimonial cognition (pkt. *suanāṇa*, skt. *śrutajñāna*). Strangely, while doing so, the author does not seem to take the first classification, given in the *sūtras* 3–5, into account any more. He clearly puts sensuous cognition under the head of *parokṣa*:

> What is indirect cognition? Indirect cognition is taught to be twofold: indirect [cognition consisting in] sensuous cognition and indirect [cognition consisting in] testimonial cognition.[17]

Thus, if we want to propose a single *pramāṇa* table that would hold true for the whole text, we are faced with two difficulties. First, sensory cognition appears twice, once integrated into *pratyakṣa* and once into *parokṣa* (this double occurrence is underlined in Figure 9.3). Second, combining both classifications raises a problem of terminology: in NSū 5, the term *noindriya-* referred to the three kinds of cognition that never involve sensory faculties, insofar as they manifest the pure capacity of soul when the *karman* obscuring them have been pacified or destroyed (i.e. clairvoyance, telepathy and omniscience).[18] In contradistinction to this first use, while investigating sensuous cognition (*ābhinibodhikajñāna*) in agreement with the older classification, NSū 30 enumerates six kinds of object apprehension (pkt. *atthuggaha*, skt. *arthāvagraha*) according to the sensory faculty involved. At the end of the list, once the five senses of hearing, sight, taste, smell and touch have been mentioned, the last object apprehension which results from the activity of understanding (*manas*), that is from the quasi-sensory perception, is called *noindriya*,[19] where we would have rather expected the word *anindriya-* that usually denotes the *manas*.[20] This twofold meaning of the word *no-indriya* is underscored by bold characters in Figure 9.3.

2.3. However, the same hesitation is found in another text, without its testifying to a lack of consistency in the classification of *pramāṇas*. The fact that the philosophical terminology was at some moment subject to a wavering in the Jaina circles is evidenced by the comparison between the *Tattvārthādhigamasūtra* and the *Tattvārthādhigamabhāṣya* (TSBh). When the *manas* is expressed by a term meant to show a relationship with sensory faculties,[21] the word *anindriya-*, though used most of the time, is not found systematically in TSBh: we can sometimes read the word *noindriya-* instead. The fluctuation is especially obvious, if we have a closer look at TS I.19 and the commentary given by TSBh. To replace the *sūtra* in its context, two kinds of apprehension (*avagraha*) have been enumerated just before (TS I.18). But Umāsvāmi has to make clear in TS I.19 that one subdivision of apprehension, named *vyañjanāvagraha*, does not arise in case of sight and of *manas*. Even if the term *anindriya* is used in the *sūtra* to refer to *manas*, the commentary chooses *noindriya*, but the meaning is indeed exactly

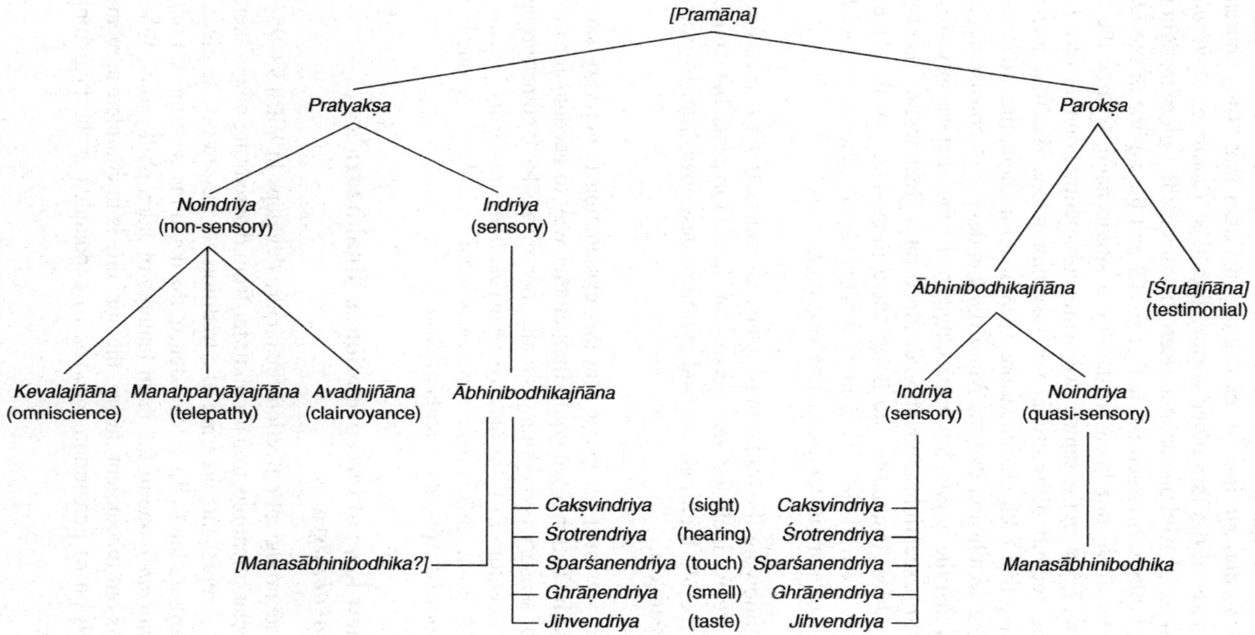

Figure 9.3 Classification of *pramāṇa* according to NSū 1–30.

the same. Let us compare both texts in Sanskrit. To express the idea that "there is no *vyañjanāvagraha* in case of sight and of the quasi-sense", the *sūtra* says: *na cakṣuranindriyābhyām*,[22] whereas the commentary says: *cakṣuṣā noindriyena ca vyañjanāvagraho na bhavati*, explaining just after that "[this apprehension] exists in the case of the four other sensory faculties" (*caturbhir indriyaiḥ śeṣair bhavatīty arthaḥ*).[23] And one cannot assert that this is the sign of a slight discrepancy of terminology between the author of TS and the author of the *bhāṣya* in case both texts have not been written by a single hand,[24] since the last one employed *anindriya-* in the same sense while commenting on the *sūtra* I.14.[25]

2.4. If the second difficulty is not insurmountable, the first one is more serious. Stating that both classifications seem incompatible, the modern scholars often draw the conclusion that the *Nandīsūtra* is devoid of consistency. At best, one assumes that the innovation represented by the fact that sensory cognition is integrated into perception, innovation destined for a great destiny, is responsible for a philosophical instability and is sufficient to explain that its place has not been definitely fixed in the *Nandīsūtra* yet. This idea is especially voiced by I.C. Shastri who wrote in his *Jaina Epistemology* (1990: 209):

> Nandī, following the tradition of Anuyoga and feeling the pressure of non-jaina systems, included sense-cognition into Pratyakṣa; but could not go against the old tradition also and therefore described Mati as Pratyakṣa as well as Parokṣa.

Nevertheless, we must recognize that this explanation is not very satisfactory. And it would be better if we could find another way to account for this double occurrence of sensory perception. Actually, our wishes have come through. Jinabhadra (sixth century CE)[26] in his *Viśeṣāvaśyakabhāṣya* (ViBh)[27] seems to have been the first Jaina philosopher to offer a solution able to reconcile the two apparently contradictory statements of NSū.

Towards new keys of interpretation in Jinabhadra's *Viśeṣāvaśyakabhāṣya*

3.1. The epistemological reflection Jinabhadra develops in ViBh 94–95 attempts to take both classifications into account: far from discrediting one of them letting us think that it represents the trace of a tradition not passed yet, he gives a philosophical interpretation to their coexistence, thanks to the doctrine of multilateralism (*anekāntavāda*), one of the main features of Jaina philosophy. Whereas the stanza 94 sets out the ancient theory, the next one is in complete agreement with the new division of perception (*pratyakṣa*) expounded at the beginning of the *Nandīsūtra*:

> Sensuous cognition and testimonial cognition are the indirect means of knowledge, because they are caused by [something] else than soul, inasmuch as it is based on the memory of a relation grasped before, as inference.[28]

According to an unilateral thesis, **(a)** a [cognition] based on an inferential sign is [a variety of the] indirect means of knowledge while **(b)** clairvoyance, etc. is perception; **(c)** the [cognition] produced by sensory faculties or by understanding is conventional perception.[29]

The possible problem of an incompatibility between both views is focused on in the *bhāṣya* Jinabhadra himself wrote in order to comment on the stanza 95. The passage consists of a succession of answers thanks to which Jinabhadra rejects the objections an opponent may raise. The debate shed light on our difficulty very well, because the adversary's view, based on NSū 3, allows Jinabhadra to explain how this passage can be reconciled with more traditional teachings. The first objection disputes the statement set out at the beginning of ViBh 95, namely the idea that the cognition based on an inferential sign, cognition which in fact also depends on a sensory faculty or on understanding, belongs to *parokṣa*:

[O_1] [An opponent] says: The utterance: "[cognition] caused by sensory faculties [is] the indirect means of knowledge" deviates from the sacred books. But then, it is explained in the *sūtra* that "perception is taught to be twofold: sensory perception and no-sensory perception!" [$NSū_1$ 3 = $NSū_2$ 9][30]

3.2. This objection let us put forward an assumption concerning the identity of the rival. It is especially noteworthy that he does not take as a starting point of his objection the conception admitted in the *Āgamas*, but precisely the view that seems the least traditional of all. This clue may prove itself helpful: it is unlikely that Jinabhadra's co-religionists are unaware of the usual conception that is found in the *Āgamas*; even though the adversary is a Jaina neophyte, he is at least supposed to know TS, which was considered as a handbook. No doubt that a Jaina would voice his astonishment while stating the apparent impossibility of reconciling the traditional tenets with the view newly introduced by the author of the *Nandīsūtra*; thus he would rather quote traditional teachings so as to refute NSū 3 than refer to this singular *sūtra* in order to reject the usual conception. Inversely, if the opponent embodies an heterodox system, quoting NSū 3 is easily understandable, since the dichotomy between sensory and no-sensory perceptions makes sense in a theory where the cognition derived from senses is called "perception".

3.3. Jinabhadra's reply aims at showing that the way he divides up the different varieties of cognition among two means of knowledge is consistent. With this end in view, he proves that the characterizations of *pratyakṣa* or *parokṣa* cannot always be given absolutely: the point of view according to which a cognition is said perceptual or indirect must sometimes be considered, otherwise one might fall into an unilateral (*ekānta*) view. Such a necessity is evidenced by a threefold illustration:

[A_1] It is answered [by us]: That is true, but in this [stanza], [we] say that **(a)** the cognition of an external sign which is produced by sensory faculties and

> understanding is indirect (*parokṣa*) towards sensory faculties and soul – according to an unilateral thesis – because [such a cognition] is an inference, as the cognition of fire from smoke; **(b)** and the cognition [that consists in] clairvoyance, etc. is direct (i.e. perceptual, *pratyakṣa*) towards soul – according to a unilateral thesis –because it does not depend on an inferential sign, as a cognition [produced by sensory faculties] which does not depend on an [inferential] sign is direct (i.e. perceptual, *pratyakṣa*) towards sensory faculties. **(c1)** On the other hand, the cognition which is directly caused by sensory faculties and understanding is direct towards these [faculties] only, as clairvoyance, etc. [is a direct cognition] towards soul; **(c2)** but [this cognition is] not [a direct one] towards soul; towards soul it is only an indirect cognition, "because it is caused by [something] else [than soul], as inference" is it said [in ViBh 94]. And towards these [faculties], this [cognition] is direct only from the conventional standpoint, but not from the transcendental standpoint. Why? "because [these faculties] are devoid of consciousness, as a pot".[31]

This answer, in which Jinabhadra develops ViBh 95, follows exactly the same structure as the stanza. First (a), Jinabhadra studies the case of a cognition that, though produced with the help of sensory faculties and understanding, is also based on an external inferential sign (*bāhyaliṅga*); as the power of *indriyas* and of *manas* would not be sufficient to cause this cognition, it cannot be viewed as their exclusive and direct production. Nor can it be considered as a direct production of soul, because *indriyas* and *manas* are necessary to its production. Therefore the cognition depending on a mark that is external to the cognizer constitutes the indirect cognition *par excellence*. Conversely, the second case (b) provides an instance of the direct cognition *par excellence*, since soul produces this cognition without its using any helper. Both kinds of cognition share a common feature: their association with a means of knowledge does not require a differentiated dividing up according to the standpoint adopted. Jinabhadra justifies this single treatment by the expression "according to a unilateral thesis" (pkt *egaṃteṇa*, skt. *ekāntena*), which occurs in the stanza as in the *vṛtti*. Here, the term *ekānta* does not aim, as it often does, at suggesting the partiality of the statement and implying that another analysis, itself also unilateral, could be provided if we adopt another standpoint. Characterizing a statement as unilateral does not necessarily reduce its truth-value, insofar as a description can be true in spite of its unilateralism.[32] The word *ekānta* enables Jinabhadra to show a strong difference in the treatment of the third kind of cognition, since he adopts two standpoints successively.

In this manner, the cognition focused on in the third case provides the most significant illustration: devoted to the cognition produced thanks to the activity of senses and of *manas* alone, it comprises two levels of analysis (called c_1 and c_2). What is partly suggested in the stanza, because ViBh merely mentions one level of interpretation (c_1), becomes clearer when one reads the *vṛtti*.[33] In the first part of the investigation (c_1), the philosopher explains that the absence of any inferential sign (*liṅga*) constitutes a sufficient reason to consider the cognition acquired by sensory and quasi-sensory faculties as belonging to perception, insofar as that cognition is direct (*pratyakṣa*) from the standpoint of these faculties, because no other faculty is involved in its production. But the second part of his account (c_2) qualifies this first statement: the cognition acquired by sensory and quasi-sensory faculties must not be absolutely viewed as an integral part of perception, because from the standpoint of soul, this is an indirect cognition, since its nature precisely proves the inability of soul to cognize a thing solely by itself. Of course, this second assertion comes within the framework of the traditional conception, according to which only a cognition produced by the soul without its using any helper (sensory faculty, understanding) can be held to be perceptual. The fact that the two different explanations do not lead to a contradiction reveals the existence of two levels of mediacy and of immediacy, depending on whether the standpoint taken into consideration is the soul or the sensory and quasi-sensory faculties, as it appears in Table 9.1.

Such a distinction is especially meant to explain the possible ambiguity found in NSū, as it is clearly expressed while Jinabhadra answers the second objection. According to him, NSū 3 views sensuous cognition as *pratyakṣa* because the *sūtra* is taught from the conventional point of view, while NSū 24 adopting the transcendental point of view considers sensuous cognition as *parokṣa*.

> **[O_2]** [The opponent] says: It is not specified in the *sūtra* that "the [cognition] caused by sensory faculties is direct (i.e. perceptual, *pratyakṣa*) from the conventional [standpoint], but not from the transcendental one".
>
> **[A_2]** It is answered [by us]: But then, it is explained in a *sūtra* that "indirect cognition is taught to be twofold: sensuous cognition and testimonial cognition" [$NSū_1$ 24 = $NSū_2$ 42]. And there is no [cognition] caused by sensory faculties other than sensuous cognition and testimonial cognition that would be absolutely direct (i.e. perceptual).[34]

Nevertheless, the opponent conceives another way of resolving the difficulty: instead of considering one and the same cognition from two different standpoints,

Table 9.1 Two levels of immediacy according to Jinabhadra

	Cognition	*Standpoint*		*Kind of pramāṇa*
		jīva	***indriya and manas***	
b	*avadhijñāna*, etc.	*pratyakṣa*	—	*pratyakṣa* (*paramārthataḥ*)
c_1				
c_2	*alaiṅgika matijñāna*	*parokṣa*	*pratyakṣa*	*pratyakṣa* (*saṃvyavahārataḥ*) *parokṣa* (*paramārthataḥ*)
a	*laiṅgika matijñāna*	*parokṣa*	*parokṣa*	*parokṣa*

he suggests to introduce a dichotomy, based on the cognition nature, depending on whether it depends on an inferential sign or not. This constitutes the content of the third objection:

> **[O_3]** [The opponent] says: But then only the [cognition] caused by sensory faculties which does not depend on an inferential sign will be absolutely direct (i.e. perceptual), while the [cognition] caused by sensory faculties which depends on an inferential sign [will] belong to sensuous [cognition] and testimonial [cognition].[35]

Nevertheless this idea is unacceptable to Jinabhadra, since the cognition at issue is precisely devoid of all the mental processes that make it similar to inference. No doubt that a *laiṅgika* sensuous cognition is a kind of *parokṣa*, as has already been settled in the gloss of ViBh 95 (**A_1**). On the other hand, if one considers that sensory perception does not belong to the indirect means of knowledge because this cognition is not based on an inferential sign, it necessarily follows that sensory perception is different from the set composed of *matijñāna* and *śrutajñāna*. And, inasmuch as sensory perception, as its name shows, has to be distinguished from no-sensory perception, namely composed of clairvoyance, telepathy and omniscience, one should postulate the existence of a sixth kind of knowledge. But reading NSū 1 is sufficient to reject such an hypothesis.[36]

Thus, Jinabhadra rules out convincingly the opponent's attempts to explain NSū, and thanks to his distinction between two points of view the conception held in the *Nandīsūtra* does not appear as inconsistent anymore. But Jinabhadra's philosophical interpretation introduces changes in denominations revealing a more fundamental change in the criterion which the distinction between both kinds of perception is based on: whereas NSū considers the cognition nature, sensory or no-sensory, the author of ViBh makes the opposition dependent on two levels of reality. First and foremost, Jinabhadra's distinction pertains to a meta-epistemological analysis; one can reconstruct only subsequently the dichotomy implied among perception, so as to distinguish the conventional one ("sensory" according to NSū's wording) from the transcendental one (or "no-sensory").

3.4. A final problem can now be elucidated that was left aside in the *Nandīsūtra*: to which *pramāṇa* does the quasi-sensory cognition (*manas-ābhinibodhika* according to NSū's wording) belong? On the one hand, when according to NSū 30 sensory cognition is put under the head of *parokṣa*, quasi-sensory cognition is treated in the same way, and both constitute sensuous cognition. On the other hand, while specifying the various sorts of *indriyapratyakṣa*, the fourth *sūtra* only gives five subdivisions, corresponding to the five senses, but there is no mention at all of a perception produced by *manas*. Therefore, we wondered whether this kind of cognition belongs to *pratyakṣa*, following the example of sensory cognition, or to *parokṣa* (cf. our question marks in Figures 9.2 and 9.3). Jinabhadra solves the difficulty present in the *Nandīsūtra*; for he clearly states in the first part of the third illustration that the characterization of perception does not only concern the cognition caused by sensory faculties but also that caused by *manas* (*indriyamanonimittaṃ*): it belongs to conventional perception or to the indirect means of knowledge, in accordance with the rule applying to the cognition produced by senses.[37]

Besides, ViBh removes the possible ambiguity concerning the meaning of the word *noindriya-* in NSū. When the opponent – thinking perhaps that the word *noindriya-* designates the *manas* in the context of NSū 24 – understands that the perception called *noindriya* in NSū 3 refers to a cognition produced by *manas*,[38] Jinabhadra retorts that the negation *no-* expresses a total negation:[39] the sorts of cognition meant by the term *noindriyapratyakṣa* are those which require nothing else than soul itself. And Jinabhadra makes it clear that such a cognition comprises clairvoyance and the other intuitive types, namely telepathy and omniscience.[40] If we follow the reasoning until its end, we may assume that a partial negation expressing a relationship between sensory faculties and understanding would be expressed by the prefix *an-*.

Conclusion

To conclude, the *Nandīsūtra* is an essential evidence of the transition that has occurred from the oldest *Āgamic* conception to the new one: the wavering in the wording just as the fact that two typologies are taught in two different parts of the text reveal a classification not yet absolutely systematized. However, far from combining inconsistently two heterogeneous typologies, NSū represents the first stage of a fundamental epistemological process destined to be achieved by some of the greatest Jaina philosophers. While distinguishing two levels of immediacy, Jinabhadra embodies a second epistemological stage. For he offers a solution so as to avoid regarding the apparent fluctuation as incoherent, and the way he applies the same distinction to the quasi-sensory cognition makes the coherence of the system stronger: according to him, sensuous cognition in its totality can be viewed either as conventional perception or as indirect means of knowledge. This philosophical explanation has attained its goal since it has been adopted by some Jaina logicians, among whose the great Akalaṅka (720–780),[41] perhaps the foremost Digambara philosopher, has also contributed to preserving the memory of this conceptual evolution.[42]

Notes

1 Cf. SthSū 71f. 49a–b (the *sūtra* consists of a series of dichotomies of which we only quote those that are relevant to our purpose):

> *duvihe nāṇe pannatte, taṃ jahā: paccakkhe ceva parokkhe ceva (1); paccakkhe nāṇe duvihe pannatte, taṃ jahā: kevalanāṇe ceva ṇokevalanāṇe ceva (2) (...); ṇokevalanāṇe duvihe pannatte, taṃ jahā: ohināṇe ceva maṇapajjavanāṇe ceva (12) (...); parokkhe nāṇe duvihe pannatte, taṃ jahā: ābhiṇibohiyanāṇe ceva suyanāṇe ceva (17) (...).*

Cognition is taught to be twofold: perceptual (i.e. direct) and indirect (1); perceptual cognition is taught to be twofold: perfect (i.e. omniscient) cognition and

> imperfect cognition (2) (...); imperfect [perceptual] cognition is taught to be twofold: clairvoyant cognition and telepathic cognition (12) (...); indirect cognition is taught to be twofold: sensuous cognition and testimonial cognition (17) (...).

The evolution of the epistemological conceptions has been treated more or less extensively, among others, by Schubring (1935: 156–159), Tatia (1951: chapter II and especially 27–30), Sanghvi (1961: 50–54), Bothra (1976: 18–20) and Shashtri (1990: 196–211), among others. We just propose a brief survey of the tradition within which the theory found in the *Nandīsūtra* comes. The *Bhagavatīsūtra* (BhSū) reveals a conceptual stage which seems older than in SthSū, but it is of no interest for our present purpose. Epistemological matters are only analysed from the standpoint of cognition (*jñāna*), not from the standpoint of means of knowledge (*pramāṇa*), so that the main problem, i.e. dividing the five *jñānas* among two *pramāṇas*, cannot arise.

> BhSū 318, f. 342b:
>
> *(...) paṃcavihe nāṇe pannatte, taṃ jahā: ābhiṇibohiyanāṇe suyanāṇe ohināṇe maṇapajjavanāṇe kevalanāṇe (...).*
>
> Cognition is taught to be fivefold: sensuous cognition, testimonial cognition, clairvoyant cognition, telepathic cognition and omniscient cognition.

The standpoint of *pramāṇa* is meaningless in the context of BhSū, because the criterion according to which a cognition is valid or not does not pertain to epistemology at all, but to faith: a cognition is false if the cognizer's faith is erroneous; inversely, a cognizer whose faith is right has necessarily a right knowledge, whatever the content of the cognition and its conformity with reality are.

2 TS I.9–12, pp. 12–13:

> *matiśrutāvadhimanaḥparyāyakevalāni jñānam* || 9 || *tat pramāṇe* || 10 || *ādye parokṣam* || 11 || *pratyakṣam anyat* || 12 ||
>
> (9) Cognition [is fivefold]: sensuous, testimonial, clairvoyant, telepathic and omniscient. (10) The set made up of these [five kinds of divides (are divided) into] two means of knowledge. (11) The first two [kinds of cognition] (i.e. *mati* and *śruta*) constitute the indirect means of knowledge. (12) The remaining [kinds] constitute perception.

Dating TS precisely poses a serious problem and scholars now waver between the first century CE and the end of the fifth century AD. A brief survey of the various proposals as to the dating of TS, as well as convincing arguments for the second half of the fourth century, are given in Balcerowicz (2008: 35, n. 23).

3 *Stricto sensu*, unlike TS, SthSū does not use the term *pramāṇa* in this context, unlike TS. Nevertheless, there is not the slightest doubt that the dividing up of five *jñānas* is already combined with the dichotomy between *pratyakṣa* and *parokṣa*, a dichotomy that will later lay the foundations of the *pramāṇa* theory. We use square brackets in order to distinguish the elements which appear only in TS, but not in SthSū.

4 The problem pertains to etymology, even though the disagreement does not concern the way the word *pratyakṣa* is analysed (into the prefix *prati-* and the substantive *akṣa*), but the meaning of the noun *akṣa*. Whereas the other *darśanas* regard the *akṣas* as the sensory organs, *akṣa* is, according to ancient Jainism, equivalent to soul (*ātman*) or, in other words, to the life-monad (*jīva*). Cf. Bothra (1976: 31). In a system that conceives cognition as an innate faculty of soul and not as an adventitious property, *pratyakṣa* is thus the means of cognition which involves soul alone and thanks to which soul can contemplate directly its object. On the other hand, every kind of cognition that forces soul to use other instruments of knowledge, for instance sensory faculties, belongs to *parokṣa*.

5 See, for instance, Sanghvi (1961: 51–52):

> Under the influence of the logical systems of philosophy like the Nyāya-Vaiśeṣika, etc., the Buddhist monks had long since left the field assigned to them by *Piṭakas* (*piṭakocitamaryādā*) and had entered the arena of debate and of the logical treatment of *pramāṇas* (that goes with debate). Gradually, the Jaina monks too could not remain immune from the influence of this logical treatment undertaken by the Vedicist and Buddhist philosophers.

See also Tatia (1951: 28) and Shastri (1990: 199–200), who concerning the stage represented by the *Anuyogadvārāṇi* insists on the influence of the four-part division admitted among the Naiyāyikas which might have reflected conceptions that were popular at that time.

6 The *aṅgas* constitute in the main the oldest material – fixed ca. 300 BC – while ADv and NSū, both summing up teachings drawn from the whole scriptures, are considered as forming the youngest material. According to Folkert (1993: 44–46), they may have been fixed after the second Valabhī council (453 or 466 CE).

7 Among the three properties inherent to soul, cognition (*ṇāṇa*), faith (*daṃsaṇa*) and conduct (*caritta*), ADv 144, f. 211a–b distinguishes four subdivisions:

> *cauvvihe paṇṇatte, taṃ jahā: paccakkhe anumāne ovamme āgame. se kiṃ taṃ paccakkhe? duvihe paṇṇatte, taṃ jahā: iṃdiapaccakkhe a ṇoiṃdiapaccakkhe a. se kiṃ taṃ iṃdiapaccakkhe? paṃcavihe paṇṇatte, taṃ jahā: soiṃdiapaccakkhe cakkhuriṃdiyapaccakkhe ghāṇiṃdiapaccakkhe jibbhiṃdiapaccakkhe phāsiṃdiapaccakkhe, se taṃ iṃdiyapaccakkhe. se kiṃ taṃ ṇoiṃdiyapaccakkhe? tivihe paṇṇatte, taṃ jahā: ohiṇāṇapaccakkhe maṇapajjavanāṇapaccakkhe kevalaṇāṇapaccakkhe, se taṃ ṇoiṃdiyapaccakkhe, se taṃ paccakkhe.*
>
> [Cognition] is taught to be fourfold: perception, inference, analogy and tradition. What is perception? It is taught to be twofold: sensory perception and no-sensory perception. What is sensory perception? It is taught to be fivefold: perception [based on] the sense of hearing, perception [based on] the sense of sight, perception [based on] the sense of smell, perception [based on] the sense of taste and perception [based on] the sense of touch; these [constitute] sensory perception. What is no-sensory perception? It is taught to be threefold: perception [consisting in] clairvoyant cognition, perception [consisting in] telepathic cognition and perception [consisting in] omniscient cognition; these [constitute] sensory perception; these [sensory and no-sensory perceptions constitute] perception.

Concerning the division in four means of valid cognition, compare the underlined passage with NS I.1.3, p. 2: *pratyakṣānumānopamānaśabdāḥ pramāṇāni.* In spite of the lexical variant – *āgama* in ADv instead of *śabda* in NS – the fourth *pramāṇa* refers in both cases to a reliable testimony. Of course, the fourfold division does not reveal an innovation in itself, inasmuch as this typology already existed in SthSū and BhSū; but combining it with the division of cognition is a novelty.

8 The fact that the denomination *parokṣa* disappeared in ADv confirms the supremacy of the Naiyāyika framework over the Jaina one, for *parokṣa* could have included inference, analogy and tradition. Cf. Schubring (1935: 159).

9 See *infra* note 41.

10 $NS\bar{u}_1$ 1, f. 65a [= $NS\bar{u}_2$ 7, p. 13.9–10]: *nāṇaṃ paṃcavihaṃ pannattaṃ, taṃ jahā: abhiṇibohianāṇaṃ suanāṇaṃ ohināṇaṃ maṇapajjavanāṇaṃ kevalanāṇaṃ.*

11 $NS\bar{u}_1$ 2, f. 71b [= $NS\bar{u}_2$ 8, p. 14.13]: *taṃ samāsao duvihaṃ paṇṇattaṃ, taṃ jahā: paccakkhaṃ ca parokkhaṃ ca.*

12 $NS\bar{u}_1$ 3, f. 75a [= $NS\bar{u}_2$ 9, p. 14.20–21]:

> *se kiṃ taṃ paccakkhaṃ? paccakkhaṃ duvihaṃ paṇṇattaṃ, taṃ jahā: iṃdiyapaccakkhaṃ ṇoiṃdiyapaccakkhaṃ ca.* "What is perception? Perception is taught to be twofold: sensory perception and no-sensory perception."

13 NSū$_1$ 5, f. 76b [= NSū$_2$ 11, p. 15.6–7]:

> *se kiṃ taṃ noiṃdiapaccakkhaṃ? noiṃdiyapaccakkhaṃ tivihaṃ paṇṇattaṃ, taṃ jahā: ohināṇapaccakkhaṃ maṇapajjavaṇāṇapaccakkhaṃ kevalaṇāṇapaccakkhaṃ.* "What is no-sensory perception? No-sensory perception is taught to be threefold: perception [consisting in] clairvoyant cognition, perception [consisting in] telepathic cognition and perception [consisting in] omniscient cognition."

14 A similar reasoning, aiming at rejecting the existence of a sixth kind of cognition, is found in ViBhV 95 (see 3.3 and note 36).

15 NSū$_1$ 4, f. 76a [= NSū$_2$ 10, p. 14.22–24]: *se kiṃ taṃ iṃdiapaccakkhaṃ? iṃdiapaccakkhaṃ paṃcavihaṃ paṇṇattaṃ, taṃ jahā: soiṃdiapaccakkhaṃ cakkhiṃdiapaccakkhaṃ ghāṇiṃdiapaccakkhaṃ jibbhiṃdiapaccakkhaṃ phāsiṃdiapaccakkhaṃ, se taṃ iṃdiapaccakkhaṃ.* "What is sensory perception? Sensory perception is taught to be fivefold: perception [based on] the sense of hearing, perception [based on] the sense of sight, perception [based on] the sense of smell, perception [based on] the sense of taste and perception [based on] the sense of touch; these [constitute] sensory perception." This *sūtra* is an exact quotation of a part of ADv 144 (cf. *supra*, note 7).

16 One must pay careful attention to the words used to express this dichotomy, for despite the similarity to the terms employed in NSū to distinguish two types of *pratyakṣa* (cf. NSū 3), the opposition between *indriya-* and *anindriya-* appears in an absolutely different context, inasmuch as they designate here the subdivisions of *matijñāna*, which is itself a kind of *parokṣa*.

TS I.14:

> *tad indriyānindriyanimittam.*
>
> Sensory cognition is caused by sensory faculties and by the quasi-sense.

TSBh 1.14, p. 16.11–14 explains the division of *matijñāna* in the following way:

> *indriyanimittam anindriyanimittaṃ ca. tatrendriyanimittaṃ sparśanādīnāṃ pañcānāṃ sparśādiṣu pañcasv eva svaviṣayeṣu. anindriyanimittaṃ manovṛttir oghajñānaṃ ca.*
>
> [One] is caused by sensory faculties and [the other one] is caused by the quasi-sensory faculty. Among these [two subtypes], the one caused by sensory faculties is the result of the five [sensory faculties], i.e. touch, etc.; it is concerned with their respective domains, [which are] also five, i.e. tangibility, etc. The one caused by the quasi-sensory faculty is the activity of mind and the *ogha* cognition.

Tatia defines *oghajñāna* (1951: 33) as the "instinctive incipient intuitions of the plant world as well as the undeveloped animal organisms, which are independent of both the sense-organs and the mind". We may assume that the *oghajñāna* corresponds to *manonimittajñāna* for living beings that are devoid of understanding.

17 NSū$_1$ 24, f. 140a [= NSū$_2$ 42, p. 31.3–4]: *se kiṃ taṃ parukkhanāṇaṃ?, parukkhanāṇaṃ duvihaṃ pannattaṃ, taṃ jahā: ābhiṇibohianāṇaparokkhaṃ ca suanāṇaparokkhaṃ ca (...).*

18 Let us remember that his meaning is also attested in ADv (cf. *supra* note 7).

19 NSū$_1$ 30, f. 173b [= NSū$_2$ 50, p. 35.8–10]: *se kiṃ taṃ atthuggahe? atthuggahe chavvihe paṇṇatte, taṃ jahā: soiṃdiaatthuggahe cakkhiṃdiaatthuggahe ghāṇiṃdiaatthuggahe jibbhiṃdiaatthuggahe phāsiṃdiaatthuggahe noimdiaatthuggahe.* "What is object apprehension? Object apprehension is taught to be sixfold: the object apprehension [occurring in the case] of hearing, the object apprehension [occurring in the case] of sight, the object apprehension [occurring in the case] of smell, the object apprehension [occurring in the case] of taste, the object apprehension [occurring in the case] of touch [and] the object apprehension [occurring in the case] of the quasi-sense."

20 Cf. for instance TS I.14 and TSBh I.14 previously quoted (note 16).

21 In the word *anindriya-*, the prefix *an-* does not express a total negation, but indicates a close relationship, so that the *anindriya* points out what is similar to a sixth sense, namely the *manas*, even though it does not absolutely share the status of the five senses that are traditionally listed: sight, hearing, smell, taste and touch. Whereas these five senses are considered to be external, *manas* is an internal sense.

22 TS I.19, p. 18.

23 TSBh I.19, p. 19.2–3.

24 Cf. Balcerowicz (2008: 35).

25 TS and TSBh I.14 have been quoted before (cf. note 16).

26 It is generally admitted that Jinabhadra Gaṇi Kṣamāśramaṇa flourished during the second half of the sixth century CE: CE 484–588 according to Vidyabhusana (1971: 181), CE 489–593 according to Malvania (introduction to ViBh, volume I, p. 1).

27 The *Viśeṣāvaśyakabhāṣya* is a commentary on the first chapter of the *Āvaśyakaniryukti*, which itself comments on the third *mūlasūtra*, namely the *Āvaśyakasūtra*. Concerning the quasi-canonical status of the *Āvaśyakaniryukti*, cf. Dundas (2002: 75).

28 ViBh 94, I p. 24.20–21: *honti parokkhāiṃ maisuyāiṃ jīvassa paraṇimittāo | puvvovaladdhasaṃbandhasaraṇao vāṇumāṇaṃ va ||*.

29 ViBh 95, I p. 24.26–27: *egaṃteṇa parokkaṃ liṃgiyam ohāiyaṃ ca paccakkhaṃ | iṃdiyamaṇobhavaṃ jaṃ taṃ saṃvavahāra-paccakkhaṃ ||*.

30 ViBhV 95, I p. 25.1–3: **[O_1]** *āha: ucchāstram ucyate "parokṣam indriyanimittam" iti. nanu sūtropadiṣṭaṃ "paccakkhaṃ duvidhaṃ paṇṇattaṃ, taṃ jahā: iṃdiyapaccakkhaṃ ca ṇoiṃdiyapaccakkhaṃ ca" [nandī 10].* Malvania may have had an edition of NSū with a sligh different numbering when he edited ViBh. For a greater clarity, we add in square brackets the capital letters **O** and **A** in order to indicate respectively an objection and its answer.

31 ViBhV 95, I p. 25.3–9: **[A_1]** *ucyate: satyam idam, atra tu* **(a)** *yad indriyamanobhir bāhyaliṅgapratyayam utpadyate, tad ekāntenaivendriyāṇām ātmanaś* ca parokṣam, anumānatvāt, dhūmād agnijñānavat.* **(b)** *yac cāvadhyādi tad ekāntenaiva pratyakṣam ātmanaḥ, aliṅgatvāt, indriyāṇām aliṅgajñānavat.* **(c_1)** *yat punaḥ sākṣād indriyamanonimittaṃ tat teṣām eva pratyakṣam, aliṅgatvāt, ātmano 'vadhyādivat,* **(c_2)** *na tv ātmanaḥ, ātmanas tu tat parokṣam eva, 'paranimittatvāt, anumānavat' ity uktam. teṣām api ca tat saṃvyavahārata eva tat pratyakṣam, na paramārthataḥ. kasmāt? 'acetanatvāt, ghaṭavat' ity uktam. * ātmanaś* em. Malvania: *ātmakaś* ||. I have failed to identify the last quotation. The same reasoning has been adopted by Jinadāsa Gaṇi Mahattara, latter quarter of the seventh century CE according to Singh (2001: 4556) in his *cūrṇi* on NSū 42 ($NSū_2$ 42, p. 31.5–10): *akkhassa iṃdiyamaṇā parā, tesu jaṃ ṇāṇaṃ taṃ parokkhaṃ. matiśrute parokṣamātmanaḥ, paranimittatvāt, anumānavat. ṇanu sutte iṃdiyapaccakkhaṃ bhaṇitaṃ? ucyate: saccam iṇaṃ, etthaṃ jaṃ iṃdiyamaṇohiṃ bahiliṃgapaccayam uppajjati tam egaṃteṇeva iṃdiyāṇa attaṇo ya parokkhaṃ, aṇumāṇattaṇato, dhūmāo aggiṇāṇaṃ va. jaṃ puṇa sakkhā iṃdiyamaṇonimittaṃ taṃ tesiṃ ceva paccakkhaṃ, aliṃgattaṇato, attaṇo avadhimādi vva, attaṇo tu taṃ egaṃteṇeva parokkhaṃ. iṃdiyāṇaṃ pi taṃ saṃvavahārato paccakkhaṃ, ṇa paramatthato. kamhā? jamhā davviṃdiyā acetaṇā iti. taṃ duvihaṃ: matiṇāṇaṃ sutaṇāṇaṃ ca.*

32 Commenting on TS 1.9, Akalaṅka clearly indicates the existence of right *ekānta* statements (RVār I, p. 35.23–28), even though this term is often employed by Jaina philosophers in order to reject an opponent's thesis, pointing out its insufficiency. An *ekānta* statement becomes wrong, deserving then the denomination *durnaya* ("wrong viewpoint") when the cognizer, misunderstanding its partiality and its inadequacy to describe reality, claims that this perspective is the only one valid. See, for example, Shastri (1987: 75–76), Bossche (1993: 462–464), Balcerowicz (2003: 40–41). Nevertheless, the doctrine of multilateralism does not imply that Jainism is a relativism.

Every unilateral assertion is not wrong by its sole unilateralism: few statements, especially meta-epistemological, can escape the *anekāntavāda* and hold true absolutely. Such assertions are indicated by the use of terms, like *añjasā*, *tattvātaḥ*, *paramārthataḥ*, implying that the utterance is not uttered from the empirical and conventional standpoint, but from the transcendental one. This peculiar issue has been extensively studied in our doctoral dissertation entitled *The Theory of Knowledge in Akalaṅka's Laghīyastraya* (forthcoming).

33 However, while characterizing the cognition based on *indriyas* and on *manas* as a conventional perception (*saṃvavahārapaccakkhaṃ*), ViBh 95 lets us assume that there must be another kind of perception, otherwise the precision would be useless.

34 ViBhV 95, I p. 25.9–12:

> **[O₂]** *āha: na sūtre viśeṣitam "indriyanimittaṃ saṃvyavahārataḥ pratyakṣam, na paramārthataḥ" iti.*
>
> **[A₂]** *ucyate: nanu sūtropadiṣṭaṃ "parokkhaṃ duvihaṃ, taṃ jahā: ābhiṇibohiyaṇāṇaṃ suyaṇāṇaṃ ca" [nandī 43] iti. na ca matiśrutābhyām indriyanimittam anyad asti yat pratyakṣam añjasā bhavet.*

35 ViBhV 95, I p. 25.12–13:

> **[O₃]** *āha: nanv etad evendriyanimittaṃ pratyakṣam añjasā bhaviṣyati yad alaiṅgikam, matiśrute tu yal laiṅgikam indriyanimittam iti.*

36 ViBhV 95, I p. 25.13–15:

> **[A₃]** *ucyate: na, laiṅgikasya aindriyanimittābhāvād, indriyasya pratyutpannamātraviṣayatvāt, na matiśrutayoś ca, indriyānindriyanimittatvāt; indriyapratyakṣasya ca matiśrutābhyām anyatve ṣaṣṭhajñānaprasaṅgāt.*

37 This peculiarity of Jinabhadra's conception has already been noticed by Tatia (1951: 28) and Mahendra Kumar (introduction to SVi, p. 36). Nevertheless, Shastri (1990: 210) seems incoherent: he first acknowledges that Jinabhadra calls *sāṃvyavahārikapratyakṣa* the cognition produced by sensory faculties and understanding, but then in his later conclusions, he maintains that sensuous cognition caused by *manas* belongs totally to *parokṣa*, whatever the standpoint.

38 We can notice that the opponent's misunderstanding concerning the meaning of *noindriya-* confirms that he may be impregnated with the naiyāyika conception.

39 ViBhV 95, I p. 25.16–20:

> **[O₄]** *āha: indriyanimittaṃ parokṣam iti śraddadhmahe, manonimittaṃ tu katham?*
>
> **[A₄]** *ucyate: nanūktaṃ "paranimittatvāt, anumānavat" iti.*
>
> **[O₅]** *āha: na sūtre viśeṣyābhihitaṃ "parokṣaṃ manonimittam" iti.*
>
> **[A₅]** *ucyate: tat pratyakṣam api naivoktam.*
>
> **[O₆]** *āha: "iṃdiyapaccakkhaṃ ca noiṃdiyapaccakkhaṃ ca" [nandī 10] iti. noindriyaṃ ca mana iti.*
>
> **[A₆]** *ucyate: na, sarvaniṣedhamātravacanatvād nośabdasya.*
>
> **[O₄]** [The opponent] says: We assent to [the idea] that the cognition caused by sensory faculties is indirect, but how [the cognition] caused par understanding [could be indirect]?
>
> **[A₄]** It is answered [by us]: But then, it is said: "because [this cognition] is caused by [something] else [than soul], as inference" [ViBh 94].
>
> **[O₅]** [The opponent] says: It is not specifically declared in the *sūtra* that "the [cognition] caused by understanding is indirect".

[A_5] It is answered [by us]: Nor is it said that this [cognition] is direct (i.e. perceptual)!

[O_6] [The opponent] says: [But] it is said that "sensory perception and no-sensory perception [are the two different kinds of perception]" [$NS\bar{u}_1$ 3 = $NS\bar{u}_2$ 9], and the "no-sensory" is the understanding (*manas*).

[A_6] It is answered [by us]: No, because the word "no" [in "no-sensory"] expresses only the total negation.

40 ViBhV 95, I p. 25.20–25: **[end of A_6]** *katham? avadhyādiviśeṣaṇāt, avadhyāditrayasya ca manonimitta*prasaṅgāt, tataś ca manaḥparyāptiśūnyasyāvadhijñān opayogābhāvaḥ syāt; aniṣṭaṃ caitat, yasmād uktaṃ "cutemi tti jāṇati" [kalpa° 3] siddhasya cājñānitva°prasaṅgaḥ, amanaskatvāt. tasmād yathendriyajñānaṃ† pratyakṣam apy uktaṃ matiśrutayoḥ parokṣavacanāt parokṣam iti gamyate, tathā matiśrutaparokṣavacanād eva manonimittam anuktam api gamyate tadantarbhāvāt‡ parokṣam iti, aṣṭāviṃśatibhedatvāc ca mater iti, anyathāsyāpi ṣaṣṭhajñānaprasaṅgaḥ syād iti.*

* *manonimitta°* em. Malvania: *manonimitvā°* || ° *cājñānitva°* em. Malvania: *cājñāni°* || † *jñānaṃ* em. Malvania: *jñāna* || ‡ *antarbhāvāt* em. Malvania: *antarbhāva* ||

41 LT 3, p. 1.16–17: *pratyakṣaṃ viśadaṃ jñānaṃ mukhyasaṃvyavahārataḥ | parokṣaṃ śeṣavijñānaṃ pramāṇe iti saṅgrahaḥ* ||. "Perception [is] clear cognition, [it is twofold] because of [the division between the] transcendental [standpoint] and [the] conventional [standpoint]; the indirect means of knowledge [comprises] the remaining cognition. These are the two means of knowledge in summary." The same division also appears in other philosophical works. See, for example, Māṇikyanandin's *Parīkṣāmukham* (PMS), where the term *mukhyam* ("absolute, primary") amounts to *paramārthikam* ("transcendental"). PMS 5, p. 60: *indriyānindriyanimittaṃ deśataḥ sāṃvyavahārikam.* PMS 11, p. 72: *sāmagrīviśeṣa-viśleṣitākhilāvaraṇam atīndriyam aśeṣato mukhyam.*

42 NVi 3.88, II p. 363.23 and 33: *ādye parokṣam aparaṃ pratyakṣaṃ prāhur āñjasam | kevalaṃ lokabuddhyaiva mater lakṣaṇasaṅgrahaḥ* ||. "Absolutely, the first two [kinds of cognition (i.e. *mati* and *śruta*)] are called "indirect means of knowledge", [whereas] the remaining is called "perception". Sensuous cognition is included in the definition [of perception] only in order to be in accordance with people's opinion."

Bibliography

Primary sources and abbreviations

ADv = *Anuyogadvārāṇi*. Ed. Veṇīcand Sūrcand. Bombay: Agamodaya Samiti, 1924.

BhSū = *Bhagavatīsūtraṃ*. Ed. Veṇīcand Sūrcand. 3 vol. Mehesana: Agamodaya Samiti, 1917–1922.

LT = Akalaṅka, *Laghīyastraya* in *Śrīmadbhaṭṭākalaṅkadevaviracitam Akalaṅkagranthatrayam. Svopajñavivṛtisahitam Laghīyastrayam, Nyāyaviniścayaḥ, Pramāṇasaṅgrahaś ca*. Ed. Mahendra Kumar. Ahmedabad: Sarasvatā Pustak Bhaṇḍār (Singhi Jaina Granthamālā 12), 1996, 2nd edn. 1–26; 1st edn. 1939.

NS = Gautama, *Nyāyasūtra* in *Die Nyāyasūtra's Text, Übersetzung, Erlaüterung und Glossar*. Ed. W. Ruben. Leipzig: Deutsche morgenländische Gesellschaft (Abhandlungen für die Kunde des Morgenlandes XVIII), 1928.

$NS\bar{u}_1$ = *Nandīsūtra*. Ed. Veṇīcand Sūrcand. Bombay: Agamodaya Samiti, 1924.

$NS\bar{u}_2$ = *Nandīsūttaṃ by Devavācaka, with the cūrṇi by Jinadāsa Gaṇi Mahattara*. Ed. Muni Shri Punyavijayaji. Ahmedabad: Prakrit Text Society, 2004.

NVi = *Nyāyaviniścayavivaraṇa of Śrī Vādirāja Sūri, the Sanskrit Commentary on Bhaṭ Akalaṅkadeva's Nyāyaviniścaya*. Ed. Mahendra Kumar Jain [ed.], 2 vols. Delhi: Bhāratīya Jñānapīṭha Prakāśana, 2000, 2nd edn; 1st edn Varanasi: 1949 & 1954.

PMS = *Parīkṣāmukham* of Māṇikyanandī. Ed. and tr. S.C. Ghoshal. New Delhi: Today & Tomorrow's Printers & Publishers (The Sacred Books of the Jainas XI), 1990, reprint; 1st edn Lucknow: The central Jaina Publishing House, 1940.

RVār = *Tattvārthavārttika [Rājavārttika] of Śrī Akalaṅkadeva*. Ed. Mahendra Kumar Jain. 2 vols. Delhi: Bhāratīya Jñānapīṭha Prakāśana (Jñānapīṭha Mūrtidevī Jaina Granthamālā 10), 2001, 6th edn; 1st edn 1953 & 1957.

SthSū = *Sthānāṅgasūtra*. Ed. Veṇīcand Sūrcand. 2 vols. Mehesana: Agamodaya Samiti, 1918–1920.

SVi = *Siddhiviniścaya of Akalaṅka edited with the commentary Siddhiviniścayaṭīkā of Anantavīrya*. Ed. Mahendra Kumar Jain. 2 vols. Delhi: Bhāratīya Jñānapīṭha Prakāśana (Jñānapīṭha Mūrtidevī Jaina Granthamālā 22–23), 1959.

TS = Umāsvāti, *Tattvārthādhigamasūtra* in *Tattvārtha Sūtra, That Which Is*. Tr. N. Tatia. San Francisco: Harper Collins, 1994.

TSBh = Umāsvāti, *Tattvārthādhigamabhāṣya* in *Tattvārthādhigamasūtram Śrīmadumāsvātinā racitam svakṛtabhāṣyasahitam*. Ed. K.P. Mody. Calcutta: Asiatic Society (Bibliotheca Indica 1044), 1903.

ViBh = *Ācārya Jinabhadra's Viśeṣāvaśyakabhāṣya*, 3 vols. Vol. I & II: *with autocommentary*, Ed. D. Malvania; Vol. III: *with Śrīkoṭyāryavādigaṇi's vivaraṇa*. Ed. D. Malvania & B.J. Doshi. Ahmedabad: L.D. Institute of Indology (Lalbhai Dalpatbhai Series 10, 14 & 21), 1966–1968.

ViBhV = Jinabhadra, *Viśeṣāvaśyakabhāṣyavṛtti*. See ViBh.

Secondary sources

Balcerowicz, Piotr. 2003. "Some Remarks on the Naya Method." *Essays in Jaina Philosophy and Religion*. Ed. Piotr Balcerowicz & Marek Mejor, 37–68. Delhi: Motilal Banarsidass.

Balcerowicz, Piotr. 2005. "Pramāṇas and Language: A Dispute between Diṅnāga, Dharmakīrti and Akalaṅka." *Journal of Indian Philosophy* 33, 343–400.

Balcerowicz, Piotr. 2008. "Some Remarks on the Opening Sections in Jaina Epistemological Treatises." *Śāstrārambha. Inquiries into the Preamble in Sanskrit*. Ed. Walter Slaje, 25–81. Wiesbaden: Harrassowitz.

Bossche, Frank van den. 1993. "Jain Relativism: An Attempt at Understanding." *Jain Studies in Honour of Jozef Deleu*. Ed. Rudy Smet & Kenji Watanabe, 457–474. Tokyo: Hon-No-Tomosha.

Bothra, Pushpa. 1976. *The Jaina Theory of Perception*. Delhi: Motilal Banarsidass.

Dundas, Paul. 1992. *The Jains*, London – New York: Routledge, 2002, 2nd revised edn, 1st edn.

Folkert, Kendall W. 1993. *Scripture and Community: Collected Essays on the Jains*. Ed. John E. Cort. Atlanta (Georgia): Scholars Press.

Sanghvi, Sukhlalji. 1961. *Advanced Studies in Indian Logic and Metaphysics*. Calcutta: Indian Studies Past and Present.

Schubring, Walther. 1935. *Die Lehre der Jainas, nach den alten Quellen dargestellt*. Berlin – Leipzig: de Gruyter.

Shah, Nagin J. 1967. *Akalaṅka's Criticism of Dharmakīrti's Philosophy. A Study*. Ahmedabad: L.D. Institute of Indology.

Shastri, Indra C. 1990. *Jaina Epistemology*. Varanasi: P.V. Research Institute (P.V. Research Series 50).

Shastri, Yajneshwar S. 1987. "Reconciliation of Different Philosophical View-points – An Attempt Made by Jaina Philosophers." *Jain Journal* 21/3, 71–85.

Singh, Narendra K. (ed.). 2001. *Encyclopaedia of Jainism*. 30 vol. New Delhi: Anmol Publishers.

Tatia, Nathmal. 1951. *Studies in Jaina Philosophy*. Varanasi: P.V. Research Institute.

Vidyabhusana, Satis C. 1920. *A History of Indian Logic*. Delhi: Motilal Banarsidass, 1971, 1st edn, Calcutta.

10 Vasudeva the philosopher

Soul and body in Saṅghadāsa's *Vasudevahiṇḍī*[1]

Anna Aurelia Esposito

Story-telling was always considered an ideal means for the transmission of moral and religious teachings in a form which can be both easily understandable and absorbing. We owe especially to the Jains a huge amount of lively and entertaining stories with more or less concealed messages for the audience. Among the less concealed messages[2] are parables, allegories, sermons and philosophical passages, which are often intertwined in a quite artistic way with the main narrative, as is, for example, the case in Saṅghadāsa's *Vasudevahiṇḍī*.[3] The *Vasudevahiṇḍī*, written in Jaina-Māhārāṣṭrī,[4] is not only the earliest work of Jain narrative literature, but also the oldest witness[5] to the lost *Bṛhatkathā* of Guṇāḍhya.[6] In its main character, King Vasudeva, the father of Kaṇha (Kṛṣṇa), the last *Vāsudeva* of this descending world period, the *Vasudevahiṇḍī* combines the story of King Naravāhanadatta's adventures of the *Bṛhatkathā* with the universal history of the Jains.

While doctrinal passages are quite frequent in the *Vasudevahiṇḍī*, philosophical parts are very rare. I would like to elaborate here on one of these passages, *Vh.* 202.13–203.8, that contains a discussion about the existence of the soul, *āyā* (*ātmā*).[7] Dialogue partners are Puṇṇāsa, a materialist, and Vasudeva, who is defending the Jaina concept of soul. Disputes between materialists and followers of the Jain faith occur also elswhere in Jain literature. Prominent examples are the *Paesikahāṇayaṃ* of the Śvetāmbara canon and a passage in Haribhadra's poem *Samarāiccakahā*. As these texts bear a certain affinity to the passage in the *Vasudevahiṇḍī* and a comparison between the three texts could be fruitful, I would like to introduce first shortly the *Paesikahāṇayaṃ* and the *Samarāiccakahā*. After an analysis of the passage of the *Vasudevahiṇḍī* I will look closer at the similarities and the differences of the three texts.

Prince Paesi and the princely renouncer Kesi

"The Story of Paesi", *Paesikahāṇayaṃ* (Skr. *Pradeśikathānaka*), forms the kernel of the *Rāyapaseṇiya* (Skr. *Rājapraśnī*?),[8] the second Upāṅga of the Śvetāmbara canon.[9] The *Rāyapaseṇiya* starts with god Sūriyābha (Skr. Sūryābha), coming from the Sohammakappa[10] to pay homage to Jina Mahāvīra. Mahāvīra describes to his pupil Goyama (Skr. Gautama) the magnificence of Sūriyābha and his *vimāna*[11] of the same name. Then Mahāvīra narrates, how god

Sūriyābha got all this glory – and here the *Paesikahāṇayaṃ* starts: In his last birth, god Sūriyābha had been born as Paesi (Skr. Pradeśin), ruler of Seyaviyā.[12] He was a wicked, impious[13] materialist. His charioteer Citta, who had become a follower of the princely renouncer Kesi (Skr. Keśin),[14] managed to bring about a meeting between Paesi and Kesi. A lively dialogue develops, in which the king's thesis or objection and the renouncer's antithesis or refutation succeed one another.[15] Finally Paesi, convinced by Kesi's arguments, is ready to hear the doctrine. The very next day he starts a new life: He spends a quarter of the revenue he got from the city Seyaviyā and its seven thousand villages to build a large hall; there he gives orders to hand out food to many *śramaṇa*s. Furthermore, he no longer pays attention to his affairs, his subjects or even his harem – which was a mistake, as his further biography shows: Feeling neglected, his queen Sūriyakantā puts an end to his life. He is reborn in the Sohammakappa as god Sūriyābha. There he will live for four *paliovama*s.[16] In his following birth he will attain final emancipation.[17]

Piṅgakesa the *nāstika* versus Vijayasiṃha the Jain Ācārya

The *Samarāiccakahā* of Haribhadra (eighth century CE) is, as the author explicitly states in his *Bhūmikā*, a *dharmakathā*.[18] Its main plot describes nine births (*bhava*) of the hero and the antagonist, in which they were connected with each other. In their first birth the hero, King Guṇasena, provokes through his negligence the hatred of the antagonist, Aggisamma (Skr. Agniśarman). This hatred is so intense, that Aggisamma, at that time being a monk famous for keeping his vows and practising severe penance, uttered an awful resolve (*nidāna*): He vowed to kill his enemy in every one of his future births.[19] And so he did, as Haribhadra describes in the nine chapters (*bhava*) of his *Samarāicchakahā*. In their ninth birth, however, the hero succeeds to sow the first seed of righteousness in the antagonist. In this birth the hero reaches *mokṣa*, and the antagonist at least enters the path that will lead him after countless rebirths to salvation.

In the third *bhava* the former monk Aggisamma is reborn as Jāliṇī, wife of minister Bambhadatta (Skr. Brahmadatta), and the former King Guṇasena as her son Sihi (Skr. Śikhin). Due to her former hatred, Jāliṇī already detested the unborn child and tried to abandon him after birth. Bambhadatta, however, brought him up secretly in some other place. As Jāliṇī discovered, that her son whom she had thought dead still lived, she flew into a passion and told her husband to choose between her or him. Sihi, who came to know this, left the town without taking leave even of his father. At the park Asogavaṇa (Skr. Aśokavana) he met the *ācārya* Vijayasiṃha, to whom the account of his former births told by a *tīrthaṃkara* had made such an impression that he had renounced the world. After Sihi had questioned him about various aspects of the *dharma*, he expressed his wish to become a monk. While they were conversing the minister Bambhadatta arrived with some followers. Sihi asked his permission to enter the Order, but his father objected because Sihi was too young to renounce the world. He was supported by one of his followers, a *nāstikavādin* named Piṅgakesa (Skr. Piṅgakeśa), who tried to dissuade Sihi from his decision. A discussion between the materialist and the Jain monk arose.[20] Vijayasiṃha refuted Piṅgakesa's arguments one by one and in the end reduced him to silence. By this discussion both Bambhadatta and Piṅgakesa were awakened and adopted the Law of laymen. The minister now readily consented to the ordination of Sihi.

Instructor Puṇṇāsa in discussion with his opponent Vasudeva

The discussion about the existence of the soul takes place in the *Paümālaṃbha* (Skr. *Padmālambha*), the eighth chapter of the *Sarīra* (Skr. *Śarīra*), the central part of the *Vasudevahiṇḍī*.[21] At the beginning of this chapter, Vasudeva's enemy, the *Vidyādhara*[22] Nīlakaṇṭha,[23] carries him off by air and drops him finally into a pond.[24] Vasudeva is able to rescue himself and reaches a park near the city Salaguhā. There he encounters the sons of King Abhaggaseṇa,[25] practising archery.[26] After Vasudeva has revealed himself as master in this art, he teaches them at their request without the knowledge of Puṇṇāsa (Skr. Pūrṇāśa), the official teacher of the princes. Eventually Puṇṇāsa comes to know this. In the presence of the king he poses Vasudeva some questions. Here arises the opportunity to divagate into Jain mythology: Asked by Puṇṇāsa about the origin of archery (*dhaṇuvveda*/*dhanurveda*),[27] Vasudeva goes back to the time of Usabha (Ṛṣabha), the first *Tīrthaṅkara* and king of this world age. Under his reign weapons had not been necessary; his son Bharaha (Bharata), however, the first *Cakravartin*, laid the foundation for weaponry by means of a compilation called "Māṇava". In the course of time cruel kings and their ministers made up different kinds of weapons, and experts produced them (*Vh.* 202.4–12).

This relatively concise (and by no means remarkable) excursus into Jain universal history serves merely as a starting point for a much more interesting passage, in which Vasudeva proves himself to be also an expert of Jain philosophy. Vasudeva is accomplished in the arts,[28] he knows both the Aryan and the non-Aryan Veda[29] and he is an authority in weaponry; as philosopher he is depicted – except for our present passage – only once,[30] a role that is rather more fitting for an ascetic than for a warrior. Our passage starts with a concluding remark, that has but little to do with his previous exposition:

> *karaṇa-sahito puṇa āyā kaya-payatto cakkh'-iṃdiya-so'-iṃdiya-ghāṇ'-iṃdiya-paütto lakkha-dese*[31] *cittaṃ niveseūṇa hiya-icchiyam attha-kajjaṃ samāṇeti.*
>
> (*Vh.* 202.13 f.)
>
> [Vasudeva said:] Moreover, the soul (*āyā*), united with the sense organs, accomplishes the desired action[32] in making an effort through employing the organs of sight, hearing and smell and turning the mind towards the indicated places.

This remark seems at a first glance quite startling. Vasudeva had answered in his foregoing explanations completely and utterly Puṇṇāsa's question about the origin of archery. The sentence in question seems to be not only redundant, but even out of place. When I said above, the foregoing excursus "serves merely as a starting point for a much more interesting passage", I refered to the *Vasudevahiṇḍī* as it is available to us now, with all the interpolations that have slipped in over the course of the centuries – and this passage is quite suspicious to be one of them. The connection between Vasudeva's actual answer and the following philosophical discourse, made by this quite unfitting sentence, is rather clumsy. Besides, the following "discussion" does actually not deserve this designation, as it consists of two quite monolitic blocks: Puṇṇāsa's rejection of Vasudeva's remark, followed by Vasudeva's refutation of Puṇṇāsa's world view. It seems that the whole passage, starting with Vasudeva's concluding remark (i.e. *Vh.* 202.13–203.8), dates from a more recent period and has originally nothing to do with Vasudeva's interrogation. Most probably, after Vasudeva's answer to Puṇṇāsa's question (*Vh.* 202.5–12) followed immediately *Vh.* 203.9 *tato kei sadde chaṃde aṇṇesu ya kalā-vihānesu sikkhiyā pucchaṃti* (After that others learned in grammar, metrics and other arts asked me questions).

Be it as it may, in our present text of the *Vasudevahiṇḍī* Vasudeva's concluding remark invites Puṇṇāsa's contradiction:

> *tato bhaṇati joggâriyao – sāmi! hou bharaha-raṇṇo māṇaveṇa ṇihiṇā pavattiyaṃ paharaṇâvaraṇa-vihāṇaṃ, jaṃ bhaṇaha – "āyā satthāṇaṃ*[33] *saṃdhāṇe nissaraṇe ya raṇe ya pamāṇaṃ" ti taṃ ṇa hoti.*
>
> (*Vh.* 202.15–17)
>
> Then the instructor [Puṇṇāsa] said: Sir, all right, the method of weapons and armours was introduced by King Bharaha's compilation "Māṇava"; but when you say "the soul (*āyā*) is the authority behind the aiming and the throwing of the weapons and the fight [with them]" – that can't be true.

***pamāṇaṃ*:** A means of acquiring certain knowledge; out of the six *pramāṇa*s in the Vedānta the *nāstika*s acknowledge only *pratyakṣa*, perception through the senses, as Maṇibhadra states in his commentary *Laghuvṛtti* to Haribhadra's *Ṣaḍdarśanasamuccaya*, verse 81[34] (see also Tucci 1925: 39).

Puṇṇāsa fully agrees to Vasudeva's answer per se, his objection concerns only Vasudeva's last remark. In the following he reveals his *Weltanschauung*:

> *āyā bhūya-samavāya-atiritto na koi uvalabbhati, savvaṃ ca bhūyamayaṃ jagaṃ. bhūyāṇi ya saṃhatāṇi*[35] *tesu tesu kajjesu uvaüjjaṃti, tāṇi puḍhavi-jala-jalaṇa-pavaṇa-gagaṇa-saṇṇiyāṇi.*[36] *jo thiro bhāvo so patthivo, jo davo so udayaṃ, umhā*[37] *aggeyā, ciṭṭhā vāyavvā, chiddam ākāsaṃ. karaṇāṇi vi tappabhavāṇi – soyaṃ āyāsa-saṃbhavaṃ sadda-ggahaṇe samatthaṃ, tatī vāyavvā phāsaṃ paḍisaṃvedeti, cakkhuṃ teya-saṃbhavaṃ rūvaṃ geṇhati, nāsā patthivā gaṃdha-gāhiyā, rasaṇam udaga-saṃbhavaṃ rasa-saṃveyagaṃ*[38] *ti. viṇaṭṭhe sarīre sa-bhāvaṃ paḍivajjaṃti bhūyāṇi. kayaro ettha āyā jatthaṃ sāmittaṃ vaṇṇeha?*
>
> (*Vh.* 202.17–23)

> Nobody can perceive a soul (*āyā*) which is different from the aggregate of material elements (*bhūya*), and the whole world is consisting of [the five] elements. The combined elements are employed in all sorts of things, they are called earth (*puḍhavi*), water (*jala*), fire (*jalaṇa*), wind (*pavaṇa*) and space (*gagaṇa*). Whatever has a solid nature is coming from earth, whatever is liquid from water, heat is belonging to fire, moving is connected to wind, the opening to space. The sense organs (*karaṇa*) are also derived from them – the ear, that is produced from space, is capable of catching the sound; the skin, connected to wind, recognizes touch; the eye, that is produced from glow, grasps the form; the nose, coming from earth, causes to grasp smell; the tongue, that is produced from water, perceives flavour. When the body has perished, the elements return to their natural state. Which [of these elements] is here the soul (*āyā*), of whom you describe the lordship?

***āyā bhūya-samavāya-atiritto na koi uvalabbhati*:** The beginning of the first sentence reminds one of a similar passage in Haribhadra's *Samarāiccakahā* (165.1 f.): *na khalu ettha pañca-bhūya-vaïritto* [...] *jīvo samatthīyaï*, "By no means in this world can (the existence of) a soul be assumed which is different from the five elements" (Transl. Bollée 2002: 357).

***uvaüjjaṃti*:** The present of *yuj* can be besides *juñjaï* also *jujjaï*, according to Hemacandra 4.109 (cf. also Pischel § 507). In the present case, however, *uvaüjjaṃti* has to be taken as passive (Skr. *upayujyante*).

***puḍhavi-jala-jalaṇa-pavaṇa-gagaṇa-saṇṇiyāṇi*:** Contrary to Haribhadra's and Prabhācandra's presentation of the materialists' views,[39] Puṇṇāsa accepts five elements instead of originally four. As Frauwallner (1973: 14 f.) remarks, the nature-philosophical schools, whose theory of the elements does principally not differ from that of the materialists, know initially four elements (earth, water, fire and air), which are characterized by definite qualities. At the time of Buddha, the four elements are still unconnected with the five objects of sense-perception, in the doctrine of the Epic, however, the connection is already carried through. Form, taste, smell and touch could, without further ado, be ascribed to the four known elements. Form was considered as the quality of fire, taste as the quality of water, smell as the quality of earth and touch as the quality of air. Only the sound created a difficulty, because there was no fifth element which could be its bearer. Relief came from the old idea of world-space (*ākāśa*). Already in the *Upaniṣad*s, *ākāśa* was considered as material; later on, similar to the four elements, a quality was described to it, viz. non-hindrance (*anāvaraṇam*) or allowing space (*avakāśadānam*). It could, therefore, be made, without further problems, the bearer of sound. Thereby it moved in step with the other elements, as is obviously the case in Puṇṇāsa's remarks.[40]

Puṇṇāsa answers his rhetorical question:

> *bhūya-saṃjoge ceyaṇā saṃbhavati, jahā majj'-aṃga-samavāde pheṇa*[41]*-bubuya-sadda-karaṇāṇi; mada-sattī ya ṇa ya majja-vatirittā tab-bhavā, tahā bhūyāṇaṃ visaya-paḍivattī. na vijjae āyā.*
>
> (*Vh.* 202.23–25)

[The answer is:] The consciousness (*ceyaṇā*) arises from the conjunction of the elements, like the production (*karaṇa*) of the sound "budbuda" and froth from the combination of the ingredients of liquor. And [as] the power of intoxication, that is not separate from the liquor, has this [i.e. the liquor] as origin, so is the perception of the objects of sense (*visaya*) regarding the elements. [Therefore], the soul (*āyā*) does not exist.

bhūya-saṃjoge ceyaṇā saṃbhavati: The same is expressed by Haribhadra in his *Ṣaḍdarśanasamuccaya*.[42] According to Jinabhadra Gaṇi,[43] the materialists ascribed to the elements incorporeal units of knowledge. Knowledge becomes manifest, when the material elements have been joined together and transformed into the body. The moment that the elements dissolve (i.e. the body perishes), knowledge becomes again subtle and disappears into the separate elements (cf. Uno 1999: 239 f.).

majjaṃga-samavāde: I read *samavāya* instead of *samavāda* that makes no sense here. Incorrect *-d-* (or *-t-*) instead of *-y-* or dropped consonant is not only common in the *Vasudevahiṇḍī*, as Weber (1883: 235) already noted, referring to the manuscripts of the Jaina canon. As the knowledge becomes manifest through the union of the elements, froth and the sound "budbuda" (or: froth, bubbles and sound, see below) become manifest through the union of the different ingredients of liquor.

pheṇa-bubuya-sadda-karaṇāṇi: *bubuya* should be actually *bubbuya*, Skr. *budbuda*, like in Vasudeva's answer *Vh.* 202.27. It is also possible to understand the compound as "the producing of froth, bubbles and sound" (as Soorideva does in his Hindī-translation), but due to the variant readings "*-pulupulusadda-*" and "*-kulukulusadda-*" (see n. 40) the translation above seemed more plausible.

mada-sattī: The power of intoxication never occurs separately from the liquor, as it is an inherent quality (*guṇa*) of the same (i.e. it has the liquor as origin). Likewise, the perception of the objects (or: the knowledge) is an inherent quality of the (combined) material elements and can never appear separate from them. Haribhadra uses in his *Ṣaḍdarśanasamuccaya* a similar example concerning the relation of the power of intoxication and the ingredients of a spiritous drink to illustrate the dependence of the consciousness on the material elements.[44]

na vijjae āyā: As, according to Puṇṇāsa, the knowledge has its origin in the combination of the material elements, there is no need for (and no proof of) a soul separate from the material world.

Thereupon Vasudeva takes up Puṇṇāsa's arguments:

> *mayā bhaṇio – jaï bhūya-*[45]*saṃjoge ceyaṇā-pasūï*[46] *tti ciṃtesi, na ya vaïritto āya-bhāvo; evaṃ jahā sarīrī āyā majj'-aṃga-saṃjogaṃ maya-vigamaṃ ca jāṇati tahā majjeṇa vi ṇīyaka-guṇo vi ṇāyavvo. jahā majj'-aṃgesu kammii kāle pheṇu-bubbuyâdao vi karaṇā tahā sarīriṇo ceyaṇā. jāva āyā sarīraṃ na pariccayaï tāva viṇṇāṇa-guṇā uvalabbhaṃti. jati bhūya-guṇo hojja to jāva sarīraṃ na vāvajjati tāva vedejja suha-dukkhaṃ.*
>
> (*Vh.* 202.25–29)

> I [Vasudeva] said to him – "If you think, the consciousness (*ceyaṇā*) is produced from the conjunction of the elements, and [therefore] there is no separate existence of the soul (*āyā*) – in this way, like the embodied soul (*āyā*) knows the union with the ingredients of liquor [= intoxication] and the going away of intoxication, thus in spite of the liquor [the soul] should know its innate quality. [You say,] like with the ingredients of liquor after some time froth, bubbles and so on are produced, so is the consciousness (*ceyaṇā*) [produced] for the embodied being. [Furthermore you claim,] as long as the soul (*āyā*) does not abandon the body, so long the qualities of conscious knowledge (*viṇṇāṇa*) are perceived. [But,] if [the consciousness] would be a quality of the elements, then the body would experience happiness and sorrow, as long as he does not disappear [i.e. even the dead body would experience happiness and sorrow, as long as he is not decomposed].

***ṇīyaka-guṇo*:** For *ṇīyaka* read *ṇiyaka* = *nijaka*; *nīyaka* = *nīcaka* "low" makes no sense. Here arises the question, whether *ṇiyaka-guṇa* refers to the innate quality of the soul or to the innate quality of the liquor, i.e. the *mada-sattī*, the power of intoxication (as Soorideva understands it in his Hindī-translation). In my opinion, both options are possible and make, ultimately, the same sense: The soul is always aware of its own innate quality as contrasted with temporary conditions like intoxication.

***jahā majj'-aṃgesu … viṇṇāṇa-guṇā uvalabbhaṃti*:** These two sentences reflect exactly the foresaid opinion of Puṇṇāsa, Vasudeva simply takes up again its opponent's words. Unlike the first sentence of Vasudeva's speach, however, the quotation is here not marked by *tti ciṃtesi* or the like.

***jati*:** Mistake for *jaï* (Skr. *yadi*). As noted above, incorrect *-t-* instead of *-y-* or dropped consonant appears sometimes in the *Vasudevahiṇḍī*.

> *jaïyā iṃdiyāṇi sa-visaya-gāhaṇāṇi*[47] *āyā, to so'-iṃdieṇa uvaütto vattaṃ saddaṃ soūṇa jibbhôṭṭha-tālu-dasaṇa-saṃjogeṇa kaya-payatto ṇa koya paḍivayaṇaṃ dejjā; saddaṃ ca soūṇa cakkhu-visae sadda-vehī na rūve saraṃ ṇivāejja; jamm'-aṃtarâṇubhūte*[48] *ya atthe ṇa koi sumarejjā, sutta-vibuddho*[49] *iva daṃsei, suvvaṃti ya jāi-ssarā.*
>
> (*Vh.* 202.29–203.4)

> Or if the organs of sense (*iṃdiya*) that are grasping [only] their proper object are the soul (*āyā*), then one who is fit with the organ of hearing would hear a sound that has occurred, [but] making an effort with the combination of tongue, lip, palate and teeth could not give an answer; and after hearing a sound, a person who is piercing [an object] by mere sound, could in the sphere of the eye not direct his arrow on forms; and nobody could remember the things that were perceived in former lives, like one awakened from sleep demonstrates by telling memories from [former] births (literally: and memories from [former] births are heard).

***jaïyā*:** Has to be taken as Skr. *yadi vā*.

sadda-vehī: Skr. *śabdavedhin*; the archer locates the target merely by sound, cf. Haribhadra's *Samarāiccakahā*, where King Guṇadhara wanted to show to Queen Jayāvalī his proficiency in hitting an invisible aim by the sound; he shot an arrow by which he killed two crowing birds (who were, by the way, in their former birth his father and his grandmother).[50]

> *jaï ya bhūya-saṃjogo evaṃ sarīra-hetū, na kamma-vasa-vattiṇo attaṇo*[51] *sāmatthaṃ, tato sarisa-vaṇṇa-gaṃdha-rasa-phāsa-saṃṭhāṇāṇi sarīrāṇi hojjā; na kiṇho bhamaro, hario suko, lohio iṃdagovo, citto kavoo, sukkilā balāgā. je ya vigalā jaṃtavo dīsaṃti tesiṃ kayar'-atthaṃ bhūya-guṇaṃ? taṃ mā evaṃ hohi a-sag-gāhī. atthi āyā bhūya-vaïritto, subhâsubhāṇaṃ kammāṇaṃ kārago, vipaccamāṇāṇa ya bhotta tti.*
>
> (*Vh.* 203.4–8)

> And if the conjunction of elements would be thus the cause of the body [and] not the force of the soul (*attaṇo*, gen. sg.), which is acting according to the power of *karman*, then [all] bodies would be similar in colour, smell, taste, touch and shape; the bee would not be black, the parrot green, the cochineal red, the pigeon speckled, the crane white. And what is the cause, regarding the quality of the elements, for those beings, who are manifested as crippled? Therefore, don't be thus one who does not grasp the truth. There exists a soul, distinct from the elements, the producer of good and bad and the enjoyer of ripened *karman*.

vipaccamāṇāṇa: According to Pischel § 370, the gen. plur. of masculine and neuter stems in *-a* ends in all the dialects in *-āṇaṃ*. In Māhārāṣṭrī, Ardhamāgadhī, Jaina Māhārāṣṭrī and Jaina Śaurasenī, however, the denasalized form in *-āṇa* may also occur, in Ardhamāgadhī particularly before enclitics, as it is the case with *vipaccamāṇāṇa*, followed by *ya* (Skr. *ca*).[52]

Contrary to the *Samarāiccakahā*, where the materialist Piṅgakesa is "somehow embarrassed, because he could not reply",[53] or the *Paesikahāṇayaṃ*, where Prince Paesi is converted by the Jain monk Kesi and starts to act according to his new faith, in the *Vasudevahiṇḍī* neither Puṇṇāsa's reaction is reported nor is he mentioned again. He simply vanishes from our narrative. The story continues:

> *tato kei sadde chaṃde aṇṇesu ya kalā-vihāṇesu sikkhiyā pucchaṃti. ahaṃ pi tesiṃ avisaṇṇo āgama-baleṇaṃ paḍivayaṇaṃ demi.*
>
> (*Vh.* 203.9 f.)

> After that others learned in grammar, metrics and other arts asked me questions. I, undaunted, gave them answers by means of the doctrine.

King Abhaggaseṇa is so impressed by the stranger, that he marries even his daughter Paümā (Skr. Padmā) to him. But this is by no means the end of Vasudeva's adventures…

The materialists and their Jain opponents – a comparison

In Jain canonical and narrative literature we can find quite often dialogues between the religious specialists, normally monks or nuns, and Jain laymen or heretics. While the dialogues of Jain layman and renouncer are normally limited to short questions or the request for religious instruction of the former, the conversations of Jain monks with people from other faiths assume the form of (more or less) lively discussions. So it is the case in the *Rāyapaseṇiya* and the *Samarāiccakahā*, where the heretic's thesis or objection and the monk's antithesis or refutation succeed one another. As opposed to this, Vasudeva's controversy with Puṇṇāsa is composed quite crude: Puṇṇāsa presents all he has to say at a single blow, followed by Vasudeva's rejection – two monolithic blocks of arguments instead of a vivid discussion.

Another important difference that sets the *Vasudevahiṇḍī* apart from the *Rāyapaseṇiya* and the *Samarāiccakahā* is that Vasudeva, a nobleman but certainly not a renouncer, takes the place of the religious specialist. This is in the context of the *Vasudevahiṇḍī* not overly surprising, as Vasudeva is depicted as a kind of "allrounder", well versed not only in the 64 arts, but also in Jain doctrine. He represents the ideal Jain layman, who is not only successful in worldly affairs, but also in matters concerning the "other world", as Mahāvīra told king Seṇia[54] (*Vh.* 26.11 f.).

If we look closer at the arguments put forward in the discussions, the *Vasudevahiṇḍī* holds again a special position. The most prominent analogies of the *Rāyapaseṇiya* and the *Samarāiccakahā* are absent in the *Vasudevahiṇḍī*: Both Paesi in the *Rāyapaseṇiya* and Piṅgakesa in the *Samarāiccakahā* argue, if an afterlife would exist, their evil grandfather and their pious grandmother (Piṅgakesa: father) would have returned from their infernal and heavenly abode respectively and issued a warning to them. Furthermore, the rather striking experiments with criminals sentenced to death that Paesi and Piṅgakesa carried out in search of a soul are missing in the *Vasudevahiṇḍī*. There, Puṇṇāsa confines himself to a concise description of the ideology of the materialists: He declares the five material elements to be the source of the body, the sense organs and the consciousness. Therefore, he reasons, a soul independent from the body cannot exist. Only the beginning of Puṇṇāsa's discourse shows parallels to the *Samarāiccakahā*, his closer depiction of the elements' nature and his comparison of the consciousness with the power of intoxication are absent, as are Vasudeva's counter-arguments.

It is quite striking that the passage in the *Vasudevahiṇḍī* shows no affinity at all with the *Rāyapaseṇiya*, that in all probability has been known by the author. The beginning of Piṅgakesa's discourse in the *Samarāiccakahā* might have been influenced by the *Vasudevahiṇḍī*; afterwards, Haribhadra follows quite closely the authoritative canonical text. It is quite typical for the *Vasudevahiṇḍī* to go also in this philosophical passage its own way: Just as it is not the author's intention to create a new version of the *Bṛhatkathā* by borrowing the main plot from this tradition, but to use instead the material from the popular *Bṛhatkathā* as background for religious and instructive stories,[55] the author tries also in this philosophical passage not to draw on tradition, but to create a new story fitting more or less in this context, however clumsy the connection to the main plot may be. It is quite obvious that the main focus of the *Vasudevahiṇḍī* is not on literary innovation, but on the transmission of moral and doctrinal contents.

Notes

1 As already indicated by the title, this chapter follows Willem B. Bollée's book *The Story of Paesi (Paesi-kahāṇayaṃ). Soul and Body in Ancient India*, published in 2002. I owe this and many other books and articles of Prof. Bollée a significant part of my knowledge about Jainism; I can't thank the jubilarian enough for the numerous information, suggestions and advice during the last years. For this reason, I am extremely happy to contribute an article to his felicitation volume.

2 For more concealed messages resulting e.g. from rebirth stories see Esposito (2010b).

3 The means to connect the numerous secondary narratives with the main plot is the embedding of stories within stories including further stories; up to nine different narrative layers sometimes pile up. The strategy of building up successive narrative layers enables the author to insert more examples, more philosophical and didactical material inside one frame story; see, for example, the story of Jina Usabha (Esposito 2014).

4 As already Alsdorf pointed out in his article "The Vasudevahiṇḍi, a Specimen of Archaic Jaina-Māhārāṣṭrī" (1935–37), the language of the *Vasudevahiṇḍī* is an archaic form of Jaina-Māhārāṣṭrī, often very close to Ardhamāgadhī, the language of the Jaina canon. For the characteristics of Ardhamāgadhī, see von Hinüber (2001: 98–100 (§§ 74–78)); for a study of the Prakrit of the *Vasudevahiṇḍī* see Esposito (2012b).

5 The *Vasudevahiṇḍī* is mentioned three times in Jinadāsa's *Āvaśyaka-Cūrṇi* (1st vol. 164.12 and 460.3, 2nd vol. 324.1 [the figures refer to the pages and lines of the printed text], see Balbir 1993: 101), dated sixth-seventh century CE (Balbir 1993: 45). Therefore, it cannot be later than the sixth century (see also Jacobi 1932: vii f.). Alsdorf (1935–37: 320) assigns a much earlier date because of the *Vasudevahiṇḍī*'s archaic Jaina-Māhārāṣṭrī, von Hinüber (2001: 76) assumes a time of origin before CE 450. Later Sanskrit versions of the *Bṛhatkathā* are Buddhasvāmin's *Bṛhatkathāślokasaṃgraha*, the *Kathāsaritsāgara* of Somadeva and the *Bṛhatkathāmañjarī* of Kṣemendra. Furthermore, in the *Peruṅkatai* of Koṅku Vēḷir a Tamil version survived. For an attempt to reconstruct the lost "ur-text" see Nelson (1978).

6 Alsdorf (1938: 345 f.) dates the *Bṛhatkathā* due to literary considerations back to the second or first century BC, the same does Warder (1990: 118 f.) on the basis of historical reasons and reflections concerning the language. If, however, the connection between Guṇāḍhya and the Śātavāhanas should be based on a later legend, as von Hinüber (2001: 111, § 101) supposes, Warder's argumentation loses an important evidence. Winternitz (1966: 347) assigns to Guṇāḍhya a date of the third century CE or earlier, because he must be prior to Bhāsa, who has taken the plot of his dramas *Svapnavāsavadatta* and *Pratijñāyaugandharāyaṇa* from the *Bṛhatkathā*. As neither the attribution of these dramas to Bhāsa nor their date can be considered as reliable (see Esposito 2004: 2–4 and 2010a: 2–13), Winternitz's approach is untenable.

7 The form *āyā* (*ātmā*), attested by Pischel only for Ardhamāgadhī, occurs also in the *Vasudevahiṇḍī* (e.g. 130.16, 202.13, 16, 17, 23, 26, 203.1, 7; 361.13 *ātā*), although *atta* is more common; besides, *attaya* (*ātmaka*, e.g. *Vh*. 141.7) sometimes appears (see Esposito 2012b: 31). As Mette (2010: 233, fn. 65) remarks, older sources use for "soul" often *āyā* instead of *jīva*.

8 Already Weber (1883: 382–384) and Leumann (1883: 2, 1885: 536) had various suggestions concerning the origins viz. the sanskritized forms of "Rāyapaseṇiya/

Rāyapaseṇaïyya" and "Paesi"; for a summary and further suggestions see Bollée (2002: 9 f.) as well as Balcerowicz (2005: 571 f.). For a German translation of the *Rāyapaseṇiya* see Leumann (1885: 503–527), for an English translation with valuable annotations Bollée (2002: 15–221).

9 Bollée (2002: 1) considers the *Rāyapaseṇiya* to be older than CE 350, for it is quoted twice by the *Viyāhapannatti* (dated CE 350–450 by Ohira 1994: 163 f.) and because of the Buddhist canonical parallel. The *Viyāhapannatti*, the fifth Aṅga, quotes twice the *Rāyapaseṇiya*. As Bollée (2002: 1) states, the *Rāyapaseṇiya* has to be older than the *Viyāhapannatti*, the fifth Aṅga.

10 The Sohamma (Skr. Saudharma) is the southern half of the lowest heaven. The eight lowest heavens are called *kappa* (*kalpa*).

11 *Vimāna*s are heavenly palaces that can have the expanse of whole cities. In the middle of each heaven is the round central or Indraka-*vimāna*, round which the remaining *vimāna*s are situated.

12 For Seyaviyā, Skr. Setavyā, see Bollée (2002: 19).

13 *Adhammia* (Skr. *adharmika*), see also Bollée's explanation (2002: 24 f.).

14 Kesi is called a follower of Pāsa, the twenty-third *tīrthaṃkara*. In Bollée's (2002: 273) opinion, Passa/Pāsa is "wrongly sanskritized as Pārśva". He proposes a new etymology and suggests "(U)pāśva(sena)". For a discussion of this suggestion and some futher notes see Balcerowicz (2005: 577–579).

15 Paesi's arguments can be summarized in the following way: If a soul independent from the body existed, his grandparents would have warned him from their infernal or heavenly abode, respectively. Furthermore, in experiments with the bodies of criminals he found no evidence of a soul. And if a soul different from the body existed, all beings should have the same abilities, independent from their age, size etc.

16 One *paliovama* (Skr. *palyopama*) is the time it takes to empty a receptacle of one *yojana* diameter and heigth, that is tightly filled with tiny hair, when every hundred years only one hair is taken out (Kirfel 1920: 339).

17 As an omniscient person, Mahāvīra knows everything about past, present and future events. He is thus not only able to narrate the past, but also to predict the future of the former Paesi.

18 *Samarāiccakahā* 4.13: *tao ahaṃ pi iyāṇiṃ divva-māṇusa-vatthu-gayaṃ dhamma-kahaṃ c' eva kittaïssāmi*. As Jacobi (1926: xviii) states in the introduction of his edition of the *Samarāiccakahā*, almost all *kathā*s by Jain authors may be ranged in this category. Whatever the adventures of the hero or the heroine may be, the end is always their renouncement of the world. Furthermore, the narrative is usually interspersed with a great deal of religious instruction.

19 As Jacobi (1926: xviii) states, the idea of retribution which underlies the main story of the *Samarāicchakahā* and most of the tales inserted in it are also characteristic for a *dharmakathā*. Koch (2009) draws attention to the narration of the former birth of King Śreṇika and his son Kūṇika in Jinadāsa's *Āvaśyakacūrṇī*, that might provide the source for Haribhadra's story of King Guṇasena and Aggisamma. A similar story is recorded in Saṅghadāsa's *Vasudevahiṇḍī* (*Vh.* 368.7–17), in which King Ugrasena and his son Kaṃsa appear to be counterparts of Śreṇika and Kūṇika.

20 Piṅgakesa's arguments show strong parallels to Paesi's: Also he argues, if a soul independent from the body existed, his evil grandfather and his pious father would have warned him from their infernal or heavenly abode, respectively. Furthermore, in experiments with the bodies of criminals he found no evidence of a soul. Additionaly he presents a short summary of the materialists' world view: As the body consists exclusively of the five material elements (and thus produces also the consciousness), there is no soul independent from the body. On the basis of this precept he deconstructs Sihi's motives for renouncing the world. Sihi asks Vijayasiṃha to answer Piṅgakesa's claims, and so the discussion between the materialist and the Jain Ācārya starts.

21 The *Śarīra* is divided into 28 chapters (*lambhas*, "conquests"), that are named after the respective heroine "conquered" and married by Vasudeva. The *lambhas* 19 and 20 and the end of the last *lambha* seem to be lost (see also Jain 1975 and 1977: 18).

22 A *Vidyādhara* is essentially a being that possesses certain magical powers, *vidyās*. Since these powers can be gained or even conferred, it is possible for a human being to become a *Vidyādhara* – as in the case of King Naravāhanadatta, the protagonist of the *Bṛhatkathā*. For a detailed description of *Vidyādharas* in Indian literature see Grafe (2001). Being a *Vidyādhara*, Nīlakaṇṭha masters the art of flying and is thus able to carry Vasudeva off through the air.

23 Nīlakaṇṭha is the cousin of Vasudeva's wife Nīlajasā, to whom she was promissed by her mother even before her birth. Because she as a woman had no right to dispose of her children, Nīlakaṇṭha's claim was denied, see *Vh.* 180.17–181.8.

24 The motif of Vasudeva's abduction by various *Vidyādharas* and his subsequent falling from the sky is quite prevalent in the *Vasudevahiṇḍī*. Vasudeva is always fortunate to fall into a pond (*Vh.* 201.14 f., 309.6, 358.27), into a river (*Vh.* 217.28 f., 229.18, 352.26 f.), on a heap of straw (*Vh.* 247.11), on a vine (*Vh.* 359.8) or even into a dry well filled with straw (*Vh.* 125.29; for the affinity of this passage with the story of Tṛta in the *Nārāyaṇīya* in the *Mahābhārata* see Oberlies 1997: 113–115).

25 Skr. Abhagnasena or Abhāgyasena? Hemacandra's *Triṣaṣṭiśalākāpuruṣacarita* has Bhāgyasena.

26 In *Vh.* 201.17 the kind of weapons the princes are practising with are not specified (*āuha-paricaya*, Skr. *āyudha°*), but in the following Vasudeva is showing his skills in archery.

27 The mention of archery just before a philosophical discussion about the *ātman* is quite meaningful. In her translation of *Vh.* 15.7–14 ("Das Wirken der Sinne und des Gemüts"), Mette (2010: 308) refers with regard to the (unidentified) quotation " 'ins Ziel treffen die Pfeile', heißt es" ("to the target the arrows strike, it is said", *lakkhe sarā ṇivayaṃti tti*, *Vh.* 15.13) to *Muṇḍakopaniṣad* 2.2.3–4, which addresses the Brahmanical ascetic searching for enlightenment. Here the syllable Ōṃ is identified with the bow, the arrow with the *ātman* and the *brahman* with the target. Unfailingly the ascetic should try to hit the target to become, like the arrow, one with it (*praṇavo dhanuḥ, śaro hy ātmā, brahma tadlakṣyam ucyate. apramattena veddhavyaṃ, śaravat tanmayo bhavet*) (Mette 2010: 308, fn. 183).

28 In his "autobiography" Vasudeva relates that he was taken to a teacher to learn the arts when he was eight years old. He was able to satisfy his teacher due to his "distinguished intelligence and understanding" (*visiṭṭha-mehā-mati-guṇeṇa*, *Vh.* 118.25).

29 In order to gain Somasirī, the daughter of Devadeva, the head man of the village Girikūḍa, Vasudeva decided on learning both the Aryan and the non-Aryan Veda; for the difference between the two kinds of Vedas and their origin see *Vh.* 183.1–193.20. In the following interrogation (*Vh.* 194.9–19) Vasudeva's answers indicate that the Vedas studied by him have a thoroughly Jain content.

30 In a discussion with an ascetic near the city Kañcaṇapura about the relationship between *prakṛti* and *puruṣa* (*Vh.* 360.20–361.21).

31 °*kkhaṃse* Mss. lī 3 (= Mss. lī, ya and ḍe, see *Prāstāvikaṃ nivedanam* of the *Vasudevahiṇḍī*, ed. Caturvijaya Muni and Puṇyavijaya Muni). Probably *lakkhaṃ* (acc. of the aim of *lakkha*, Skr. *lakṣa*) *se* (gen. sg. m. of pronoun *sa-*), "turning its mind towards the target".

32 Lit.: the thing to be done that was desired by the heart.

33 °*ṇaṃ saṃbaṃdhissaraṇe raṇe ya pamāṇaṃ ti āyā* all Mss. except Ms. śāṃ. *saṃbaṃdhissaraṇe* is written instead of *saṃdhāṇe nissaraṇe ya* (and *āyā* is repeated after the quotation). *saṃbaṃdhissa* as gen. sg. of *saṃbaṃdhi* (Skr. *sambandhin*, 'related, connected by marriage, a relative) makes no sense here, nor the doubling of *raṇe*. Probably a writing mistake.

34 *iti pañca-prakāra-pratyakṣa-dṛṣṭam eva vastu-tattvaṃ pramāṇa-padavīm avagāhate, śeṣa-pramāṇānām anubhavâbhāvād eva nirastatvād gagana-kusumavat* (210.27 f.): "Thus, only things which can be known by these five kinds of perception would be things really established by *pramāṇa*. The other *pramāṇa*-s, there being no evidence for their existence, are to be rejected like flowers blooming in the sky" (Transl. Chattopadhyaya 1990: 259).

35 °*ṇi kajje*° all Mss. except Ms. śāṃ. As *tesu tesu* is missing, the translation would run "The combined elements are employed in things", which does not really make sense.

36 °*sahiyā*° all Mss. except Ms. śāṃ. *sahiyāṇi* (Skr. *sahita*, joined, united, connected) instead of *saṇṇiyāṇi* (Skr. *saṃjñita*, called, named, termed) makes no sense here.

37 *uṇhā* all Mss. except Ms. śāṃ. *uṇhā* (Skr. *uṣṇa*) has, like *umhā* (Skr. *ūṣman*), the meaning "heat", but *uṇha* is neuter and can't possibly take the ending -*ā* as nom. sg.

38 *rasaṃ saṃvedayati* Ms. lī 3 (= Mss. lī, ya and ḍe). Same meaning, lectio facilior.

39 *kiṃ ca pṛthvī jalaṃ tejo vāyur bhūta-catuṣṭayam* (Haribhadra, *Ṣaḍdarśanasamuccaya* 83a + b); *nanu cārvākamate pṛthivī-ap-tejo-vāyurūpāṇi catvāry eva tattvāni* (Prabhācandra, *Nyāyakumudacandra* 341.17). Space (*ākāśa*) was, according to Prabhācandra, not accepted as element, for its existence could not be established by perception: *na khalu pratyakṣam ākāśādisadbhāve pravarttate tasya rūpādau tadvati cārthe pravṛttipratīteḥ, na ca ākāśādau etat saṃbhavati arūpidravyatayāsyābhyupagamāt* (341.22–24). Prabhācandra, the author of the *Nyāyakumudacandra* and the *Prameyakamalamārtaṇḍa*, a commentary on Māṇikyanandin's *Parīkṣāmukhasūtra*, is in all probability not identical with the same Prabhācandra who was a pupil of Akalaṅka. According to the epilogue (*praśasti*) of the second work, this work was written in Dhārā in the reign of King Bhoja (CE 1019–1060), cf. Winternitz (1933: 582). Haribhadra, a pupil of Jinabhadra (or Jinabhaṭa) and Jinadatta, lived presumably in the eighth century CE, cf. Winternitz (1933: 479).

40 Guṇaratna (fifteenth century CE) mentions in his commentary *Tarkarahasyadīpikā* (introduction to Haribhadra's *Ṣaḍdarśanasamuccaya* 80), that some sections of the *Cārvākās*, considering *ākāśa* as the fifth element, declare that the world consists of five elements: *kecit tu cārvākaikadeśīyā ākāśaṃ pañcamaṃ bhūtam abhimanyamānāḥ pañca-bhūtâtmakaṃ jagad iti nigadanti* (450.12–451.1).

41 Only attested by Mss. lī 3 (= Mss. lī, ya and ḍe). °*ṇapulupulusadda*° Mss. ka 3 (= Mss. ka, mo and saṃ), Mss. go 3 (= Mss. go, vā and khaṃ), Ms. u and Ms. me. "the sound 'pulupulu' and froth". °*ṇakulukulusadda*° Ms. śāṃ. "the sound 'kulukulu' and froth".

42 *kiṃ ca pṛthvī jalaṃ tejo vāyur bhūta-catuṣṭayam| caitanya-bhūmir eteṣāṃ* (83a–c); *eteṣāṃ* refers according to Maṇibhadra's commentary *Laghuvṛtti* (fourteenth century CE) to the *Cārvākas*. Instead of *caitanya-bhūmir eteṣāṃ* Guṇaratna has in his commentary *Tarkarahasyadīpikā* the reading *ādhāro bhūmir eteṣāṃ*, "earth is the substratum of all these [i.e. the four elements mentioned in 83a + b]", which sounds less convincing.

43 Jinabhadra Gaṇi (sixth century) discusses in the *Gaṇadharavāda*, one of the sections of the *Viśeṣāvaśyakabhāṣya*, a materialistic view, based on a Upaniṣadic passage (*Bṛhadāraṇyakopaniṣad* 2.4.12). For further details see Uno (1999: 238).

44 *pṛthvyâdi-bhūta-saṃhatyāṃ tathā dehâdi-sambhavaḥ| mada-śaktiḥ surâṅgebhyo yadvat tadvat sthitâtmatā* (Haribhadra's *Ṣaḍdarṣanasamuccaya* 84 with commentary of Maṇibhadra; the edition with Guṇaratna's commentary has slightly different readings).

45 *bhūisaṃ*° Mss. ka 3 (= Mss. ka, mo and saṃ), go 3 (= Mss. go, vā and khaṃ), lī 3 (= Mss. lī, ya and ḍe). *bhūi* (Skr. *bhūti*, "existence, being; power, wealth") makes no sense. Besides, Vasudeva is quoting Puṇṇāsa, who used *bhūya* in his foregoing speach.

46 °*sūya tti* Ms. śāṃ. Probably *pasūyā* (Skr. *prasūtā*, corresponding to *ceyaṇā*; final long

vowel followed by an enclitic is shortened, see Pischel § 92). The meaning of the sentence does not chance.

47 °*ṇi ṇe ṇa ā*° all Mss. except Ms. śāṃ. Probably *ṇeṇa* instr. sg. neut. from stem *ena-* (Pischel § 431), "thus, thereby, in this way".

48 °*bhūe ṇa atthe* all Mss. except Ms. śāṃ. *ṇa* instead of *ya* makes no sense, probably a writing mistake.

49 °*budhā iva dīsaṃti, suvvaṃti* Ms. śāṃ. Pl. instead of sg. and passive instead of parasm. of the causative: "like people awakened from sleep would prove". In this case the following *suvvaṃti ya jāi-ssarā* could be also translated as "and they who remember their former births are heard".

50 *gahiyam aṇeṇa pāsattham dhaṇu-varaṃ, sandhio tīriyāsaro, 'devi peccha me sadda-vehittaṇaṃ' ti bhaṇiūṇa mukko, tao ṇeṇa vāvāiyāiṃ amhe, Samarāiccakahā* 267.12–14. Also in Hemacandra's *Triṣaṣṭiśalākāpuruṣacaritra* this practice is mentioned in a vivid scene: Prince Aparājita, one of the former births of *Tīrthaṅkara* Ariṣṭanemi, hears a woman's cry in the night, and, "thinking 'a woman is crying' the hero (i.e. Aparājita), an ocean of compassion, followed the sound like an arrow that strikes merely from sound" (transl. Johnson 1962: 21), *kāpy eṣā roditi strīti niścitya sa kṛpānidhiḥ| anuśabdaṃ yayau vīraḥ śabdāpātīva sāyakaḥ||* (VIII.295).

51 *attiṇo* Ms. śāṃ. Probably writing mistake because of foregoing °*vattiṇo*.

52 As already mentioned above (n. 3), the language of the *Vasudevahiṇḍī* is often very close to Ardhamāgadhī.

53 *uttara-ppayāṇâbhāveṇa viliyam iva Piṅgakesaṃ, Samarāiccakahā* 175.1.

54 Seṇia is identical with King Bimbisāra of Buddhist sources, his son Koṇia (also Kūṇia) with Ajātasattu.

55 For the relationship of the main plot and the secondary stories in the *Vasudevahiṇḍī* see Esposito (2012a).

Bibliography

Alsdorf, Ludwig. "The Vasudevahiṇḍi, a Specimen of Archaic Jaina-Māhārāṣṭrī." *BSOAS* 8 (1935–37) 319–333 [= *Kleine Schriften* 56–70].

Alsdorf, Ludwig. "Eine neue Version der verlorenen Bṛhatkathā des Guṇāḍhya." *Atti del XIX Congresso Internationale degli Orientalisti, Roma* (1938) 344–349 [= *Kleine Schriften* 101–106].

Alsdorf, Ludwig. *Kleine Schriften.* Ed. Albrecht Wezler. Wiesbaden: Franz Steiner Verlag (Glasenapp-Stiftung 10), 1974.

Balbir, Nalini. *Āvaśyaka-Studien. Introduction générale et Traductions.* Stuttgart: Franz Steiner Verlag, 1993 (Alt- und Neu-Indische Studien 45.1).

Balcerowicz, Piotr. "Monks, Monarchs, and Materialists." *Journal of Indian Philosophy* 33 (2005) 571–582 [Review Article of Bollée 2002].

Bollée, Willem B. *The Story of Paesi (Paesi-kahāṇayaṃ). Soul and Body in Ancient India. A Dialogue on Materialism. Text, Translation, Notes and Glossary.* Wiesbaden: Harrassowitz, 2002 (Beiträge zur Kenntnis südasiatischer Sprachen und Literaturen 8) [Reprint Mumbai: Hindi Granth Karyalay, 2005].

Chattopadhyaya, Debiprasad (ed.). *Cārvāka/Lokāyata. An Anthology of Source Materials and Some Recent Studies.* Ed. Debiprasad Chattopadhyaya, in collaboration with Mrinal Kanti Gangopadhyaya. New Delhi: Indian Council of Philosophical Research, 1990.

Esposito, Anna Aurelia. *Cārudatta. Ein indisches Schauspiel. Kritische Edition und Übersetzung mit einer Studie des Prakrits der 'Trivandrum-Dramen'.* Wiesbaden: Harrassowitz, 2004 (Drama und Theater in Südasien 4).

Esposito, Anna Aurelia. *Dūtavākya. Die Worte des Boten. Ein Einakter aus den 'Trivandrum-Dramen'. Kritische Edition mit Anmerkungen und kommentierter Übersetzung*. Wiesbaden: Harrassowitz, 2010a (Drama und Theater in Südasien 10).

Esposito, Anna Aurelia. "Who Was Who? Eine komplexe Wiedergeburtsgeschichte aus der *Vasudevahiṇḍī* des Saṅghadāsa." *From Turfan to Ajanta. Festschrift for Dieter Schlingloff on the Occasion of his Eightieth Birthday*. Ed. Eli Franko & Monika Zin, 315–328. Lumbini: Lumbini International Research Institute, 2010b.

Esposito, Anna Aurelia. "How to Combine the *Bṛhatkathā* with Jain World History – Reflections on Saṅghadāsa's *Vasudevahiṇḍī*." *Jaina Studies. Proceedings of the DOT 2010 Panel in Marburg, Germany*. Ed. Jayandra Soni, 201–212. New Delhi: Aditya Prakashan, 2012a.

Esposito, Anna Aurelia. "The Prakrit of the *Vasudevahiṇḍī* – an Addendum to Pischel's *Grammar*." *Zeitschrift für Indologie und Südasienstudien* 28 (2011 [2012]), 29–50, 2012b.

Frauwallner, Erich. *History of Indian Philosophy. Transl. from Original German into English by V. M. Bedekar. Vol. 2: The Nature-philosophical Schools and the Vaiśeṣika System. The System of the Jaina. The Materialism*. Delhi: Motilal Banarsidass, 1973 [Original: *Geschichte der indischen Philosophie*. Salzburg: Otto Müller Verlag, 1956].

Grafe, Jörg. *Vidyādharas. Früheste Zeit bis zur Kaschmirischen Bṛhatkathā*. Frankfurt a. M.: Peter Lang, 2001 (Europäische Hochschulschriften, Reihe XXVII, 82).

Haribhadra, *Ṣaḍdarśanasamuccaya*. In: Jaina, Mahendrakumāra (ed.). *Śrīharibhadrasūri viracita Ṣaḍdarśanasamuccaya. Śrīguṇaratnasūrikṛta Tarkarahasyadīpikā, Somatilakasūrikṛta Laghuvṛtti tathā ajñātakartṛka avacūrṇi sahita*. Nayī Dillī: Bhāratīya Jñānapīṭha Prakāśana, 1989 (Jñānapīṭha Mūrtidevī Granthamālā, Saṃskṛta Granthāṃka 36).

Haribhadra, *Ṣaḍdarśanasamuccaya*. In: Śarmā, Śrīnivāsa (ed.). *Paramārhaddharibhadra sūripraṇītaḥ Ṣaḍdarśanasamuccayaḥ Maṇibhadrasūrikṛta'Laghuvṛtti'saṃvalitaḥ, 'Sudhā'saṃskṛtavyākhyāsahita, 'Bhāṣā-prakāśa'hindīvyākhayā samalaṅkṛtaś ca. Vyākhyākāraḥ Ācārya Rudraprakāśa Darś-anakeśarī*. Vārāṇasī: Kṛṣṇadāsa Akādamī, 2002 (Kṛṣṇadāsa Saṃskṛta Sīrīja 175).

Haribhadra, *Samarāiccakahā*. In: Jacobi, Hermann (ed.). *Samarāicca Kahā. A Jaina Prākṛta Work. Volume I: Text and Introduction*. Calcutta: Asiatic Society of Bengal, 1926 (Bibliotheca Indica 169).

Hemacandra, *Siddhahemacandram*. In: Pischel, Richard (ed.). *Hemacandra's Grammatik der Prākritsprachen (Siddhahemacandram Adhyāya VIII). Mit kritischen und erläuternden Anmerkungen. I. Theil: Text und Wortverzeichniss. II. Theil: Übersetzung und Erläuterungen*. Halle: Verlag der Buchhandlung des Waisenhauses, 1877, 1990.

Hemacandra, *Triṣaṣṭiśalākāpuruṣacaritra*. In: Śrīramaṇīkavijayajī Gaṇi; Vijayaśīlacandrasūri (eds.). *Kalikālasarvajña Śrīhema-candrācāryaviracitaṃ Triṣaṣṭiś alākāpuruṣacaritamahākāvyam. Vol. 4: Aṣṭama-navamaparvaṇī*. Amadāvāda: Kalikālasarvajña Śrīhemacandrācārya Navama Janmaśatābdī Smṛti Śikṣaṇa Saṃskāranidhi, 2006.

Hinüber, Oskar von. *Das Ältere Mittelindisch im Überblick*. 2., erweiterte Auflage. Wien: Verlag der österreichischen Akademie der Wissenschaften, [1986]2001 (Österreichische Akademie der Wissenschaften, Philosophisch-Historische Klasse, Sitzungsberichte 467. Veröffentlichungen der Kommission für Sprachen und Kulturen Südasiens 20).

Jacobi, Hermann [Georg] (ed.). *Sthavīrāvalicarita or Pariśiṣṭaparvan, Being an Appendix of the Triṣaṣṭi-Śalākāpuruṣacarita*. Calcutta: Asiatic Society of Bengal, 1891 (Bibliotheca Indica 96).

Jain, Jagdish Chandra. "The Missing Lambhas in the Vasudevahiṇḍi and the Story of Pabhāvatī." *Indo-Iranian Journal* 17 (1975) 41–46.
Jain, Jagdish Chandra. *The Vasudevahiṇḍi. An Authentic Jain Version of the Bṛhatkathā. With Selected Translations Compared to the Bṛhatkathāślokasaṅgraha, Kathāsaritsāgara, Bṛhatkathāmañjarī and Some Important Jaina Works, Including the Unpublished Majjhimakhaṇḍa and with Extensive Notes, Introduction and Appendices.* Ahmedabad: L. D. Institute of Indology, 1977 (L. D. Series 59).
Jinadāsa, *Āvaśyakacūrṇī.* In: *Śrīmadgaṇadharagautamasvāmisaṃdṛbdhaṃ Śrutakevaliśrīmadbhadrabāhu-svāmi-sūtritaniryukticūrṇiyutaṃ Śrīmajjinadāsagaṇima hattarakṛtayā sūtracūrṇyā sametaṃ Śrīmadāvaśyakasūtram.* 2 vols. Ratalāma: Śrī Ṛṣabhadevajī Keśarīmalajī Paḍhā Jukāma, 1928–29.
Johnson, Helen. *Triṣaṣṭiśalākāpuruṣacaritra or the Lives of Sixty-three Illustrious Persons by Ācārya Śrī Hemacandra. Translated into English by Helen M. Johnson.* Vol. V. Baroda: Oriental Institute, 1962 (Gaekwad's Oriental Series 139).
Kirfel, Willibald. *Die Kosmographie der Inder. Nach den Quellen dargestellt.* Bonn, Leipzig: Kurt Schroeder, 1920 [Reprint Hildesheim: Georg Olms Verlag, 1990].
Koch, Rolf Heinrich. "On the Interrelation of Certain Prakrit Sources." *Indologica Taurinensia* 35 (2009) 275–286.
Leumann, Ernst. *Das Aupapātika Sūtra, erstes Upāṅga der Jaina. I. Theil: Einleitung, Text und Glossar.* Leipzig: Deutsche Morgenländische Gesellschaft, 1883 (Abhandlungen für die Kunde des Morgenlandes VIII.2) [Reprint Nendeln, Liechtenstein: Kraus Reprint Ltd, 1966].
Leumann, Ernst. "Beziehungen der Jaina-Literatur zu anderen Literaturkreisen Indiens." In: *Actes du VIe congrès international des Orientalistes* III.2 (1885) 469–564 [= *Kleine Schriften* 29–124].
Leumann, Ernst. *Kleine Schriften.* Ed. Nalini Balbir. Stuttgart: Franz Steiner Verlag, 1998 (Glasenapp-Stiftung 37).
Mette, Adelheid. *Die Erlösungslehre der Jaina. Legenden, Parabeln, Erzählungen. Aus dem Sanskrit und Prakrit übersetzt und herausgegeben.* Berlin: Verlag der Weltreligionen, 2010.
Nelson, Donald Allan. "Bṛhatkathā Studies: The Problem of an Ur-text." *Journal of Asian Studies* 37, 4 (1978) 663–676.
Oberlies, Thomas. "Die Textgeschichte der Śvetadvīpa-Episode des Nārāyaṇīya (MBh. 12,321–326)." *Nārāyaṇīya-Studien.* Ed. Peter Schreiner, 75–118. Wiesbaden: Harrassowitz, 1997 (Purana research publications Tübingen 6).
Ohira, Suzuko. *A Study of the Bhagavatī Sūtra. A Chronological Analysis.* Ahmedabad: Prakrit Text Society, 1995 (Prakrit Text Series 28).
Paesikahāṇayaṃ. See Bollée 2002.
Pischel, Richard. *Grammatik der Prakrit-Sprachen.* Hildesheim: Georg Olms Verlag, [1900] 1973.
Saṅghadāsa, *Vasudevahiṇḍī.* In: Caturvijaya Muni; Puṇyavijaya Muni (eds.). *Pūjyaśrīsaṅghadāsagaṇivācakavinirmitā Vasudevahiṇḍī.* Gandhinagar: Gujarat Sahitya Akadami, [1930–31] 1989.
Tucci, Giuseppe. "A Sketch of Indian Materialism." *Proceedings of the Indian Philosophical Congress* 1 (1925) 34–44 [Reprint in: *Cārvāka/Lokāyata. An Anthology of Source Materials and Some Recent Studies.* Ed. Debiprasad Chattopadhyaya & Mrinal Kanti Gangopadhyaya, 384–393. New Delhi: Indian Council of Philosophical Research, 1990].
Uno, Tomoyuki. "A Debate between Materialists and Jainas on the Interpretation of *Bṛhadāraṇyakopaniṣad* 2.4.12." *Approaches to Jaina Studies.* Ed. Narendra K. Wagle

& Olle Qvarnström, 238–249. Toronto: Univ. of Toronto, Centre for South Asian Studies, 1999.

Warder, A[nthony] K[ennedy]. *Indian Kāvya Literature. Vol. II: The Origins and Formation of Classical Kāvya*. Delhi: Motilal Banarsidass, [1974]1990.

Weber, Friedrich Albrecht. "Über die heiligen Schriften der Jaina (Teil 1)." *Indische Studien* 16 (1883) 211–479 [Reprint Hildesheim: Georg Olms Verlag, 1973].

Weber, Friedrich Albrecht. "Über die heiligen Schriften der Jaina (Teil 2)." *Indische Studien* 17 (1885) 1–90 [Reprint Hildesheim: Georg Olms Verlag, 1973].

Winternitz, Moriz. *A History of Indian Literature. Vol. II: Buddhist Literature and Jaina Literature*. Calcutta: University of Calcutta, 1933.

Winternitz, Moriz. *A History of Indian Literature. Vol. III: Part 1: Classical Sanskrit Literature. Part 2: Scientific Literature*. Delhi: Motilal Banarsidass, 1966.

11 Do attempts to formalize the *Syād-vāda* make sense?

Piotr Balcerowicz

Ontology and epistemology of the *Syād-vāda*

A contribution of Jainism to Indian philosophy which seems most stimulating, inspiring, debated and controversial, one which provoked most opposition from other systems of India is beyond doubt the doctrine of multiplexity of reality (*anekānta-vāda*). Indisputably it is also the most interesting Jaina contribution to Indian philosophy. The doctrine involved both a very particular realist ontology as well as a corresponding epistemology that was structured in such a way as to most aptly handle certain ontological presuppositions.

The Jaina ontology entailed by the doctrine of multiplexity of reality (*anekānta-vāda*) viewed the world structure as consisting of four interrelated aspects: substance (*dravya*), quality (*guṇa*), mode (*paryāya*) and ineffable, transient occurrence (*vivarta, vartanā*), often overlooked in both Jaina expositions of the theory and in analyses carried out by modern researchers. However, the point to emphasize was that things, especially when conceived as substances, were believed to preserve their identity and in this aspect they were immutable and permanent; at the same time, however, when conceived as modes, they appeared to change and transform continuously. This seemed to have led to contradictions in ontology. Besides, in order to explain the process of change, Jaina ontology also distinguished three modes of existence, that actually coexisted: origination (*utpāda, udaya*), continued existence (*sthiti, dhrauvya*) and cessation, or disintegration (*bhaṅga, vyaya, apavarga*) and sometimes the fourth one is added, i.e. ineffable transient occurrences (*vartanâ, vivarta*). These four closely corresponded to the Buddhist Sarvâstivāda's and Abhidharma's four (or three) conditioned factors, known as "markers" (*saṃskṛta-lakṣaṇa*) – origination (*utpāda*), continuity (*sthiti*), deterioration (*jarā, vyaya*) and extinction (*bhaṅga, nirodha*) – or second-order elementary constituents of reality (*dharma*) that were believed to attach themselves to every other first-order elementary constituent of reality "marked" (*lakṣya*) by them and thereby determined in its momentary existence (*kṣaṇika*).

The emphasis (which gradually became more pronounced after the second/third centuries CE) of Jaina ontology on both permanence and imperishability of substances, worked out against the Buddhist theories of momentariness (*kṣaṇika-vāda*) and insubstantiality (*nairātmya, niḥsvabhāvatā*), as well as constant mutability and change of substances in form and occurrence, developed in contrast to the theory of the immutable substance of the Vaiśeṣika, seemed to lead to a contradiction: how to reconcile the idea of a permanent substance with its incessant mutability? Both the dual nature of things and a solution of the paradox was expressed by Umāsvāmin (c. 350–400) in the *Tattvârtha-sūtra*:[1]

> [29] The existent is furnished with origination, annihilation and permanence. [30] It is indestructible in its essentiality, i.e. permanent. [31] [The existent is both], because [it is] established as having emphasized [property] and not-emphasized [property].[2]

It seems that this juxtaposition of two seemingly incompatible natures of the real were the starting point for the doctrine of multiplexity of reality (*anekānta-vāda*).

The complexity of the nature of everything that exists was further emphasized by the fact that the existent was thought, under the influence of the Vaiśeṣika, to be qualified by the universality, or universal character (*sāmānya*), and particularity, or particular character (*viśeṣa*). The idea is expressed as early as by Siddhasena Divākara in the *Saṃmati-tarka-prakaraṇa*.[3]

The dual nature of the existent is reflected in the language, which is expressed by Samantabhadra in the *Yukty-anuśāsana*:

> Manifold particulars are grounded in universality. Word [by its nature] is furnished with an access into (*sc.* pertains to) the particular. Another [variety of word (speech element)] leads to (*sc.* conveys) a particular, that is of the universal nature, because [such a word] functions with regard to intermediate particulars.[4]

It is also found in the *Āpta-mīmāṃsā*:

> The manifest thing neither originates nor disintegrates as something that has universal character, because of its continuity. It does disintegrate and originate because it is particular. These two [universal and particular character occur] jointly in one [thing]. The existent consists in origination and [continued existence as well as disintegration].[5]

The idea was also repeatedly mentioned by Akalaṅka (eighth century), for instance in the *Laghīyas-traya*:

> The defining feature of time and other [categories], which should be reflected upon, has been examined elsewhere in its entirety [with the conclusion that] this [defining feature] is grounded in an object that consists in substance, modes, the universal character and the particular character.[6]

The conviction that world substances, and their qualities, modes and transient occurrences cannot even be conceived to exist entirely independently, as if separated from other elements and that they all simultaneously originate, are endowed with continued existence and disintegrate in every moment again and again, while at the same time preserve their integrity and self-identity, led further to a belief that the world is a complex network within which all the existents are related with all the remaining ones and that their essential character and nature is not only determined by what is in things themselves but also by all the relations in which they enter vis-à-vis all other existents.

These ontological concepts, as usually is the case (e.g. two cognitive criteria (*pramāṇa*) to cognize two aspects of the world (*sva-lakṣaṇa* and *sāmānya-lakṣaṇa* in Dignāga's system), necessitated a particular epistemology to most efficiently and competently handle accepted ontological constitution of the world.

Originally, ontological or metaphysical considerations eventually led to exuberant development of corresponding epistemology, which ultimately involved what came to be known as the theory of multiplexity of reality (*anekānta-vāda*), that comprised three analytical methods: the method (historically the oldest) of the four standpoints (*nikṣepa-vāda, nyāsa-vāda*), the (usually) sevenfold method of conditionally valid predications, known as the doctrine of viewpoints (*naya-vāda*),[7] and the method of the seven-fold modal description (*sapta-bhaṅgī, syād-vāda*).

A clear reflection of the awareness that the Jaina theory serves to handle a very particular ontology, based on the idea of coexistence of seemingly incompatible features in one and the same locus, can be found in the *Nyāya-viniścaya* on a few occasions:

> They have correctly explained that the defining feature of perception is lucid percipience of definite contents consisting in an object which is both substance and modes as well as is of universal character and of particular character;[8]

and

> The seven-fold modal description operates by way of affirmation and negation [expressed with the functor] "in a certain sense" in keeping with the complex structure (lit. divisions) consisting in substance and modes as well as in the universal character and the particular character.[9]

Since the term "*bhaṅga*" ("angle"), or figure, may denote either an "expressed option" or a "sentence" (*vākya*),[10] esp. an attributive or qualitative one, that predicates a certain attribute or its absence to an object, and this understanding applies both to *naya-vāda* and *syād-vāda*, and since both the theories coincided as regards the number of their elements, these two came to be called *naya-sapta-bhaṅgī* ("seven-fold description through viewpoints") and *pramāṇa-sapta-bhaṅgī* ("seven-fold description through cognitive criteria"), respectively, in the mediaeval period. Further, since – in opposition to both *naya-vāda* and *syād-vāda* which were considered true and reliable – one could also distinguish a third analytical description of the world, a flawed one called "erroneous viewpoint" (*durnaya*) or "erroneous presentation" (*durnīti*),[11] a third *sapta-bhaṅgī* method was invented called *durnīti°/durnaya-sapta-bhaṅgī* ("seven-fold description through erroneous viewpoints").[12] It didactically and rhetorically served to demonstrate how it is possible that other philosophical and religious systems can err, what analytical methods they unknowingly apply so that they achieve wrong results, and what doctrinal errors they commit.

The present chapter will deal only with one component of the doctrine of multiplexity of reality (*anekānta-vāda*), i.e. with the method of the seven-fold modal description (*sapta-bhaṅgī, syād-vāda*).

Its most important component, most hotly criticized by other schools of thought, were the conjunctions of three basic figures (*bhaṅga*), or ways of analysing an object within a consistent conceptual framework, usually – at an earlier stage – expressed *roughly* as follows:

(1) *syād asti* ("*x* is, in a certain sense, *P*"),
(2) *syān nâsti* ("*x* is, in a certain sense, not-*P*"),
(3 or 4) *syād avaktavyam* ("*x* is, in a certain sense, inexpressible").

The remaining four figures were, as it is widely known, permutations of the three basic ones.

In the first part, the chapter asks the question whether attempts, and they are quite numerous, to formalize *syād-vāda* really make sense, or if they were to make any sense what requirements they would have to fulfil in the first place in order to approach any degree of being an accurate (and correct from formal logical point of view) description of what the Jainas attempted to say through their theory. By implication, the chapter will show what approaches to the formalization issue are flawed at the very outset. In the second part, the chapter presents an attempt to formalize the *syād-vāda* which, in my opinion, fulfils the formal requirements or an accurate representation of the doctrine.

Formalization attempts and requirements of the *Syād-vāda*

Generally speaking, I would distinguish two kinds of modern approach to the method of the seven-fold modal description (*syād-vāda*): constructivist method (interpretation) and reductionist method (interpretation), decisively most of the modern interpretations belong to the former category.

What is called the "constructivist method" is such a strategy of examination that, while trying to meaningfully analyse the theory, makes use of modern tools of logic and epistemology which were not explicitly known in ancient or mediaeval India, although one can see no objection to their application and one thinks their use helps one illuminate the issue by "dismembering" its muddled structure or by disambiguating expressions which seem to us either indeterminate, obscure or equivocal precisely because no such disambiguation tools were available at that time. It is the lack of original clarity or ambiguity on part of ancient or mediaeval Jaina thinkers that supposedly calls for the application of modern logical terms and apparatus to clearly see logical relations and logical structures that lie behind the *syād-vāda* theory. The outcome of this approach is generally richer in logical terms, philosophical concepts and theoretical apparatus than what seemed to be the original concepts expressed by Indian thinkers centuries ago. As a matter of fact, this methodological approach dominates in research and many have felt inspired by the apparent ambiguity of the *syād-vāda*, viewing it as an expression of current fashions and tendencies in Western philosophy and logic. Since the relativity seemingly embedded in the theory easily yields to various interpretations and trends in vogue as well as to various levels of individual understanding and formal (often inadequate) schooling and appears to be applicable to various fields of human activity, ranging from formal logic, philosophy of language, logical pragmatics to theories of conflict solution, intercultural relations, multiculturalism, ethics and tolerance, a plenitude of papers and articles of various quality have been produced by serious scholars, perhaps less serious amateurs and inspired Jaina lay persons. Even stimulating and philosophically valuable works are far too many to be listed here; I have to confine myself just to mentioning a handful of selected papers written in the last quarter of a century or so: Barlingay (1965), Mukerji (1977), Matilal (1981), Bharucha and Kamat (1984), Matilal (1985: 301–319),[13] Pandey (1984), Matilal (1991), to some extent (as regards the interpretation of *syāt* ... *eva*) Cort (2000), Gokhale (2000), Jain (2000), Kothari (2000), Kulkarni (2000), Uno (2000), Ganeri (2001: 137–144), Ganeri (2002), Priest (2008), Schang (2008a: 78–80; 2008b; 2010). Especially Ganeri's presentation, lucid in its form, is a serious attempt to offer a truly consistent logical model of the *syād-vāda*, an attempt in which the author hopes to take into account most ramifications of the Jaina system. Heretofore researchers had largely been satisfied with offering a more or less plausible exposition for the first three or four figures of the doctrine, without exploring the implications of their models for the fifth, sixth and seventh compounded propositions. Had they done it, they would have immediately discovered inconsistencies in *their own* proposals, which were subsequently projected onto the original Jaina model. Not only expositions of Bharucha and Kamat's and Matilal's interpretations, mentioned by Ganeri (2002), suffered from this flaw, but a range of other attempts, such as that of Mukerji (1977), or quite recent ones of Kothari (2000), Uno (2000) and Gokhale (2000), the latter being perhaps most faithful of them.

What is perhaps a little surprising, most of the above-mentioned authors hardly acknowledge what has been said on the *syād-vāda* prior to *their* times and they expound their interpretation of the *syād-vāda* without entering into discussion of earlier interpretations. A good exemplification of this approach is that almost none of eleven authors of a monograph on *anekānta* edited by J. Nagin Shah (2000) ever refers to his predecessors or argues in favour of his own interpretation as better representing the *syād-vāda* than any other.

To recapitulate, the constructivist method explores what respective authors believe are hidden, unexpressed logical structures and logical and philosophical implications of the *syād-vāda*, such as multiple values or paraconsistency of the *syād-vāda*. A real danger of this approach is that it may read modern concepts into an ancient theory, albeit the theory allowed no room for them.

What I call the "reductionist method" is an approach that tries to do without modern tools as much as possible by not postulating more than ancient or mediaeval authors express themselves explicitly. There are very few who have followed this track and one could call them more traditionally oriented, just to mention a few names: Nahar and Ghosh (1917: 103–135, and thereafter), Bharadwaja (1984), Padmarajiah (1986: 333–378), to some extent (as regards the interpretation of the seven *bhaṅgas*) V.M. Kulkarni (2000) and Atsushi Uno (2000). The involvement of modern tools of logic basically is reduced merely to a limited set of symbols which do not involve more than the texts say themselves explicitly. The reason for that is often what the authors, e.g. Nahar and Ghosh (1917: 110), feel is "inadequacy of Formal Logic" to handle the complexities of the *syād-vāda* and the intricate and highly complex structure of the world as well as the conviction, expressed for instance by Nahar and Ghosh (1917: 115), that "*Saptabhangi* supersedes formal logic as the latter is inadequate to explain unity in difference". Another possible reason may also be inadequate knowledge of modern logic and its tools on the part of some scholars romancing with the *syād-vāda*. The outcome of such an approach should, in principle, not entail more than ancient or mediaeval thought contained and expressly reflected upon. The result may not be as stimulating as that of the former method, and indeed very few authors refrain from venturing an exciting "constructivist" journey into the realms of modern logic. No wonder, this methodological approach may thus seem a bit disappointing to a philosophically oriented mind.

Let us have a closer look at the approach adopted by some of the representatives of what I call the constructivist method. Due to lack of space I cannot discuss every single interpretation, and I will restrict myself to singling out some most conspicuous points of a selected few.

Mukerji (1977: 230–233) directly establishes a link between "Syādvāda and modern many-valued logic", frames the seven figures (*bhaṅga*) and assigns (almost) each of them as separate truth value ranging from 1/6 up to 6/6, or 1, in a six-valued probability logic, "rather like the throw of six-faced dice in games of chance", as follows:

a	a_1	A	1/6
	a_2	~(~A)	1/6
b	(= 2a)	A • ~(~A)	2/6 or 1/3
c		~[A ⊙ ~(~A)]	3/6 or 1/2
d	d_1 (= c • a)	A • ~[A ⊙ ~(~A)]	4/6 or 2/3
	d_2	~(~A) • ~[A ⊙ ~(~A)]	4/6 or 2/3
e	(= c + b)	A • ~(~A) • ~[A ⊙ ~(~A)]	5/6
f	(= 2c)	A ⊙ ~(~A)	6/6 or 1

The symbols ⊙ and • stand for "*sahārpaṇa*" and "*kramārpaṇa*" respectively, which R.N. Mukerji (1977: 227) explains as follows: "in words the partially grasped aspects are stated serially (*kramārpaṇa*), and cannot be stated together in their integral unity (*sahārpaṇa*)", whatever that "integrity" could mean and irrespective of how "the games of chance" and dice could relate to chances of hitting truth by expressing a particular statement out of seven options, or figures (*bhaṅga*). R.N. Mukerji makes use of two separate conjunction symbols ⊙ and • in order to combine sentences based on one predicate (either asserted or negated). What is problematic with this representation, as we shall see later, is among other things the fact that what is denied in negative sentences of the *syād-vāda* is never one and the same predicate, but always a different predicate than the one which has been previously asserted, viz. it is never the case that A and ~A,[14] but always the case that A and ~B.

Bimal Krishna Matilal (1981: 54–56;[15] 1991: 12–16) follows suit, with some modifications though. He specifically distinguishes "three primary and non-compound predicates, positive, negative and the neutral (+, –, 0)", and represents how "a simple mathematical computation will generate only seven varieties, if we use these three units in three ways, one at a time, two at a time and three at a time". In addition he introduces "three predication-units … represented by *x*, *y*, and *z*" as follows:

x,	y,	z,	xy,	yz,	zx,	xyz
+,	–,	0,	±,	-0,	+0,	±0 ‘

What is completely misleading and wrong in his presentation of 1981 is that he takes the three symbols +, –, 0 to stand for "three primary and non-compound predicates", and treats them as three separate basic truth value symbols! This mistake is somehow corrected in his exposition of 1991, when he speaks of "the three basic evaluative predicates (truth-values?)" (Matilal 1991: 13), although he simultaneously speaks of "a separate and non-composite value called '*avaktavya*' ('inexpressible'), side by side with 'true' and 'false'". He further replaces R.N. Mukerji's two separate conjunction symbols ⊙ and • that combine sentences based on one predicate (asserted or negated) with three separate sentential symbols, and not really predicate symbols, "*x*, *y*, and *z*" (despite the fact that he ambiguously calls them "predicate-units") that stand for three different options/figures (*bhaṅga*): *syād asti*, *syān nâsti* and *syād avaktavyam*. Although to use three separate symbolic expressions (+, –, 0) for three different basic options (*asti*, *nâsti*, *avaktavyam*) is a welcome move, at the same time it – as much as we use three sentential symbols instead of three predicate symbols – actually conceals or evades the real problem which the *syād-vāda* posits, which basically is a case of a predicate calculus, namely how to assert and deny a property of a thing at the same time and not to bypass the law of non-contradiction.

This lack of clarity as regard the treatment of what really the symbols +, –, 0 and ± represent ("truth values", also referred to as "evaluative predicates" or "predication-units" whatever the latter two could really mean) and how they then differ from symbols *x*, *y* and *z*, if both are series of predicates, what Bimal

Krishna Matilal (1981) does not do, and what Mukerji (1977) does, is to explain how the three primary truth values add up from the lowest truth value up to truth value 1 (Mukerji: 6/6). What is certain, he does use the symbols +, – and 0 in order to demonstrate "combinability of values" (Matilal 1991: 13), which clearly goes in the direction of many-valued logic. Further, while referring to non-bivalence logic and paraconsistent logic that applies to the *syād-vāda* (p. 14 f.), he is aware (p. 15) that what the Jainas developed was not a typical system of "multiple-valued logics or the para-consistent logics". He also claims that "the Jainas, in fact, set the limit to our usual understanding of the law of non-contradiction" (p. 15). This claim is, as we shall see, based on a wrong reading and analysis of sources.

In fact, both R.N. Mukerji and Matilal find their predecessor in Barlingay (1965: 6, 65), who takes the *syād-vāda* as a case of modal logic apparently with three values, with *syāt* being expressive of "perhaps", "possibly" or "probably". Especially recent decades abound in interpretations that cast the *syād-vāda* in the mould of many-valued logic, albeit with various modifications that try to explain how different truth values are applicable and in what sense. For instance, Pradeep P. Gokhale (1991: 83–84) takes *syāt* as an existential qualifier qualifying possible viewpoints. To him, "'*syāt*' … does not appear as an antecedent of a conditional but it looks more like an existential quantifier of the following sort: There is a standpoint such that…, There is a way in which…, There is a respect in which…" In his interpretation a sentence, say, *syāt jīvaḥ nityaḥ*, "would rather mean: (a) There is a standpoint such 'that Self is permanent' is the case", or in more general terms: "(b) There exist some x such that x makes p true", i.e.: "(c) (∃x) (xTp)".

Not everyone would agree that the *syād-vāda* represents a six-valued logic, as R.N. Mukerji (1977) claims, or is a case of a three-valued logic, as the interpretations Matilal (1981), (1991) and Barlingay (1965) contend. Some scholars, e.g. Bharucha and Kamat (1984), Ganeri (2002) and Fabien Schang, speak in favour of a seven-valued logic, each of them for different reasons though. Ganeri (2002: 274, 276) speaks of Jaina seven-valued logic **J7**, with three primitive values, t, f and u, and explains that

> The Jainas have a seven-valued logic because, if we allow for the existence of non-optimal standpoints, standpoints which are just neutral with respect to some propositions, then, for each proposition, *p* say, the total discourse has exactly seven possible states.
>
> (p. 274)

Ganeri's (2002) model finds its continuation in a recent interpretation by Schang (2008b), who constructs a $\mathbf{J}_7$ model, trying to compromise two interpretations, Ganeri's (2002) and Matilal's (1991), which assume that *avaktavya*, i.e. "'non-assertability' refers to incompleteness (*à la Ganeri*) or inconsistency (*à la Matilal*)," and "both result in a unique quasi-truthfunctional logic with either many-valued or classical, two-valued entailment relations". Ultimately, Schang develops "a syncretist approach of Jaina logic … constructed in order to do justice to both interpretations of non-assertability; the subsequent many-valued logic is a 24–1 = 15-valued logic that is shown to be reducible to Priest's paraconsistent logic **P3**".

Further, many scholars maintain that the *syād-vāda* violates the law of non-contradiction. An example is Sangam Lal Pandey (1984: 163), who is of the opinion that "…only that logic is indicated by *syādvāda* which challenges the law of contradiction and gives some truth value to contradictory statements". According to Pandey, the *syād-vāda* represents many-valued logic, or three-valued logic resembling that of Łukasiewicz, to be exact. Also Ganeri (2002: 273 f.) is of the opinion that the Jainas reject the law of non-contradiction in the sense that although they are committed to "(a) the thesis that '¬ (p & ¬p)' is a theorem in the system", they "reject (b) the thesis that it is not the case that both 'p' and '¬p' are theorems".

Others, e.g. Bharucha and Kamat (1984), argue to the contrary, viz. that the *syād-vāda* does challenge the law of non-contradiction, albeit it is a case of paraconsistent logic. Further contemporary models that are applied to the *syād-vāda* are those of modal logic (e.g. Barlingay 1965 and Ganeri 2002), of probability logic (R.N. Mukerji 1977) or modal logic that is not truth-functional (Ganeri 2002: 274–278).

The problem with all the above instances of the constructivist approach is that, in order to make an appearance to faithfully and consistently represent the *syād-vāda*, they presuppose far more theoretical logical tools than ever existed in India.

Formalized interpretations that see a breach of bivalence assume that ancient or mediaeval Jainas for all practical purposes developed a notion of logic that does not respect the law of contradiction, and that when the Jaina speak that the *syād-vāda* relies on "notions of affirmation and negation applied to numerically one real thing in all cases without any contradiction"[16] they mean something completely different than what they expressly state.

And what the Jainas communicate on various occasions is a rather straightforward expression of their conviction that their theory involves no logical contradiction (*avirodhena*), no conflict with empirical observation and no inconsistency with their system of beliefs (*pratyakṣâdi-bādhā-parihāreṇa*):[17]

> What is called the seven-fold modal description is an arrangement of statements that are expressed in seven forms, which is marked with the term "in a certain sense", which considers numerically one real thing, such as the living element (soul) etc., by way of affirmation and negation, either taken separately or compounded, in accordance with queries whose contents are properties such "existence" (sc. "*x* being P") etc. taken one by one, while avoiding contravention with perception and other [cognitive criteria] without any contradiction.[18]

Interpretations which want to see a case of many-valued logic in the *syād-vāda* overlook that there was neither a term nor concept for additional truth values other than "true" and "false". The proponents of this approach also overlook the most important fact that the crucial expression *avaktavya*, which to them seems to provide a justification for their many-valued logical theories, is not about four[19] out of seven propositions of the *syād-vāda* but is about the object, or rather about its properties that are predicated of.

An approach to see probability logic in the *syād-vāda* relies on the assumption that the Jainas had a *logical* notion of probability, a notion which is a relatively recent concept and it is rather problematic whether ancient Indians had it or whether it could be formulated in terminology and the conceptual framework of ancient Indian philosophers.

A close reading of the paraconsistent interpretations will reveal a lot of logical apparatus that is a modern invention, and it is not possible to have paraconsistent logic without having a clear notion of certain basic conceptual components of it. Most importantly, we should in the first place distinguish actual cases of reasoning or statements that at least seem to be inconsistent (as is the case with the *syād-vāda*), although the authors are either not aware of such inconsistencies or do not consciously make any formal attempt to explain away these inconsistencies from the cases when authors consciously express something which they know is inconsistent under classical or common-sensical interpretation but they make a conscious attempt to reformulate basic logical relations and they expressly state new logical rules. The latter attempt is not really observed in the case of the *syād-vāda* on the part of ancient and mediaeval Jaina philosophers. As we know paraconsistent logic was developed mostly in order to bypass the logical principle that anything follows from contradictory premises, and it entails a number or explicitly accepted semantics and redefinition of traditional terms as well as introduces new logical rules. Again, we do not see anything in the history of the *syād-vāda* that would match this kind of development. In order to ascribe paraconsistency to the *syād-vāda* as a logical theory we would have to first demonstrate that its creators had, for instance, a clear notion of a principle of non-adjunction or an idea of a non-truth-functional logic (as Ganeri argues in favour of the *syād-vāda* as an example of both). But do we really see that Jaina thinkers accepted that in a discourse various participants formulate their own beliefs in a consistent way, albeit these may not be consistent with those propounded by others, and the sum of these beliefs makes a paraconsistent system, and, in addition, have a clear idea of the principle of non-adjunction? I seriously doubt it.

Similarly, any attempt to present an axiomatization of the Jaina system, e.g. those proposed by Ganeri (2002: 278 f.) or by Schang (2008b) as ingenuine as they may be, presupposes that the Jainas had a clear concept of "axiom" and "derivation of theorems", and that they consciously applied it to the *syād-vāda*. However, I find no evidence for that. That is why such attempts will fail to accurately reflect the real structure of the *syād-vāda*, albeit they may be interesting pieces of modern logical exercise inspired by the *syad-vāda*.

To clarify my objections to the constructivist approach, let me avail myself of the following analogy (although analogies are never a logically sound argument but can serve as a useful didactic device). Would it make sense to interpret Anaximenes' idea of τό πνεῦμα ("the breath [of life]", cf. *prāṇa*), identified with ἡψυχή ("soul"),[20] as an indication of ontological dualism of mind and matter which he accepted? After all Anaximenes does speak of various forms of existence, including what we would call "matter" as a result of condensation (DK 13A5). However, we know that a prerequisite of such a dualism is the acceptance of the idea of intelligibility, or a similar one, as a criterion that distinguishes the mind from insentient matter, something that originates first with Plato's *Phaedo*, and the idea of intelligibility does not play any role in Anaximenes' understanding of ἡψυχή. To project later concepts on Anaximenes' theory would be methodologically as mistaken as reading modern logical concepts into the ancient *syād-vāda*, because theoretical requirements that would make constructivist interpretations meaningful were still absent at the time when Jaina thinkers developed their ideas. The indispensability of the theoretical apparatus of modern logic lies in its making a reflection on certain logical concepts at all possible: without this apparatus any formulation of logical ideas formulated in terms of, say, paraconsistent logic or many-valued logic is simply not possible. If one claims that, say, the Jainas do not understand bivalence in a classical way, one should first produce a piece of textual evidence attesting to the fact that indeed there was at least one Jaina philosopher who expressly stated that contradiction (*virodha*) should be reinterpreted or understood a little different than we usually do. If we wish to maintain that there are other truth values at work in the *syād-vāda*, we are expected to pinpoint at least one passage which explicitly argues in favour of the stance that there are other notions apart from truth (*satya*) and falsehood (*asatya*), which are as real as these two. If we merely rely on how *we* understand the *syād-vāda* theory, we merely project our modern concepts. That is why I have serious reservations as regards this method and its results as a genuine description of the *syād-vāda*. Their usefulness may lie only in approximation or metaphor (*upacāra*), the usefulness of which is rather limited in extra-poetical context.

Furthermore, one can see that as a matter of fact some scholars, e.g. Ganeri (2002), to some extent, and Fabien Schang *en masse*, no longer offer a genuine interpretation of the *syād-vāda* but use some ideas of the theory in order to develop independent systems of many-valued logic which may be of considerable interest in their own right but of little interest as formalization attempts of the *syād-vāda*. Many interpretations either neglect original textual sources and rely on a very superfluous popular understanding of the *syād-vāda*, or they misconstrue the sources.

A good example is Ganeri (2002), with all respect to his ingenuity, whose attitude to Sanskrit sources is quite liberal in the sense that he reads ideas and notions into textual layers that are simply not there, and mistranslates crucial terms, for instance in a passage of PKM 6.74, p. 683.7 ff.:

OPPONENT: Just as the values "true" and "false", taken successively, form a new truth-value "true-false", so do the values "true" and "true-false". Therefore, the claim that there are seven truth-values is wrong.

REPLY: No: the successive combination of "true" and "true-false" does not form a new truth-value, because it is impossible to have "true" twice. … In the same way, the successive combination of "false" and "true-false" does not form a new truth-value.

OPPONENT: How then does the combination of the first and the fourth, or the second and the fourth, or the third and the fourth, form a new value?

REPLY: It is because, in the fourth value "non-assertible", there is no grasp of truth or falsity. In fact, the word "non-assertible" does not denote the simultaneous combination of truth and falsity. What then? What is meant by the truth-value "non-assertible" is that it is impossible to say which of "true" and "false" it is.

(Ganeri 2002: 273)

A number of philological misinterpretations in Ganeri's rendering of this brief passage seem to me quite considerable: his "values" are merely properties (*dharma*) predicated of a real thing (*vastu*) being examined through the *syād-vāda*, his "true" and "false" are the existence (*sattva*) and non-existence (*asattva*) of particular properties in the real thing; "the claim that there are seven truth-values" is in fact "the limitation to properties of seven kinds" (*sapta-vidha-dharma-niyamaḥ*), viz. a conviction that there cannot be more than seven properties; instead of his "combination of" truth values we have properties that either coexist or not (*sahita*); "the successive combination of 'true' and 'true-false'" as truth values is simply "[two properties] emphasized consecutively" (*kramārpitayoḥ*); "it is impossible to have 'true' twice" is in fact "it is not possible to have existence twice" (*sattva-dvayasyāsambhavād*), viz. when we express existence of a property twice, it does not add up to "two existences".

The methodological flaw here lies also in the following fact: Ganeri ascribes what he takes to be truth values, but what is called in Sanskrit texts "properties" (*dharma*), to sentences, and rightly so in the sense that truth and falsehood can indeed be properties of propositions *only*. However, what Prabhācandra speaks of are *properties* of a real thing (*vastu-viṣaya*), i.e. he – as *all* Jaina authors known to me – speaks of "*syāt* sentences" as predicating of particular properties of an object under examination. But doing so, Ganeri is in good company: most interpreters commit the same mistake. The properties (*dharma*) are, therefore, not of propositions (and only in such a case there might be some justification to interpret them as truth values) but of objectively existing things that are being talked about.

The most serious problem with Ganeri's interpretation is that he uses the passage as an attestation to an explicit reference to many-valued logic. However, in the *real* text there is no mention of logical truth values at all! We have here a case of pouring new theory into old "theoryskins". Interesting and highly appealing as it really is, his project of **J7** (Jaina seven truth values) remains his **J7** (Ganeri's seven values); it is not, in my opinion, a rendering of a theory that was developed centuries ago in India and should not be treated as such. Here is exactly the same passage translated anew, without, I hope, projecting any external ideas onto the original text (the braces {} mark a portion omitted by Ganeri):

OBJECTION: Just as it is the case with the property [predicated of in] the first and second [figures], it is established (sc. clear) that the properties [predicated of in] the first and third etc. [figures] when emphasised either consecutively or reversely (i.e. simultaneously) become still another property, therefore the limitation to properties of seven kinds will not be established (sc. there will be more properties than seven).

REPLY: This is not proper, because one never cognises two [predicated properties] which are emphasised consecutively as still another (sc. third) property, because it is not possible to have existence twice, {and because the existence [of a property in an object] is one with its intrinsic nature etc. which one intends to express.[21]} . . .

OBJECTION: How would it then be possible that the first and the fourth, or the second and the fourth, or the third and the fourth combined are still another [property]?

REPLY: Because in the fourth [statement], in which the [expressed] property is "inexpressibility", there is no comprehension of existence and non-existence. As one should realise, it is not the case that one can express these two [existence and non-existence], when emphasised simultaneously, with a word "inexpressible". Rather, because it is completely impossible to express these two when emphasised in such a way (sc. simultaneously), one wants to demonstrate with this [fourth sentence] still another property "inexpressibility".[22]

The background for Prabhācandra's above discussion and the passage misunderstood by Ganeri is the question which Prabhācandra asks in the *Prameya-kamala-mārtaṇḍa*:

> So why either in the verbal method of viewpoints or in the verbal method of cognitive criteria (i.e. *syād-vāda*) there are exactly seven options? Because only as many (sc. seven only) questions on the part of the debater are possible. For such a limitation to seven options [only] is [the case] precisely because of [the number of possible] queries. Why can the query be only sevenfold? Because inquisitiveness [in this case] can only be sevenfold. How come it is sevenfold? Because the doubt arises in seven ways. Why is then doubt sevenfold? Because a property of a real thing that becomes an object of doubt can be sevenfold. For it is as follows: the existence [of the thing as P], to begin with, is a property of a real thing, because if one does not accept this [existence of the thing as P], it is not consistent to assume that the real thing is a real thing, like a horn of a donkey. Similarly, non-existence [of the thing as Q] is somehow a property of the very same [real thing]; [otherwise] there would be a contradiction as regards the exact determination of the real thing, because the own form (sc. intrinsic nature) [of a real thing] cannot be determined if its non-existence [as Q] is not taken into account on the basis of a different form [belonging to other things] too, like [*mutatis mutandis* its existence as P is determined] on the basis of [the real thing's] own form

> (sc. intrinsic nature). Through such [a method], one can demonstrate the fact, which has [just now] been demonstrated, that both properties (sc. existence as P and non-existence as Q) etc. when emphasised consecutively[23] are properties of the real thing, because if it were not the case, it would contradict the everyday practice based on words [that] consecutively [express] notions of existence or non-existence [as P or Q], and because there would be an undesired consequence that there could be no everyday practice based on words [expressive] of the notion of the additional three properties distinguished with [the term] "simultaneous inexpressibility". And those types of everyday practice [based on the additional three properties or inexpressibility] are certainly not without their objects, because [they do lead to] certainty [derived] from the actual cognition of the real thing and from successful execution of activity [aimed at the real thing],[24] just as everyday practice [based on the real thing's] form of such a kind (i.e. the object's existence [as P]) etc.[25]

As we can see, Prabhācandra sets off with the idea of doubt (*saṃśaya*), well known from its classical exposition in the *Nyāya-bhāṣya*:

> First one sees a property common to a pillar and a person a [particular] height or a [particular] circumference [which could be a feature of both], and becomes curious as regards that particular characteristic [which can be applicable] to both [a pillar and a person] which he has seen before. Then he cannot determine any of the two [possibilities and decide] what it is. Doubt is such a cognition that fails to determine what it is. "I apprehend a property which is common to both [but] I do not apprehend a particular characteristic which belongs only to one of these two" – such a reflection is the basis [of doubt]. This [reflection] emerges as [a cause] that prompts doubt. Such an inquisitive reflection that depends on [this] particular characteristic [which one needs to determine what object one actually sees] is doubt.[26]

The nature of doubt, both as it is described by Vātsyāyana Pakṣilasvāmin and by Prabhācandra, is a particular property one is in search of in order to distinguish one thing from another, similar one. Since one may entertain a range of doubts, one can also ask questions (*praśna*) to clear the doubt.[27] One can, as Prabhācandra maintains, approach one and the same thing (*vastu*) in order to determine its particular character (*sva-rūpa*) and distinguish it from other things (*para-rūpa*) by examining all possible figures, which are said to be not more and not less than seven. But there can be no doubt that the properties are of the real thing (*vastu*) and not of the sentences that predicate a property of a thing. Therefore, the properties in question cannot be truth values.

In contradistinction to the constructivist method, the reductionist approach, as we have seen above, simply restates, in modern languages, which are natural languages, what was said centuries ago in Sanskrit or Prakrits, in many cases hardly adding anything that would enrich our understanding of the structure of the *syād-vāda* and its implications. In addition, the use of natural languages may conceal hidden implications, inconsistencies and structures or may expose apparent inconsistencies, paradoxes and contradictions which perhaps are not there.

Attempts to formalize the *syād-vāda*, which promise to reveal the structure of the *syād-vāda* and to deconstruct apparent contradictions, generally presuppose concepts that were originally, historically not there and therefore present a theory called "*syād-vāda*" that has never existed in such a form. Do such attempts make sense at all? Are we justified in any way in our endeavours to formalize it? I think we are under a condition that we do not presuppose more that existed already in India in ancient times. And this approach entails a close philological reading of the sources.

We should certainly not attempt to formalize the *syād-vāda* as it existed in a way that hopefully yields a logically sound system of logic, which can preferably even be axiomatized, but rather to use formalization, if we at all think we should, only in order to *reproduce* the real structure of the *syād-vāda*, even if it ultimately turns out to be incoherent! Nonetheless, the researcher's task should here be restricted merely to a possibly faithful representation through which one may, perhaps, easier discover its logical flaws or appreciate its logical rigidity, whatever the case may be. Otherwise we shall be devising our own system of logic that is a distant echo of the historically attested *syād-vāda*.

The relevance of the foregoing remarks is not restricted to the treatment of the *syād-vāda*, but it concerns the methodological approach of modern scholars, especially philosophers, who try to make sense of ancient theories by applying modern tools. Such an approach is not entirely innocuous and one should always proceed with utmost care not to impose modern conceptual frameworks onto old theories and derive from them implications which are not necessarily entailed by them, but it is their combination with modern tools that yields such implications. One should always ask what questions were at all possible given a particular conceptual framework and presuppositions in a particular historical context, and what questions result from the theories and their underlying presuppositions that were current in ancient times only.

To mitigate the apparent impression that all the above is criticism directed against the constructivist approach, I should add that there is undeniable value in this approach's opening new possibilities of expressing ingenious intuitions ancient Indian philosophers had by applying modern tools. But as researchers and philosophers we should always, at each stage of our investigation, remind ourselves that modern tools can make such intuitions more transparent and visible, but at the same time they create new intuitions, which would otherwise not have been possible. And we should not confuse these two kinds of intuitions.

Description of the *Syād-vāda*

Perhaps the most conspicuous feature of the *syād-vāda* figures is that they *all are true*, and it is not possible to formulate a range of truth values either as **J3**,

J6 or **J7**. All constructivist interpretations in terms of many-valued logic seem to tacitly assume that at least some *bhaṅga*s can be hierarchically ordered with respect to their truth value, ranging from false and indeterminate to true. The matter of fact is, however, that all seven statements are true:

	bhaṅga	**truth value**
1	*syād asti*	1
2	*syān nâsti*	1
3	*syād avaktavyam*	1
4	*syād asti nâsti*	1
5	*syād asty avaktavyam*	1
6	*syān nâsty avaktavyam*	1
7	*syād asti nâsty avaktavyam*	1

It is not the case that each member of this septuplet has a different truth value; what each of these figures actually expresses is a different property! No text ever says that, as for instance Mukerji (1977) proposes, that the *syāt* sentences can be ordered according to their truth values from the least true to the most true as follows: 1/6, 1/6, 1/3, 1/2, 2/3, 5/6 and 1.

There is no single author, to my knowledge, who would claim, as Mukerji (1977: 227) does (*vide supra*, p. 6), that the *syād-vāda* is "a game of chance" and the sentences *syād asti, syān nâsti*, etc. hit the truth with different probabilities, therefore we can speak of different "grades of truth". No Jaina text ever says that at least one of the seven *syāt* sentences is false or is not really true, or it is not possible to say that a sentence is neither true nor false, i.e. the sentence cannot be assigned any truth value. All the Jaina sources are quite unequivocal that *all* these statements are true.

Suppose, however, as basically most interpreters do, that the figures have different truth values. What would it mean then, as e.g. Matilal (1981: 54–56; 1991: 12–16) wants, and in the same spirit Ganeri (2002) as well as most other scholars, that (1) the truth value of "*syād astī*" is true, (2) the truth value of "*syān nâstī*" is false, whereas (3) the truth value of "*syād avaktavyam*" is "neutral"? What it would yield is the following:

1 If "*syād astī*" is true, then it is the case that *syād asti*.
2 If "*syān nâstī*" is false than it is not the case that *syān nâsti*, hence *syād asti*!
3 If "*syād avaktavyam*" is "neutral", or neither true nor false, or true-false (depending on interpretation), than it is not really the case that *syād avaktavyam*, although we are unable to say what the case is!

This is certainly not what the *syād-vāda* entails.

As has been noticed before, the term *syāt* is a sentential functor which means "somehow", "in a certain sense", a particle "expressive of multiplexity of reality".[28] The seven sentences, as all textual sources show, are in fact incomplete sentences for which we search for a meaningful context, but they all concern one and the same object (*ekatra vastuni, eka-vastu, ekatra jīvâdau vastuni*)[29]:

> Difference and identity, which are the domain of cognitive criteria, are not empirical deceptions. For you, [Jina,] these two [coexist] without contradiction in one and the same [thing] consistent with the secondary or primary expressive intent [respectively].[30]

These seven sentences predicate a particular property (*dharma*) of the object in logically possible ways.

The meaning of "existence" in the Syād-vāda

Although it seems rather obvious, the three primary terms used in the *syād-vāda*, i.e. (1) *asti* ("*x* is") and *astitva/sattva* ("existence of *x*"), (2) *nâsti* ("*x* is not") and *nāstitva/asattva* ("non-existence of *x*") and (3) *avaktavya/avācya* ("*x* is inexpressible") and *avaktavyatva/avācyatā* ("inexpressibility of *x*") do not represent any truth values, as suggested e.g. by Matilal (*vide supra*, p. 6) and Ganeri (*vide supra*, p. 10). These are clearly used in a copulative meaning of "is", viz. (1) "x is P", (2) "x is $\neg Q$", and (3) "x is inexpressible as being P and $\neg Q$ at the same time". In this sense, all the *syāt* sentences are incomplete sentences in which predicates should be supplied. All the examples supplied by Jaina authors unanimously point in the same direction. Samantabhadra in the *Āpta-mīmāṃsā* (*vide infra*, p. 16) and Malliṣeṇa in the *Syād-vāda-mañjarī*,[31] give some examples.

Contradiction in the Syād-vāda

Any model genuinely faithful to original intentions of the Jainas should take into account their insistence on the lack of contradiction in any of the seven propositions, which has been explicitly articulated on numerous occasions, e.g. by Hemacandra-sūri in the *Anya-yoga-vyavaccheda-dvātriṃśikā*:

> Non-existence, existence and inexpressibility with regard to things are not contradictory [when taken as] conditioned by differentiation through conditioning factors. Only when they do not realise the above, idiots who fear contradiction, who are led to destruction by their simplistic interpretation (absolutism) of these [three], stumble.[32]

It is reiterated by Malliṣeṇa (c. 1229) in the *Syād-vāda-mañjarī*:

> Existence [combined] with non-existence does not present any contradiction. Neither does inexpressibility, composed of assertion and denial, present any internal contradiction, nor does inexpressibility combined with expressibility yield any contradiction. And that is why the whole theory of the seven-fold modal description, which is based on the three figures whose defining features are non-existence, existence and inexpressibility, respects non-contradictoriness.[33]

Accordingly, the Jainas, it seems, consistently defined contradiction as based on negation in its classical sense, viz.

x, y are contradictory iff $x = \neg y$.

Such understanding transpires from various passages, e.g. from Hemacandra's *Pramāṇa-mīmāṃsā*:

> If, in the presence of x, y is not comprehended, x stands in contradiction to y.[34]

Malliṣeṇa repeats the same idea:

> If x and y appear by way of their mutual exclusion, this is contradiction, defined as mutual non-occurrence, just like cold and heat. But here [with the *syād-vāda*] it is not the case, because existence and non-existence occur as being non-reciprocal with respect to each other.[35]

Much earlier the impossibility of co-occurrence of two contradictory properties in the same substratum was expressed by Samantabhadra in the *Āpta-mīmāṃsā* nine (!) times, which highlights Jaina emphasis on non-contradictoriness of their theory:

> Because of the contradiction, there cannot be selfsameness of nature of both [phenomena that are opposed in nature, which is incriminated] by the enemies of the method of the seven-fold modal description. Also when [a charge is expressly formulated by the opponents] that if [a thing is] indescribable[36] it [must be indescribable] in the absolute sense, then [such a charge] is not logically tenable because, [that being the case, the charge itself] is [seen to be] expressible.[37]

Each of the instances of the above verse are meant to illustrate the impossibility of a conjunction of a set of contradictory properties: presence and absence (13: *abhāva–bhāva*), universality and particularity (32: *sāmānya–viśeṣa*), permancence and impermanence (55: *nitya–anitya*), being an effect and being a cause (70: *kārya–kāraṇa*), dependent and independent (74: *apekṣika–anapekṣika*), perception and tradition (77: *pratyakṣa–āgama*), mental congoscible thing and objective congoscible thing (82: *antar-jñeya–bahir-jñeya*), fate and opposite of fate (90: *daiva–adaiva*), merit and demerit (94: *puṇya–pāpa*), nescience and cognition (97: *ajñāna–jñāna*). These are just examples of properties (*dharma*) that might appear to stand in contradiction.

In the same spirit, the question how the notions of universality and particularity (*sāmānya–viśeṣa*) are possible with respect to one and the same real thing (*vastu*) is discussed by Malliṣeṇa[38] as a case of *seeming* contradiction. On another occasion, he maintains:

> For, just as there is [seven-fold modal description] of the existence and non-existence, similarly there is also the seven-fold modal description, and only seven (*eva*), of [the thing's] universal character and particular character. For it is as follows: in a certain sense, *x* is universal; in a certain sense, *x* is particular; in a certain sense, *x* is both; in a certain sense, *x* is inexpressible; in a certain sense, *x* is universal and inexpressible; in a certain sense, *x* is particular and inexpressible; in a certain sense, *x* is universal, particular and inexpressible. And one should not claim that in these [statements], there is no form of affirmation and negation, because the universal character has the form of affirmation, whereas the particular character consists in negation as having the form of exclusion.[39]

Such a clearly defined idea of non-contradiction is especially important in propositions (3) "inexpressible" or (4) "both existence and non-existence", and all their derivative propositions (5)–(7). This certainly leaves no room for a non-classical or paraconsistent interpretation of contradiction.[40]

Accordingly, the Jainas' understanding does not appear to be very much different from the classical definition of contradiction formulated by Aristotle:

> It is impossible that the same thing at the same time both belongs and does not belong to the same object and in the same respect (and all other conditions which one can specify, let them be specified, so that dialectal objections be met).[41]

Disambiguation of incomplete sentences

An important question is what the semantic background of the *syād-vāda* actually is? In general, textual sources are quite unanimous that the idea behind "doctrine of the seven-fold modal description" (*sapta-bhaṅgī*) is to disambiguate statements, which after a closer inspection are a sort of shorthand for more complex assertions, e.g. "in a certain sense, it (some object) indeed exists" is a truncated statement, which should be read as "in a certain sense, it (some object) indeed exists ***as …*** (something)", or "in a certain sense, some object *x* indeed has a property P". In a natural language, all statements stand in need of additional analysis which has to take into account the context. The idea that every sentence is incomplete and its intent should be delimited by or derived from a particular context to which it applies is occasionally expressed by the Jainas with a maxim (*nyāya*): "Every sentence functions with a restriction."[42] This is, perhaps, the most crucial aspect when it comes to the proper understanding of the *syād-vāda*.

The mechanism how statements expressed in natural languages, by nature ambiguous, could be converted into propositions whose meaning is unequivocal as well as the practical need for such a mechanism is well exemplified in what Malliṣeṇa demonstrates, availing himself of a verse of the *Manusmṛti*:

> There is nothing wrong with consumption of meat, with alcohol and with having sex – this is a natural activity of living beings. However, abstention [from such activities] brings a great reward.[43]

Mallişeṇa argues that

> If this [verse] is interpreted to have the meaning as it stands, it is incoherent twaddle. If there is nothing wrong in [activity] which is practised, how is it possible that abstention from it could bring a great reward? That would lead to an undesired consequence that abstention from sacrifice, studying the Veda, donations etc. [would also bring a great reward]. Therefore this verse must have a different intent. For it is as follows: it is not the case that there is nothing wrong when one eats meat, on the contrary: it is really wrong. Similarly, it is the case also with alcohol and sex. Why does he then say that there is nothing wrong [with these] because this is a natural activity of living beings? That with respect to which they act, i.e. which they encounter, is activity, i.e. a situation of encounter. That means that – [if we take] "living beings" [to mean] ordinary creatures – this is a cause of acquaintance of ordinary creatures with such [an activity, although they do not follow it]. It is well known from tradition that consumption of meat, alcohol and sex are main causes of the acquaintance of creatures [with such a custom].... Alternatively, this is activity of "living beings" taken to stand for monsters. The sense is that only these [monsters] act in the sense that they consume meat, drink alcohol and have sex, but not reasonable creatures.[44]

Clearly, no verse and no sentence can be read out of context and every proposition and sentence requires a closer analysis of its meaning. With the above analysis and examination of similar traditional maxims, Mallişeṇa opens his exposition of the *syād-vāda*. The way he proceeds is highly significant: by quoting a well-known passage he demonstrates how semantics is at play: this is something all of us do in our ordinary lives; we never take propositions as they stand but we always supply additional information from the context in order to reach an accurate understanding of it.

Quoting a verse of the *Visesâvassaya-bhāsa* (VĀBh 115), Mallişeṇa explains that sometimes humans commit a mistake of a false interpretation even of an authoritative text (*āgama*), which is by definition true:

> "From incapacity to distinguish true and false, from apprehension conditioned by causes of existence (sc. *karman*), from absence of results of cognition [comes] nescience of the wrong believer (*mithyā-dṛṣṭi*)."[45]
>
> Precisely from such causes [the heretics], when overpowered by these [causes of nescience], interpret even the Twelve Canonical Books as false testimony.[46]

By implication, as Malliṣeṇa wants to convince us, a remedy that safeguards one from committing such a mistake is, of course, a proper methodology, i.e. the *syād-vāda*, which disambiguates enigmatic and equivocal natural language.

The process of disambiguation not only allows one to determine a proper application of a proposition and its accurate meaning but also proves indispensable to eliminate other possible meanings the proposition can in theory convey, as Vidyānanda Pātrakesarisvāmin (c. 850) explains:

> One should in the first place carry out the process of [semantic] determination of a proposition in order to eliminate [its] undesirable meanings. Otherwise, because the [meaning of the proposition] would be equivalent to anything unsaid, it [could be taken] in any possible meaning.[47]

Thus, the primary task of a philosopher, as Jaina thinkers understood it, is to develop adequate tools that should make our language precise and unequivocal. They try to achieve this goal by formulating an appropriate semantic model that would provide reliable instruments to read any statement within its intended context. As Akalaṅka in the *Pravacana-praveśa* puts it, such a disambiguating strategy is indispensable in any successful communication:

> Even if it is not explicitly pronounced, the functor "in a certain sense" is understood from the context in all cases, both with respect to an affirmation and negation as well as with respect to any other case (sc. these two combined), if one should successfully convey [the intended meaning].[48]

As the verse indicates, any successful and, therefore context-sensitive communication procedure should consistently read the functor *syāt* into any sentence, which by nature is incomplete and cannot convey its meaning while taken alone: the crucial semantic elements necessary for its proper understanding have to be supplied from the context. And that is what, as Akalaṅka claims, we regularly do in our daily life.

The Syāt particle and the basic figures (bhaṅga)

One of the most conspicuous early components of the Jaina seven-fold modal description is the three basic figures (*bhaṅga*), or ways of analysing an object within a consistent conceptual framework:

(1) *syād asti* ("x is, in a certain sense, P"), i.e. σ (x is P).
(2) *syān nâsti* ("x is, in a certain sense, not-Q"), i.e. σ (x is $\neg Q$),
(3 or 4) *syād avaktavyam* ("x is, in a certain sense, inexpressible"), σ (x is (P & $\neg Q$)).

where the symbol σ represents the sentential functor *syāt*. As we shall see, the above formalization, which is here treated only as an approximation, is not the most accurate one.

The idea of the three basic figures (*bhaṅga*), viz. *syād asti, syān nâsti, syād avaktavyam*, was not a Jaina invention. It seems to have been a common intellectual property shared by various philosophically oriented groups of early Indian thinkers, including the Ājīvikas, e.g. Makkhali Gosāla (Pāli)/Gosāla Maṅkhaliputta (Buddh. Skt.) = Gośala Maskariputra (Jaina).[49]

It is not impossible that the true inventors of a crude form of this manner of describing the world were Makkhali Gosāla and his followers, with whom Mahāvīra Vardhamāna and early Jainas had a lot in common. As the *Naṃdī-sutta* informs us much later:

> So these Ājīvikas are called "Three-tiers". Why? It is explained: because they accept the whole world as consisting in three natures, namely: the soul, the non-soul and both the soul–non-soul; the world, the non-world and the world–non-world; the existent, the non-existent and the existent–non-existent, etc. Because of reflection based on viewpoints, they accept three viewpoints, namely: substance-expressive, mode-expressive and both-expressive. It is for this reason that is has been said: the heretics of the three-tiers conceive of kinds of reflection [in the form] of viewpoints in sevenfold manner as seven computations – such is the meaning.[50]

The Jainas were to develop the three primary statements into a more complex system by permutating them and giving them a more specific meaning, and then applied them to their ontology.

It should be noted, however, that a crude form of the three basic figures – "x is P", "x is $\neg$Q" and "x is both P and $\neg$Q" – is present in some canonical works, e.g. in the *Viyāha-pannatti*.[51] However, the basic figures (*bhaṅga*) augmented with the particle *syāt* are absent from early portions of the Jaina Canon. They emerge gradually both in much later canonical strata and, especially, in non-canonical literature.[52] I just list a couple of examples where the *bhaṅgas* are used as well as some occurrences of the sentential functor *siya/siyā/syāt*:

(a) Viy 12.10 (pp. 608–614): *…siya atthi siya natthi…*, esp.: 610.15 ff.: *rayaṇa-ppabhā puṭhavī siya āyā, siya no āyā, siya avattavyaṃ – āyā ti ya, no ātā ti ya*; and 611.20 ff.: *du-paesie khaṃdhe siya āyā, siya no āyā, siya avattavvaṃ – āyā ti ya no āyā ti ya, siya āyā ya no āyā ya, siya āyā ya avattavvaṃ – āyā ti ya no āyā ti ya, siya no āyā ya avattavvaṃ – āyā ti ya no āyā ti ya.*

(b) Viy 5.7.1 (pp. 210.20–21 ff.): *paramāṇu-poggale ṇaṃ bhaṃte! eyati veyati jāva taṃ taṃ bhāvaṃ pariṇamati? goyamā! siyā eyati veyati jāva pariṇamati, siya ṇo eyati jāva ṇo pariṇamati.*

(c) Paṇṇ 784 (pp. 195.21 ff.): *cau-paesie ṇaṃ khaṃdhe siya carime no acarime siya avattavvae no carimāiṃ no acarimāiṃ no avattavvayāiṃ, … siya carimāiṃ ca acarime ya siya carimāiṃ ca acarimāiṃ ca siya carime ya avattavvae ya siya carime ya avattavvayāiṃ ca…*, etc.

(d) AṇD 415 (pp. 166.22 ff.): *tathā ṇaṃ je te baddhellayā te ṇaṃ siyā atthi siyā natthi, jai atthi jahaṇṇeṇaṃ ego vā do vā tiṇṇi vā…*

(e) AṇD 473 (p. 182): *siyā dhamma-padeso siyā adhamma-padeso siyā āgāsa-padeso siyā jīva-padeso siyā khaṃdha-padeso.*

It is not always the case that the three basic figures (*bhaṅga*) invariably co-occur with the *syāt* particle. There are numerous cases when the sentential functor *syāt* (*siya, siyā*) is missing, which most probably reflects an earlier historical layer and attests to a slow gradual development of the concept of the *syād-vāda* in Jainism:

(a) Paṇṇ 781–788 (p. 194 ff.), e.g. pp. 194.25 ff.: *paramâṇu-poggale ṇaṃ bhaṃte! kiṃ carime acarime avattavaye carimāiṃ acarimāiṃ avattavayāiṃ, udāhu carime ya acarime ya udāhu carime ya acarimāiṃ ca udāhu carimāiṃ ca acarime ya udāju carimāi ca acarimāiṃ ca…*, etc.

(b) Viy 8.2.29 (p. 337.20 ff.): *jīvā ṇaṃ bhaṃte! kiṃ nāṇi annāṇī? goyamā jīvā nāṇī vi, annāṇī vi.*

Perhaps the earliest non-canonical Jaina thinker who mentions the basic figures (*bhaṅga*) and occasionally appends the sentential functor *syāt* to them (but not always!) is the collective author called Kundakunda, to whom a number of works composed between the third and sixth centuries are traditionally ascribed. The *Paṃcatthiya-saṃgaha* already offers what is later known as *pramāṇa-sapta-bhaṅgī* and contains an expression *ādesa-vaseṇa* (*ādeśa-vaśāt*) which clearly foreshadows later tradition that speaks of a "complete account" (*sakalâdeśa*), in contradistinction to "incomplete account" (*vikalâdeśa*):[53]

> Substance is possible, as one should realise, as "seven-figured" (sc. can be predicated of with the help of seven figures) by force of the account (sc. way of predication): in a certain sense it is, it is not, it is both, it is inexpressible and it is a combination of the three.[54]

Kundakunda's *Pavayaṇa-sāra* offers another instance:

> [22] From the substance-expressive viewpoint everything is a substance. From the mode-expressive viewpoint, [any thing] becomes different. It is [nevertheless] non-different, because it consists in that [substance] at the time of its [existence].[55] [23] The substance is said – on account of any particular mode – to be…, and not to be…, and again [the substance] becomes inexpressible; but further [the substance] is both, [viz. is … and is not … at the same time] or is otherwise, [viz. any other permutation of the three basic figures (*bhaṅga*)].[56]

Not much later than the *Pavayaṇa-sāra*, perhaps even contemporaneous with it in view of the simplicity of the exposition of idea of "path of verbal characterisation which has seven possibilities",[57] i.e. the *syād-vāda*, Siddhasena Divākara in the *Saṃmati-tarka-prakaraṇa* (ca. 450–500) describes all the seven figures (*bhaṅga*), albeit he does so without the functor *syāt*:

> [36] A substance which is simultaneously beyond verbal characterisation through [either of] the first two [modes (*paryāya*)] that are either of another thing (sc. "*x* is not-Q") or that are determined [as one's own] (sc. "*x* is P") turns out to be inexpressible. [37] If one aspect is determined with respect to its occurrence and another aspect [is determined] with respect to its mode of absence, such a substance both is [with respect to one aspect] and is not [with respect to the other aspect] (sc. "*x* is P and is not-Q"), because it is characterised by some account[58] (sc. through some predication). [38] Such a substance whose [one] aspect is mentioned with respect to its occurrence and whose [another] aspect is [mentioned] in both ways (sc. simultaneously is and is not), it is something that both is and is inexpressible according to [the fifth] possibility. [39] Such a substance whose [one] aspect is mentioned with respect to its non-occurrence and whose [another] aspect is [mentioned] in both ways (sc. simultaneously is and is not), it is something that both is not and is inexpressible according to [the sixth] possibility. [40] Such a substance whose [one] aspect is mentioned with respect to its occurrence and non-occurrence and whose [another] aspect is [mentioned] in both ways (sc. simultaneously is and is not), it is something that is, is not and is inexpressible according to [the seventh] possibility.[59]

Although the functor "in a certain sense" is missing, the picture presented here is not an altogether undeveloped concept. Besides, Siddhasena Divākara, who does not use the sentential functor *siya*/*siyā* (*syāt*) at any section of his work, supplies additional parameters (*vide infra*, p. 31 f.) which he calls "aspects" (*deso*) from which the substance can be predicated of in each of the seven possibilities: it can be said to exist with respect to a certain aspect, and not to exist with respect to another.

Certain discrepancies in Kundakunda's and Siddhasena Divākara's presentations, most probably either contemporaneous or not much distant in time from each other, which are conspicuous in the above juxtaposition may be taken as an indication that the period of the fifth century, to which I would assign both the expositions, was a time when the method of the seven-fold modal description (*syād-vāda*) was not a definite concept but, instead, was at a stage of development, and the sentential functor *syāt* was still not obligatory.

Typical examples in genuine sentences of the *syād-vāda* are generally restricted to the terms: *jīva*, *paṭa*, *ghaṭa* and *kumbha*, and it seems that the earliest point of reference, when the subject of the proposition is at all mentioned is *jīva*, which reflects a general soteriological concern of Jaina thinkers. Other standard subject terms (*paṭa*, *ghaṭa* and *kumbha*), which I would take as secondary examples, were taken from a general tradition of Indian inference (*anumāna*). An interesting reference is found in Jinabhadra-gaṇin's *Viśeṣâvaśyaka-bhāṣya* (sixth/seventh century) which does not use the standard set of expressions: *atthi/ asti, nâsti/ṇatthi, avattavvam/avaktavyam*, typical of the method of the seven-fold modal description, but instead he uses the expressions *kuṃbha* ("pitcher"), *akuṃbha* ("not pitcher"), *avattavyam* ("inexpressible"):

> Being something the existence, non-existence and both [the existence and non-existence] of [a particular property of it] is emphasised through [the pitcher's] own mode and through the mode of something else, this [pitcher] is differentiated as "a pitcher", as "something else than a pitcher", as "something inexpressible" and as "both [a pitcher and something else than a pitcher]".[60]

This seemingly innocuous mode of expression may attest to an older strand of Jaina tradition, preserved in the Āvaśyaka tradition that preserves terminology that has much affinity to the way Ājīvikas employed the three figures: P, non-P, P & non-P, for instance *jīva, ajīva, jīvājīva* (*vide supra*, p. 20, n. 50).[61] This "*syāt*-free" tradition apparently was continued as a marginal phenomenon until early mediaeval times, because Hemacandra Maladhārin, who aptly elaborates on the verse, does not use the functor in his explanations at all:

> The idea is that [the author of the verse] demonstrates the seven-fold modal description, namely: a [particular] pitcher is called "pitcher" when, being predicated of, it is emphasised, through its own modes such as an upward neck, a hull, a spherical shape, a base etc., as something existent (sc. as something which is a member of a class A). That is what is meant by the first figure: "the vessel is existent [as $a \in A$]". Similarly, [a particular pitcher] is [taken to be] something else than a pitcher when, being predicated of, it is emphasised, through the modes of another [thing] such as the protection of the skin, as something non-existent (sc. as something which is a member of a class $\neg A$). When the expressive intent is [to emphasise] the non-existence (sc. its being something else) [in the case] of any pot whatever through the modes [typical] of another [thing], that is what is meant by the second figure: "the vessel is non-existent [as $a \in A$]". By the same token, when one wishes to speak of any pot with no exception when, being predicated of, it is simultaneously emphasised – through its own modes, through the modes of another [thing] and through both [in the same breath] – as something [both] existent and non-existent, then it becomes inexpressible. [It becomes inexpressible], because it is not possible to speak, by means of any conceivable, numerically singular speech element which is not convention-bound, of any thing at all simultaneously as both existent and non-existent. These [figures] present a complete account [of a thing]. Now, the [remaining] four are explained in its turn explained as incomplete account [of a thing]...[62]

The second essential element of the theory in its developed form is, as it is well-known, beside the idea of the "figures" (*bhaṅga*), the sentential functor *syāt* ("in a certain sense"), usually explained as *kathaṃcit* ("somehow"). It is well attested in most Jaina sources, including the latest strata of the Jaina Canon, but entirely absent in earlier canonical phases. The particle is the most pronounced element of each of the seven basic figures (*bhaṅga*). It is said to operate by means of affirmation (*vidhi*) and negation (*niṣedha, pratiṣedha, niyama*). The various combinations of affirmation and negation are extensively detailed and elaborated, for instance, by Mallavādin Kṣamāśramaṇa in the *Dvādaśāra-naya-cakra.*[63] Also Samantabhadra refers to them in his *Svayambhū-stotra*:

> Affirmation and negation are accepted [in the sense of] "somehow". [Thereby] the distinction between primary and secondary [figure] is established. Such is the guideline of the wise (or: of the fifth Tīrthaṃ-kara Sumati). That is your most excellent creed. Let the worshipper praise you.[64]

In the *Āpta-mīmāṃsā*, he states:

> The application domain of the speech element should be qualified, inasmuch as it consists in aspects that should be affirmed and in aspects that should be negated, just as a [positive] logical reason is a property [related] to the inferable property, and likewise a negative logical reason [is not related to it], respectively.[65]

Closer examination of the development of the *syāt* particles and the figures (*bhaṅga*) leads us to a conclusion that a mature theory of the seven-fold modal description took final shape by approximately the turn of the fifth and sixth centuries at the earliest.

To recapitulate, what were historically only three basic figures (*bhaṅga*) later came to be permutated so that the total of seven basic figures was reached, making up a complete version of the doctrine of the modal description (*syād-vāda*):

1 "In a certain sense, *x* [indeed] is P" – *syād asty* [*eva*].
2 "In a certain sense, *x* [indeed] is not-Q" – *syān nâsty* [*eva*].
3 "In a certain sense, *x* [indeed] is P and [indeed] is not-Q" – *syān asty* [*eva*] *nâsty* [*eva*].
4 "In a certain sense, *x* [indeed] is inexpressible" – *syād avaktavyam* [*eva*].
5 "In a certain sense, *x* [indeed] is P and [indeed] is inexpressible" – *syād asty* [*eva*] *avaktavyam* [*eva*].
6 "In a certain sense, *x* [indeed] is not-Q and [indeed] is inexpressible" – *syān nâsty* [*eva*] *avaktavyam* [*eva*].
7 "In a certain sense, *x* [indeed] is P, [indeed] is not-Q and [indeed] is inexpressible" – *syān asty* [*eva*] *nâsty* [*eva*] *avaktavyam* [*eva*].

A significant step was an introduction of the particle *eva* – altogether absent in all earlier formulations – by Samantabhadra (c. 580–640?), who was apparently influenced by Dharmakīrti's use of *eva* as a delimiting particle (*vyavaccheda*).[66] The particle *eva* was a highly useful semantic tool to restrict the applicability of the property (*dharma*) predicated of the real thing (*vastu*), or a semantic method to restrict the range of the term that denotes the property.

I find it rather difficult to determine when and by whom the term *sapta-bhaṅgī* as such was used for the first time. Although the expression is, to my knowledge, absent from the canon, it is, however, already used by a pre-Diṅnāga author Kundakunda in PAS 14 (*vide supra*, n. 54, p. 21), albeit in the form *satta-bhaṃgaṃ* ("seven-figured"), which is a *bahu-vrīhi* adjective compound relative to *davvaṃ* ("substance"), which indicates that any substance can be *predicated of with the help of seven figures.*

Further, the same author refers to the *sapta-bhaṅgī* method applicable to (or as a capacity of) the soul:

> [71] The great soul is one (viz. either "self-same", or "one perceiving organ" (*akṣa*) or "it is possessed of cognitive application (*upayoga*)"). It is [also] two (viz. "it is possessed of two-fold cognitive application: cognition and perception"). It becomes of threefold characteristics, it is said to roam in four [types of existence]. And it is grounded in five primary qualities (viz. karmic states (*bhāva*)). [72] It is endowed with the capability to move in six [directions]. It is cognitively apt as *having the existence to which the seven figures apply.* It has eight substrata (viz. qualities). It has nine objects (sc. the nine categories (*tattva*)) [to cognise]. It has ten states. It is called the living element.[67]

Interestingly, also in this passage Kundakunda makes reference to the method not directly through the expression *sapta-bhaṅgī*, so well-established later on, but again through a *bahu-vrīhi* adjective compound which describes the ultimate soul: *mahātmā … sapta-bhaṅga-sadbhāvaḥ* – "the great soul … has the existence to which the seven figures apply".[68]

Although Siddhasena Divākara does not use the term *sapta-bhaṅgī* in STP, he speaks of "a verbal procedure that consists of seven options" (*sapta-vikalpaḥ vacana-panthaḥ*) instead, with which he concludes the description of the seven figures in STP 1.36–40 (*vide supra*, n. 59, p. 22):

> In this way, there emerges a verbal procedure that consists of seven options, taking into account the substantial modes. However, while taking into account the modes [in the form] of momentary manifestations, [the method of analysis] either has options [of description, viz. the object can be predicated of from various figures,] or it has no options.[69,70]

This may be an indication that the term *sapta-bhaṅgī* was not so well-established or not universally widespread among Jaina theoreticians even still around CE 500 as it is popularly thought.

The parameters and aspects

Most Jaina descriptions of the *syād-vāda* make a clear mention of what is called by them variously as aspects (*deśa*/*deso*) or facets (*aṃśa*), and what I propose to call parameters. Most Jaina thinkers distinguish four such basic parameters that qualify the way we predicate of a thing: substance (*dravya*), place (*kṣetra*), time (*kāla*), condition (*bhāva*).[71]

The four classical parameters have a longer history. They gradually developed during the so-called "canonical period", that ranges from the fourth/third century BCE till CE 450–480 and are reflected in the Jaina Canon eventually codified in the second half of the sixth century. They assumed their more or less classical form before the fourth/fifth century within a complex strategy of "dialectical ways of analysis" (*anuyoga-dvāra*). Initially these tools of analysis were crucial theoretical determinants known as the four standpoints (*nikṣepa*, *nyāsa*):[72] substance (*dravya*), place (*kṣetra*), time (*kāla*) and actual condition (*bhāva*) of an entity analysed. Occasionally, other parameters were added in canonical literature, such as a particular quality (*guṇa*), a mode (*paryaya*), spatial extension (*pradeśa*), name (*nāma*), form (*rūpa*), material representation (*sthāpanā*), transformation (*pariṇāma*) etc.[73] Also the post-canonical literature enumerated similar parameters that served the same purpose. Some authors distinguished more than the classical four. A good example is Siddhasena Divākara (c. CE 450–500) in the *Saṃmati-tarka-prakaraṇa*, who regularly speaks of aspects (*deso*) from which the substance can be predicated of. He mentions eight such parameters which qualify our statements about a thing, although he is rather unique:

> The proper method of exposition of entities [in accordance with *syād-vāda*] is based on substance (*dravya*), place (*kṣetra*), time (*kāla*), condition (*bhāva*) as well as mode (*paryāya*), aspect (or part, *deśa*) and relation (or combination of elements, *saṃyoga*), and also distinction (*bheda*).[74]

Later on, with the development of the Nyāya school and emergence of the concept of *upādhi*, variously translated as "subsidiary condition", "extraneous condition", "limiting adjunct", "conditioning factor", i.e. additional factors which should be taken into account in inference (*anumāna*) and in establishing the relation of invariable concomitance (*vyāpti*), the idea of the parameters came to be identified with *upādhi*. Hemacandra-sūri, in the *Anya-yoga-vyavaccheda-dvātriṃśikā* 24 (*vide supra*, p. 15), uses this new term and applies it in the sense of "an additional semantic factor" one should take into account while analysing the meaning of a sentence. In his opinion, the meaning of every statement is "conditioned by differentiation through conditioning factors", i.e. it should be disambiguated through additional semantic criteria. Commenting on Hemacandra-sūri's phrase *upādhi-bhedôpahitaṃ*, Malliṣeṇa develops the idea and establishes an explicit link between the "conditioning factors" and an earlier idea of aspects or facets (*deso*/*deśa*/*aṃśa*; *vide supra*, p. 25):

> From incapacity to distinguish true and false, from apprehension [non-existence, existence and inexpressibility] are conditioned by, i.e. are emphasised by way of, differentiation, i.e. diversity, of conditioning factors, i.e. delimiters which are the modes which express an aspect. This [differentiation] is a qualifier of non-existence. When conditioned by differentiation through conditioning factors, non-existence does not stand in contradiction with existent objects. One should correlate it to existence and inexpressibility having introduced such differentiation in utterances.[75]

As for the number of such basic parameters, Siddhasena Divākara was not unique in devising his own set of parameters. At a certain point also Malliṣeṇa,[76] following Akalaṅka,[77] offers his own set of eight parameters with regard to which the thing is being predicated of: time factor (*kāla*), the thing's own essence (*ātma-rūpa*), the thing in its substantial aspect, i.e. its material substratum (*artha*), its relation (*sambandha*), the thing's serviceability, i.e. its role as assisting factor or auxiliary condition (*upakāra*), the location of the thing as the property-possessor (*guṇi-deśa*), the thing as a combination of related attributes, or its concurrence with other properties (*saṃsarga*), and verbal designation (*śabda*). However, these additional parameters are usually treated as second-order parameters (*vide infra*, p. 35) that help determine the exact context of the four first-order parameters (*vide infra*, p. 31).

The relevance of the four basic parameters, and the same holds valid for more parameters than the classical four, is explained by Malliṣeṇa:

> For there would be contradiction only if both existence and non-existence had one and the same conditioning factor. But it is not the case [in the *syād-vāda*], because the existence [of the object as *P*] is not [predicated of] with respect to the same fact with respect to which non-existence [as Q is predicated of]. Rather, existence [of the object as P] has a different conditioning factor and non-existence [of the object as Q] has a different conditioning factor. For existence is with respect to the own form [of a real thing], whereas non-existence is with respect to a different form [belonging to another thing].[78]

Such an account clearly avoids an apparent contradiction that "*x* is both P and ¬P"; what we have instead is a statement to the effect that "*x* is both P and ¬Q". It is never the case under the *syād-vāda* scheme, that one and the same property is affirmed and denied from one and the same viewpoint or under one and the same set of circumstances.

But how should we read and apply this scheme in practice? Malliṣeṇa provides a lengthy example of how one should interpret modal sentences by applying the parameters for all the seven figures, and what semantic implications the figures carry:

> [1] As for these [modal sentences, the first figure is:] "in a certain sense", or "somehow", [i.e.] through its own substance, place, time and condition,

> everything, for instance a pot etc., indeed exists; [it does] not [exist] through another thing's substance, place, time and condition. For it is as follows: With respect to substance, a pot exists as being made of clay and does not exist as something made of water etc. With respect to place, a pot exists as related to [the city of] Pāṭaliputra, it does not exist as related to [the city of] Kanyakubja etc. With respect to time, it exists as related to autumn, not does not exist as related to spring etc. With respect to condition, it exists as something black, not as something red etc. Otherwise, an undesired consequence would follow that [the thing] would abandon its own form by assuming the other form. And in this method the process of [semantic] determination the aim of which is to exclude unintended meanings is employed, because otherwise it would absurdly follow that the same proposition would equally have the meaning which has not been expressed, because its own meaning would not be clearly defined in every case.[79]

As it seems, every affirmative sentence predicates certain properties of a real thing with respect to its particular, individually specific substance, place, time and condition. At the same time it carries a hidden meaning which excludes a range of alternative properties predicable of the thing with regard to the same parameters: substance, place, time and condition. However, what can be, for all practical reasons, explicitly conveyed by an affirmative sentence is merely the former range of meanings.

Accordingly, ordinary sentences should always be interpreted through the parameters, and what the particle *syāt* actually expresses are various perspectives one can take while predicating a particular property of a particular object. Accordingly, if we wish to formally symbolize the *syād-vāda*, we should first distinguish (positive and negative) sentences that consist of a subject and a range of predicates R {A, C, E, G,…} of the form: Px, and its hidden implied counterpart is: ¬Qx, with a range of predicates Q {B, D, F, H,…}. For instance, the example given by Malliṣeṇa can be said to represent, at its face value, the following situation:

> x is A = "x is made of clay",
> x is ¬B = "x is not made of water etc.";
> x is C = "x is related to the city of Pāṭaliputra",
> x is ¬D = "x is not related to the city of Kanyakubja etc.",
> x is E = "x is existing in autumn",
> x is ¬F = "x is not existing in spring etc.",
> x is G = "x is something black",
> x is ¬H = "x is not something red etc."

It should be noted that all negative predicates ¬Q {¬B, ¬D, ¬F, ¬H,…} are merely implied by the affirmative predicates R {A, C, E, G,…}, but they are not expressly stated in sentences of the first figure: *syād asti*. It is only in the second sort of sentences, negative ones, that the exclusion comes to the fore:

> [2] "In a certain sense", or "somehow", the pot etc. indeed does not exist; for in a certain sense there cannot be a thorough determination of the real thing, because its own form is not determined thoroughly when the real thing's non-existence [as Q] is not accepted also on the basis of a different substance etc. [belonging to other things], like [*mutatis mutandis* its existence as P is determined] on the basis of [the real thing's] own substance. And someone who maintains that [the pot] exists in an absolute sense cannot claim that the non-existence [as Q] with respect to the [pot] is not established, because it is somehow established to be congruous with the real thing, just as a proof [requires both positive and negative concomitance].[80,81]

The idea of a description of the thing's essence in a negative manner is related to a considerably common conviction among Indian philosophers that any definition determines the nature of a thing by indicating "a property which excludes all that is not the thing's nature".[82] Accordingly, the negative aspect of exclusion, so much emphasized by semantic theory of *anyâpoha* ("exclusion of the other") developed by the Buddhist tradition of Diṅnāga, plays an important role in the Jaina theory of the *syād-vāda.* The same conviction led, for instance, Dharmakīrti, following Diṅnāga, to formulate his theory that inference – comprising also all verbal communication based on linguistic signs[83] – is a process which proceeds by the exclusion of false superimposition (*samāropa*), i.e. properties wrongly superimposed on the thing, or by removing cognitive error (*bhrānti*), that stems from the doubt as to what characteristics a thing possesses. Accordingly, what inference, including verbal communication, leads to is the determination of the thing by excluding the properties which do not belong to it.[84] As Dharmakīrti observes, the determination of the thing's nature is directly related to the exclusion of all properties that do not constitute its nature, although the cognitive process that leads to the correct knowledge of the thing takes the negative path through elimination:

> Since determinate cognition and false superimposition stand in a relation of [a cognitive act] that sublates [false superimposition] and [a cognitive act] that is sublated [by determinate cognition], it is understood that the former operates when the determination (sc. exclusion) of the false superimposition takes place.[85]

Similarly, when the Jainas speak of thing's non-existence (*vastuno 'sattva*) they mean precisely such an exclusion of the properties that do not constitute the thing's essence. Although logically equivalent to "*x* is P", to say "*x* is not non-*P*" reveals an additional intensional, semantically relevant information, which is precisely the line of thought that motivated Diṅnāga to develop his theory of exclusion (*apoha*).

In Malliṣeṇa's laconic exposition, the combination of the first and second figure should not present any difficulty:

[3] The third one, [i.e. the combination of the two: *syād asti nâsti,*] is absolutely clear.[86]

Since the first and the second figures are logically equivalent, although they do carry different semantic contents, their conjunction involves no contradiction. In addition, it is within our verbal means to express their conjunction. Similarly, the fourth figure which involves the conjunction of the positive and negative statements cannot yield any contradiction, although it is practically inexpressible in the sense that there are no verbal means to express the conjunction with one word:

> [4] If there is a desire to express both properties of existence and non-existence, which are simultaneously emphasised as primary, with respect to one and the same real thing, then a real thing such as the soul etc. [understood in this way] is inexpressible, because a word of such kind [to denote both properties] is impossible. For it is as follows, a pair of qualities, i.e. of existence [as P] and non-existence [as Q], cannot be simultaneously articulated with respect to one [and the same real thing] with the [expression]: "*x* is [P]", because this [expression] is not capable of conveying the non-existence [of *x* as Q]. Similarly, [a pair of qualities cannot be simultaneously articulated with respect to one and the same real thing] with the [expression]: "*x* is not [Q]", because it is not capable of conveying existence [of *x* as P]. Further, no numerically one conventionally accepted word, like "flower-toothed" (Puṣpadanta),[87] is capable of expressing such a [complex] meaning, because even this [compound] name [Puṣpadanta] is seen to have the capacity to demonstrate the pair of meaning ["flower" and "teeth"] consecutively, like for instance the conventional (sc. artificial) term SaT [which is used to denote] both Śatṛ and ŚānaC affixes.[88] And for this very reason, no copulative compound and no descriptive determinative (appositional) compound as well as no sentence can denote this [compounded meaning]. That is why the real thing [in question], which remains inexpressible, because there is no [verbal means] to denote the compounded whole, is [here] established as determined by simultaneous existence and non-existence, [both] emphasised as the primary meaning. But it is not inexpressible completely, because that would lead to an undesired consequence that it would not be communicable even with the term "inexpressible"![89]

The outcome of this kind of approach may seem rather trivial and disappointing because all that is meant by the statement *syād avaktavyam* is linguistic incapacity, or human incapability, to express an affirmation of certain properties and negation of some others in one breath, and not some kind of logical third value. It is simply not possible to expressly communicate two ideas simultaneously, even though they can be logically closely related. Both the singular name "Puṣpadanta", belonging to the natural language, for one and the same individual which conveys two distinct ideas, i.e. "flower" (*puṣpa*) and "teeth" (*danta*), and the term SaT, artificially created within the technical language of the grammarians, to denote two different affixes Śatṛ and ŚānaC, symbolize the idea that whatever the linguistic means, either evolved naturally or devised in order to suit practical needs of a linguistic convention, any compounded idea is always expressed or brought to mind in a sequence, never simultaneously. Under such circumstances, the theory seems to lose its stimulating flavour for a logician and becomes of interest rather for a linguist.

In conclusion, Malliṣeṇa expresses what is already well known, namely that the fifth to seventh figures are mere permutations of the first four options:

> [5–7] The intent of the remaining three can be easily deduced.[90]

As it transpires from the foregoing, the sentential functor *syāt* is itself a kind of variable the actual values of which are various parameters. We can distinguish two types of such parameters (for the second-order parameters see below), whose actual values happen to be, as in the above example: "made of clay", "made of water etc.", "related to the city of Pāṭaliputra", "related to the city of Kanyakubja etc.", "existing in autumn", "existing in spring etc.", "something black", "something red", etc. What I call first-order parameters are the traditionally accepted following four:

substance (*dravya*) = S,
place or occurrence (*kṣetra*) = O,
time (*kāla*) = T,
condition (*bhāva*) = C.

Their number can be extended (*vide supra*, p. 26 f.) and can include other parameters, such as mode, aspect, relation, distinction, material substratum, relation, serviceability, verbal designation, etc., depending on the requirements of the analysis.

In other words, if we want to be more accurate, the ranges of predicates R {A, C, E, G,…} and ¬Q {¬B, ¬D, ¬F, ¬H,…} turn out to be a predicate P indexed with the set of the four basic parameters $\{P^{S}x, P^{O}x, P^{T}x, P^{C}x, \ldots\}$, for instance as follows:

"With respect to substance, *x* is…": $P^{S}x$,
"With respect to place, *x* is…": $P^{O}x$,
"With respect to time, *x* is…": $P^{T}x$,
"With respect to condition, *x* is…": $P^{C}x$, etc.

However, a closer reading of textual sources shows that this is still a simplification, insofar as what we really have is a case of double indexicality or double parameterisation, i.e. the four basic, first-order parameters are also indexed in at least twofold fashion as follow: $R^{S1}x$, $\neg Q^{S2}x$, $P^{O1}x$, $\neg Q^{O2}x$, $P^{T1}x$, $\neg Q^{T2}x$, $P^{C1}x$, $\neg Q^{C2}x, \ldots$, for instance:

"with respect to substance S_1, x is..." : $R^{S}{}_{1}x$,
"with respect to substance S_2, x is not..." : $\neg Q^{S}{}_{2}x$,
"with respect to place O_1, x is..." : $R^{O}{}_{1}x$,
"with respect to place O_2, x is not..." : $\neg Q^{O}{}_{2}x$,
"with respect to time T_1, x is..." : $R^{T}{}_{1}x$,
"with respect to time T_2, x is not..." : $\neg Q^{T}{}_{2}x$,
"with respect to condition C_1, x is..." : $R^{C}{}_{1}x$, etc.
"with respect to condition C_2, x is not..." : $\neg Q^{C}{}_{2}x$, etc.

We can restate the above set of propositions as a general rule as follows:

$$\forall x \,.\, \exists\sigma\ \sigma\colon P^{\pi}x,$$

For every real thing (*vastu*) x, there is a particular perspective σ such that it can be interpreted as parameter π with respect to which x is P, where $\pi = \{S, O, T, C\}$ is the set of the first-order parameters of substance = S, place (occurrence) = O, time = T and condition = C.

Thus, every sentence should be taken as embedding a set of hidden parameters that delineate the context, and a predicate, say, P of any statement x: Px is in fact a compound predicate that should be analysed by way of additional parameters.

Emphasis

There is still one more important element to take account of, namely emphasis (*arpaṇa*/*arpaṇā*). The idea comes to the surface from relatively early works onwards, perhaps the earliest being Umāsvāmin's *Tattvârtha-sūtra*, where we find the expression "*arpitânarpita*" ("emphasized [property] and not-emphasized [property]", *vide supra*, p. 2). The idea of an emphasized property (*arpita*) is subsequently elaborated by Pūjyapāda Devanandin in the *Sarvârtha-siddhi* and explained as "a property to which prominence is extended" (*prādhānyam ... upanītam*):

> On account of the purpose [which] a real thing, being of multiplex nature, [is to serve or is to be referred to], prominence is extended to, or is emphasised, i.e. [prominence] is given to a certain property in accordance with the expressive intent [of the speaker]. [The property] which is contrary to that [emphasised property] is not-emphasised [property]. Since [such a not-emphasised property serves] no purpose [at a particular time], even though it exists, there is no expressive intent [to assert it]; hence it is called subordinate [property]. Since these two [kinds of properties] are established, viz. "because emphasised [property] and not-emphasised [property] are established", there is no contradiction.[91]

The opposite of the emphasized property in a not-emphasized property (*anarpita*), taken as subordinate property (*upasarjanīta*). These two are sometimes also called "primary" (*mukhya*) and "secondary" (*gauṇa*).

The emphasis has been variously understood by various authors and an exact analysis of its historical development and its different interpretations would serve no direct purpose here. In most cases, however, it is understood that two properties can be emphasized, this way or another, either simultaneously (*yugapad*, *yaugapadyena*) or consecutively (*krama*, *krameṇa*). What emphasis (*arpaṇa*) actually means is a verbal pronouncement of a property, whereas "non-emphasis" (*anarpaṇa*) means that a property is not explicitly mentioned in a sentence although it is logically implied or entailed. What is important, the emphasis applies only when we want to express two properties, but it is never mentioned when one expresses just one property.

Other relatively early examples of the idea of emphasis are found in Siddhasena Divākara's *Saṃmati-tarka-prakaraṇa* 1.36–40 (*vide supra*, p. 22) and in Samantabhadra's *Āpta-mīmāṃsā*:

> The pair [of existence and non-existence is possible] because both are emphasised consecutively. [Their pair] is inexpressible because it is impossible [to express them] together. The last three figures consist of the inexpressible and the remaining [figures], according to their own reasons.[92]

Samantabhadra makes a reference to the idea of emphasis also in the *Yuktyanuśāsana*:

> To establish [absolute] distinction of substance and modes is not [possible]. Double nature is contradictory when emphasised singly. Both property and property-possessor are mutually related in threefold manner. These two are not accepted by you (sc. by the Jina) to be contradictory in an absolute sense.[93]

A fairly early date of first occurrences of the idea of emphasis attests to its being a vital component of the theory of the *syād-vāda* from its outset. The idea becomes a standard element in all expositions of the theory. It is usually used to explain the difference between the figures *syād asti nâsti* and *syād avaktavyam*. Referring to the idea of emphasis and its consecutive or simultaneous application in the *Tattvârtha-rāja-vārttika*, Akalaṅka clarifies the difference between the third and fourth statements precisely as a difference in a consecutive and simultaneous emphasis:

> The third alternative holds good, insofar as one wants to predicate two [distinct] qualities simultaneously of a numerically one undifferentiated [thing] without any differentiation [between the two]. In this case, when one thing as a whole is consecutively denoted by way of [accentuating] one property of a whole [composite] thing as such with [just] one speech element at one

> time for each of the first and the second alternatives (figures), [this is consecutiveness]. Similarly, when one wishes to ascribe two opposing qualities, each restricted (sc. expressible by separate words of different denotation), to numerically one thing as an indivisible whole with numerically one speech element at one time simultaneously, without any differentiation [between the two], then it is inexpressible (sc. inexpressible), because there is no such speech element [to convey] this [complex meaning]. In this case, simultaneity (sc. the fourth figure "inexpressible") operates with regard to implied properties without differentiation with respect to time and other [factors], and their differentiation in the case of [the inexpressible proposition] is not possible.[94]

Clearly, for all practical reasons the third statement (*syād asti nâsti*) *consecutively* expresses two distinct properties, that are not contradictory, because they refer to two different contexts, or they have two different sets of parameters. On the other hand, in the fourth statement (*syād avaktavyam*), we have a case of, again, two distinct parameterized properties, which do not stand in contradiction, but there is no linguistic tools at our disposal to express them *simultaneously*. It seems that the "inexpressible" figure is not a case of indeterminateness or undecidedness either understood as a third logical truth value or in the sense that we are unable to determine which of possible sets of parameters apply.

On the other hand, the claim that the figure "inexpressible" refers to a situation when the truth value of a proposition is undecided or undetermined, or when neither of two alternatives can be affirmed or denied, finds some corroboration in what Malliṣeṇa incidentally, in a slightly different context, says in the *Syād-vāda-mañjarī*:

> As regards [the predication expressing] "existence", because it is inexpressible, [we speak of] the third sex (viz. neither male nor female), [when we reply to the question]: "what is conceived in her womb".[95]

Apparently, on his reading, inexpressibility (*avaktavyatva*) fills in the lacuna in our knowledge, when we are unable to determine either of two values, i.e. "male" or "female", and instead we use a third term. The practical application of the three terms (existence, non-existence and inexpressibility) to the linguistic usage shows that apparently "inexpressibility" might be used, one could argue, as a third logical value. However, this is probably not what Malliṣeṇa wants to say: although the term *napuṃsaka* does normally refer to a third sex ("neither male [nor female]"), in this case such an interpretation can easily be dismissed on the ground that, under ordinary conditions, what is born of the womb can either be a girl or a boy, not a hermaphrodite ("a third value"). The inability to determine whether "a girl will be born of the womb" or "a boy will be born of the womb" resembles the problem of a future sea battle discussed by Aristotle in Chapter 9 of Περὶ 'Ερμηνείας (*De Interpretatione*), esp. 18a29–39. Out of two contradictory statements about a future sea battle, either "it is the case that a sea battle will take place tomorrow" is true, and the latter false, or "it is not the case that a sea battle will take place tomorrow" is true, and the former false. However, "since propositions are true as they correspond with facts" (18a33), so, as long as there is no tomorrow yet, both affirmation and denial have the same character: they remain undecided. There is one important difference, though, between Malliṣeṇa's "either boy or girl" case and Aristotle's "sea battle" dilemma: as long as a new day has not dawned yet, there is no corresponding fact, as an objective criterion of truth of propositions, against which we could determine which of two contradictory propositions is true, whereas in the former case the objective fact, in the form of a foetus in the womb, is there, but we are merely incapable of determining which of the two propositions corresponds to it. One could argue that, apparently, what this practical usage of the *syād-vāda* reveals is that a proposition "in a certain sense, the foetus *x* conceived in the womb is inexpressible" simply means that it is impossible to express jointly that "*x* is a boy" and "*x* is a girl", but this only evades the real problem of how to relate this practical example to the theoretical structure devised by the Jainas. Clearly what it demonstrates is that inexpressible propositions are also such the truth value of which we are unable to determine, although the facts to which the propositions correspond are there but remain beyond our knowledge.

The idea of simultaneity can, as Akalaṅka points out, easily be replaced with the idea of "equal expressive force" applied to both properties one wishes to predicate of the thing:

> Alternatively, [the figure] is inexpressible because two properties of equal force, inasmuch as both function as primary, cannot be expressly predicated of a real thing as qualities both of which one intends to express, due to the fact that, when verbal designation of one impedes verbal designation of the other, that would entail either that [the object] would be contrary to what one accepts or it would have no qualities.[96]

As he indicates,[97] various other parameters, not necessarily the time factor alone, can be used as criteria of emphasis, the main idea of which is to facilitate a reference point that determines what particular feature can either be affirmed or denied of an object, viz. in what sense a particular thing "is P" and in what sense it "is not-Q". Due to purely practical or verbal limitations, but certainly not logical constraints, the affirmation or denial cannot be asserted of one and the same object simultaneously.

That the problem of inexpressibility of the third (or fourth) figure does not concern logic but is a matter of limited verbal means at our disposal is quite a popular stand, and Akalaṅka is not an exception. The idea is echoed, e.g., by Abhayadeva-sūri (early eleventh century) in the *Tattva-bodha-vidhāyinī*:

> The first figure is used in the sense of demonstrating existence [of *x* as P], in which the subordinate element is non-existence [of *x* as Q]. The second [figure] is used in the sense of demonstrating the [non-existence of *x* as Q]

> by the transposition of the [first figure]. However, there is no single term capable of demonstrating these two properties either as [simultaneously] primary or as [simultaneously] secondary, because in the first place there is no compounded expression that can demonstrate these [two] nor a [singular] sentence [expressive of both] is possible.[98]

His analysis of all verbal means that could potentially be handy in expressing first two figures in one breath,[99] Abhayadeva-sūri concludes with the claim that

> Simultaneous [application] of these two figures (sc. assertion and denial) is inexpressible, because such [a statement that could express the two jointly] is void of the form [conforming to that] which could be predicated of in such a way, [i.e. affirmatively or negatively].[100]

The above quotations, as well as a number of other passages, including those of the *Tattvârtha-rāja-vārttika* 4.42 (*vide infra*, p. 38), attest to the fact that, within in the framework of the seven figures, the elements of seemingly contradictory attributes ("existence" and "non-existence"), taken either alone or in combinations, are not given equal treatment but are treated in a qualified manner, i.e. as primary or secondary.

The idea of consecutiveness and simultaneity, especially embedded in the "inexpressible" proposition, does not refer only to the time factor, but there are certain other parameters that should not to be confused with the first-order parameters of substance, place, time and condition, mentioned above (p. 31 f.), which determine the context of the predicate P. The traditional enumeration of second-order parameters[101] comprises additional reference points, which may be instrumental in determining from what perspective we can speak of "simultaneous" application or "equal expressive force" (*tulya-bala*), to use Akalaṅka's expression, of the predicates. To be exact, they provide the context for the idea of emphasis applicable in each and every case.[102]

What is called "simultaneity" (*yaugapadya*) involves the application of one and the same parameter taken as the point of reference which one wishes to apply to various properties affirmed or denied of one and the same thing. In other words, "simultaneous" predications are those which predicate two incompatible sets of properties of numerically one object from exactly the same reference point, which is elucidated by Akalaṅka:

> As regards these [second-order parameters], [when some] properties happen to be contradictory with respect to one factor α, and the relevance of these [factors] αs is not observed with regard to one and the same thing at one and the same point of time β; hence there is no speech element to express both of them, because [speech] does not function in this way.[103]

In a longer section Malliṣeṇa[104] replicates more or less the contents of respective sections of the *Tattvârtha-rāja-vārttika*, and explains in more detail how the second-order parameters operate. We have seen that the list of second-order parameters includes also second-order time-parameters, i.e. exact temporal reference points that index a basic parameter of time as distinguished from basic parameters of substance, place and condition. For instance we can both assert and deny particular properties of a given object with reference to time (as distinguished from predication with reference to, e.g., place, substance and condition), but we can apply different time points:

> As regards these [second-order parameters], in the figure: "in a certain sense, a real thing such as the soul etc. is indeed [P]", existence [is predicated of] at a given time *t*, but all the remaining innumerable properties existing at the same time *t* also occur in the same numerically one object [which are not expressed] – this is the procedure of non-differentiation with respect to time.[105]

As we have seen, the idea of emphasized property means that the property not emphasized is implied but not expressed, and the relationship between the emphasized and not-emphasized properties is often likened to the case of the inference (*anumāna*) based on the negative concomitance (*vyatireka*), which is necessarily implied by a positive proof formula that is based on positive concomitance (*anvaya*), albeit it is not expressed. Just as positive and negative kinds of concomitance are logically equivalent, but one still sees the need to state them both consecutively out of practical, rhetorical or didactic considerations, likewise it is not completely meaningless to formulate a separate negative proposition of the *syān nâsti* type that explicitly denies certain not-emphasized properties, although such denial is already implied by the positive proposition of the *syād asti* type, as Mallişeṇa explains:

> For the existence of a proving property such as existent character etc. with respect to a particular inferable property such as impermanence etc. is not explicable without [implying its] non-existence in dissimilar instances, because [otherwise] that would lead to an undesired consequence that this [proving property] could not have the status of a proving property. Therefore, the existence of a real thing is inseparably connected with its non-existence, and its non-existence is [inseparably connected] with its [existence]. And their main and subordinate characters depend on the intention [of the speaker].[106]

As we know, the occurrence of a proving property (*sādhana*) in all loci of an inferable property (*sādhya*), i.e. in similar instances (*sapakṣa*), which is the scope of positive concomitance (*anvaya*), is logically related to the non-occurrence of the inferable property (*sādhya*) in all loci that are not loci of the proving property (*sādhana*), i.e. in all dissimilar instances (*vipakṣa*), which is a case of negative concomitance (*vyatireka*). That is precisely the link which Mallişeṇa wishes to establish also in the case of a *syāt* figure that affirms a certain property and a *syāt* figure that denies other properties.

How closely the concepts of two kinds of invariable concomitance (*vyāpti*) and the idea of properties affirmed and denied in the *syād-vāda* correspond to each other is highlighted in another passage of the *Syād-vāda-mañjarī*, devoted mainly to the idea of the particular (*viśeṣa*) and negative concomitance (*vyatireka*) and in which no direct reference is made to the doctrine of multiplexity of reality (*anekānta-vāda*):

> And it is this [negative concomitance] that excludes itself from other [entities] belonging to the same class (sc. similar) and from [entities] belonging to a different class (sc. dissimilar) by means of substance, place, time and condition, and acquires the designation "the particular". For this reason one should not come to the conclusion that the universal and the particular are two different as two separate ontological categories.[107]

The passage attempts to establish a link between the particular and the universal as two opposites that are based on the negative idea of exclusion the basis of which is the logical rule of negative concomitance. What is conspicuous in the passage is an explicit reference to "substance, place, time and condition" as criteria that make the exclusion possible; and these are precisely the same four parameters that are at play in the *syād-vāda*, called here first-order parameters.

We can therefore introduce a new symbol ε for "emphasis" to a model sentence in our formalization attempt as follows:

$$\forall x \,.\, \exists\sigma\ \sigma\colon \mathrm{P}^{\pi\varepsilon}x$$

For every real thing (*vastu*) x, there is always a particular perspective σ such that it can be interpreted as parameter π with respect to which x is P and the property P is emphasized under condition ε.

I will use the symbol ε "property under emphasis", or "emphasized property", and ε for "property under no emphasis", or "property not emphasized".

Let us see, at least provisionally, before a final attempt of formalization (pp. 38 ff.), how the idea of emphasis can accordingly be applied formally. Closely following Malliṣeṇa's interpretation of SVM_1 23.113–119, p. 143.12–18 (*vide supra*, p. 27 f.), in a manner which is a recurrent theme in many other earlier works, Yaśovijaya (c. 1600) describes, in his *Jaina-tarka-bhāṣā*,[108] the first figure *syād asty eva ghaṭaḥ* under four parameters:

[1] "In a certain sense, i.e. with respect to substance ***S***, a given pot x exists as being made of clay" ($\mathrm{A}^{S1}x$) and "with respect to substance ***S***, a given pot x does not exist as something made of water" ($\neg\mathrm{B}^{S2}x$): $\mathrm{A}^{S1\varepsilon 1}x$ & $\neg\mathrm{B}^{S2\varepsilon 0}x$;

[2] "In a certain sense, i.e. with respect to place ***O***, a given pot x exists in the city of Pāṭaliputra" ($\mathrm{C}^{O1}x$) and "with respect to place ***O***, a given pot x does not exist in the city of Kānyakubja" ($\neg\mathrm{D}^{O2}x$): $\mathrm{C}^{O1\varepsilon 1}x$ & $\neg\mathrm{D}^{O1\varepsilon 0}x$;

[3] "In a certain sense, i.e. with respect to time ***T***, a given pot x exists in the

autumn" ($E^{T_1}x$) and "with respect to time ***T***, a given pot *x* does not exist in the spring" ($\neg F^{T_2}x$): $E^{T_1\varepsilon_1}x$ & $\neg F^{T_2\varepsilon_0}x$;

[4] "In a certain sense, i.e. with respect to condition ***C***, a given pot *x* exists as something black" ($G^{C_1}x$) and "with respect to condition ***C***, a given pot *x* does not exist as something red" ($\neg H^{C_2}x$): $G^{C_1\varepsilon_1}x$ & $\neg H^{C_2\varepsilon_0}x$.

How exactly the process of disambiguation takes place through the application of the idea of emphasis is further explained by Akalaṅka in the *Tattvârtha-rāja-vārttika*:

> All figures are useful and meaningful because they aim at demonstrating particular distinction between secondary and primary character. Namely, (1) when substance-expressive [perspective] is considered as primary and modes (qualities) are taken to be secondary, this is the first [figure: P*x*]. (2) When mode-expressive [perspective] is considered as primary and substance is taken to be secondary, this is the second [figure: ¬Q*x*]. In this case, the primary character depends on verbal means, because it is expressly intended (sc. conveyed) by the speech element; whereas that which is not expressed by the speech element and what can be understood from the context has non-primary (sc. secondary) character. (3) In the third [figure "inexpressible"] on the other hand, which is of simultaneous character, both have non-primary (sc. secondary) character, because neither of them is expressed by the speech element as the subject-matter (sc. content) [of the statement]. (4) The fourth [figure], in its turn, has both [aspects] as primary, because both are expressed consecutively by the speech element "exists" etc. In this manner, the remaining figures will be explained.[109]

For Akalaṅka, the figure "inexpressible" is equivalent to the situation when neither of the two properties is expressed, i.e. both of them are subordinate, or "non-primary" (*aprādhānya*). This stand will have important implications for my attempt at formalization.

Formalization

Having taken all the above, I propose the following way to formalize the seven propositions of the *syād-vāda*:

	bhaṅga	**formalization 1:**
1	*syād asti*	$P^{\pi_1\varepsilon_1}x$
2	*syān nâsti*	$\neg P^{\pi_2\varepsilon_1}x$
3	*syād avaktavyam*	$P^{\pi_1\varepsilon_0}x$ & $\neg P^{\pi_2\varepsilon_0}x$
4	*syād asti nâsti*	$P^{\pi_1\varepsilon_1}x$ & $\neg P^{\pi_2\varepsilon_1}x$
5	*syād asty avaktavyam*	$P^{\pi_1\varepsilon_1}x$ & $P^{\pi_1\varepsilon_0}x$ & $\neg P^{\pi_2\varepsilon_0}x$
6	*syān nâsty avaktavyam*	$\neg P^{\pi_2\varepsilon_1}x$ & $P^{\pi_1\varepsilon_0}x$ & $\neg P^{\pi_2\varepsilon_0}x$
7	*syād asti nâsty avaktavyam*	$P^{\pi_1\varepsilon_1}x$ & $\neg P^{\pi_2\varepsilon_1}x$ & $P^{\pi_1\varepsilon_0}x$ & $\neg P^{\pi_2\varepsilon_0}x$

where P is a predicate variable, and comprises a range of positive predicates R {A, C, E, G,…} and a range of negative predicates Q {B, D, F, H,…} (*vide supra*, p. 28); π is a set of the first-order parameters {*S*, *O*, *T*, *C*} of substance, place (occurrence), time and condition (*vide supra*, p. 32), which determine in what sense predicate P is to be understood; ε is emphasis, which indicates that a given property is either expressed (ε_1) or suppressed (ε_0).

How to read this? For instance, $P^{\pi 1 \varepsilon 1}x$ states that an assertion that an object x is P should be understood through a certain first-order parameter π (π_1), e.g. "in view of its substance, a jar is made of clay", and it is verbally emphasized (ε_1), i.e. the predicate is expressly stated in language. The second figure $\neg P^{\pi 2 \varepsilon 1}x$ means a proposition stating that the same object x is not P should be understood through some other first-order parameter π (π_2), e.g. "in view of its substance, a jar is not made of water", and likewise it is verbally emphasized (ε_1). The third figure $P^{\pi 1 \varepsilon 0}x$ & $\neg P^{\pi 2 \varepsilon 0}x$ expresses an idea that the object x is both $P^{\pi 1}$ and is not $P^{\pi 2}$, but no single term or expression can convey this complex meaning, hence the properties in question are verbally suppressed (ε_0).

On this reading, we can see that all the seven figures do not overlap and in each of them the component predicates are not repeated, for instance in figure 7 ($P^{\pi 1 \varepsilon 1}x$ & $\neg P^{\pi 2 \varepsilon 1}x$ & $P^{\pi 1 \varepsilon 0}x$ & $\neg P^{\pi 2 \varepsilon 0}x$) no element occurs twice. It is because the "inexpressible" proposition holds only when both properties are not emphasized at the same time. This corresponds to Akalaṅka's reading of the figure "inexpressible", in which both properties are not emphasized, or "non-primary" (*vide supra*, p. 38), viz. both are conveyed with equally suppressed "expressive force".

The compound predicates $P^{\pi 1}$ (affirmed) and $P^{\pi 2}$ (denied) can be easily replaced with simpler predicate variables, say, A and ¬B, respectively, however first-order parameter π that indexes predicate P, or rather a predicate variable P, shows that we move in the same range of properties or with the same "onto-logical context", e.g. we refer either to a certain substantial aspect of the thing only (predicate: substance), or to its certain situational aspect only (predicate: place/occurrence) etc., and these levels are not confused or intermixed.[110] For instance, if we take substance S as the value of first-order parameter π, then we have the following table:

1	*syād asti*	$P^{S_1 \varepsilon_1}x$
2	*syān nâsti*	$\neg P^{S_2 \varepsilon_1}x$
3	*syād avaktavyam*	$P^{S_1 \varepsilon_0}x$ & $\neg P^{S_2 \varepsilon_0}x$
4	*syād asti nâsti*	$P^{S_1 \varepsilon_1}x$ & $\neg P^{S_2 \varepsilon_1}x$
5	*syād asty avaktavyam*	$P^{S_1 \varepsilon_1}x$ & $P^{S_1 \varepsilon_0}x$ & $\neg P^{S_2 \varepsilon_0}x$
6	*syān nâsty avaktavyam*	$\neg P^{S_2 \varepsilon_1}x$ & $P^{S_1 \varepsilon_0}x$ & $\neg P^{S_2 \varepsilon_0}x$
7	*syād asti nâsty avaktavyam*	$P^{S_1 \varepsilon_1}x$ & $\neg P^{S_2 \varepsilon_1}x$ & $P^{S_1 \varepsilon_0}x$ & $\neg P^{S_2 \varepsilon_0}x$

Similarly, one can take place, time and condition as reference points, and in each of such sets of predications one remains within the range delimited by one and the same parameter, albeit it can assume various values. Akalaṅka's suggestion to take the properties in figure 3 "inexpressible" as not emphasized produces a relatively simple model that involves no further problems.

In contradistinction to Akalaṅka's solution, however, for whom inexpressibility concerns verbal communication in which no positive and no negative aspect is expressed and what follows is silence, most authors take *avaktavya* to be the case when both properties are emphasized at the same time, viz. when one intends to expressly convey both of them but lacks the appropriate verbal means. In their opinion, inexpressibility is the case when one intends to verbally highlight two aspects, one positive and one negative, but simply lacks verbal means to accomplish this. That being the case, our table should be changed to the following:

	bhaṅga	**formalization 2:**
1	*syād asti*	$P^{\pi_1\varepsilon_1}x$
2	*syān nâsti*	$\neg P^{\pi_2\varepsilon_1}x$
3	*syād avaktavyam*	$P^{\pi_1\varepsilon_1}x \;\&\; \neg P^{\pi_2\varepsilon_1}x$
4	*syād asti nâsti*	$P^{\pi_1\varepsilon_1}x \;\&\; \neg P^{\pi_2\varepsilon_1}x$
5	*syād asty avaktavyam*	$P^{\pi_1\varepsilon_1}x \;\&\; P^{\pi_1\varepsilon_1}x \;\&\; \neg P^{\pi_2\varepsilon_1}x$
6	*syān nâsty avaktavyam*	$\neg P^{\pi_2\varepsilon_1}x \;\&\; P^{\pi_1\varepsilon_1}x \;\&\; \neg P^{\pi_2\varepsilon_1}x$
7	*syād asti nâsty avaktavyam*	$P^{\pi_1\varepsilon_1}x \;\&\; \neg P^{\pi_2\varepsilon_1}x \;\&\; P^{\pi_1\varepsilon_1}x \;\&\; \neg P^{\pi_2\varepsilon_1}x$

This reading, with the two properties emphasized in figure 3 "inexpressible", reveals that figure 3 is basically identical to figure 4 "affirmation and denial". We should, therefore, introduce a third kind of emphasis ε_2, beside lack of emphasis ε_0, to account for the distinction between simultaneity (both properties are equally emphasized: ε_1) and consecutiveness (one property is emphasized as ε_1, whereas the other property is subsequently emphasized as ε_2):

	bhaṅga	**formalization 3:**
1	*syād asti*	$P^{\pi_1\varepsilon_1}x$
2	*syān nâsti*	$\neg P^{\pi_2\varepsilon_1}x$
3	*syād avaktavyam*	$P^{\pi_1\varepsilon_1}x \;\&\; \neg P^{\pi_2\varepsilon_1}x$
4	*syād asti nâsti*	$P^{\pi_1\varepsilon_1}x \;\&\; \neg P^{\pi_2\varepsilon_2}x$
5	*syād asty avaktavyam*	$P^{\pi_1\varepsilon_1}x \;\&\; P^{\pi_1\varepsilon_1}\mathrm{x} \;\&\; \neg P^{\pi_2\varepsilon_1}x$
6	*syān nâsty avaktavyam*	$\underline{\neg P^{\pi_2\varepsilon_1}x} \;\&\; \underline{P^{\pi_1\varepsilon_1}x} \;\&\; \neg P^{\pi_2\varepsilon_1}x$
7a	*syād asti nâsty avaktavyam* [conjunction of fig. 1, 2, 3]	$\underline{P^{\pi_1\varepsilon_1}x} \;\&\; \underline{\underline{\neg P^{\pi_2\varepsilon_1}x}} \;\&\; \underline{P^{\pi_1\varepsilon_1}x} \;\&\; \underline{\underline{\neg P^{\pi_2\varepsilon_1}x}}$
7b	*syād asti nâsty avaktavyam* [conjunction of fig. 4, 3]	$\underline{P^{\pi 1\varepsilon 1}x} \;\&\; \neg P^{\pi 2\varepsilon 2}x \;\&\; \underline{P^{\pi_1\varepsilon_1}x} \;\&\; \neg P^{\pi_2\varepsilon_1}x$

This interpretation reveals serious redundancy: the elements which are repeated are underlined.

Furthermore, the problem with the above formalization is that it does not take into account all what Malliṣeṇa and Yaśovijaya say (p. 27 and 37). For instance, this approach overlooks the idea that affirmation of $P^{\pi 1}$ entails negation of $\neg P^{\pi 2}$, albeit it is implied ("not emphasized") and not explicit. That being the case, we would have to redraft the table as follows:

	bhaṅga	**formalization 4:**
1	*syād asti*	$P^{\pi_1\varepsilon_1}x \,\&\, \neg P^{\pi_2\varepsilon_0}x$
2	*syān nâsti*	$\neg P^{\pi_2\varepsilon_1}x \,\&\, P^{\pi_1\varepsilon_0}x$
3	*syād avaktavyam*	$P^{\pi_1\varepsilon_1}x \,\&\, \neg P^{\pi_2\varepsilon_1}x$
4	*syād asti nâsti*	$P^{\pi_1\varepsilon_1}x \,\&\, \neg P^{\pi_2\varepsilon_2}x$
5	*syād asty avaktavyam*	$P^{\pi_1\varepsilon_1}x \,\&\, \neg P^{\pi_2\varepsilon_0}x \,\&\, P^{\pi_1\varepsilon_1}x \,\&\, \neg P^{\pi_2\varepsilon_1}x$
6	*syān nâsty avaktavyam*	$\neg P^{\pi_2\varepsilon_1}x \,\&\, P^{\pi_1\varepsilon_0}x \,\&\, P^{\pi_1\varepsilon_1}x \,\&\, \neg P^{\pi_2\varepsilon_1}x$
7a	*syād asti nâsty avaktavyam*	$\underline{P^{\pi_1\varepsilon_1}x} \,\&\, \neg P^{\pi_2\varepsilon_0}x \,\&\, \underline{\underline{\neg P^{\pi_2\varepsilon_1}x}} \,\&\, P^{\pi_1\varepsilon_0}x \,\&$
	[conjunction of fig. 1, 2, 3]	$\underline{P^{\pi_1\varepsilon_1}x} \,\&\, \underline{\neg P^{\pi_2\varepsilon_1}x}$
7b	*syād asti nâsty avaktavyam* [conjunction of fig. 4, 3]	$\underline{P^{\pi_1\varepsilon_1}x} \,\&\, \neg P^{\pi_2\varepsilon_2}x \,\&\, \underline{P^{\pi_1\varepsilon_1}x} \,\&\, \neg P^{\pi_2\varepsilon_1}x$

However, also in the fourth attempt we discover that again some components (underlined) turn out to be redundant! The case is that whatever variants we can conceive of, granted both are properties emphasized in the "inexpressible" figure, we will always find some elements in the final analysis redundant, especially in figures 5, 6 and 7. Therefore, for the sake of relative elegance, consistency and, perhaps, optimality, one should follow Akalaṅka in his interpretation of figure 3, in which both properties are not emphasized (formalization 1).

Worth noting here is a compromising position taken by Abhayadeva-sūri who maintains that the figure "inexpressible" may be due to the fact that either both properties are emphasized or that both properties are not emphasized, i.e. it is the case whenever the properties share the same kind of emphasis.[111] As a matter of fact, his position is foreshadowed by Akalaṅka's mention of "equal expressive force" (*tulya-bala*).[112]

Such reformulations, conspicuous in formalizations 2–4, reveal certain inconsistencies which are, in my opinion, not of logical nature but concern redundancy. My claim is that with Malliṣeṇa's and Yaśovijaya's interpretations, and these are most representative of Jaina tradition, according to which both properties are equally emphasized in figure 3 "inexpressible", we will never bypass redundancies in figures 5, 6 and 7, and that is why I would rather take formalization 1 (Akalaṅka) as the most consistent representation of the *syād-vāda*.

Final remarks

A major concern of all interpretations of the *syād-vāda* is whether the Jaina model indeed yields any type of inconsistency or paraconsistency, and if it does, on which level. These inconsistencies, of still new nature, that surfaced in the above exposition of two different takes at the *syād-vāda* – Akalaṅka's, on the one hand, and Malliṣeṇa's and Yaśovijaya's, on the other – reveal an important feature of the theory of the seven-fold modal description: we should no longer speak of a uniform Jaina tradition or a homogenous interpretation of the theory, whereas the modern formalization attempts discussed in § 2 tend to conceal this important historical fact, inasmuch as the tendency has usually been to present the theory as a consistent project. Rather, researchers should compare and separately analyse different expositions of the *syād-vāda* theory produced by various Jaina thinkers instead of imposing their preconceived beliefs in the homogeneity of Jaina intellectual tradition.

Further, it seems that a solution to the redundancy problem of the *syād-vāda* that surfaces if one takes the "inexpressible" to mean that two properties are simultaneously emphasized (Malliṣeṇa's and Yaśovijaya's interpretation) lies in accepting the fact that what the theory is about is not really logical relations but rather semantics and our usage of natural languages: its main practical import is to demonstrate to what degree every proposition is context-dependent. The "logical" approach will probably never solve the problem of redundancy in the sense that it is unlikely that one will once present the theory as an absolutely consistent, redundancy-proof and error-free model. Rather, the purpose of formalization attempts and formal models should be a lucid presentation through which one could more clearly see the limitations of a particular interpretation of all the seven figures adopted by presented by a particular Jaina thinker. As we have seen, the problematic predication "inexpressible" (*avaktavya*) is a result neither of logically indeterminate character of a variable nor of undecided nature or status of an entity, either logically or ontologically or otherwise. That is lucidly demonstrated through the instances of the name "Puṣpadanta" and the term "SaT" (*vide supra*, p. 30).

There arises a very important question in the general context of the Jaina doctrine of multiplexity of reality (*anekānta-vāda*), which is known to comprise three theories: *nikṣepa-vāda*, *naya-vāda* and *syād-vāda*, which complement each other. Especially the latter two make an impression that somehow their application overlaps and, indeed, most researchers seem to have treated them jointly, without making a conscious effort to distinguish them or to keep their respective applications distinct. What is then a practical difference of the doctrine of viewpoints (*naya-vāda*) and the method of the seven-fold modal description (*sapta-bhaṅgī, syād-vāda*)?

The former takes any potentially meaningful sentence as context-dependent and assigns to it a context within which the sentence is true. The *naya-vāda* states that, as far as a real thing (*vastu*) is considered, only one aspect of it can be taken into account, albeit the whole range of possible applications and references of the sentence can be conceived of, but these would become meaningful only within a correspondingly delimited range of context. That is why the *naya-vāda* is called an "incomplete account" (*vikalâdeśa*), because only one context, out of many, can be verbally expressed by a sentence and is applicable to a particular object under a particular viewpoint. In other words, the *naya-vāda* takes a sentence as an object of its analysis and selects a particular context as its proper reference, out of many possible applications. According to this theory, all utterances are in fact incomplete sentences, and the task of the theory is to determine a proper context for a particular sentence by assigning to it its proper point of reference, which is a particular viewpoint. In other words, one sets off with a particular utterance, which is by nature ambiguous, and searches for such a viewpoint, or for an "indexed level of description",[113] under which the sentence is true and relevant. Thus, the primary object of the *naya-vāda* are statements and their application.

The idea of the "incomplete account" (*vikalâdeśa*), or partial description of an object, which is merely a "side-effect" of the strategy to assign proper reference to a proposition, is crucial in the way viewpoints operate, whereas cognitive criteria are characterized by the "complete account" (*sakalâdeśa*). The idea is often repeated in Jaina philosophical works and finds its succinct form in an unidentified, often quoted passage:

> Complete account rests on cognitive criteria, [whereas] incomplete account rests on viewpoints.[114]

In contradistinction to the *naya-vāda*, the seven-fold modal description takes a real thing (*vastu*) as the object of its analysis and searches for all possible statements that can be made about it. That is why it is called a "complete account" (*sakalâdeśa*),[115] insofar as all possible perspectives relevant in the verbal description of a thing are thereby taken into account. This idea was rather to accommodate all propositions that are conceivable with regard to one and the same object: each of the figures as a distinct locutionary act presents a new context or reveals its new aspect (*deśa*), but does not necessarily have its own distinct truth-value different from truth or falsity.[116] Also, the theory of the seven-fold modal description acts on the presumption that all utterances are incomplete sentences, but the difference as compared to a similar assumption of the *naya-vāda* concerns the fact that a sentence undergoes the process of disambiguation through the process of establishing a referential link with its object, which is merely one of innumerable aspects of a real thing. To put it more precisely, one tries to offer a complete account of a real thing and formulates a whole spectrum of assertions and denials about the thing, and the meaning of each and every particular sentence in the seven-fold scheme of such assertions and denials is thereby determined, as if incidentally: it is, so to say, a side effect of the description of a particular real thing in its various aspects. These aspects are proper denotata of a particular sentence, not the real thing as such.

Last but not least, Bimal Krishna Matilal is reported to once have expressed his conviction that

> The Jainas contend that one should try to understand the particular point of view of each disputing party if one wishes to grasp completely the truth of the situation. The total truth ... may be derived from the *integration* of all different viewpoints.[117]

This and similar opinions expressed by Matilal,[118] repeatedly circulated, were reiterated by Ganeri (2002: 279) who maintained "'that every standpoint reveals a facet of reality, and that, to get a full description of the world, what we need to do is to *synthesise* the various standpoints". This opinion seems to be dominant among modern researchers and, in my opinion, should be revised.

Interestingly enough, in order to incorporate various theories or worldviews into a consistent whole, the Jainas in their textual expositions never apply the *syād-vāda*; instead they use a different model, which is the sevenfold method of "conditionally valid predications" (*naya-vāda*). As a rule, we find their attempt to give a meaning to each of various philosophical schools and standpoints in a consistent holistic framework in the context of the *naya-vāda*, contrary to what some researchers would expect. On the other hand, "the doctrine of the sevenfold modal description" (*sapta-bhaṅgī*) is primarily discussed in three contexts: that of the triple nature of reality, which is believed to consist of "origination, continuation and decay", that of the relation between the universal and the particular,[119] and that of the relationship between the substance and its properties/modes. In short, all these questions could be reduced to that of "the identity problem": how it is possible that a complex entity, composite and extended in space and time, is one and preserves its identity despite its transformations and similarities to other entities. This finds corroboration in Hemacandra's *Anya-yoga-vyavaccheda-dvātriṃśikā* 25:

> In a certain sense, any thing (lit. "this very [thing]") is [both] perishing and permanent. In a certain sense, any thing is [both] similar (sc. universal) and unique (particular). In a certain sense, any thing is communicable and incommunicable. In a certain sense, any thing is existent and non-existent. O Lord, this [seven-fold modal description] is the tradition the stream[120] of which proceeds forth as nectar of truth enjoyed by the wise.[121]

In this poetically rather awkward verse, Hemacandra aptly sketches the four main thematic groups to which usually the *syād-vāda* is most commonly applied. And indeed, most examples of the application of "the doctrine of the seven-fold modal description" we come across in various works essentially pertain to one and the same issue: how to preserve the integrity of a composite thing, a problem which is entailed by the question of the relation between permanence and change, also phrased in terms of the question of how to relate the whole and its parts. However, the *syād-vāda* is never applied to doxographic analysis or as an instrument to construct typologies of various doctrines or to pigeonhole the opponents.

Hemacandra, followed by his commentator Malliṣeṇa,[122] as well as all other Jaina authors[123] I have come across correlate particular theories and views represented by particular thinkers and philosophical schools only under the scheme of the viewpoints (*naya-vāda*). Malliṣeṇa is not unique in the way he maps doxography onto respective erroneous viewpoints (*durnaya*):

> The Naiyāyika and Vaiśeṣika are the followers of the view of the comprehensive viewpoint. All monistic doctrines with no exception and the Sāṃkhya school are prompted by the intention [expressed] through the

> collective viewpoint. The materialist school predominantly falls into [the category] the empirical viewpoint. The Buddhists[124] are those whose minds are prompted by the perspective of the direct viewpoint. The grammarians etc. stick to verbal and other viewpoints, [i.e. the etymological viewpoint and the factual viewpoint].[125]

Clearly, an attempt to classify the whole spectrum of philosophical doctrines is undertaken in a separate section of Malliṣeṇa's work, after he has concluded the examination of the *syād-vāda,* and it is only in this context of the viewpoints (*naya*) that one can meaningfully talk of integrating various doctrinal positions and opinions. In the same spirit, Siddhasena Divākara establishes a correlation between the number of viewpoints which can be accommodated within the scheme of the *naya-vāda* and the multitude of doctrines and opinions:

> There are as many accounts via viewpoints as there are possibilities of expressing [views]. Likewise, there are as many heretic doctrines as there are accounts through viewpoints.[126]

This verse demonstrates that, from relatively early times, it was the doctrine of viewpoints, not the method of the seven-fold modal description, that was exclusively used by the Jainas to handle doctrinal divisions and allocate them within particular compartments of the *naya-vāda*. Following this reasoning, the Jainas could indeed say that one reaches truth if one integrates all partial positions which are false when taken uncompromisingly as only true, as it was put by Matilal (*vide supra,* p. 42). That conviction is expressed in a concluding verse of the *Saṃmati-tarka-prakaraṇa*:

> [Let there be] prosperity to Jina's words that are made of an amassment of false views, that are conducive to immortality, that are venerable, and lead to the salvific happiness.[127]

In every viewpoint, as Siddhasena claims, there is some grain of truth because every opinion, even erroneous, has been formulated as relying on some kind of justification or empirical data. Just as, for an epistemic realist, no false mental image can be absolutely mistaken, and its falsity may be due to some kind of misapprehended correlation of real components that are true reflections of reality this way or another, in the same way even false beliefs are somehow grounded in facts, at least to a minimum degree. One can, therefore, make a claim that, metaphorically, the whole truth encompasses all such partial false views that result from a restricted vision or limited understanding of the world. But even the above opinion of Siddhasena shows that spheres of application of the *syād-vāda* and of the *naya-vāda* should not be conflated or confused: all Siddhasena says concerns only the latter. Such a conflation of the two separate realms must have been responsible for Bimal Krishna Matilal's (1991: 15) opinion, and that mistake is occasionally committed, that

> The Jainas ... believe that each proposition, at least each metaphysical proposition, has the value "Inexpressible" (in addition to having other values, true, false etc.). That is, there is some interpretation or some point of view, under which the given proposition would be undecidable so far as its truth or falsity is concerned, and hence could be evaluated as "Inexpressible". Likewise the same proposition, under another interpretation, could be evaluated "true" and under still another interpretation, "false".

A situation when one seeks an accurate point of view under which a given proposition can be interpreted as true, false etc., viz. when one attempts to determine a proper context for the proposition, is not, as we have just seen, a domain of application of the *syād-vāda*, but that of the *naya-vāda*. It is also never the case, under the *naya-vāda*, that the truth value of a proposition is indeterminate, because the interpretative scheme is optimal and allows to always allocate a proper context to a meaningful proposition.

There is still one more remark to make and it concerns what I would call the "tolerance myth" of Jainism, repeated in large circles of scholars and Jaina laity. In its popular form the tolerance myth states that the doctrine of multiplexity of reality was developed by the Jainas, or even by Mahāvīra himself, both as an expression of their intellectual non-violence and tolerance as well as in order to accommodate all conflicting worldviews with the aim of achieving reconciliation or promoting tolerance. In his relatively widely circulated book Matilal (1981) expresses this conviction on numerous occasions, just to mention a few citations:

> It is possible that the well-known moral doctrine of Jainism, i.e. *ahimsā* "non-violence" was partly responsible for the development of the *anekānta* attitude in Jaina philosophy
>
> (p. 4)

> Mahāvīra thus developed a philosophy of synthesis and toleration, which later came to be designated as the *anekānta-vāda*.... Mahāvīra's method was one of commitment, for he attempted to understand the points of view of the fighting parties (in a philosophical dispute) so that their dispute could be resolved and reconciled
>
> (p. 23)

> I think the Jainas carried the principle of non-violence to the intellectual level, and thus propounded their *anekānta* doctrine. Thus the hallmark of the *anekānta* was toleration. The principal embodied in the respect for the life of others was transformed by the Jaina philosophers at the intellectual level into respect for the view of others
>
> (p. 61)

Such an approach has penetrated the minds of researchers and students of Jainism to a degree that it has actually become a silent presupposition underlying a number of papers and books. One of the plausible sources of such an opinion, or at least of a corresponding term, is Dhruva (1933: lxxiv) where the seminal expression "intellectual *ahiṃsā*" appears for the first time. Dhruva's phrasing had an impact on similar opinions which Kāpaḍīā (1947: cxiv) expressed later.[128]

In his well-researched review of the dissemination and propagation of the myth, John Cort (2000: 324 f.) argues, and I could not agree more, that the modern understanding of Jaina tradition as intellectually pluralistic and tolerant

> is at odds with the one gained from investigating a wider range of sources than just the logic texts themselves.... If one looks at other aspects of the Jain religious worldview, in particular the Jain position on the proper path to liberation (*mokṣa-mārga*), one finds that the Jains accept other points of view as being at best only partially correct and therefore, inevitably, for the most part incorrect. In return, the Jains assert that only the Jain perspective is based on correct perception (*samyag-darśana*) and correct knowledge (*samyak-jñāna*), which are correct because they are rooted in the omniscience of the enlightened and liberated Jinas. Further, if one looks at narrative texts and other sources in which one finds expressions of Jain intellectual and social interaction with non-Jains, one finds that the Jains are frequently intolerant and disputatious in their interactions with non-Jains ... nowhere in traditional Jain sources is this spirit of toleration and coexistence characterized as "intellectual *ahiṃsā*".

Not only stories and narratives, legendary accounts or historical records belie a belief that Jaina spirit of *ahiṃsā* pervades the *anekānta-vāda*,[129] a belief that has in the meantime assumed a status of a prevalent article of faith of most modern Jainas, but we find absolutely nothing in Jaina philosophical texts, in which Jaina philosophers reflect either on the nature of non-violence or on the multiplexity of reality but never establish any link between these two themes, until the twentieth century which could lend even symbolic degree of justification for such a belief. On the contrary, the *anekānta-vāda* could be more accurately viewed both as an effective ideological weapon wielded against other religious traditions and philosophical schools,[130] which are thereby demonstrated to be merely one-sided and true in a very limited sense, and as an expression of the conviction on the part of the Jainas that, since they have such a powerful tool that comprises all partially true worldviews, it is them who enjoy intellectual superiority over other traditions and the supremacy of their salvific doctrine is thereby well grounded.

Jaina doctrine of multiplexity of reality pretends to provide a meta-philosophical vantage point, or present a supra-doxastic scheme that enables one to evaluate the truth and falsity, always said to be partial, of all particular philosophical claims and beliefs in a wider model of truth, available only to the Jainas. However, this claim, instead of promulgating tolerance and equal respect for other convictions, introduces a doctrine of two truths, in a way similar to what we know from, e.g., Mādhyamika or Yogācāra schools. The difference is that the ultimate truth (*paramârtha-satya*) is in Jaina hands. And it is in this sense that the *anekānta-vāda* can be treated, contrary to modern claims, as a kind of concealed intellectual violence (*hiṃsā*). Of course, this aspect of Jaina theory is in no way different from similar cases of intellectual violence exercised by other religious and philosophical traditions in a context of debate and rivalry in the sense that the latter, too, would waste no opportunity to take advantage of the strength of their own merits and arguments to secure their own privileged position in philosophical or public discourse. This should not obscure, however, obvious philosophical merits of the *syād-vāda*, and other components of the *anekānta-vāda*, which can justifiably be reckoned among most important contributions of Indian philosophy and continue to be a source of inspiration for logicians and philosophers. And the progression from earlier position to modern stance that takes the *anekānta-vāda* as an expression of *ahiṃsā* is socially noteworthy.

Notes

1 In my opinion there are strong intratextual reasons (putting the Digambara tradition aside) to claim that the author of the *Tattvârtha-sūtra* (c. 350–400) was a different person from the author of the *Tattvârthâdhigama-bhāṣya* (c. 400–450), a Śvetāmbara commentary thereon. That is why, in order to distinguish between these two authors, I take Umāsvāmin to be the author of the *Tattvârtha-sūtra* and Umāsvāti the author of the *Tattvârthâdhigama-bhāṣya.*

2 TS_1 5.29–31/TS_2 5.30–32: [29] *utpāda-vyaya-dhrauvya-yuktaṃ sat.* [30] *tad bhāvāvyayaṃ nityam.* [31] *arpitânarpita-siddheḥ.*

3 STP 3.1:

sāmaṇṇammi viseso visesa-pakkhe ya vayaṇa-viṇiveso /
davva-pariṇāmam aṇṇaṃ dāei tayaṃ ca ṇiyamei //

4 YA 40, p. 94:

sāmānya-niṣṭhā vividhā viśeṣāḥ padaṃ viśeṣântara-pakṣa-pāti /
antar-viśeṣântara-vṛttito 'nyat samāna-bhāvaṃ nayate viśeṣam //

5 ĀMĪ 57:

na sāmānyâtmanôdeti na vyeti vyaktam anvayāt /
vyety uedti viśeṣāt te sahâikatrôdayâdi sat //

6 LT 47:

kālâdi-lakṣaṇaṃ nyakṣeṇâyatrêkyaṃ parīkṣitam /
dravya-paryāya-sāmānya-viśeṣâtmârtha-niṣṭhitam //

7 See Balcerowicz (2001) and (2003).

8 NVi 1.3_1:

pratyakṣa-lakṣaṇaṃ prāhuḥ spaṣṭaṃ sākāram añjasā /
dravya-paryāya-sāmānya-viśeṣârthâtma-vedanam //

9 NVi_1 3.66_2 = NVi_1 451cd–452ab:

dravya-paryāya-sāmānya-viśeṣa-pravibhāgataḥ /
syād-vidhi-pratiṣedhābhyāṃ sapta-bhaṅgī pravartate //

10 E.g. SBhT. p. 16.10: ... *bhaṅgānāṃ vākyānāṃ*...

11 See. e.g. Hemacandra-sūri (1088–1172) in AYVD 28ab:

sad eva sat syāt sad iti tridhârtho mīyate durnīti-naya-pramāṇaiḥ /

A thing *x* can be determined in threefold manner as "*x* only is…", "in a certain sense, *x* is…", "*x* is…" by means of, respectively, erroneous presentations (viewpoints), viewpoints and cognitive criteria.

12 See e.g. Māilla-dhavala-[deva] (c. 1200) in ṆC 254ab, p. 128: *satteva huṃti bhaṅgā pamāṇa-ṇaya-duṇaya-bheda-juttāvi*/ ("There are as many as seven conditional perspectives with divisions as regards cognitive criteria, viewpoints and defective viewpoints"); Prabhācandra (eleventh century) in PKM 6.74, pp. 482 ff.; Vimaladāsa (fifteenth century) in SBhT 1.7, p. 16.1: *iyaṃ eva pramāṇa-sapta-bhaṅgī naya-sapta-bhaṅgīti ca kathyate*. See Balcerowicz (2003: 37).

Comp. also $JTBh_1$ 1.22 § 64, pp. 20.7–10: *sêyaṃ sapta-bhaṅgī pratibhaṅga(ṃ) sakalâdeśa-svabhāvā vikalâdeśa-svabhāvā ca. tatra pramāṇa-pratipannânanta-dharmâtmaka-vastunaḥ kālâdibhir abheda-vṛtti-prādhānyād abhedôpacārād vā yaugapadyena pratipādakaṃ vacaḥ sakalâdeśaḥ. naya-viṣayī-kṛtasya vastu-dharmasya bheda-vṛtti-prādhānyād bhedôpacārād vā krameṇâbhidhāyakaṃ vākyaṃ vikalâdeśaḥ.* Yasovijaya prefers a term *nayābhāsa* ("fallacy of a viewpoint") for *durnaya*, see $JTBh_1$ 2.2 § 11 (pp. 24.15 ff.) = $JTBh_2$, pp. 24.15 ff.

13 This is a shortened version of Matilal (1981).

14 For another case of this common mistake see e.g. Ganeri (2001: 138): "(1) asserting that the object is *F*; (2) denying that it is *F*; or (3) both asserting and denying that it is *F* (with different values of the hidden parameters)", etc.

15 John Cort (2000: 326 f.) copies the analysis of Matilal (1981) without acknowledging it.

16 PKM 6.74, pp. 681.22–23: *pratiparyāyaṃ vastuny ekatrâvirodhena vidhi-pratiṣedha-kalpanāyāḥ*.

17 Even for this reason alone the interpretation of the *syād-vāda* as a non-adjunctive system (see e.g. Ganeri 2002: 278, echoed by Schang 2008b: 5), which tries to bring meaningfulness into a discourse held by various parties, does not apply because we have here one and the same party and not really a multi-party discussion.

18 SVM_1 23.100–104, pp. 142.23–143.3: *ekatra jīvâdau vastuny ekâika-sattvâdi-dharma-viṣaya-praśna-vaśād avirodhena pratyakṣâdi-bādhā-parihāreṇa pṛthag-bhūtayoḥ samuditayoś ca vidhi-niṣedhayoḥ paryālocanayā kṛtvā syac-chabda-lāñchito vakṣyamānaiḥ saptabhiḥ prakārair vacana-vinyāsaḥ sapta-bhaṅgīti gīyate*. Cf. also SBhT, p. 3.1–2: *eka-vastu-viśeṣyakâviruddha-vidhi-pratiṣedhâtmaka-dharma-prakāraka-bodha-janaka-sapta-vākya-paryāpta-samudāyatvam*. This goes back to Prabhācandra's PKM 6.74, pp. 684.12–13: "*avirodhena*" *ity-abhidhānāt pratyakṣâdi-viruddha-vidhi-pratiṣedha-kalpanāyāḥ sapta-bhaṅgī-rūpatā pratyuktā*. – "With the term 'without contradition' we deny that the character of the seven-fold modal description consist of combinations of assertion and denial that stand in contradiction to perception etc."

19 Namely *syād avaktavyam, syād asty avaktavyam, syān nâsty avaktavyam* and *syād asti nâsty avaktavyam*.

20 DK 13B2: οἷον ἡψυχή ... ἡμετέρα άἡε οὖσα συγκρατεῖ ἡμᾶς, καὶ ὅλον τὸν κόσμον πνεῦμα καὶ ἀὴρ περιέχει. – "Like our soul, being the air, which holds us together and controls us, so does air and breath embrace the world around."

21 In other words, to say that "*x* has a property P" and to say that "*x* exists as having a property P" is one and the same thing.

22 PKM 6.74, pp. 683.7–19: *nanu ca prathama-dvitīya-dharma-vat prathama-tṛtīyâdi-dharmāṇāṃ kramêtarârpitānāṃ dharmântaratva-siddher na sapta-vidha-dharma-niyamaḥ siddhyet; ity apy asundaram. kramârpitayoḥ dharmântaratvenâpratīteḥ, sattva-dvayasyâsambhavād {vivakṣita-svarūpâdinā sattvasyâikatvāt} … katham evaṃ prathama-caturthayor dvitīya-caturthayor tṛtīya-caturthayoś ca sahitayor*

dharmântaratva syād iti cet? caturthe 'vaktavyatva-dharme sattvâsattvayor aparāmarśāt. na khalu sahārpitayos tayor avaktavya-śabdenâbhidhānam. kiṃ tarhi, tathârpitayos tayoḥ sarvathā vaktum aśakter avaktavyatvasya dharmântarasya tena pratipādanam iṣyate.

23 The background for above use of the expression *arpita* is the passage of TS_1 5.29–31/TS_2 5.30–32 quoted above (p. 1, n. 2). See also relevant portion of SSi 5.32 referred to below (p. 32, n. 91).

24 These two notions clearly correspond to the Naiyāyika and Buddhist criteria of the truth of our cognitions respectively: the cognition of the object (*vastu-pratipatti*) as correspondence of the cognition to facts and *pravṛtti-prāpti*) and causal efficacy (*artha-kriyā-sāmarthya*).

25 PKM 6.74, p. 682.18 ff.: *kasmāt punar naya-vākye pramāṇa-vākye vā saptâiva bhaṅgāḥ sambhavantîti cet? pratipādya-praśnānāṃ tāvatām eva sambhavāt. praśna-vaśād eva hi sapta-bhaṅgī-niyamaḥ. sapta-vidha eva praśno 'pi kuta iti cet? sapta-vidha-jijñāsā-sambhavāt. sāpi sapta-dhā kuta iti cet? sapta-dhā saṃśayôtpatteḥ. so 'pi sapta-dhā katham iti cet? tad-viṣaya-vastu-dharmasya sapta-vidhatvāt. tathā hi—sattvaṃ tāvad vastu-dharmaḥ, tad-anabhyupagame vastuno vastutvâyogāt khara-śṛṅgavat. tathā kathaṃcid asattvaṃ tad-dharma eva, sva-rūpâdibhir iva para-rūpâdibhir apy asyâsattvâniṣṭau pratiniyata-svarūpâsaṃbhavād vastu-pratiniyama-virodhaḥ syāt. etena kramârpitôbhayatvâdīnāṃ vastu-dharmatvaṃ pratipāditaṃ pratipattatvyam. tad-abhāve krameṇa sad-asattva-vikalpa-śabda-vyavahāra-virodhāt, sahâvaktavyatvôpalakṣitôttara-dharma-traya-vikalpasya śabda-vyavahārasya câsattva-prasaṅgāt. na câmī vyavahārā nirviṣayā eva; vastu-pratipatti-pravṛtti-prāpti-niścayāt tathā-vidha-rūpâdi-vyavahāravat.* This idea of doubt, crucial to understand this passage, is much earlier and is present already in NS 1.1.23: *samānâneka-dharmôpapatter vipratipatter upalabdhy-anupalabdhy-avyavasthātaś ca viśeṣâpekṣo vimarśaḥ saṃśayaḥ.* – "Doubt is an inquisitive reflection that depends on a particular characteristic [about which one is not certain and it is] due to perceived possibility of a property common [to different loci], due to perceived possibility of numerous properties, contradictory apprehension, incongruity of apprehension or incongruity of non-apprehension."

26 NBh 1.1.23: *sthāṇu-puruṣayoḥ samānaṃ dharmam āroha-pariṇāhau paśyan pūrva-dṛṣṭaṃ ca tayor viśeṣaṃ bubhutsumānaḥ kiṃsvid ity anyataraṃ nâvadhārayati, tad-anavādharaṇaṃ jñānaṃ saṃśayaḥ. samānam anayor dharmam upalabhe viśeṣam anyatarasya nôpalabha ity eṣā buddhir apekṣā. sā saṃśayasya pravarttikā vartate. tena viśeṣâpekṣo vimarśaḥ saṃśayaḥ.* For NS 1.1.23, see n. 25.

27 The idea of positing questions (*praśna*) with respect to one and the same thing goes back to Akalaṅka, RVār 1.6, p. 33.15: *praśna-vaśād ekasmin vastuny avirodhena vidhi-pratiṣedha-vikalpanā sapta-bhaṅgī. ekasmin vastuni praśna-vaśād dṛṣṭenêṣṭena ca pramāṇenâviriddhā vidhi-pratiṣedha-vikalpanā sapta-bhaṅgī vijñeyā.*

28 SVM_1 5.7, p. 13.11: *syād ity avyayam anekānta-dyotakam.*

29 PKM 6.74, p. 681.22–23, SVM_1 23.100–104, pp. 142.23–143.3, SBhT, p. 3.1–2, see p. 8.

30 ĀMī 36:

pramāṇa-gocarau santau bhedâbhedau na saṃvṛtī /
tāv ekatrâviruddhau te guṇa-mukhya-vivakṣayā //

31 See SVM_1 24.58 ff., pp. 150.14 ff. = SVM_2, pp. 225.4 ff.

32 AYVD 24:

upādhi-bhedôpahitaṃ viruddhaṃ nârtheṣv āsattvaṃ sad-avācyate ca /
ity aprabuddhâiva virodha-bhītā jaḍās tad-ekānta-hatāḥ patanti //

33 SVM_1 24.10–11, p. 148.14–16: *astitvaṃ nāstitvena saha na virudhyate. avaktavyatvam api vidhi-niṣedhâtmakam anyonyaṃ na virudhyate. athavā avaktavyatvaṃ*

vaktavyatvena sākaṃ na virodham udvahati. anena ca nāstitvâstitvâvaktavyatva-lakṣaṇa-bhaṅgaka-trayeṇa sakala-sapta-bhaṅgyā nirvirodhatôpalakṣitā.

34 PMĪ$_1$ 1.1.32 § 130, p. 32.18; PMĪ$_2$, p. 28.10: *yat-sannidhāne yo nôpalabhyate sa tasya virodhīti niścīyate.*

35 SVM$_1$ 24.22–23, p. 149.3–6: *paraspara-parihāreṇa ye vartete tayoḥ śītôṣṇavat sahânavasthāna-lakṣaṇo virodhaḥ. na câtrâivam. sattvâsattvayor itarêtaram aviṣvag-bhāvena vartanāt.*

36 Here: *avācya* = *avaktavya*, in the sense of the third (or fourth) figure (*syād avaktavyam*).

37 ĀMī 13, 32, 55, 70, 74, 77, 90, 94, 97:

virodhān nôbhayâikātmyaṃ syād-vāda-nyāya-vidviṣām /
avācyatâikānte 'py uktir nāvācyam iti yujyate //

38 SVM$_1$ 24.58–78, pp. 150.14–151.9 = SVM$_2$, pp. 225.4 ff.

39 SVM$_1$ 23.158–162, p. 145.7–12: *yathā hi sad-asattvābhyām evaṃ sāmānya-viśeṣābhyām api sapta-bhaṅgy eva syāt. tathā hi. syāt sāmānyaṃ syād viśeṣaḥ syād ubhayaṃ syād avaktavyaṃ syāt sāmānyâvaktavyaṃ syād-viśeṣâvaktavyaṃ syāt sāmānya-viśeṣâvaktavyam iti. na câtra vidhi-niṣedha-prakārau na sta iti vācyam. sāmānyasya vidhi-rūpatvād viśeṣasya ca vyāvṛtti-rūpatayā niṣedhâtmakatvāt.*

40 Clearly, as Ganeri (2002: 271 f.) rightly notices, models proposed by Bharucha and Kamat and Matilal place the contradiction where it is not there, viz. $|p| = \mathrm{I}$ iff ∇ (p & $\neg p$) (Bharucha and Kamat (1984: 183)) or $|p| = 0$ iff ∇ (p, $\neg p$) (Matilal 1991: 10 f.).

41 *Met* 1005b19–22: τὸ γὰρ αὐτὸ ἅμα ὑπάρχειν τε καὶ μὴ ὑπάρχειν ἀδύνατον τῷ αὐτῷ καὶ κατὰ τὸ αὐτό (καὶ ὅσα ἄλλα προσδιορισαίμεθ' ἄν, ἔστω προσδιωρισμένα πρὸς τὰς λογικὰς δυσχερείας).

42 *sarvaṃ vākyaṃ sāvadhāraṇaṃ, sarvaṃ vacanaṃ sāvadhāraṇaṃ*, quoted e.g. by Siddharṣi-gaṇin in NAV 1.9, p. 341, NAV 29.28, p. 472; Guṇaratna-sūri in TRD 9, p. 35.1–2. The maxim is also used by non-Jaina authors, e.g. Jayanta-bhaṭṭa in NMa vol. 2, p. 555.10; NĀ 372, p. 96; Bhāsarvajña in NBhū, p. 282; Karṇakagomin in PVSVṬ, p. 248; Bhāskara in BĪPVV 1.5.15, vol. 1, p. 269.19; 2.3.1, vol. 2, p. 70.9; BĪPVV 2.4.16, vol. 2, p. 192.17. See also NUK, p. 95.

43 MDhŚ 5.56:

na māṃsa-bhakṣaṇe doṣo na madye na ca maithune /
pravṛttir eṣā bhūtānāṃ nivṛttis tu mahā-phalā //

Quoted in SVM$_1$ 23.58–59, p. 141.5–6.

44 SVM$_1$ 23.60–86, pp. 141.7–142.11: *asya ca yathā-śrutârtha-vyākhyāne 'saṃbaddha-pralāpa eva. yasmin hy anuṣṭhīyamāne doṣo nâsty eva tasmān nivṛttiḥ katham iva mahā-phalā bhaviṣyati? ijyâdhyayana-dānâder api nivṛtti-prasaṅgāt. tasmād anyad aidaṃparyam asya ślokasya. tathā hi na māṃsa-bhakṣaṇe kṛte adoṣaḥ api tu doṣa eva. evaṃ madya-maithunayor api. kathaṃ nâdoṣa ity āha yataḥ pravṛttir eṣā bhūtānām. pravartante utpadyante 'syām iti pravṛttiḥ utpatti-sthānam. bhūtānāṃ jīvānāṃ tat-taj-jīva-saṃsakti-hetur ity arthaḥ. prasiddhaṃ ca māṃsa-madya-maithunānāṃ jīva-saṃsakti-mūla-kāraṇatvam āgame ... athavā bhūtānām piśāca-prāyāṇāṃ eṣā pravṛttiḥ. ta evâtra maṃsa-bhakṣaṇâdau pravartante na punar vivekina iti bhāvaḥ.*

45 This is the first *guṇa-sthāna* and should not be confused with *mithyā-darśana*; *mithyā-dṛṣṭi* is a possessor of *mithyā-darśana*. See SSi. 18, 9,1, and H. von Glasenapp (1942: 75–92).

46 SVM$_1$ 23.42–45, p. 140.14–17:

sad-asad-avisesеṇāu bhava-heu-jahicchiôvalaṃbhāu /
ṇāṇa-phalâbhāvāu micchyā-diṭṭhissa aṇṇāṇaṃ //
ata eva tat-parigṛhītaṃ dvādaśâṅgam api mithyā-śrutaṃ āmananti.

47 TŚVA$_1$ 1.6.53, vol. 2, p. 431:

vākye 'vadhāraṇaṃ tāvad aniṣṭârtha-nivṛttaye /
kartavyam anyathânukta-samatvāt tasya kutracit //

The verse is quoted also by Malliṣeṇa in SVM$_1$ 23.121–122, p. 143.20–21, and by Vimaladāsa in SBhT, p. 21.3–4.

48 LT 63:

aprayukto 'pi sarvatra syāt-kāro 'arthāt pratīyate /
vidhau niṣedhe 'py anyatra kuśalaś cet prayojakaḥ //

Comp. also Prabhācandra's explication in NKC, p. 692.6–7: ***aprayukto 'pi** na kevalaṃ prayuktaḥ **sarvatra** vākye **syāt-kāraḥ**, upalakṣaṇam etat tena eva-kāro 'pi **pratīyate**.* – "the functor 'in a certain sense', even when it is not explicitly pronounced, i.e. when it is not pronounced at all [is understood] in any sentence. This is an implication. By force of this [implication] also [the delimiting particle] 'only' is understood [too]."

49 But see also the Buddhist approach of the *vibhājya-vāda* and the "unanswered questions" (*avyākata pañha/avyākṛta-praśna*), described in Matilal (1981: 7–18); See also relevant remarks in Matilal (1981: 47–51).

50 NaṃSCū 105, p. 73.26: *te cêva ājīvikā terāsiyā bhaṇitā. kamhā? ucyate—jamhā te sarvaṃ jagaṃ trayâtmakaṃ icchaṃti, jahā—jīvo ajīvo jīvâjīvaś ca, loe aloe loyâloe, saṃte asaṃte saṃtāsaṃte evam-ādi. ṇaya-ciṃtāe vi te tivihaṃ ṇayam icchaṃti, taṃ jahā—davvaṭṭhito payyav'aṭṭhito ubhay'aṭṭhito, ato bhaṇiyaṃ—"satta terāsiyāiṃ" tti satta parikammāiṃ terāsiya-pāsaṃḍ'atthā tividhae ṇaya-ciṃtāe ciṃtayaṃtîty-arthaḥ*. The passage, in mixed Prakrit and Sanskrit, is basically identical with NaṃVṛ 107, p. 87.5–8; *te cêva ājīviyā terāsiyā bhaṇiyā. kamhā? ucyate, jamhā te savvaṃ jagat trayâtmakam icchanti, yathā jīvo 'jīvo jīvâjīvo, loe aloe loyâloye, saṃte asaṃte saṃtâsaṃte evam-ādi. ṇaya-ciṃtāe te tivihaṃ ṇayam icchaṃti, taṃ jahā—davv'aṭṭhito pajjav'aṭṭhito ubhay'aṭṭhio, ao bhaṇiyaṃ—"satta terāsiya" tti, satta parikammāiṃ terāsiya-pāsaṃḍatthā tivihāe ṇaya-ciṃtāe cintayantîty-ārthaḥ.* Cf. also Basham (1951: 274 f., n. 5): '*Nandi comm.*: *tathā ta eva gośāla-pravarttitā ājīvikāḥ pāṣaṇḍinas trairāśikā ucyante, yatas te sarvaṃ vastu try-ātmakam icchanti, tad yathā: jīvo 'jīvo jīvâjīvaś ca, loko 'loko lokâlokaś ca, sad asat sad-asat. naya-cintāyāṃ dravyâstikaṃ paryāyâvastikaṃ ca. tatas tribhī rāśibhiś carantîti trairāśikaḥ.*'

51 E.g. Viy 10.2.4, pp. 488.21–489.1: *kati-vidhā ṇaṃ bhaṃte! joṇī paṇṇatā? goyamā! tivihā joṇī paṇṇattā, taṃ jahā—sīyā usiṇā sītôsīṇā. evaṃ joṇīpayaṃ nikhasesaṃ bhāṇiyavvaṃ*. And similarly it is applied to *vedaṇā* in Viy 10.2.4, p. 489.3–5: *kati-vidhā ṇaṃ bhaṃte! vedaṇā paṇṇatā? goyamā! tivihā vedaṇā paṇṇattā, taṃ jahā—sīyā usiṇā sītôsīṇā. evaṃ vedaṇā-padaṃ bhāṇiyavvaṃ java neraiyā ṇaṃ bhaṃte.*

52 Some canonical instances are enumerated, e.g., by Kāpaḍīā (1940–1947: cxi ff.), Upadhye (PSā: 81–84); they are also discussed by Schubring (1962: 163–165) and occasionally in Shah (2000); stray occurrences are listed also in JSK (entry '*syād-vāda*', Vol. 4, pp. 496–502).

53 See pp. 42 ff.

54 PAS 14:

siya atthi ṇatthi uhayaṃ avvattavvaṃ puṇo ya tat-tidayaṃ /
davvaṃ khu satta-bhaṃgaṃ ādesa-vaseṇa saṃbhavadi //

55 The verse is rather obscure. Another possibility to translate it as follows: "From the substance-expressive viewpoint and from the mode-expressive viewpoint, any substance is [both] different and non-different, because [the particular] consists in that [universal] at the time of its [existence]", where *aṇṇam* corresponds to *viśeṣam* and *aṇaṇṇaṃ* to *sāmānyam*. The difficulty with such a translation is that the idea it renders is that "everything is different from the substance-expressive viewpoint, and

everything is the same from the mode-expressive viewpoint". On the other hand *dravyârthika* relates to *sāmānya*, whereas *paryāyârthika* to *viśeṣa* (comp. STP 3.57), which finally yields a contradiction. That is why the commentators Amṛtasena and Jayasena (pp. 144–145) are at pains to relate *dravyârthika–sāmānya–ananya* and *paryāyârthika–anya–viśeṣa*.

56 PSā 2.22–23, pp. 146 ff.:

davv'aṭṭhieṇa savvaṃ davvaṃ taṃ pajjay'aṭṭhieṇa puṇo /
havadi ya aṇṇam aṇaṇṇaṃ tak-kāle tam-mayattādo // 22 //
atthi tti ya ṇatthi ya havadi avattavvam idi puṇo davvaṃ /
pajjāyeṇa du keṇa vi tad ubhayam ādiṭṭham aṇṇaṃ vā // 23 //

57 STP 1.41a: *satta-viyappo vayaṇa-paho.*

58 Comp. the expression *ādesa-vaseṇa* (*ādeśa-vaśāt*) in PAS 14 above, p. 21.

59 STP 1.36–40:

atth'aṃtara-bhūehi ya ṇiyaehi ya dohi samayam āīhiṃ /
vayaṇa-visesāīyaṃ davvam avattavvayaṃ padai // 36 //
aha deso sabbhāve deso abbhāva-pajjave ṇiyao /
taṃ daviyam atthi ṇatthi ya āyesa-visesiyaṃ jamhā // 37 //
sabbhāve āiṭṭho deso deso ya ubhayahā jassa /
taṃ atthi avattavvaṃ ca hoi daviaṃ viyappa-vasā // 38 //
āiṭṭho 'sabbhāve deso deso ya ubhayahā jassa /
taṃ ṇatthi avattavvaṃ ca hoi daviyaṃ viyappa-vasā // 39 //
sabbhāvāsabbhāve deso deso ya ubhayahā jassa /
taṃ atthi ṇatthi avattavvayaṃ ca daviyaṃ viyappa-vasā // 40 //

Compare a completely misconstrued and erroneous translation of the passage in Saṅghavi and Dośi (2000: 29).

60 VĀBh 2232 (p. 910):

sabbhāvâsabbhāvôbhayappio sa-para-pajjaôbhayao /
kuṃbhâkuṃbhâvattavyôbhaya-rūvāibheo so //

61 See also VĀBh, p. 911.9 ff.: *kumbhaḥ akumbhaḥ avaktavyaḥ* … and p. 912 (on *paṭa*).

62 VĀVṛ, pp. 910.12 ff.: *sapta-bhaṅgīṃ pratipadyata ity arthaḥ, tad yatha—ūrdhva-grīvā-kapāla-kukṣi-budhnâdibhiḥ sva-paryāyaiḥ sadbhāvenârpito viśeṣitaḥ kumbhaḥ kumbho bhaṇyate—"san ghataḥ" iti prathamo bhaṅgo bhavatîty arthaḥ. tathā paṭâdi-gatais tvak-trāṇâdibhiḥ para-paryāyair asadbhāvenârpito viśeṣito 'kumbho bhavati—sarvasyâpi ghaṭasya para-paryāyair asattva-vivakṣāyāṃ "asan ghaṭaḥ" iti dvitīyo bhaṅgo bhavatîty arthaḥ. tathā sarvo 'pi ghaṭaḥ sva-parôbhaya-paryāyaiḥ sadbhāvâsadbhāvābhyāṃ sattvâsattvābhyām arpito viśeṣito yugapad vaktum iṣṭo 'vaktavyo bhavati, sva-para-paryāya-sattvâsattvābhyām ekena kenâpy asāṃketikena śabdena sarvasyâpi tasya yugapad vaktum aśakyatvād iti. ete trayaḥ sakalâdeśāḥ. atha catvāro 'pi vikalâdeśāḥ procyante…*

63 E.g. DNC, p. 6.2 ff. (*vidhi-bheda*), and DNC, p. 9.7: *vidhi-niyama-bhaṅga-vṛtti-vyatiriktatvād* … All the permutations of *vidhi* and *niyama* are enumerated also in DNC, pp. 10.1–11.2.

64 $SvSt_1$ 5.5 = $SvSt_2$ 25:

vidhir niṣedhaś ca kathañcid iṣṭau vivakṣayā mukhya-guṇa-vyavasthā /
iti praṇītiḥ sumates taveyaṃ mati-pravekaḥ stuvato 'stu nātha //

For later descriptions see e.g. RVār 2.8, pp. 122.15 ff., esp. RVār 1.6, pp. 33.15 ff.

65 ĀMī 19:

vidheya-pratiṣedhyâtmā viśeṣyaḥ śabda-gocaraḥ /
sādhya-dharmo yathā hetur ahetuś câpy apekṣayā //

66 See Balcerowicz (2009: ix–x) and (2011). The use of the particle *eva* is one of a few points that, in opinion, force us to re-examine traditional (i.e. pre-Dharmakīrtian) dating of Samantabhadra.

67 PAS 71–72, p. 123:

eko cêva mahappā so duviyappo tti-lakkhaṇo hodi /
cadu-saṃkamaṇo bhaṇido paṃcagga-guṇa-ppadhāṇo ya // 71 //
chakkāpakkama-jutto uvautto satta-bhaṅga-sabbhāvo /
aṭṭhāsao ṇavattho jīvo dasa-ṭṭhāṇago bhaṇido // 72 //

68 Or less likely: "the great soul … has the existence which applies the seven figures".

69 i.e. it is not possible to predicate of an object because momentary manifestations, being transient and infinite, are beyond the scope of the language (sc. there are not enough words, numerically speaking, to describe each of them). The verse offers another possibility of interpretation, see TBV.

70 STP 1.41:

evaṃ satta-viyappo vayaṇa-paho hoi attha-pajjāe /
vaṃjaṇa-pajjāe uṇa saviyappo ṇivviyapppo ya //

71 E.g. RVār 4.42 (pp. 254.14 ff.), SVM_1 23.113 (pp. 143.12), $JTBh_1$ 1.22 § 63 (p. 19)/ $JTBh_2$ 1.22 (p. 19).

72 See Alsdorf (1973) and Bhatt (1978), esp. the "general catalogue" of the *nikṣepas* (1978: 15–32), in which the combination of *davvao khettao kālao bhāvao* is a recurring theme, next to other parameters such as *guṇao* or *ṭhavaṇao*. In a subsequent development, the paths of the standpoints (*nikṣepa*) and the parameters of the *syād-vāda* bifurcated in two different directions, with the *nikṣepas* "canonized" as the quadruplet of the name, material representation, substance and condition in TS 1.5: *nāma-sthāpanā-dravya-bhāvatas tan-nyāsaḥ*.

73 Cf. the general catalogue of such parameters in Bhatt (1978: 15–32).

74 STP 3.60:

davvyaṃ khittaṃ kālaṃ bhāvaṃ pajjāya-desa-saṃjoge /
bhedaṃ ca paḍucca samā bhāvāṇaṃ paṇṇavaṇa-pajjā //

75 SVM_1 24.17–20, pp. 148.21–149.1 = SVM_2, pp. 223.4 ff.: *upādhayo 'vacchedakā aṃśa-prakārāḥ teṣāṃ bhedo nānātvam, tenôpahitam arpitam. asattvasya viśeṣaṇam etat. upādhi-bhedôpahitaṃ sad-artheṣv asattvaṃ na viruddham. sad-avacyatayoś ca vacana-bhedaṃ kṛtvā yojanīyam.*

76 SVM_1 23.189–206, pp. 177.13–178.5 = SVM_2, pp. 214.8–215.7.

77 RVār 4.42, p. 257.17: *kāla ātma-rūpam arthaḥ sambhandhaḥ upakāro guṇi-deśaḥ saṃsargaḥ śabda iti.*

78 SVM_1 24.28–31, p. 149.9–12 = SVM_2, pp. 224.1 ff.: *tadā hi virodhaḥ syād yady ekôpadhikaṃ sattvam asattvaṃ ca syāt. na câivam. yato na hi yenâivâṃśena sattvaṃ tenâivâsattvam api. kiṃ tv anyôpādhikam sattvam, anyôpādhikaṃ*[a] *punar asattvam. sva-rūpeṇa hi sattvaṃ para-rūpeṇa câsattvam* [[a] SVM_1 misprints: *sattvanyôpādhikaṃ*].

79 SVM_1 23.113–119, p. 143.12–18 = SVM_2, p. 210.7–12: *tatra syāt kathaṃcit sva-dravya-kṣetra-kāla-bhāva-rūpeṇâsty eva sarvaṃ kumbhâdi na punaḥ para-dravya-kṣetra-kāla-bhāva-rūpeṇa. tathā hi kumbho dravyataḥ pārthivatvenâsti nāpa-ādi-rūpatvena*[a]. *kṣetrataḥ pāṭaliputrakatvena na kānyakubjâditvena. kālataḥ śaiṣiratvena na vāsantikāditvena. bhāvataḥ śyāmatvena na raktâditvena. anyathêtara-rūpāpattyā sva-rūpa-hāni-prasaṅga iti. avadhāraṇaṃ*[b] *câtra bhaṅge 'nabhimatârtha-vyāvṛtty-artham upāttam. itarathânabhihita-tulyatâivâsya vakyasya prasajyeta. pratiniyata-svârthânabhidhānāt.* [[a] SVM_1/SVM_2 read *nāpy ādi-rūpatvena*, but this reading does not make sense. An almost identical passage found in JTBh 1.22 § 63.23: reads: *na jalāditvena*, therefore I suggest to emend the text

taking *āpas*, a synonym of *jala*, as the first member of the compound. [b] SVM$_1$ reads *avadhāraṇāṃ*].

80 See pp. 36 f.

81 SVM$_1$ 23.132–140, p. 144.6–14 = SVM$_2$, p. 211.7–9: *syāt kathaṃcin nâsty eva kumbhādiḥ sva-dravyâdibhir iva*[a] *para-dravyâdibhir api vastuno 'sattvâniṣṭau hi pratiniyata-sva-rūpâbhāvād vastu-pratiniyatir na syāt. na câstitvâikānta-vādibhir atra nāstitvam asiddham iti vaktavyam. kathaṃcit tasya vastuny yukti-siddhatvāt sādhanavat*. [[a] SVM$_1$ reads *eva*].

82 NBh$_2$ 1.1.2, p. 8. 6: *tatrôddiṣṭasyâtattva-vyavacchedako dharmo lakṣaṇam.*

83 See *Pramāṇa-samuccaya* 5.1:

> *na pramāṇântaraṃ śābdam anumānāt tathā hi tat*[a] /
> *kṛtakatvâdivat svārtham anyâpohena bhāṣate* // —
>
> – "Verbally acquired cognition is not an additional cognitive criterion, different from inference, because it names its object through [the procedure known as] 'exclusion of the other' in the same way as [the inference: '*x* is impermanent, because it is produced', determines its object to have the quality of 'impermanence' on the basis of the already known quality of] 'being produced' etc."

The verse is quoted by Kamalaśīla in TSaP 1515, p. 441.6–7 ([a]*saḥ* {*tat*?}), partly quoted by Siṃha-sūri in DNCV, p. 612.13–14; quoted in DNC ed., vol. 2, p. 607.7–8. Cf. the translations in: Hayes (1988: 300) and Herzberger (1986: 145 f.). See also Hayes (1988: 188–193) and Dunne (2004: 145 f.) on Dharmakīrti.

84 See, e.g., PVSV, p. 27.13: *anumānena samāropa-vyavacchedaḥ kriyate*. – "Through inference, one accomplishes the exclusion of false superimposition"; PVSV, pp. 27.14 f.: *samāropa-vyavacchedād anya-vyavacchedaḥ kṛto bhavatîti tad-artham anyat pravartate*. – "The exclusion of the other (i.e. all that is not the particular thing) is accomplished through the exclusion of false superimposition…"

85 PV$_1$ 3.49 = PV$_2$ 3.49:

> *niścayâropa-manasor bādhya-bādhaka-bhāvataḥ* /
> *samāropa-viveke 'sya pravṛttir iti gamyate* //

86 SVM$_1$ 23.142, p. 144.16 = SVM$_2$, p. 212.3: *tṛtīyaḥ spaṣṭa eva.*

87 This passage is translated in Ganeri (2001: 143), who – instead of "one conventionally accepted word, like 'flower-toothed' (Puṣpadanta)" – speaks of "a single conventional term such as *puṣpavant* [meaning 'sun or moon']". Ganeri does not justify his reading (emendation?), which apparently is: *puṣpavant-ādivat*, although both editions read: *puṣpadantâdivat*. Indeed, his suggestion does seem very attractive at first, because the term *puṣpavant* in dual (*puṣpavantau*) means "both the sun and the moon", and the term *puṣpavant* serves the purpose better than Puṣpadanta, inasmuch as *puṣpavant* ("one which has the flower") seems to be a uniform word and as a homogenous term indicates two objects in one take, whereas the name Puṣpadanta is clearly a copulative compound (*puṣpa-danta*) and appears to also convey two ideas. However, what is at stake in the passage is the question whether one linguistic unit (word) can convey two different properties that can pertain to one and the same referent. Clearly, it is only Puṣpadanta that meets this condition, whereas *puṣpavant* has two referents, so it is not what Malliṣeṇa originally could have had in mind.

88 For the ŚatṚ and ŚānaC *kṛt*-affixes see e.g. A 3.2.124: *laṬaḥ ŚatṚ-ŚānaCāv aprathamā-samānādhikaraṇe*. – "The [*kṛt*-affixes] ŚatṚ and ŚānaC [are used to replace] laṬ affix when it has the same reference except the first case-affix." The ŚatṚ and ŚānaC affixes of the *kṛt* category express the activity that occurs simultaneously with the activity expressed by the main verb, provided they are used in all other cases than the nominative case. ŚatṚ affix, as participial ending, forms active participles with °*ant* ending: *pacantaṃ devadattaṃ paśya* ("Watch Devadatta who is

cooking"); similarly ŚānaC affix forms medium participles: *pacamānaṃ devadattaṃ paśya* ("Watch Devadatta who is cooking"). Malliṣeṇa's idea is that even the artificially created term ŚaT does not have the capacity to denote both ŚatR̥ and ŚānaC *kr̥t*-affixes, but it projects both the ideas to the mind one after the other. This example is taken over by Yaśovijaya in JTBh₁ 1.22 § 63, p. 20.1.

89 SVM₁ 23.143–147, pp. 144.17–145.2 = SVM₂, p. 212.3–10: *dvābhyām astitva-nāstitva-dharmābhyāṃ yugapat-pradhānatayârpitābhyām ekasya vastuno 'bhidhitsāyāṃ tādr̥śasya śabdasyâsaṃbhāvād avaktavyam jīvâdi-vastu. tathā hi sad-asattva-guṇa-dvayaṃ yugapad ekatra sad ity-anena vaktum aśakyam, tasyâsattva-pratipādanâsamarthatvāt. tathâsad ity-anenâpi, tasya sattva-pratyāyana-sāmarthyābhāvāt. na ca puṣpadantâdivat sāṅketikam ekaṃ padaṃ tad vaktuṃ samartham, tasyâpi krameṇârtha-dvaya-pratyāyane sāmarthyôpapatteḥ, śatr̥-śānayoḥ saṅketita-sac-chabdavat. ata eva dvandva-karma-dhāraya-vr̥ttyor vākyasya ca na tad-vācakatvam iti sakala-vācaka-rahitatvād avaktavyam vastu yugapat-sattvâsattvābhyāṃ pradhāna-bhāvârpitābhyām ākrāntaṃ vyavatiṣṭhate. na ca sarvathâvaktavyam, avaktavya-śabdenâpy anabhidheyatva-prasaṅgāt.* Cf. the translation in Ganeri (2001: 143).

90 SVM₁ 23.154, p. 145.3: *śeṣās trayaḥ sugamâbhiprāyāḥ.*

91 SSi 5.32 ad loc., § 588, pp. 231.9. ff.: *anekāntâtmakasya vastunaḥ prayojana-vaśād yasya kasyacid dharmasya vivakṣayā prāpitaṃ prādhānyam arpitam upanītam iti yāvat. tad-viparītam anarpitam. prayojanâbhāvāt sato 'py avivakṣā bhavatîty upasarjanītam iti ucyate. tābhyāṃ siddher "arpitânarpita-siddher"* [TS 5.32] *nâsti virodhaḥ.*

92 ĀMī 16:

kramârpita-dvayād dvaitaṃ sahâvācyam aśaktitaḥ /
avaktavyôttarāḥ śeṣās trayo bhaṅgāḥ sva-hetutaḥ //

93 YA 48:

na dravya-paryāya-pr̥thag-vyavasthā dvaiyātmyam ekârpaṇayā viruddham /
dharmaś ca dharmī ca mithas tridhêmau na sarvathā te 'bhimatau viruddhau //

94 RVār 4.42, p. 257.10–15: *tr̥tīyo vikalpaḥ ucyate—dvābhyāṃ guṇābhyām ekasyâiva abhinnasyâbheda-rūpeṇa yupagad vaktum iṣṭatvāt. tatra yathā prathama-dvitīyayor vikalpayor ekasmin kāle ekena śabdena ekasyârthasya samastasyâiva ekena gūṇa-rūpeṇâbhidhānam kramāt, evaṃ yadā dvābhyāṃ pratiyogibhyāṃ guṇābhyām avadhāraṇâtmabhyāṃ[a] yugapad ekasmin kāle ekena śabdena ekasyârthasya kr̥tsnasyâivâbheda-rūpeṇâbhidhitsā tadā avācyāḥ tad-vidhârthasya śabdasya câbhāvāt. tatra yugapad-bhāvo guṇānāṃ kālādibhir abhedena vivikṣitānāṃ vr̥ttiḥ, na ca tair abhedo 'tra sambhavati.*
[a] RVār ed. proposes to read: *avadhāraṇāt kābhyāṃ*; varia lectio in n. 10: *avadhāraṇâtmakābhyāṃ.*

95 SVM 28.12–13, p. 159.16–17: *sad iti avaktavyatvān napuṃsakatvaṃ yathā kiṃ tasyā garbhe jātam iti.*

96 RVār 4.42, p. 258.13–14: *athavā vastuni mukhya-pravr̥ttyā tulya-balayoḥ parasparâbhidhāna-pratibandhe sati iṣṭa-viparīta-nirguṇatvâpatteḥ vivakṣitôbhaya-guṇatvenânabhidhānād avaktavyam.*

97 RVār 4.42, pp. 257.17 ff.

98 TBV ad STP 1.36, p. 443.2–4: *asattvôpasarjana-sattva-pratipādane prathamo bhaṅgaḥ. tad-viparyayeṇa tat-pratipādane dvitīyaḥ. dvayos tu dharmayoḥ prādhānyena guṇa-bhāveṇa vā pratipādane na kiṃcid vacaḥ samartham yato na tāvat samāsa-vacanaṃ tat-pratipādakam nâpi vākyaṃ sambhavati.* In what follows Abhayadeva-sūri analyses various kinds of compounds etc. and their inefficacy to express both assertion and denial at the same time.

99 TBV ad STP 1.36, p. 443.2–12.

100 TBV ad STP 1.36, p. 443.23: *tat-prakārābhyāṃ yugapad avācyam tathâbhidheya-pariṇāma-rahitatvāt tasya.*

101 E.g. time factor, the thing's own essence, the thing in its substantial aspect, i.e. its material substratum, its relation, the thing's serviceability, the location of the thing, its status as the property-possessor, the thing as a combination of related attributes, the thing's concurrence with other properties, the thing's verbal designation etc.; *vide supra*, p. 27.

102 Akalaṅka does not use the word *arpaṇā* explicitly in his exposition, nor does he use the term *arpita* ("emphasized") in the afore-quoted passages, which might lead one to a mistaken impression that he does not know of the idea of emphasis or he understood it somehow differently. On the contrary, both the idea of emphasis and the term *arpita* are actually present in his works; the latter occurs several times in his exposition of the *syād-vāda* in RVār 4.42, pp. 253.9–262.13, esp. while dealing with the third (*syād avaktavyam*) and fourth (*syād asti nâsti*) figures, for instance: p. 258.21 = 259.1 (*ayam api syād ity evārpitavyaḥ*), 252.31 (*ābhyām eva krameṇârpitābhyām ubhaya-rūpaṃ vastûcyate*), etc.

103 RVār 4.42, pp. 257.16 ff.: *tatra yena kāraṇena viruddhā bhavanti guṇās teṣāṃ ekasmin kāle kvacid eka-vastuni vṛttir na dṛṣṭā, atas tayor nâsti vācakaḥ śabdaḥ tathā-vṛtty-abhāvāt.*

104 SVM_1 23.189–225, pp. 146.13–147–24.

105 SVM_1 23.191–193, p. 146.14–16: *tatra syāj jīvâdi vastv asty evêty atra yat-kālam astitvam tat-kālāḥ śeṣânanta-dharmā vastuny ekatrêti teṣāṃ kālenâbheda-vṛttiḥ.*

106 SVM_1 23.136–139, p. 144.10–14 = SVM_2, pp. 211.9–212.2: *na hi kvacid anityat-vâdau sādhye sattvâdi-sādhanasyâstitvaṃ vipakṣe nāstitvam antareṇôpapannam, tasya sādhanatvâbhāva-prasaṅgāt. tasmād vastuno 'stitvaṃ nāstitvenâvinābhūtam, nāstitvaṃ ca teneti. vivakṣā-vaśāc cânayoḥ pradhānôpasarjana-bhāvaḥ.*

107 SVM_1 4.20–22, p. 11.14–16 = SVM_2 p. 13.14–16: *sa* [*vyatirekaḥ*] *eva cêtarebhyaḥ sajātīya-vijātīyebhyo dravya-kṣetra-kāla-bhāvair ātmānaṃ vyāvartayan viśeṣa-vyapadeśam aśnute. iti na sāmānya-viśeṣayoḥ pṛthak-padârthântaratva-kalpanaṃ nyāyyam.*

108 $JTBh_1$ 1.22 § 63, 19.21 ff.: *tatra syād asty eva sarvam iti prādhānyena vidhi-kalpanayā prathamo bhaṅgaḥ. syāt kathaṃcit sva-dravya-kṣetra-kāla-bhāvâpekṣayêty arthaḥ. asti hi ghaṭādikaṃ dravyataḥ pārthivâditvena, na jalâditvena. kṣetrataḥ pāṭaliputrakâditvena, na kānyakubjâditvena. kālataḥ śaiśirâditvena, na vāsantikâditvena. bhāvataḥ śyāmāditvena, na raktâditveneti. evaṃ syān nâsty eva sarvam iti prādhānyena niṣedha-kalpanayā dvitīyaḥ. na câsattvaṃ kālpanikam, sattvavat tasya svātantryeṇânubhavāt, anyathā vipakṣâsattvasya tāttvikasyâbhāvena hetos trairūpya-vyāghāta-prasaṅgāt. syād asty eva syān nâsty evêti prādhānyena kramika-vidhi-niṣedha-kalpanayā tṛtīyaḥ. syād avaktavyam evêti yugapat prādhānyena vidhi-niṣedha-kalpanayā caturthaḥ, ekena padena yugapad ubhayor vaktum aśakyatvāt*, etc.

109 RVār 4.42, p. 253.21–26: *guṇa-prādhānya-vyavasthā-viśeṣa-pratipādanârthatvāt sarveṣāṃ bhaṅgānāṃ prayogo 'rthavān. tad yathā—dravyârthikasya prādhanye paryāya-guṇa-bhāve ca prathamaḥ. paryāyârthikasya prādhānye dravya-guṇa-bhāve ca dvitīyaḥ. tatra prādhānyaṃ śabdena vivakṣitatvāc chābdâdhīnam, śabdenânupāttasyârthato gamyamānasyâprādhānyam. tṛtīye tu yugapad-bhāve ubhayasyâprādhānyaṃ śabdenâbhidheyatayânupāttatvāt. caturthas tûbhaya-pradhānaḥ krameṇa ubhaysyâsty-ādi-śabdena upāttatvāt. tathôttare ca bhaṅgā vakṣyante.*

110 This prevents, for instance, the conjunction: "in a certain sense, *x* is made of clay and *x* is not present in Kanyakubja", because "made of clay" and "present/not present in Kanyakubja" belong to different levels, and the parameter π does not allow for it.

111 "There is no single term capable of demonstrating these two properties either as

[simultaneously] primary or as [simultaneously] secondary" (*dvayos tu dharmayoḥ prādhānyena guṇa-bhāveṇa vā pratipādane na kiṃcid vacaḥ samartham*), *vide supra*, p. 35, n. 98.

112 *Vide supra*, pp. 34, 35 and n. 96.

113 Balcerowicz (2001: 392).

114 RVār 1.6, p. 33.9–10 = YAṬ 47, p. 106.7: *sakalâdeśaḥ pramāṇâdhīno vikalâdeśo nayâdhīnaḥ*. For the idea see also LT 62 and LTV ad loc. (*Pravacana-praveśa*), pp. 686.2–688.2:

upayogau śrutasya dvau syād-vāda-naya-saṃjñitau /
syād-vādaḥ sakalâdeśo nayo vikala-saṃkathā //

Comp. NAV 29.28: *ataḥ sampūrṇa-vastu-pratipādanâbhāvād vikalâdeśo 'bhidhīyate, naya-matena sambhavad-dharmāṇāṃ darśana-mātram ity arthaḥ*. – "Hence, [such a statement] – inasmuch as it does not demonstrate the whole real thing – is called the incomplete account, which means that it merely shows [selected] properties that are possibly there in consonance with the opinion of (sc. according to) a [respective] viewpoint."

Again, also when it comes to the distinction into "complete account" (*sakalâdeśa*) and "incomplete account" (*vikalâdeśa*), Jaina tradition was not unanimous. For instance, Hemacandra Maladhārin designates the role of both accounts to the *syād-vāda* only: the complete account is the first three figures (assertion, denial and inexpressibility), whereas the incomplete account is the remaining three combinations, see VĀVṛ, pp. 910.12 ff.

115 The concept of the "complete account" (*sakalâdeśa*), or the idea of completeness of the system, is reflected in Ganeri's (2002: 278) idea of "optimality", axiomatized by Ganeri as axiom A4 $\neg(\exists\sigma)$ $(\neg\sigma\text{: } p \ \& \ \neg\sigma\text{: } \neg p)$. In this interpretation, "optimality" is not about the fact that there are no other truth values than seven, but that there is no other way to predicate of a property than through the seven figures.

116 See RVār 4.42. pp. 253 ff.

117 I quote this opinion after Ganeri: this opinion, in exactly the same form and omission (indicated by "…") as reproduced above, is quoted by Ganeri (2001: 149) who refers to Matilal (1981) as its source, without mentioning any page number, and by Ganeri (2002: 279), who mentions a 1977 publication of Matilal, which is later, in the bibliography, identified as: "Matilal, B. K. 1977. *The Central Philosophy of Jainism*. Calcutta: Calcutta University Press", i.e. a publication which does not exist. I have closely examined Matilal (1981, 1985, 1991), and have failed, perhaps due to my oversight, to find such a quotation. However, what is quoted by Ganeri is not different in spirit from what Matilal stated on numerous occasions in his publications just mentioned, e.g. Matilal (1981: 2):

> Jaina philosophers claim that no philosophic or metaphysical proposition can be true if it is simply asserted without any condition or limitation.… [T]he philosophic propositions of rival schools could be integrated together under the *Anekānta* system. In other words, these rival propositions can be said to capture the truth when and only when they are asserted with proper qualifications or conditions.

> Other philosophers suffer from partiality of their outlook while the Jainas try to overcome partiality and one-sidedness and search for the totality of outlook[s], for omniscience.
>
> (p. 30)

> The *anekānta-vāda* is thus a philosophy of synthesis and reconciliation since it tries to establish a rapprochement between seemingly disagreeing philosophical schools.
>
> (p. 61)

118 For some opinions see n. 117 and see below, p. 46.
119 E.g. RVār 4.42, pp. 258–259.
120 Lit. "spittle", "vomit" or "discharge"! Malliṣeṇa (SVM$_1$ 25.27–36, pp. 152.20–153.4) is not quite comfortable with the simile and proposes another, alternative interpretation which he eventually called "poetical meaning" (*kāvyārtha*).
121 AYVD 25:

> *syān nāśi nityaṃ sadṛśaṃ virūpaṃ vācyaṃ na vācyaṃ sad asat tad eva /*
> *vipaścitāṃ nātha nipīta-tattva-sudhôdgatôdgāra-paramparêyam //*

See also SVM$_1$ 25.31–36, pp. 152.34–153.4.
122 See e.g. AYVD 28 and SVM thereon.
123 See for instance Vādideva-sūri in PNTĀA/SVR, chapter 7, JTBh$_1$ 2.2 § 11 (pp. 24.15 ff.) = JTBh$_2$, pp. 24.15 ff.
124 Note the pun on the Buddhists/the Buddha: °*buddhayas tathāgatāḥ*.
125 SVM$_1$ 28.155 ff., pp. 170.11 ff.: *naigama-naya-darśanânusāriṇau naiyāyika-vaiśeṣikau. saṃgrahâbhiprāya-pravṛttāḥ sarve 'py advaita-vādāḥ sāṃkhya-darśanaṃ ca. vyāvahāra-nayânupāti-prāyaś cârvāka-darśanam. ṛju-sūtrâkūta-pravṛtta-buddhayas tathāgatāḥ. śabdâdi-nayâvalambino vaiyākaraṇâdayaḥ.*
126 STP 3.47:

> *jāvaiyā vayaṇa-vahā tāvaiyā cêva hoṃti ṇaya-vāyā /*
> *jāvaiyā ṇaya-vāyā tāvaiyā cêva para-samayā //*

127 STP 3.69:

> *baddaṃ micchā-daṃsaṇa-samūha-maiyassa amaya-sārassa /*
> *jiṇa-vayaṇassa bhagavao saṃvigga-suhâhigammassa //*

128 See Cort (2000: 327 ff.).
129 For a review of some sources see Cort (2000: esp. 331–336).
130 Comp. Dundas (2002: 231):

> In Jain hands, this method of analysis became a fearsome weapon of philosophical polemic with which the doctrines of Hinduism and Buddhism could be pared down to their ideological basics of simple permanence and impermanence respectively and thus be shown to be one-pointed and inadequate as the overall interpretation of reality which they purported to be.... On the other hand, the many-pointed approach was claimed by the Jains to be immune from criticism...

Bibliography

Primary literature

A = Pāṇini: *Aṣṭādhyāyī.* (1) Sumitra Mangesh Katre: *Aṣṭādhyāyī of Pāṇini in Roman Transliteration.* Austin: University of Texas Press, 1987 [Reprinted: Delhi: Motilal Banarsidas, 1989]. (2) Śrisa Chandra Vasu: *The Aṣṭādhyāyī of Pāṇini, Edited and Translated into English.* 2 Vols. The Pāṇini Office, Al 1891 [Reprinted: Delhi: Motilal Banarsidas, 1962, 1977, 1980, 1988]. (3) Rama Nath Sharma: *The Aṣṭādhyāyī of Pāṇini.* Vols. 1–6 [Vol. 1: *Introduction ot the Aṣṭādhyāyī as a Grammatical Device,* Vols. 2–6: *English Translation of Adhāyāyas with Sanskrit Text, Transliteration, Word-Boundary, Anuvṛtti, Vṛtti, Explanatory Note, Derivational History of Examples, and Indices*]. New Delhi: Munshiram Manoharlal Publishers, 2003.

AJP Haribhadra-sūri: *Anekānta-jaya-patākā.* Hīralāl R. Kāpaḍīā (ed.): *Anekānta-jayapatākā by Haribhadra Sūri with His Own Commentary and Municandra Sūri's supercommentary*. 2 Vols. Gaekwad Oriental Series 88, 105, Baroda: Oriental Institute, 1940, 1947.

ĀMī Samantabhadra: *Āpta-mīmāṃsā*. (1) Pannālāl Jain (ed.): *Ācārya-śrī-samantabhadra-svāmi-viracitā Āpta-mīmāṃsā syād-vāda-vidyāpati-śrī-vidyānanda-svāmi-viracitā pramāṇa-parīkṣā ca*. Sanātana Jaina Granthamālā 7, 8, Kāśī 1914. (2) Vaṃśīdhar (ed.): *Aṣṭa-sahasrī tārkika-cakra-cūḍā-maṇi-syādvāda-vidyāpatinā śrī-Vidyānanda-svāminā nirākṛta*. Bombay: Nirṇaya-sāgara Press, 1915.

AṇD *Aṇuoga-ddārāiṃ* (*Anuyoga-dvārāṇi*). Muni Puṇyavijaya, Dalsukh Mālvaṇiā, Amritlāl Mohanlāl Bhojak (ed.): *Nandi-suttaṃ and Aṇuoga-ddārāiṃ*. Jaina-Āgama-Series 1, Bombay: Śrī Mahāvīra Jaina Vidyālaya, 1968.

AYVD Hemacandra: *Anya-yoga-vyavaccheda-dvātriṃśikā*. See: SVM.

BĪPVV Bhāskara: *Bhāskarī Īśvara-pratyabhijñā-vimarśinī-vyākhyā*. K.A.Subramaniya Iyer [Ko. A. Subrahmaṇya Ayyar] (ed.); K.C. Pandey [Kanticandra Pāṇḍey] (ed., trans.): *Īśvara-pratyabhijñā-vimarśinī of Abhinavagupta – Doctrine of Divine Recognition – Sanskrit Text with the Commentary Bhāskarī and English Translation*. 3 Vols. Delhi–Varanasi–Patna–Madras: Motilal Banarsidas, 1986.

De Interpretatione 'Αριστοτέλους: Περὶ 'Ερμηνείας. Immanuel Bekker: *Aristotelis Opera*. Vol. 1, *Aristoteles Graece ex recensione Immanuelis Bekkeri*. Volumen prius, apud Gregorium Reimerum, Berolini: ex Officina Academica, 1831: 17–24.

DK Diels, Hermann; Kranz, Walther: *Die Fragmente der Vorsokratiker*. Zurich: Weidmann, 1985.

DNC Mallavādin Kṣamāśramaṇa: *Dvādaśāra-naya-cakra*. Muni Jambūvijayajī (ed.): *Dvādaśāraṃ Nayacakraṃ of Ācārya Śrī Mallavādī Kṣamāśramaṇa. With the Commentary Nyāyāgamānusāriṇī of Ācārya Śrī Siṃhasūri Gaṇi Vādi Kṣamāśramaṇa*. Pt. I (1–4 Aras), Bhāvnagar: Śrī-Jaina-Ātmānaṃda-sabhā, 1966 [Reprinted: Bhāvnagar 2000]; Pt. II (5–8 Aras): Bhāvnagar 1976; Pt. III (9–12 Aras): Bhāvnagar 1988.

DNCV Siṃha-sūri: *Nyāyâgamânusāriṇī Dvādaśāra-naya-cakra-vṛtti*. See: DNC.

JSK *Jainendra Siddhānta Kośa*. Edited by Jinendra Varṇī, Parts 1–5, Jñānapīṭha Mūrtidevī Jaina Grantha-mālā, 38, 40, 42, 44, 48 [Saṃskṛta Granthāṅka], Delhi: Bhāratīya Jñānapīṭha Prakāśana, 1997, 1999, 2000.

JTBh Yaśovijaya: *Jaina-tarka-bhāṣā*. (1) Dayanand Bhargava (ed., tr.): *Mahopādhyāya Yaśovijaya's Jaina Tarka Bhāṣā with Translation and Critical Notes*. Delhi–Varanasi–Patna: Motilal Banarsidas, 1973. (2) Sukhlāljī Saṅghavī; Mahendra Kumār; Dalsukh Mālvaṇiyā (ed.): *Mahopādhyāya-Śrī-Yaśovijayagaṇi-racitā Jaina-tarka-bhāṣā*. Ahmedabad: Sarasvatī Pustak Bhaṇḍār, 1993 [1st Edition: 1938].

LT Akalaṅka: *Laghīyas-traya*. See: NKC.

LTV Akalaṅka: *Laghīyas-traya-vivṛti*. See: LT/NKC.

MDhŚ *Mānava-dharma-śāstra* [*Manu-smṛti*]. Patrick Olivelle: *Manu's Code of Law. A Critical Edition and Translation of the Mānava-dharmaśāstra*. With the editorial assistance of Suman Olivelle. Oxford–New York–Delhi: Oxford University Press, 2006.

Met 'Αριστοτέλους: Τῶν Μετά τά Φύσικά. Jaeger, Werner (ed.): *Aristotelis Metaphysica*. Oxford Classical Texts, Oxford: Clarendon Press, 1957.

NĀ *Nyāyâvali*. Bejai Singh (ed.): *Nyāyāvali*. Delhi: Nag Publishers, 1980.

NaṃS *Naṃdi-sutta/Naṃdī-sutta* [*Nandi-sūtra/Nandī-sūtra*]. Muni Puṇyavijaya (ed.): *Nandisuttaṃ by Devavācaka with the Cūrṇi by Jinadāsa Gaṇi Mahattara*. Ahmadābād–Vārāṇasī: Prakrit Text Society Series 9, 1966.

NaṃSCū Jinadāsa-gaṇin Mahattara: *Naṃdī-sutta-cūṇṇi* [*Nandi-sūtra-cūrṇi*]. See: NaṃS.

NaṃVṛ Haribhadra-sūri: *Nandi-sūtra-vṛtti*. Muni Puṇyavijaya (ed.): *Nandisūtraṃ by Śhrī Devavācaka with the Vṛtti by Śhrī Haribhadrācarya and Durgapadavhyākhyā on Vṛtti by Śhrī Śrīcandrācārya and Viṣampadaparyāya on Vṛtti*. Ahmadābād–Vārāṇasī: Prakrit Text Society Series 10, Prakrit Text Society, 1966.

NAV Siddharṣi-gaṇin: *Nyāyāvatāra-vivṛti*. See Balcerowicz (2009).

NBh Vātsyāyana Pakṣilasvāmin: *Nyāya-bhāṣya*. See: NS.

NBhū Bhāsarvajña: *Nyāya-bhūṣaṇa*. Svāmī Yogīndrānanda (ed.): *Śrīmad-ācārya-Bhāsarvajña-praṇītasya Nyāya-sārasya svopajñaṃ vyākhyānaṃ Nyāya-bhūṣaṇam*. Varanasi: Ṣad-darśana-prakāśana-grantha-mālā 1, Ṣad-darśana Prakāśana Pratiṣṭhānam, 1968.

ṆC Māilla-dhavala-[deva]: *Ṇaya-cakko* [*Dravya-svabhāva-prakāśaka-naya-cakra*]. Kailash Chandra Shastri (ed., transl.): *Ṇayacakko* [*Nayacakra*] *of Śrī Māilla-dhavala*. Delhi: Jñānapīṭha Mūrtidevī Jaina Grantha-mālā, Bhāratīya Jñānapīṭha Prakāśana 12, 1999 [1st Edition: 1971].

NKC Prabhācandra: *Nyāya-kumuda-candra*. *Nyāya-kumuda-candra of Śrīmat Prabhācandrācarya. A Commentary on Bhaṭṭākalaṅkadeva's Laghīyastraya*. Edited by Mahendra Kumār Nyāyācarya Śāstri, Vol. 1–2, Sri Garib Dass Oriental Series 121, Delhi: Sri Satguru Publications, 1991. [1st Edition: Bombay 1938–1942].

NMa Jayanta-bhaṭṭa: *Nyāya-mañjarī*. K.S. Varadacharya (ed.): *Nyāyamañjarī of Jayantabhaṭṭa with Ṭippaṇi-nyāya-saurabha by the editor*. Vol. 1 & 2, Oriental Research Institute Series 116, 139, Mysore: University of Mysore, 1969, 1983.

NS Akṣapāda Gautama: *Nyāya-sūtra*. (1) Mahāmahopadhyāya Ganganātha Jha; Pandit Dhundhirāja Shastri Nyāyopādhyāya (eds.): *The Nyaya-Darshana: The Sūtras of Gautama and Bhāṣya of Vātsyāyana with two Commentaries: (1) Khadyota by Mahāmahopādhyāya Gangānātha Jha, and (2) The Bhāṣyachandra by Raghūttama—up to Adhyāya iii, Āhnika ii, Sūtra 17 only, with Notes by Pandit Ambadās Shastri*. Chowkhambā Sanskrit Series, Vārāṇasī: Chowkhambā, 1925. (2) Anantalal Thakur (ed.): *Gautamīyanyāyadarśana with Bhāṣya of Vātsyāyana*. New Delhi: Indian Council of Philosophical Research, 1997.

NUK Chhabinath Miśra (ed.): *Nyāyokti-kośa (A Dictionary of Nyāyas in Sanskrit Śāstras)*. Delhi: Ajanta Publications, 1978.

NVi Akalaṅka Bhaṭṭa: *Nyāya-viniścaya*. (1) Nyāyācārya Mahendra Paṇḍita Kumār Śāstri (ed.): *Śrīmad-Bhaṭṭākalaṅka-deva-viracitam Akalaṅka-grantha-trayam* [*Svopajña-vivṛti-sahitam Laghīyas-trayam, Nyāya-viniścayaḥ, Pramāṇa-saṅgrahaś ca*]. Ahmadābād (Ahmedabad): Sarasvatī Pustak Bhaṇḍār, 1996 [1st Edition: Ahmedabad–Calcutta 1939]. (2) Mahendra Kumar Jain (ed.): *Nyāyaviniścaya-vivaraṇa of Śrī Vādirāja Sūri, the Sanskrit Commentary on Bhaṭṭa Akalaṅkadeva's Nyāyaviniścaya*. Vol. 1 & 2, Vārāṇasī: Bhāratīya Jñānapīṭha Prakāśana, 1949, 1955. [2nd Edition: New Delhi: Bhāratīya Jñānapīṭha Prakāśana, 2000].

PNTĀA Vādideva-sūri: *Pramāṇa-naya-tattvâlokâlaṅkāra*. (1) See: SVR. (2) Hari Satya Bhattacharya (ed., transl.): *Pramāṇa-naya-tattvālokālaṅkāra of Vādideva Sūri. English Translation and Commentary*. Bombay: Jain Sahitya Vikas Mandal, 1967.

Paṇṇ *Paṇṇavaṇā-sutta* [*Prajñāpanā-sūtra*]. Muni Puṇyavijaya, Dalsukh Mālvaṇiā, Amritlāl Mohanlāl Bhojak (ed.): *Paṇṇāvaṇāsuttam*. 2 Parts, Jaina-Āgama-Series 9 (Part 1, 2), Bombay: Śrī Mahāvīra Jaina Vidyālaya, 1969, 1971.

PAS Kundakunda: *Paṃcatthiya-saṃgaha* [*Pañcāstikāya-samaya-sāra*]. Manoharlāl (ed.): *Śrīmat-Kundakunda-svāmi-viracitaḥ Pañcāsti-kāyaḥ Tattva-pradīpikā-Tātparya-vṛtti-Bālāvabodhaka-bhāṣeti ṭīkā-trayôpetaḥ*. Agās (Gujarat): Śrī Paramaśruta-Prabhāvaka-Maṇḍala, Śrīmad Rājacandra Āśrama, 1998.

PKM Prabhācandra: *Prameya-kamala-mārtaṇḍa*. Mahendra Kumar Shastri (ed.): *Prameyakamala-mārtaṇḍa by Shri Prabha Chandra (A Commentary on Shri Manik*

Nandi's Pareeksha Mukh Sutra). Bombay: Nirnaya Sagar Press, 1941 [Reprinted: Delhi: Shri Satguru Publications, 1990].

PMī Hemacandra: *Pramāṇa-mīmāṃsā*. (1) Satkari Mookerjee and Nathmal Tatia (eds, tr.): *Hemacandra's. Text and Translation with Critical Notes*. Tara Publications, Varanasi 1970. (2) Sukhlāljī Saṅghavī; Mahendra Kumār; Dalsukh Mālvaṇiyā (eds): *Kavikālasarvajña-Śrī-Hemacandrācārya-viracitā svopajña-vṛtti-sahitā Pramāṇa Mīmāṃsā*. Ahmedabad: Sarasvatī Pustak Bhaṇḍār, 1998.

PSā Kundakunda: *Pavayaṇa-sāra* [*Pravacana-sāra*]. A.N. Upadhye (ed.): *Śrī Kundakundācārya's Pravacanasāra (Pavayaṇasāra), a Pro-Canonical Text of the Jainas, the Prakṛit Text Critically Edited with the Sanskrit Commentaries of Amṛtacandra and Jayasena*. Agās (Gujarat): Śrī Paramaśruta-Prabhāvaka-Maṇḍala, Śrīmad Rājacandra Āśrama, 1984 [1st Edition: Bombay 1935].

PV Dharmakīrti: *Pramāṇa-vārttika*. (1) Chap. 1: see: PVSV. (2) Svāmī Dvārikādās Śāstri (ed.): *Dharmakirtti Nibandhawali (1): Pramāṇa-vārttika of Acharya Dharmakīrti with the Commentary 'Vṛtti' of Acharya Manorathanandin*. Bauddha Bharati Series 3, Vārāṇasī: Bauddha Bharati, 1968 [Reprinted: 1984].

PVSV Dharmakīrti: *Pramāṇa-vārttika-svavṛtti*. Raniero Gnoli (ed.): *The Pramāṇavārttikam of Dharmakīrti, the First Chapter with the Autocommentary. Text and Critical Notes*. Serie Orientale Roma 23, Roma: Ismeo, 1960.

PVSVṬ Karṇakagomin: *Pramāṇa-vārttika-svavṛtti-ṭīkā*. Rāhula Sāṅkṛtyāyana (ed.): *Ācārya-Dharmakīrteḥ Pramāṇa-vārttikam (svārthānumāna-paricchedaḥ) svopajña-vṛttyā Karṇakagomi-viracitayā taṭ-ṭīkayā ca sahitam*. Ilāhābād [Allahabad]: Kitāb Mahal, 1943 [Reprinted: Kyoto 1982].

RVār Akalaṅka: *Tattvârtha-vārttika* (*Rāja-vārttika*). Mahendra Kumar Jain (ed.): *Tattvârtha-vārttika* [*Rāja-vārttika*] *of Śrī Akalaṅkadeva*. Edited with Hindi Translation, Introduction, Appendices, Variant Readings, Comparative Notes etc. Parts I–II. Jñānapīṭha Mūrtidevī Jaina Grantha-mālā: Sanskrit Grantha 10, 20, Delhi: Bhāratīya Jñānapīṭha Prakāśana, 1953–1957 [2nd Edition: Delhi 1982].

SBhT Vimaladāsa: *Sapta-bhaṅgī-taraṅgiṇī*. Manohar Lāl (ed.): *Śrīmad-vimaladāsa-viracitā sapta-bhaṅgī-taraṅgiṇī*. With Hindi Commentary by Ṭhākur Prasād Śarmma. Agās: Paramaśruta Prabhāvak Maṇḍal, Śrīmad Rājacandra Āśram, 1995.

SSi Pūjyapāda Devanandin: *Sarvârtha-siddhi*. Phoolchandra Shastri (ed.): *Ācārya Pūjyapāda's Sarvārthasiddhi [The commentary on Ācārya Griddhapiccha's Tattvârtha-sūtra]*. Edited and Translated [into Hindi]. Varanasi 1934 [Reprinted: Jñānapīṭha Mūrtidevī Jaina Grantha-mālā 13, Delhi: Bhāratīya Jñānapīṭha Prakāśana, 2000].

STP Siddhasena Divākara: *Saṃmati-tarka-prakaraṇa*. (1) Sukhlāl Saṅghavi; Becardās Dośi (ed.): *Saṃmatitarka-prakaraṇam by Siddhasena Divākara with Abhayadevasūri's Tattva-bodha-vidhāyinī*. *Gujarāt-purā-tattva-mandir-granthāvalī* 10, 16, 18, 19, 21, Amdāvād: Gujarāt-purā-tattva-mandir, 1924–1931 [Reprinted: 2 Vols. *Rinsen Buddhist Text Series* VI–1, 2; Kyoto 1984].

SVM Malliṣeṇa: *Syād-vāda-mañjarī*. (1) A.B. Dhruva (ed.): *Syādvādamañjarī of Malliṣeṇa with the Anyayoga-vyavaccheda-dvātriṃśikā of Hemacandra*. Bombay Sanskrit and Prakrit Series No. 83, Bombay 1933. (2) Jagadīśacandra Jain (ed., Hindi trans.): *Kali-kāla-sarvajña-śrī-hemacandrācārya-viracitā-anya-yoga-vyavaccheda-dvātriṃśikā-stavana-ṭīkā śrī-malliṣeṇa-sūri-praṇītā syād-vāda-mañjarī*. Agās: Śrī Paramaśruta Prabhāvak Maṇḍal, Śrīmad Rājacandra Āśram, 1992.

SVR Vādideva-sūri: *Syād-vāda-ratnākara*. Motīlāl Lālājī (ed.): *Śrīmad-Vādideva-sūri-viracitaḥ Pramāṇa-naya-tattvâlokâlaṅkāraḥ tad-vyākhyā ca Syād-vāda-ratnākaraḥ*. 5

Vols. Poona 1926–1930 [Reprinted: 2 Vols. Dillī (Delhi): Bhāratīya Buk Kārporeśan, 1988].

SvSt Samantabhadra: *Svayambhū-stotra.* (1) Jugal Kiśor Mukhtār "Yugavīra" (ed., introd.): *Śrīmat-svāmi-Samangabhadrācārya-viracita catur-viṃśati-jina-stavanātmaka Svayambhū-stotra (stuti-paraka jaināgama).* Vira-sevā-mandira-grantha-mālā 7, Sarasāvā Jilā Sahāranapura: Vira-sevā Mandira, 1951. (2) Devendra K. Goyal (ed., tr.): *The Path to Enlightenment. Svayambhu Stotra by Acharya Samantabhdra Svami. English Translation with Introduction.* New Delhi: Radiant Publishers, 2000.

TBV Abhayadeva-sūri: *Tattva-bodha-vidhāyinī.* Sukhlāl Saṅghavi; Becardās Dośi (ed.): *Saṃmati-tarka-prakaraṇa by Siddhasena Divākara with Abhayadevasūri's Commentary, Tattva-bodha-vidhāyinī.* Vol. I & II, Rinsen Buddhist Text Series VI-1,2; Kyoto, Rinsen Book Co., 1984 [Reprinted from the Original Edition Published in 5 vols., Gujarāt-purā-tattva-mandir-granthāvalī 10, 16, 18, 19, 21, Amdāvād: Gujarāt-purā-tattva-mandir, 1924–1931].

TRD Guṇaratna-sūri: *Tarka-rahasya-dipikā.* Luigi Suali (ed.): *Ṣaḍ-darśana-samuccaya with Guṇaratna's Commentary Tarkarahasyadipikā.* Bibliotheca Indica 167, Calcutta: Asiatic Society of Bengal, 1905–1914 [Reprinted: 1986].

TS Umāsvāmin: *Tattvârtha-sūtra.* (1) M.K. Mody (ed.): *Tattvārthādhigama by Umāsvāti Being in the Original Sanskrit with the Bhāṣya by the Author Himself.* Bibliotheca Indica/Bibliotheca Indica New Series 1044, 1079, 1118, Calcutta: Asiatic Society of Bengal, 1903, 1904, 1905 [= Śvetāmbara Recension]. (2) See: SSi [= Digāmbara Recension].

TSaP Kamalaśīla: *Tattva-saṅgraha-pañjikā.* Embar Krishnamacharya (ed.): *Tattvasaṅgraha of Śāntarakṣita with the commentary of Kamalaśīla.* 2 Vols. Gaekwad's Oriental Series 30–31, Baroda: Oriental Institute, 1926 [Reprinted: 1984, 1988].

TŚVA Vidyānanda Pātrakesarisvāmin: (1) *Tattvârtha-śloka-vārtitkâlaṃkara.* Vardhamān Pārśvanāth Śāstrī (ed.): *Śrī-vidyānanda-svāmi-viracita Tattvârtha-śloka-vārttikālaṃkara bhāṣā-ṭīkā-samanvita.* With Hindi Translation and a *Ṭīkā* by Māṇikacaṃdjī Kaundeya. 7 Vols. Solāpur: Kalyāṇ Paṃvar Priṃṭiṃg Pres, Kalyāṇ-bhavan, 1949, 1951, 1953, 1956, 1964, 1969, 1984. (2) Manoharalāl, Ramacandra Nātha Raṅgajī (eds): *Tattvârtha-śloka-vārtitkâlaṃkara.* Bombay: Nirṇāya Sāgara Press, 1918.

VĀBh Jinabhadra-gaṇin: *Visesâvassaya-bhāsa* (*Viśeṣâvaśyaka-bhāṣya*). Haragovinda Dās (ed.): *Viśeṣâvaśyaka-bhāṣyaṃ. Maladhāri-śrī-hemacandra-sūri-viracitayā śiṣya-hitānamnayā bṛhad-vṛttyā vibhūṣitam.* Śrī-Yaśovijaya-jaina-grantha-mālā 25, 27, 28, 31, 33, 35, 37, 39, Vārāṇasī: Shah Harakhchand Bhurabhai, 1915.

VĀVṛ Hemacandra Maladhārin Gandhavimukta: *Viśeṣâvaśyaka-vṛtti* (*Bṛhad-vṛtti*). See: VĀBh.

Viy *Viyāha-pannatti/Viyāha-paṇṇatti/Bhagavaī-viyāha-paṇṇaṭṭī* [*Bhagavatī Vyākhyā-prajñapti/Bhagavatī-sūtra*]. Bechardas J. Doshi; Amritlal Mohanlal Bhojak (ed.): *Viyāhapaṇṇattisuttaṃ.* 3 Parts, Jaina-Āgama-Series 4 (Part 1, 2, 3), Bombay: Śrī Mahāvīra Jaina Vidyālaya, 1974, 1978, 1982.

YA Samantabhadra: *Yukty-anuśāsana.* Indra Lāl: (ed.): *Yukty-anuśāsana of Samantabhadra.* Edited with the *Ṭīkā* of Vidyānandācārya. Māṇikacandra-Digambara-Jaina-Grantha-mālā, Bombay: Nāthūrām Premī Maṃtrī/Māṇikacandra-Digambara-Jaina-Grantha-mālā-samiti, 1921 (Saṃ.: 1977).

YAṬ Vidyānandācārya: *Yukty-anuśāsana-ṭīkā.* See: YA.

Secondary literature

Alsdorf, Ludwig. "Nikṣepa – A Jaina Contribution to Scholastic Methodology." *Journal of the Oriental Institute* (Baroda) 22 (1973) 455–463 [Reprinted in: Ludwig Alsdorf. *Kleine Schriften*. Edited Albrecht Wezler, Band X, Wiesbaden: Franz Steiner Verlag, 1974: 257–265].

Balcerowicz, Piotr. "The Logical Structure of the *Naya* Method of the Jainas." *Journal of Indian Philosophy* 29/3 (2001) 379–403.

Balcerowicz, Piotr. "Some Remarks on the Naya Method." *Essays in Jaina Philosophy and Religion*. Edited by Piotr Balcerowicz, 37–67. Delhi: Motilal Banarsidas, 2003.

Balcerowicz, Piotr. *Jaina Epistemology in Historical and Comparative Perspective. Critical Edition and English Translation of Logical-Epistemological Treatises: Nyāyāvatāra, Nyāyāvatāra-vivṛti and Nyāyāvatāra-ṭippaṇa with Introduction and Notes. Second Revised Edition.* 2 Vols. Delhi: Motilal Banarsidas, 2009 [1st Edition: Alt- und Neu-Indische Studien 53, 1–2, Stuttgart: Franz Steiner Verlag, 2001].

Balcerowicz, Piotr. "Dharmakīrti's Criticism of the Jaina Doctrine of Multiplexity of Reality (*anekānta-vāda*)." Edited by Helmut Krasser, Horst Lasic, Eli Franco, Birgit Kellner, 1–31. *Religion and Logic in Buddhist Philosophical Analysis. Proceedings of the Fourth International Dharmakīrti Conference, 23–27.08.2005*. Österreichische Akademie der Wissenschaften, Philosophisch-Historische Klasse, Denkschriften, 424. Band. Wien: Verlag der Österreichischen Akademie der Wissenschaften, 2011.

Barlingay, S.S. *A Modern Introduction to Indian Logic*. Delhi: National Publishing House, 1965.

Basham, Arthur L. *History and Doctrines of the Ājīvikas. A Vanished Indian Religion*. Luzac & and Company Ltd., London 1951 [Reprinted: Delhi–Varanasi–Patna: Motilal Banarsidas, 1981].

Bharadwaja, V.K. "The Jaina Concept of Logic." *Studies in Jainism*. Edited by M.P. Marathe, Meena A. Kelkar, P.P. Gokhale, 116–129. Indian Philosophical Quarterly Publication No. 7, Pune: Department of Philosophy, University of Poona, 1984.

Bharucha, F.; Kamat, R.V. "*Syādvāda* Theory of Jainism in Terms of Devial Logic." *Indian Philosophical Quarterly* 9 (1984) 181–187.

Bhatt, Bansidhar. *The Canonical Nikṣepa. Studies in Jaina Dialectics*. With a foreword by K. Bruhn & H. Haertel. Leiden: E.J. Brill, 1978 [Reprinted: Delhi–Varanasi: Bharatiya Vidya Prakashan, 1991].

Cort, John. "'Intellectual *Ahiṃsā*' Revisited: Jain Tolerance and Intolerance of Others." *Philosophy East and West* 50 (2000) 324–347.

Dhruva, A.B. "Introduction", see SVM, 1933.

Dundas, Paul. *The Jains*. Second Edition, London–New York: Routledge, 2002 [1st Edition: 1992].

Dunne, John Dowling. *Foundations of Dharmakīrti's Philosophy*. Boston: Wisdom, Publications, 2004.

Flügel, Peter. "Power and Insight in Jaina Discourse." *Logic and Belief in Indian Philosophy*. Edited by Piotr Balcerowicz, 85–217. Delhi: Motilal Banarsidas (Warsaw Indological Studies).

Ganeri, Jonardon. *Philosophy in Classical India: The Proper Work of Reason*. London: Routledge, 2001.

Ganeri, Jonardon. "Jaina Logic as the Philosophical Basis of Pluralism." *History and Philosophy of Logic* 23 (2002) 267–281.

Glasenapp, Helmuth von. *The Doctrine of Karman in Jain Philosophy*. Translated from the original German by G. Barry Gifford and revised by the Author, Edited by Hiralal R. Kapadia. Bombay: Viji Jivanlal Panalal Charity Fund, 1942.

Gokhale, Pradeep P. "The Logical Structure of *Syādvāda*." *Journal of Indian Council of Philosophical Research* 8 (1991) 73–81 [Reprinted in Shah (2000: 75–86)].

Hayes, Richard P. *Dignāga on the Interpretation of Signs*. Studies of Classical India 9, Dordrecht: Kluwer Academic Press, 1988.

Herzberger, Radhika. *Bhartṛhari and the Buddhists*. Studies of Classical India 8, Dordrecht: D. Reidel Publishing Company (Kluwer Academic Publishers), 1986.

Jain, Pragati: "*Saptabhaṅgī* – The Jaina Theory of Sevenfold Predication: A Logical Analysis." *Philosophy East and West* 50 (2000) 385–399.

Kāpaḍīā, Hīralāl R. "Introduction." See AJP, 1940–1947.

Kothari, D.S. "The Complementarity Principle and *Syādvāda*." In: Shah (2000: 87–94).

Kulkarni, V.M. "Relativity and Absolutism." In: Shah (2000: 61–66).

Matilal, Bimal Krishna. *The Central Philosophy of Jainism (Anekānta-vāda)*. L.D. Series 79, Ahmedabad: L.D. Institute of Indology, 1981.

Matilal, Bimal Krishna. *Logic, Language and Reality: Indian Philosophy and Contemporary Issues*. Delhi: Motilal Banarsidas, 1985.

Matilal, Bimal Krishna. "*Anekānta*: Both Yes and No?" *Journal of Indian Council of Philosophical Research* 8 (1991) 1–12 [Reprinted in Shah (2000: 1–16)].

Mukerji, R.N. "The Jaina Logic of Seven-fold Predication." *Mahāvīra and His Teachings*. Edited by A.N. Upadhye, Nathmal Tatia, Dalsukh Malvania, Mohanlal Mehta, Nemichand Shastri, Kailashchandra Shastri, 225–233. Bombay: Bhagavān Mahāvīra 2,500 Nirvāṇa Mahotsava Samiti, 1977.

Nahar, P.C.; Ghosh, K.C. *An Encyclopaedia of Jainism*. Reprint Edition, Sri Garib Dass Oriental Series 40, Delhi: Sri Satguru Publications, 1996 [1st Edition: Calcutta 1917].

Padmarajiah, Y.J. *A Comparative Study of Jaina Theories of Reality and Knowledge*. Delhi–Varanasi–Patna–Madras: Motilal Banarsidas, 1986 [1st Edition: Delhi 1963].

Pandey, Sangam Lal. "*Naya-vāda* and Many-valued Logic." *Studies in Jainism*. Edited by M.P. Marathe, Meena A. Kelkar; P.P. Gokhale, 156–166. Poona: Indian Philosophy Quarterly Publication 7, 1984.

Priest, Graham. "Jaina logic: a contemporary perspective." *History and Philosophy of Logic* 29 (2008) 263–278.

Saṅghavi, Sukhlāl; Dośi, Becardās. *Siddhasena Divākara's Sanmati Tarka with a Critical Introduction and an Original Commentary*. Translated from Hindi by A.S. Gopani, Reprinted by Jitendra B. Shah (General Editor), Ahmedabad: L.D. Institute of Indology, 2000 [1st Edition: 1939].

Schang, Fabien. "Truth-Values Are Not the Whole Story (A Semi-Paranormal Logic of Acceptance and Rejection within *n*-Valuation)." Paper presented to: 4ème Congrès Mondial sur la Paraconsistance (WCP4) – Ormond College, University of Melbourne, 13–18.07.2008a, manuscript, http://poincare.univ-nancy2.fr/digitalAssets/28005_SCHANG_WCP4__Truth-values_are_not_the_whole_story.pdf [accessed on 04.03.2009].

Schang, Fabien. "Jaina Logic in the Light of *n*-Valuation." Typescript 2008b.

Schang, Fabien. "Two Indian Dialectical Logics: *Saptabhaṅgī* and *catuṣkoṭi*." *Journal of Indian Council of Philosophical Research* 27/1 (2010) 47–76.

Schubring, Walter. *The Doctrine of the Jainas*. Translated from the German by Wolfgang Beurlen, Delhi: Motilal Banarsidas Publishers, 1962 [Reprinted: Delhi: Motilal Banarsidas Publishers, 1978. Re-edited with the Three Indices Enlarged and Added by Willem Bollée and Jayandra Soni, Delhi: Motilal Banarsidas Publishers, 2000].

Shah, J. Nagin (ed.). *Jaina Theory of Multiple Facets of Reality and Truth*. Delhi: Bhogilal Leherchand Institute of Indology, 2000.

Uno, Atsushi. "A Study of *Syādvāda*." In: Shah (2000: 33–60).

Upadhye, A.N. (PSā) "Introduction." See: PSā, pp. 1–120.

Appendix

Publications of Willem B. Bollée

Name:	Bollée, Willem B.
Born:	1927
Academic achievements:	MA, PhD, DLitt (Habilitation) Heidelberg
Honours:	Hemacandrasuri Award 2004 Prakrit Jnanabharati International Award 2005
University association:	Professor South Asia Institute
Address for communication:	Don-Bosco-Str. 2, D – 96047 Bamberg, Germany E-mail: Willem.Bollee@t-online.de

Publications

Books

1956 *Saḍviṃśa-Brāhmaṇa*. Utrecht: A. Storm [thesis].

1970 *Kuṇālajātaka*. London: Pali Text Society (Second Edition 2009).

1977 *Studien zum Sūyagaḍa I. Die Jainas und die anderen Weltanschauungen vor der Zeitenwende. Textteile, Nijjutti, Übersetzung und Anmerkungen.* Wiesbaden: Steiner (Schriftenreihe des Südasien Instituts der Universität Heidelberg Band 24).

1980 *The Pādas of the Suttanipāta*. Reinbek: Dr. Inge Wezler.

1983 *Reverse Index of the Dhammapada, Suttanipāta, Thera- and Therāgāthā Pādas with Parallels from the Āyāranga, Sūyagaḍa, Uttarajjhāyā, Dasaveyāliya and Isibhāsiyāi*. Reinbek: Dr. Inge Wezler.

1988 *Studien zum Sūyagaḍa II. Die Jainas und die anderen Weltanschauungen vor der Zeitenwende. Textteile, Nijjutti, Übersetzung und Anmerkungen.* Stuttgart: Steiner (Schriftenreihe des Südasien Instituts der Universität Heidelberg Band 31).

1991 *Materials for an Edition and Study of the Piṇḍa- and Oha-Nijjuttis of the Śvetāmbara Jain Tradition*. Vol. 1. Stuttgart: Steiner (Beiträge zur Südasienforschung Südasien-Institut Heidelberg 142).

1994 *Materials for an Edition and Study of the Piṇḍa- and Oha-Nijjuttis of the Śvetāmbara Jain Tradition*. Vol. 2: Text and Glossary. Stuttgart: Steiner (Beiträge zur Südasienforschung Südasien-Institut Heidelberg 162).

1995 *The Nijjuttis on the Seniors of the Śvetāmbara Siddhānta: Āyāranga, Sūyagaḍa, Dasaveyāliya and Uttarajjhāyā*. Text and Selective Glossary. Stuttgart: Steiner (Beiträge zur Südasienforschung Südasien-Institut Heidelberg 169).

1998 *Bhadrabāhu, Bṛhatkalpaniryukti and Saṅghadāsa, Bṛhatkalpa-bhāṣya.* Romanized and Metrically Revised Version, Notes from Related Texts, and a Selective Glossary. Part 1–3. Stuttgart: Steiner (Beiträge zur Südasienforschung Südasien-Institut Heidelberg 181,1–3).

2000 W. Schubring. *The Doctrine of the Jainas: Described After the Old Sources.* Translated from the Revised German Edition by Wolfgang Beurlen. Third English Edition. With Three Indices Enlarged and Added by Willem Bollée and Jayandra Soni. Delhi: Motilal Banarasidasa.

2002 *The Story of Paesi (Paesi-kahāṇayaṃ). Soul and Body in Ancient India. A Dialogue on Materialism.* Text, Translation, Notes and Glossary. Wiesbaden: Harrassowitz (Beiträge zur Kenntnis südasiatischer Sprachen und Literaturen 8) (Reprint: Bombay: Hindi Granth Karyalaya, 2005).

2004 W. Schubring. *Mahāvīra's Words.* Translated and Edited With Much Added Material by W. Bollée and J. Soni. Ahmadabad: L. D. Institute Series.

2006 *Vavahāra-Bhāṣya Pīṭhikā.* Edited, Translated and Annotated. Mumbai: Hindi Granth Karyalaya.

2006 *Gone to the Dogs in Ancient India.* München: Beck (Second Edition Forthcoming).

2006 L. Alsdorf. *Jaina Studies: Their Present State and Future Tasks.* Translated by B. Patil. Edited by W. Bollée. Mumbai: Hindi Granth Karyalaya.

2008 *Pārśvanāthacaritram.* Mumbai: Hindi Granth Karyalaya.

2008 *Stories from the Vyavahārabhāṣya Commentary of the Śvetāmbara Jains Selected by Ernst Leumann.* Mumbai: Hindi Granth Karyalaya.

2009 *Kuṇālajātaka.* Second Enlarged Edition. Oxford: The Pali Text Society.

2009 *Tales of Atonement.* Mumbai: Hindi Granth Karyalaya.

2010 *Samantabhadra's Ratnākaraṇḍaka-Śrāvakâcāra.* Śravaṇabeḷagoḷa: National Institute of Prakrit Studies. Reprint. Mumbai: Hindi Granth Karyalay (Pt. Nathuram Premi Research Series 41).

2010 L. Alsdorf. *The History of Vegetarianism and Cow-Veneration in India.* Translated by B. Patil. Edited by W. Bollée. London: Routledge (Routledge Advances in Jaina Studies 3).

2012 *Vavahāra Bhāṣya Pīṭhikā.* Reprint. Mumbai: Hindi Granth Karyalaya (Pt. Nathuram Premi Research Series 4).

2013 *A Cultural History of the Kathāsaritsāgara.* Studia indologica Universitatis halensis 8. Halle.

Articles

1967 Some Less Known Burmese Pali Texts. In: *Pratidānam* (Festschrift Kuiper). Ed. J. C. Heesterman *et al.*, 493–499. Gravenhage: Mouton.

1969 Die Stellung der Vinaya-Ṭīkās in der Pāli-Literatur. In: *ZDMG* Supplement I, 3: 824–835.

āhacca. In: *ZVS* 83, 1: 26–48.

Pāli mukham ulloketi (oloketi). In: *ZVS* 83, 2: 243–255.

1970 Contributions to the *Critical Pali Dictionary II.* Copenhagen: Munksgaard (until 1985).

1971 Anmerkungen zum buddhistischen Häretikerbild. In: *ZDMG* 121, 1: 70–92.

1974 Buddhists and Buddhism in the Earlier Literature of the Śvetâmbara Jains. In: *Buddhist Studies in Honour of I. B. Horner.* Ed. L. Cousins, 27–39. Dordrecht/Boston: D. Reidel.

1977 A Note on Evil and its Conquest from Indra to Buddha. In: *Prajñāpāramitā and Related Systems: Studies in Honor of Edward Conze*. Ed. L. Lancaster, 371–381. Berkeley: Group in Buddhist Studies (Berkeley Buddhist Studies Series 1).
1978 On Royal Epithets in the Aupapātikasūtra. In: *JOIB* 27, 3–4: 95–103.
1981 The Indo-European Sodalities in Ancient India. In: *ZDMG* 131, 1: 172–191.
1983 Traditionell-indische Vorstellungen über die Füße in Literatur und Kunst. In: *BAVA* 5: 227–281.
Notes on Middle-Indian Vocabulary II. In: *JOIB* 33,1–2: 108–122.
1984 Zur Typologie der Träume und ihrer Deutung in der älteren indischen Literatur. In: *StII* 10: 169–186.
1986 Le kūṭâgāra ou de la maison des hommes au manoir dans l'Inde et l'Asie du Sud-Est. In: *BEI* 4: 189–214.
1988 Pourquoi il faut respecter un savant – Uttarajjhāya XI. In: *IT* 14: 145–162.
The kūṭâgāra or from Men's House to Mansion in Eastern India and South-East Asia. In: *Shastric Traditions in Indian Arts*. Ed. A.L. Dahmen-Dallapiccola *et al.*, 143–149. Stuttgart: Steiner.
1990 Āyāranga 2, 16 and Sūyagaḍa 1, 16. In: *JIP* 18: 29–52.
Khuḍḍāga-niyaṇṭhijja (Uttarajjhāya 6): An Epitome of the Jain Doctrine. In: *ABORI* 71: 265–286.
The Peacock Egg: A Parable of Mahāvīra (Nāyādhammakahāo 1, 3). In: *The Clever Adulteress and Other Stories: A Treasury of Jain Literature*. Ed. P. Granoff, 7 16. Oakville: Mosaic Press.
1993 Die Geschichte vom Frosch. Nāyādhammakahāo 1, 13. In: *Jain Studies in Honour of Jozef Deleu*. Ed. R. Smet and K. Watanabe, 133–149. Tokyo: Hon-no-Tomosha.
Le végétarisme défendu par Haribhadrasūri contre un bouddhiste et un brahmane. In: *Studies on Buddhism in Honor of Professor A. K. Warder*. Ed. N. K. Wagle and F. Watanabe, 22–28. University of Toronto: Centre of South Asian Studies.
1994 Notes on Middle Indo-Aryan Vocabulary IV. In: *Jainism and Prakrit in Ancient and Medieval India. Essays for Prof. Jagdish Chandra Jain*. Ed. Narendra Nath Bhattacharyya, 63–70. New Delhi: Manohar, 1994.
1997 Das Aupapātika Sūtra, erstes Upânga der Jaina. II. Theil: Anmerkungen von Ernst Leumann. Edited by Willem B. Bollée. In: *BEI* 15: 311–363.
1998 Notes on Middle Indo-Aryan Vocabulary III. In: *Lex et Litterae. Studies in Honour of Professor Oscar Botto*. Ed. S. Lienhard and I. Piovano, 53–77. Alessandria: Edizioni dell'Orso.
1999 Adda or the Oldest Extant Dispute between Jains and Heretics, Sūyagaḍa 2, 6. Part Two. In: *JIP* 27: 411–437.
2002 Index to Padmanabh S. Jaini, Collected Papers on Jain Studies. In: *JIP* 30: 291–303.
Notes on Diseases in the Canon of the Śvetāmbara Jains. In: *TSAM* 7: 69–110.
Tales and Similes from Malayagiri's Commentary on the Vyavahārabhāṣya. Bhāga 1. In: *IT* 30: 41–95.
2004 Adda or the Oldest Extant Dispute Between Jains and Heretics (Sūyagaḍa 2, 6) Part One. In: *Jambū-jyoti (Munivara Jambūvijaya Festschrift)*. Ed. M. A. Dhaky and J. B. Shah, 48–84. Ahmedabad: Sharadaben Chimanbhai Educational Research Centre (Published 2006).
2005 Physical Aspects of Some Mahāpuruṣas. Descent, Foetality, Birth. In: *WZKS* 49: 6–34.
Tales and Similes from Malayagiri's Commentary on the Vyavahārabhāṣya. Bhāga 2. In: *IT* 31: 9–90.

Jain Studies in Germany. In: *German News* (Monthly Magazine of the German Embassy, New Delhi) 46: 22–23.

2006 An Important Narrative Collection Available Again. À propos Hemavijaya's Kathāratnâkara. In: *WZKS* 50: 69–139.

Adda or the Oldest Extant Dispute Between Jains and Heretics (Sūyagaḍa 2, 6) Part One. In: *Studies in Jaina History and Culture: Doctrines and Dialogues*. Ed. P. Flügel, 3–32. London: Routledge (Routledge Advances in Jaina Studies 1).

2007 Subject Index of the Inventory of the Stories in N. Balbir's Āvaśyaka Studien. In: *IJJS (Online)* 3, 1: 1–23 and *IJJS* 1–3, 2008: 60–85.

A Note on the Pāsa Tradition in the Universal History of the Digambaras and Śvetâmbaras (Guṇabhadra, Mahāpurāṇa, Utt. 73). In: *IJJS (Online)* 3, 2: 1–60 and *IJJS* 1–3: 86–145.

A Note on the Birth of the Hero in Ancient India. In: *The Concept of the Hero in Indian Culture*. Ed. H. Brückner, Hugh van Skyhawk and Claus Peter Zoller, 28. New Delhi: Manohar.

2008 Dogs in a Rare Zoological Book in Sanskrit. In: *TSAM* 8: 202–211.

Glossary of Robert Williams, Jaina Yoga. In: *IJJS (Online)* 4, 3: 1–53 and *IJJS* 4–6, 2010: 74–125.

Folklore on the Foot in Pre-Modern India. In: *IT* 34: 39–145.

Subject Index of Daṇḍin's Daśakumāracarita. In: *SI* (Warzawa) 15: 5–39.

Gomaya converts Kesi in Uttarajjhayana XXIII. In: *StII* 25: 1–33.

2010 On Nouns with Numerical Value in Sanskrit. In: *Anusandhāna* 50: 144–154.

Remarks on the Cultural History of the Ear in India. In: *Svasti. Essays in Honour of Prof. Hampa Nāgarājaiah for his 75. Birthday*. Ed. Nalini Balbir, 141–175. Krishnapuradoddhi: K.S. Muddappa Smaraka Trust (Muddushree Granthamale 75).

Willem Caland: Über den Aberglauben betreffend die Haarwirbel des Pferdes. In: *SI* (Warzawa) 17: 9–17.

Sīmantônnayana and sindūr dān. In: *From Turfan to Ajanta: Festschrift for Dieter Schlingloff on the Occasion of his Eightieth Birthday*. 2 Volumes. Ed. Eli Franco and Monika Zin, 69–74. Bhairahawa, Rupandehi: Lumbini International Research Institute.

Reviews

1969 H. Oldenberg and R. Pischel (ed.). 1966. Thera- und Therī-gāthā. 2nd Edition. Ed. K.R. Norman and L. Alsdorf (IIJ 11, 2: 146–149).

M.H. Bode. 1966. The Pali Literature of Burma (*IIJ* 11, 4: 311–318).

M. H. Aung. 1967. A History of Burma (*JESHO* 12, 2: 230–232).

T. Tun. 1967? History of Buddhism in Burma (*JESHO* 12, 3: 347–351).

1972 D. Malvania, M. Mehta and K. R. Chandra. 1970. Āgamic Index. Vol. I. Prakrit Proper Names. Part I (*BSOAS* 25, 1: 164–165).

1973 K. R. Norman. 1969. The Elders' Verses I: Theragāthā; 1971. The Elders' Verses II: Therīgāthā (*JAOS* 93, 4: 601–603).

1974 D. Malvania, M. Mehta and K. R. Chandra. 1972. Āgamic Index. Vol. I. Prakrit Proper Names. Part II (*BSOAS* 37, 1: 243).

M. C. Modi. 1972. Chakkammuvaeso of Amarakīrti (*BSOAS* 37, 2: 475).

A. K. Warder *et al.* 1971. Pāli Tipiṭakaṁ Concordance (*IF* 79: 255–256).

K. Wildhagen and W. Heraucourt. 1972. Deutsch-Englisches Wörterbuch, 2. Auflage (*Kratylos* 18, 1: 99–101).

1975 T. Ling. 1973. The Buddha (*JAOS* 95, 2: 306–307).
W. Hinz. 1973. Neue Wege im Altpersischen (*BSOAS* 38, 2: 451–454).
1977 J. Varenne. 1971. Devī Upaniṣad (*OLZ* 72, 6: 616–617).
1979 J. ver Eecke ed. & tr. 1976. Le Dasavatthuppakaraṇa (*ZDMG* 129: 201).
G. Steermann-Imre. 1977. Untersuchung des Königswahlmotivs in der indischen Märchenliteratur (*ZDMG* 129: 426–427).
H. Kopp. 1978. Buddhaghosa: Samantapāsādikā Indexes (*ZDMG* 129: 428–429).
B. Bhatt. 1978. The Canonical Nikṣepa (*ZDMG* 129: 430).
W. Schubring. 1978. Nāyādhammakahāo (*JAOS* 99, 2: 345–347).
K. Okuda. 1975. Eine Digambara-Dogmatik (*JAOS* 99, 3: 536).
1980 A.O. Franke. 1978. Kleine Schriften (*ZDMG* 130, 1: 191–192).
T. Damsteegt. 1978. Epigraphical Hybrid Sanskrit (*ZDMG* 130, 1: 192).
L.P. van den Bosch. 1978. Atharvaveda-pariśiṣṭa Chapters 21–29 (*ZDMG* 130, 1: 194).
Jambūvijaya. ed. 1977. Āyāraṅga-Suttaṃ.
Jambūvijaya. ed. 1978. Sūyagaḍaṅga-Suttaṃ.
Puṇyavijaya *et al.* ed. 1977. Dasaveyāliya-Suttaṃ, Uttarajjhayaṇāiṃ, Āvassaya-Sutta (*ZDMG* 130: 441–443).
Jambūvijaya. ed. 1978. Ācārāṅgasūtram and Sūtrakṛtāṅgasūtram (*ZDMG* 130: 196–197).
Ānandasāgarasūri. ed. 1973?. Āgamamañjūṣā (*ZDMG* 130: 197).
E. Denis. 1977. La Lokapaññatti et les idées cosmologiques du Buddhisme ancien (*ZDMG* 130: 197).
1985 N. Balbir. 1982. Dānâṣṭakakathā (*OLZ* 80, 5: 494–495).
1986 A. & P. Keilhauer. 1983. Die Bildersprache des Hinduismus (*ZDMG* 136,1: 148).
1987 R. J. Zydenbos. 1983. Mokṣa in Jainism, according to Umāsvāti (*OLZ* 82, 3: 295).
1992 A. Mette. 1991. Durch Entsagung zum Heil (*OLZ* 87, 4–5: 442–443).
1993 J. C. Jain. 1991. The Jain Way of Life (*JIP* 21, 2: 207–208).
J. Gonda. 1991. Selected Studies (*OLZ* 88, 1: 72–76).
1994 Jambūvijaya ed. 1991. Catalogue of the Manuscripts of Pāṭaṇa Jain Bhaṇḍāra (*OLZ* 89, 5–6: 593).
J. P. Jain ed. 1991. The Illustrated Manuscript of Jaina Ramayana (*ZDMG* 144, 2: 443).
1995 A. M. Ghatage ed. 1993. A Comprehensive and Critical Dictionary of the Prakrit Languages with Special Reference to Jain Literature (*OLZ* 90, 1: 80–81).
Jambūvijaya ed. 1993. Dharmabinduprakaraṇa of Haribhadra (*OLZ* 90, 5–6: 574–575).
1997 W. Johnson. 1995. Harmless Souls (*ZDMG* 147, 2: 527–528).
1999 E. Leumann. Kleine Schriften. Ed. N. Balbir. 1998 (*WZKS* 43: 257).
2000 K. Titze. 1998. Jainism: A Pictorial Guide to the Religion of Non-Violence (*WZKS* 44: 235).
Yogīndu. Lumière de l'Absolu.Tr. N. Balbir and C. Caillat. 1999 (*JIP* 28, 3: 325–326).
H. v. Glasenapp. 1999. Jainism. Tr. Shridhar B. Shroti (*JIP* 28, 3: 326–328).
2001 K. Krümpelmann. 2000. Dhuttakkhāṇa (*WZKS* 45: 219–221).
2002 P. S. Jaini. 2000. Collected Papers in Jaina Studies (*WZKS* 46: 276–277).
2003 M. Cone. 2001. A Dictionary of Pāli (*WZKS* 47: 220–222).
J. E. Cort. 2001. Jains in the World (*WZKS* 47: 233–235).
2004 K. K. Jain. 2003. Jaina Uddharaṇa Kośa (*WZKS* 48: 221–222).

2006 M. Yamazaki and Y. Ousaka. 2003. Index to the Jātaka,
M. Yamazaki and Y. Ousaka. 2004. Index to the Visuddhimagga (*WZKS* 50: 210).
N. M. Kansāra ed. 2006. Pañcagranthī Vyākaraṇa of Buddhisāgarasūri (*WZKS* 50: 211–212).
N. Shah. 2004. The World of Conquerors (*WZKS* 50: 214–215).
T. Sethia. 2004. Ahiṃsā, Anekānta und Jainism (*WZKS* 50: 215–216).
A. K. Jain. 2004. Satkhandāgama (*WZKS* 50: 216–217).
Acharya Kundkund: Barasa Anuvekkha. Ed. Dharma Rāja. 2003 (*IJJS Online* 2,1: 1–3) and *IJJS* 1–3, 2008: 16–18).

2008 K. L. Wiley. 2001. Historical Dictionary of Jainism (*ZDMG* 158, 2: 505–508).

2009 V. Kapashi. 2007. Nava Smaraṇa: Nine Sacred Recitations of Jainism (*OLZ* 104, 6: 708–709).

2010 W. M. Kelting. 2009. Heroic Wives: Rituals, Stories and the Virtues of Jain Wifehood (*OLZ* 105, 4–5: 588–592).
Ācārya Pūjyapāda: Iṣṭôpadeśa. 2010. Tr. Jaykumar Jalaj (*OLZ* 105, 3: 368–369).
A. Mette. 2010. Die Erlösungslehre der Jainas (*IJJS Online* 6, 3: 1–4).

2012 K. C. Jain. 2010. History of Jainism (*OLZ* 107, 2: 127).
C. Chojnacki. 2008. Kuvalayamala (*OLZ* 107, 3: 203–206).
M. Cone. 2010. A Dictionary of Pāli II (*WZKS* 54: 235–236).

2013 E. Leumann: Āvaśyaka-Studies. Tr. G. Baumann. 2010 (*OLZ* 108, 6: 1).

2015 J. McHugh, Sandalwood and Carrion. Oxford, 2012 (*OLZ* upcoming).
D. Habermann, People Trees. Oxford, 2013 (*OLZ* upcoming).

Abbreviations

ABORI	Annals of the Bhandarkar Oriental Research Institute
BAVA	Beiträge zur Allgemeinen und Vergleichenden Archäologie
BSOAS	Bulletin of the School of Oriental and African Studies
IF	Indogermanische Forschungen
IIJ	Indo-Iranian Journal
IJJS	International Journal of Jaina Studies
IJJS (Online)	International Journal of Jaina Studies (Online)
IT	Indologica Taurinensia
JAOS	Journal of the American Oriental Society
JESHO	Journal of the Economic and Social History of the Orient
JIP	Journal of Indian Philosophy
JOIB	Journal of the Oriental Institute Baroda
OLZ	Orientalistische Literaturzeitung
SI	Studia Indologiczne (Warzawa)
StII	Studien zur Indologie und Iranistik
TSAM	Traditional South Asian Medicine
WZKS	Wiener Zeitschrift für die Kunde Südasiens
ZVS	Zeitschrift für vergleichende Sprachwissenschaft
ZDMG	Zeitschrift der deutschen morgenländischen Gesellschaft

Index

Abhayadeva-sūri 217
abhijāti 50–3, 56
ābhinibodhika-jñāṇam (sensuous cognition) 147; identified with *indriya-pratyakṣa* 147; sensory and quasi-sensory 149
Ācāradinakara (Vardhamānasūri) 77
Ājīvika 49–54, 56, 202; twofold cosmology 52; twofold epistemology 52
ajñāna (ignorance, incorrect view, nescience) 139, 198
Akalaṅka 182, 201, 215–18, 221
ākāśa (space) 168; bearer of sound 168
Anaximenes 190f
anekānta-vāda (doctrine of multiplexity of reality) 181
anindriya (non-sensory [perception]); and manas 148
Anuyogadvārāṇi 146
Anya-yoga-vyavacche-dadvātriṃśikā 197, 208, 227
Āpta-mīmāṃsā 182, 197, 206
Aristotle 216f
arthāvagraha (object apprehension) 148
Aśoka: inscriptions of 60, 63, 65
avagraha (apprehension) 149
avaktavya (inexpressible) 190, 196, 216
āyā/ātmā (soul) 164, 166f, 169f; behind the use of weapons 167; does not exist 169

Barlingay 188
Basham 50, 51, 53
Bhagavatī Ārādhanā (Śivakoṭī/Śivarāya) 21; colophon and praśasti 23; comparative various readings 28–32; editions and translations of 22; extra gāthās 23; other manuscripts and commentaries on 22, 25–6, 27; the Pune manuscript and its Sanskrit Ṭippana 23, 24
bhaṅga (disintegration, angle, basic figure) 181, 183f; augmented without and with the particle *syāt* 202–49
bhūya (material elements) 167f
Bṛhatkathā 172

ceyaṇā/cetanā (consciousness) 169
Charpentier 5, 8, 14–15, 17
Chedasūtras 68–9, 81, 83–4, 94
cognition: arises from the conjunction of the elements 168–70, 172; consciousness 168–70, 172; integrated into *pratyakṣa* and into *parokṣa* 148; sensory (*indriya*) and non-sensory (*noindriya*) 147f
constructivist interpretation and reductionist method interpretation 184–95
contradiction 197
Cort 230

darśana 137–9
Dasaveyāliya-sutta 60–4; bee and mendicant in 60–3; *Cuṇṇi/Cūrṇi* by Agastyasiṃha on 60–5
Dhammapada 60, 62–3
Dharasena 133
dharma (property) 192, 197
Dharmakīrti 207, 211
dhīmatra 52
Dhruva 230
dialogue 172
Diṅnāga (Dignāga) 183, 211
disambiguation 199ff
doubt 8–10, 52, 95, 100, 107, 136, 140, 193f, 211
doubt, error and misapprehension 139–40, 184
doxography 49, 50